MO(VE)MENTS OF RESISTANCE

Lev Luis Grinberg

Israel: Society, Culture and History

Series Editor:
Yaacov Yadgar, Political Studies, Bar-Ilan University

Editorial Board:
Alan Dowty, Political Science and Middle Eastern Studies, University of Notre Dame
Tamar Katriel, Communication Ethnography, University of Haifa
Avi Sagi, Hermeneutics, Cultural Studies, and Philosophy, Bar-Ilan University
Allan Silver, Sociology, Columbia University
Anthony D. Smith, Nationalism and Ethnicity, London School of Economics
Yael Zerubavel, Jewish Studies and History, Rutgers University

MO(VE)MENTS OF RESISTANCE

Politics, Economy and Society in Israel/Palestine 1931-2013

LEV LUIS GRINBERG

Boston 2014

Library of Congress Cataloging-in-Publication Data:
A catalog record for this title is available from the Library of Congress.
Copyright © 2014 Academic Studies Press
All rights reserved

ISBN 978-1-936235-41-4 (hardback)
ISBN 978-1-618113-78-8 (paperback)
ISBN 978-1-618110-69-5 (electronic)

Cover illustration courtesy of *WE - Festi-Conference for Creative Collectives*, and *Af* magazine
Co-Artistic Directors: Leo Lieberman, Rotem Rozental
Branding and Concept: Yotam Kellner
Producer: Noam Kuzar
Artistic Director, Jerusalem Season of Culture: Itay Mautner
Executive Director: Naomi Bloch Fortis

Book design: Adell Medovoy

Published by Academic Studies Press in 2014
28 Montfern Avenue
Brighton, MA 02135, USA

press@academicstudiespress.com
www.academicstudiespress.com

To Yael

Contents

Acknowledgments	8
Abbreviations	9
Hebrew Terms	10
Prologue. *A Personal Account: Reflections on the Design of a Progressive Research Program*	12
1. Introduction: *Political Spaces and Mo(ve)ments of Resistance*	37
2. 1931 — *An Arab-Jewish Civil Society Struggle against the British Colonial Government*	60
3. 1959 — *Wadi Salib Riots: Culminating a Decade of Ethnic Discrimination*	90
4. 1960-1965 — *The Action Committees' Revolt: Full Employment Crisis, Failed Democratization and State Expansion*	122
5. 1971 — *The Black Panthers Movement: Ethnic Tensions and "Left-Right" Tribal Polarization*	151
6. 1980 — *Forum/13 Powerful Workers: Hyperinflation and the Challenge to State Autonomy*	181
7. 1987-1993 — *The Intifada: The Palestinian Resistance Mo(ve)ment*	217
8. 2011 — *The J14 Mo(ve)ment: The Emergence of the Occupy Repertoire of Resistance*	251
9. Conclusion: *On the Dynamics of Political Spaces—Time, Movement, Actors and Masses*	275
List of Sources	314
Bibliography	315
Index	331

Acknowledgments

Every book is a collective enterprise, personal signature and responsibility of the author notwithstanding. This book is the result of many years of work, debates with students and colleagues, and institutional support. I would like here to thank them all.

First of all, for material support. This book has been supported by a grant of the Israel Science Foundation (409/09) and the Diller Fellowship of the Center for Middle Eastern Studies at UC Berkeley. Also the President, Rector and Dean of the Humanities and Social Sciences of Ben Gurion University have given their financial support. Without this material aid I would not have been able to complete my work.

Second, for hospitality. I want to thank the Professor Nezar Al-Sayyad and Professor Emily Emight of the Center for Middle Eastern Studies and the Department of Sociology at UC Berkeley for hosting me during the writing of the book.

Third, for the initiative and encouragement to write this book I owe special gratitude to Professor Yaakov Yadgar.

Fourth, for the hard work good spirit and dedication of my research assistants, Assaf Bondy, Assaf Peled, Hagar Gutman, Rony Blank, Shahdi Rouhana and Yulia Shabshenko.

Fifth, for wisdom and friendship. I have discussed the ideas of this book and some of its chapters with colleagues and friends that enriched this book. I would like to thank Amnon Raz-Krakotzkin, Andrew Arato, Avia Spivak, Daniel Maman, Debbie Bernstein, Gil Eyal, Jackie Feldman, Michael Burawoy, Michael Shalev, Musa Budeiri, Oded Lonai, Rashid Khalidi, Roee Livne, Sarit Helman, Tova Bensky, Uri Ram, Yehuda Shenhav, and Zeev Rozenhak.

Sixth, for close involvement and generosity. I owe very special gratitude to Daniel De Malach and Rony Blank for reading and making substantial comments on the entire book. I want to thank a very sincere, clever and constructive anonymous reader that helped to improve my original version. Last and not least I thank Amy Asher for his comments and dedicated work in translating from Hebrew Chapters 2–7, and editing my English versions of the prologue and Chapters 1, 8, and 9.

Seventh, for the soul. I want to thank Yael, my companion, for her encouragement and support of this very special project designed to articulate most of my work during the last twenty years.

Abbreviations

IAI — Israel Aviation Industries
IBA — Israel Broadcasting Authority
IDF — Israeli Defense Forces
IEC — Israel Electric Corporation
LIC — Labor Institutional Complex
NUG — National Unity Government
PA — Palestinian Authority
PLO — Palestinian Liberation Organization
OT — Occupied Territories
WC — Washington Consensus
WS — Workers' Society
WZO — World Zionist Organization
ZLM — Zionist Labor Movement

Hebrew Terms

Ahdut Haavoda — United Labor Zionist Socialist party founded in 1919.
Agudat Yisrael — Ultra-Orthodox Ashkenazi Party.
Ayarot Pituach — Development towns.
Balad — National Palestinian Democratic Party established in 1999.
Dash — Democratic Party for Change, established towards 1977 elections.
Gesher — Temporary splits of David Levy from the *Likud* in 1995 and 1999.
Hadash — Democratic Front for Change. Established by the Communist Party and leaders of the Black Panthers in 1977.
Haganah — The military organization of the *Yishuv*, and forerunner of the Israeli Defense Forces.
Hapoel Hatzair — The Young Worker party, founded in 1905.
Hashomer Hatzair — Zionist Socialist and Marxist Party established in 1919.
Hevrat Haovdim — Workers Society, the name of the holding Company of enterprizes owned by the *Histadrut*.
Histadrut — Shortened version of *Hahistadrut Haclalit shel haovdim haivrim beeretz Israel*, or General Federation of Hebrew Workers in the Land of Israel.
Kadima — Namely "Forward" list formed before the 2006 elections by leaders splitting from *Likud* and Labor.
Likud — Main right wing party established towards 1973 elections.
Ma'arach — Alignment. A list of the Labor Party and *Mapam* formed leading up to the 1969 elections.
Mafdal — National Religious Party.
Mapai — Eretz Israel workers party; the ruling party of Zionism and the State of Israel from 1933 to 1977. It was founded in 1930 as a union of *Hapoel Hatzair* and *Achdut Haavoda*.
Mapam — United workers party, established in 1948 by *Ahdut Haavoda* and *Hashomer Hatzair*.
Meretz — Zionist left party established towards 1992 elections by *Ratz*, *Shinui* and *Mapam*.
Moked — Socialist list in the 1973 elections.
Moledet — Extreme right wing list supporting transfer of Palestinians

led by Gen. (res.) Rehavaam Zeevi in the 1992 elections.

Morasha — Extremist religious national party temporal split from RNP in the 1984 elections.

Ometz — Small center party list formed by former Treasury Minister Horowitz for the 1984 elections.

Palmach — Elite underground militia established by the *Haganah*.

Poalei Tzion — The Workers of Zion party founded in 1905.

Poalei Tzion Smol — Marxist split from *Poalei Tzion* in 1919.

Ra'am — Religious Muslim Party established in 1999.

Rafi — Electoral list established by Ben Gurion in 1965, joined *Mapai* in 1968 forming the Labor Party.

Ratz — Civil Rights Movement party established by Shulamit Aloni in 1977.

Shas — Religious Ultra-Orthodox party established in 1984.

Sheli — Left wing list towards 1977 elections, including *Moked, Haolam Haze*, and splinters from the Black Panthers and Labor Party.

Shinui — Liberal party that was part of *Dash* in 1977, *Meretz* in 1992-1999, and independent in 1981, 1984, 1988 and 1999-2003 elections.

Tami — Traditional *Mizrahi* list in 1981 elections.

Tehia — Extreme right wing Split from Likud in 1981.

Tsomet — Right wing list led by Gen. (res.) Raphael Eitan in 1992 elections.

Yaad — Center list towards 1984 led by Gen. (res.) Ezer Weitzman.

Yishuv — Literally, settlement. Used in Palestine (as elsewhere) to refer to the entire Jewish community.

Yesh Atid — Center list organized towards 2013 elections.

Yisrael Beiteinu — Right wing party led by Avigdor Lieberman since 2006 elections.

Prologue
A Personal Account: Reflections on the Design of a Progressive Research Program

This book was born out of an accidental sequence of events, just like the history of Israeli politics I wish to describe and analyze here. I never intended "to tell the story" of Israeli politics from its inception, precisely because I reject the idea of paradigmatic meta-narratives. I am strongly convinced that history has no necessary logic or direction; it is rather the path-dependent outcome of crucial turning points. Politics matters. The question is how political actors act and react to historical junctures, opportunities and challenges given structural constraints, competition with other actors, and the interests of dominant institutions and power-holders to maintain their position despite the resistance of subordinated populations.

The comparative research project presented here is an attempt to analyze critical turning points in Israeli/Palestinian history given the tension between political power holders and the resistance movements of subordinated, marginalized, misrecognized and underrepresented social forces. It is not at all a systematic history: it lacks many turning points, particularly those related to wars and peace-making, and several important factors and actors are ignored. It is designed rather to fill in certain vacuums in the sociology of Israel/Palestine, mainly by "bringing politics back in." It is designed as a progressive scientific plan seeking to contribute to the conceptualization of political dynamics, democracy and social movements.

I. Israeli Sociology in Historical and Political Context

Most leading political sociologists attempted to write paradigmatic meta-narratives of Israel, doomed to fail due to their teleological approach (Swirski, 1979). The first and best-known sociologist who eventually became the model for future generations of sociologists was Talcott Parsons' best disciple, Shmuel N. Eisenstadt. In 1967, Eisenstadt published the first sociological paradigmatic meta-narrative, translating Labor Zionist ideology to structural-functionalist sociology. He suggested a triumphal theory of Labor Zionism, interpreted as better suited to build nation-state institutions and power, analyzing Zionism as a revolutionary movement modernizing the Jewish people (Eisenstadt, 1967). Unfortunately for this paradigmatic project, and for the history of Israel, 1967 was a crucial turning point year, the moment when Labor Zionism ideology and power interest defeated itself, expanding the borders of the Jewish State and inserting the Palestinians in Israeli economy under a military-imposed structure of domination. The military expansion of Israel is analyzed in Chapter 4 as an accidental historical turning point that eventually provided an effective response to the challenge of working-class resistance to Labor Zionism's non-representative institutions in 1960-1966.

Eisenstadt's first disciples, Horowitz and Lissak (1978), and his most salient critic, Yonatan Shapiro (1977), did not have better luck in terms of timing with the publication of their meta-narrative paradigms. All of them developed revised paradigms explaining Labor Zionism's flexibility and capacity to adapt itself to changing conditions in the aftermath of 1967. Horowitz and Lissak attempted to correct the Parsonian functionalist model[1] using Shil's (1957) model of center and periphery. They argued that Labor Zionism was able to build functional adaptive institutions and construct the political center of Jewish society despite the external conditions of a dual society of Jews and Arabs under the pre-1948 British Mandate (Horowitz and Lissak, 1978). The direct and explicit goal of this teleological paradigm was to explain why Labor Zionism was so well prepared to continue ruling Israel after the historical turning point of 1948, and the dramatic change of its social composition with the big migration movements of Jews in and Arabs out. The indirect and implicit meaning of this paradigm was to justify and explain why Labor Zionist institutions were also able to adapt themselves to a dual society imposed on the Palestinians after 1967. Chapter 2 discusses the Labor Movement's pre-1948 institutions as a political reaction to the resistance of Jewish-Arab civil society.

Yonatan Shapiro criticized functionalist interpretations of Zionist

---

1   For an exhaustive and comprehensive analysis of Israeli sociological paradigms and schools see *The Changing Agenda of Israeli Sociology* (Ram, 1995).

Labor using elitist theories of power (Michels, 1915; Mills, 1959). He argued that Labor institutions were not designed to build an egalitarian or socialist society, as their ideology claimed, but on the contrary, ideology was used manipulatively to legitimize and conceal the extent of their power. The structure and goal of political institutions was to empower the dominant elites and to maintain them, effectively subordinating Jewish civil society—not only workers, but also the middle classes and big capital. According to Shapiro, Israeli democracy was only formal, and it did not function as a process of representing civil society forces and alternative policies; the ruling party controlled all centers of power, effectively preventing the opposition from challenging and replacing it (Shapiro, 1977).

Shapiro's theory of a non-democratic Labor superpower and Horowitz and Lissak's theory of Labor institutions' adaptive advantage to function in a dual society were published the same year the Labor Party lost the elections and its hegemonic position after dominating Zionism and the State of Israel since 1933. Chapter 5 discusses the *Likud*'s ascent to power as the effective manipulation of the of the *Mizrahi* Jews' resistance movement[2] against Labor institutions imposed on them. Since then, the political imagination of left and right identities remained closely attached to ethno-class hostility between the *Ashkenazi* middle-class and the peripheral *Mizrahi* Jews.

Apparently, the experience of these four founding fathers of Israeli sociology demonstrates that attempts to build meta-narratives with a paradigmatic teleology are doomed to fail due to the unpredictability of historical turning points. Sewell's (1996) suggestion of eventful temporality and path dependent history, where sequences of events and unpredicted turning points are crucial, seemed much more satisfactory to me. However, Shapiro's critique of democracy has provided the initial insight for my own research project on politics and turning points. I started with the critique of the Zionist Labor institutional design built to control civil society, markets and politics, aiming to explain the failure of democratization within the borders of the sovereign State of Israel, and its further colonial expansion to maintain its power.[3]

---

2   *Mizrahi* is the more or less consensual Hebrew adjective for Jews who migrated from Arab countries, in English usually referred as Oriental Jews. I'll use the Hebrew term here.
3   The late Yonatan Shapiro was my teacher and friend, and supervised my PhD thesis *The Crisis of Full Employment* (Grinberg, 1991b).

*

I owe most of my knowledge and research interests to the vibrant intellectual community of the new generation of sociology researchers in Israel. All research questions and projects presented in this book are part and parcel of a collective intellectual effort to review Israeli sociology after 1977. The founding fathers' failure to build a meta-narrative paradigm gave birth to an impressive flourishing of critical theories devoid of any pretension to formulate a single paradigmatic meta-narrative.

The resistance of *Mizrahi* Jews to Labor rule was first studied by Bernstein (1976) and Swirski (1981), who suggested applying the model of internal colonialism to explain the powerful position of European Jews, represented by Labor Zionism, which was built on the exploitation and marginalization of Jewish immigrants from Arab countries (Swirski and Bernstein, 1980). The marginal position of *Mizrahi* Jews was later analyzed by *Mizrahi* intellectuals and scholars beyond the material and economic conflict of interests using Said's (1979) critique of Orientalism and other postcolonial theories. Their goal was to explain the relationship between the subordination of Jews from Arab countries and the conflict of the Zionist European settlers with the Palestinian Arabs (Shohat, 1988; Chetrit, 2010, Shenhav, 2006). I will return to this still open puzzle in the concluding chapter of this book.

Zureik (1979) and Lustick (1980) applied the internal colonialism model to analyze the subordinated and marginal position of the Palestinians who remained in the Jewish State after 1948 and were subjected to martial law despite their official status as citizens with political rights. In the same years, Eisenstadt's most brilliant and prolific disciple, Baruch Kimmerling, caused a path-breaking paradigmatic shift in Israeli sociology when he suggested that the borders of the society to be analyzed are not those of Jewish society, but those of Jewish/Arab and Israeli/Palestinian societies framed by the state's borders (Kimmerling, 1989, 1992). In doing so, Kimmerling created a historical continuity between the pre-1948 colonial state and the post-1967 colonialist expansion of Israel's borders. Within this new paradigm Gershon Shafir (1987) and Kimmerling (1983) suggested that Israel should be analyzed as a settler society where the key questions involve institutions built to expand land appropriation, maintain and legitimize control, and the various institutions that organize and control indigenous or migrant labor.

The dominant role of Labor institutions in the construction of Israeli political power and its economic implications were analyzed by Grinberg (1991) and Shalev (1992) using neo-corporatist and dual labor market theories. In order to explain the dominant position of the military in Israeli society, several theories of militarism were adapted to the peculiar Israeli case (Kimmerling, 1993; Ben Eliezer, 1995; Levy, 2003; Helman, 1999; Grinberg, 2008).

After focusing on specific aspects of power building, domination, and conflict from 1977 to 1993, a new historical challenge appeared upon Labor's return to power: the recognition of the Palestinians and the opposition it provoked. Rabin's assassination in 1995 gave birth to three new attempts to offer meta-narratives of Israeli/Palestinian society, now suggested by critical sociologist. In my opinion, however, these improved critical attempts were not more successful than those formulated by the founding fathers. The new critical macro-paradigms of Israel were offered by Kimmerling's *The Invention and Decline of Israeliness* (2001), Shafir and Peled's *Being Israeli* (2002) and Uri Ram's *Globalization of Israel* (2008). These meta-narrative paradigms assume, like Eisenstadt, that one theory can explain all events from the inception of Zionism, now explaining why the old national solidarity declined and split into various competing factions.

The new critical paradigms suggested teleological explanations of the crisis of national identity neglecting the disastrous political performance of the Labor party and "the Left" during the 1990s. They attribute the decline of "Zionism" (Ram), "Israeliness" (Kimmerling) or "republicanism" (Shafir and Peled) to the neo-liberal economic shift after the *Likud*'s rise to power in 1977, and the ensuing expansion of Jewish settlements in the West Bank. These paradigms keep politics out of the picture, absolving Labor of responsibility for its own failure and that of the peace process during the 1990s. Instead, responsibility is shifted to the right, or "ethno-nationalism" (Shafir and Peled, 2002), "neo-Zionism" (Ram, 2008) and the national-religious settlement drive (Kimmerling, 2001). The European cultural and economic elites who lost power in 1977 somehow became the "good guys": after the *Likud*'s rise to power, they were "liberal" (Shafir and Peled), "secular" (Kimmerling), or "post-Zionist" (Ram). These critical paradigms were not pro-Labor like those of the founding fathers; rather, they involuntarily became what I have called "Labor-yearning" sociologies, despite their critique of Labor institutions and policies before 1977 (Grinberg, 2004). In addition, these latest paradigmatic efforts had bad publication timing—no less than those of the "founding fathers": they were published after the revival of Zionism, republicanism, and Israeli nationalism following the Second Palestinian Intifada in 2000.

In *Politics and Violence in Israel/Palestine* (Grinberg, 2010) I analyze the political dynamics of the years 1992-2006, emphasizing crucial turning points and the political dynamics absent in the new critical paradigmatic perspectives. As mentioned above, it is my opinion that every attempt to explain Israeli/Palestinian history with one comprehensive theory became teleological and was doomed to fail (Grinberg, 2009). Moreover, due to the predictable delay between our initial questions, research, writing and publishing, it is not surprising that all big paradigms of Israel were published after historical developments made them outdated.

II. Designing a Comparative Research Plan

I am a product of the critical sociological effort in Israel, but still somehow an outsider. This is probably due to my background as a Latin American migrant, kicked out of my continent in the 1970s by the clash between repressive military regimes supported by the US and armed revolutionary groups. Since I migrated to Israel in 1972, I had always alternative realities in mind: as a sociologist I never accepted the obvious as an explanation, and as social and political activist I rejected the conservative attitude of "real-politik." In my different research projects I applied the most critical approaches, usually focusing on specific historical "surprises," or questions existing theories were unable to explain. I sought to understand the strange society and polity I had landed in. Here was a regime that claimed to be democratic and socialist but actually imposed military rule over the Palestinian population, perpetuated extreme discrimination among Jews, and proved unable to represent and contain conflicts between them.

My historical puzzles go back and forth, and constitute the basis of this book. I attempt to explain why Jews and Arabs revolted against British colonial rule in 1931 and no one wrote about it (Grinberg, 2003;

Chapter 2 below); why Labor Zionism expanded the country's borders in 1967, contradicting its ideology and proclaimed goal of creating a separated and democratic Jewish nation-state (Grinberg, 1993; Chapter 4 below); why an apparent working-class revolt against Labor Zionist anti-democratic trade unions in 1980 ended in1985 with the aggressively anti-labor neo-liberal economic policies in 1985, implemented by the Labor-*Likud* national coalition (Grinberg, 1991; Chapter 6 here); and why the anti-colonial Palestinian revolt in 1988 ended with the re-accommodation of the Israeli military rule, improving Israel's capacity to control and subordinate Palestinians, in cooperation with the Palestinian Liberation Organization (PLO) leadership (Grinberg, 2010, Chapter 7 here).

I never pretended to write one comprehensive history of the unexpected and unpredictable development of the Israeli/Palestinian polity, and despite the fact this book may appear to be a comprehensive history or might be misinterpreted as such, it would be a serious error. This book does not suggest any new comprehensive paradigm, but rather represents a non-paradigmatic—or even anti-paradigmatic—approach. I do not believe Zionism necessarily had to deteriorate to such low ebb as it has since 2000, and I reject teleology in social sciences, which assumes that history has any direction or logic. In my previous research projects, I analyzed singular historical turning points, and here I present all of them together. I compare the cases, and analyze the relations between them as unpredictable sequences of events, using path-dependent eventful sociology (Sewell, 1996, 2005).

The sequence of events that led me to write this book includes the call for manuscripts by the Academic Studies Press immediately after I published *Politics and Violence* (Grinberg, 2010), and a delay in writing until late 2011 due to health problems. The delay was fortunate, because it enabled me to study Michael Burawoy's approach to designing comparative research. I met him during my stay at Berkeley, where I sought some distance from my tempestuous country in order to write this book. Thanks to very generous and open conversations with Burawoy, I came to deeply understand both his methodological approach and his interpretation of critical sociology. As you may recall, this was a time of social upheaval and radical enthusiasm, of the "Occupy movements" that I had the opportunity to observe both in Oakland and in Israel, providing important theoretical insights to my comparative research of resistance movements and dynamic political spaces. The final corrections made in February 2013 enabled me to finalize the theoretical argument and to add a final chapter on the occupy resistance movement against neo-liberal policies in 2011.

The last case contributed significantly to the conceptualization of resistance movements, adding a fourth category to my previous distinction between types of resistance with different social bases, countermovements and repertoires of collective action: anticolonial civil society revolts against externally imposed state institutions (Chapters 2 and 7); ethnic riots against their discrimination by the dominant cultural elites (Chapters 3 and 5), working class strike waves against employers and state economic policies (Chapters 4 and 6); and mass occupations of public space in protest against neo-liberal economic policies and the unchecked and unbalanced decision making processes imposed by international financial power (Chapter 8).

The key question that vexed me from the very start of the project was methodological: how should I compare historical cases and to what end? Burawoy argued during our talks that the goal of comparison is to discover how peoples' struggle can succeed, rather than explain why they have failed. Comparative sociological research is designed to reveal variations that contribute to a progressive scientific plan for social change. As researchers, we are not outside of history but part of it, and our investigations are part and parcel of social processes, whether we contribute to a progressive or reactionary project.

Burawoy's comparison of Theda Skocpol's and Leon Trotsky's theories of the Russian Revolution (Burawoy, 1989) is a fine example of good and bad designs of comparative research programs. The surprising argument of his article is that Trotsky understood the Russian Revolution better than Skocpol. A leader deeply involved in politics and the organization of the revolution had a better understanding of historical events before they occurred than a well-trained social scientist with historical perspective and much more information. Why? Because of a poorly designed comparative research program. Skocpol compares three revolutions (the English, French and Russian) as if they occurred out of time, namely, ignoring the influence of one revolution on the other. The sequence of events is crucial to the understanding of history (Sewell, 1996).

Following Lakatos (1978), Burawoy suggests that a progressive research method must take (any) hard-core theory and build an "expanding belt of theories that increase the corroborated empirical content and solve successive puzzles" (Burawoy, 1989: 761). This is exactly what Trotsky did: he had a theory of revolution in hand, Marxism, and was committed to it. This commitment led him to understand that Marx had been wrong, and that the revolution would start in Russia, rather than in the most developed capitalist economies of Germany or England, but the revolution could not lead immediately to socialism due to the need to industrialize Russia (Trotsky, 1906). As early as 1906, Trotsky was aware of the dangers of a revolution before the capitalist economy would develop, but in 1917, when he was already one of the leaders, he ignored his own warnings (Burawoy, 1989: 792).

My conversations with Burawoy led me to reflect on the relation between my own position in society and history—namely my political activism—and my research interests, questions and theories. I had always been designing progressive research programs that start with a historic puzzle, something that did not fit into existing theories and explanations. I adopted what seemed to me the most appropriate theoretical tool for exploring the field and in each research project I was surprised to find some resistance movement that helped solve the puzzle and expand the theory. It was the movement of resistance to the dominant power and the related, unpredictable historical turning points that helped shed light on historical shifts and manipulative political actions designed to maintain power. In this research project I compare cases aiming to expand the theoretical framework of dynamic political spaces by learning how movements of resistance challenge those in power, and how they react to the challenge.

*

Political space is an analytical tool designed to interpret the political dynamics of representation of social forces in the political sphere, as well as the peaceful containment of social and economic conflicts by political mediation, negotiation and compromise. Political space is opened to mediate between sides to a conflict—between the state and civil society, and between dominant and dominated social forces—in moments when unilateral repression by the most powerful is ineffective or not viable due to some balance of power between the parties. The concept of political space is a critical tool for analyzing democratic regimes and transitions to democracy (Grinberg, 2010). The symbolic space of representation of subordinated social forces is *dynamic*: it can be opened by recognizing their claims, identities, agendas, and representatives, but can also be closed or shrunk by the physical or symbolic violence of the dominant elites.

This theoretical conceptualization is the result of thirty years of progressive research programs designed to unlock the puzzle of Israeli politics: its incredible success in closing political space to all subordinated populations while maintaining a democratic image rarely questioned by its citizens, or the international community, for that matter. The issue that has been at the focus of all my research programs so far has been the limitations of democracy, or more precisely, the inaccessibility of democratic representation for subordinated social forces, despite the existence of democratic rules of the game. In the next two sections I will present the sequence of my research programs, motivations, questions, puzzles, initial theories, and conclusions that have progressively contributed to formulating the political space concept.

III. My Initial Research Project: The Working Class and Political Economy

a. The Historical Slip of the Tongue. In the early 1980s I was a young Argentinian immigrant in Israel, indirectly[4] influenced by the trend of socialist theories and movements that spread in Latin America in the 1960s and 1970s. Given the extremely different reality in Israel, I decided I should investigate this very strange country where capitalists were called "socialists" or "leftist," while large sections of the working class were avowed nationalists and supported the "right." My political activism and research interests converged: during the 1970s I became interested in working-class struggles, and became a "representative" in the *Histadrut* Executive Committee, despite the fact that I was not a worker but a student[5] activist in Campus, a Jewish-Arab student organization.

---

4   I was not a member of Zionist-socialist youth movements, neither of Argentinian leftist organizations, on the opposite, I was raised in a bourgeois Jewish country club. However, I was exposed to my generations' activism, interests, and preoccupations.
5   I was nominated as a "worker representative" in the *Histadrut* by my party (*Moked*) when I was not

In my first research project for an MA seminar,[6] I referred to the Marxist theory of class conflict and searched for working class solidarity between Jews and Arabs before the establishment of the Jewish State. Initially I did not find a single instance of genuine solidarity.[7] However, while reading newspapers and protocols I came across an event that was completely ignored by the historians and sociologists of the pre-state period: a joint and successful public transportation strike against the arbitrary imposition of heavy taxes, which succeeded in mobilizing the support of the entire Jewish-Arab population against the British colonial government. This was not in fact the working class, but businessmen, private owners of trucks and buses, or companies, providing a service to the whole population.

In my attempt to analyze this extraordinary moment of anti-colonial Jewish-Arab resistance, I formulated a new interpretation of the dominant trend of history leading to ethno-national confrontation, violence, and forced migration. Although class interests matter, my analysis suggested new questions: How are class and national identities articulated? What is the social basis of the dominant political elite that builds the nation, and what is its strategy to accomplish its political goals? The analytical framework I proposed to comprehend this political dynamic involved a complex matrix of class interests and intra-communal struggles and relationships (Grinberg, 2003). I explained why both the Jewish and Arab urban economic elites failed to consolidate their national communities and proved unable to take the political lead. I showed how rural conflicts over land and labor shaped relations between the two communities as a "national" conflict over exclusive state power, led by the very well-organized Zionist Labor Movement (ZLM) and the more spontaneous revolutionary Palestinian peasants (see also Shapiro, 1976; Kimmerling, 1983; Ben Eliezer, 1998; Lockman, 1996; Sayigh, 1979).

I reached four main conclusions on the basis of this MA seminar.

---

at all a worker, and even not a member of the *Histadrut*. This strange situation made clear that it was very important to understand the idea of representation and the peculiar political institution that "represented" the workers in Israel.

6 This was a seminar on the Israeli-Palestinian conflict taught by the late Professor Baruch Kimmerling. I collected the material and wrote the seminar in the early 1980s, but it was first published in Hebrew in 1995 and only in 2003 was it published in English (Grinberg, 2003).

7 There were several cases (Lockman, 1996; Bernstein, 2000) however the most famous and long-living case was of the Railway Company workers, a small group of skilled workers that never organized a struggle widely supported by the Jewish and Arab civil society.

First, class matters, but it is also influenced by ethnic identity. Second, politics are not a direct reflection of economic and class interests. Political elites define strategic goals aiming to mobilize various social identities and construct them as collective actors. Third, methodologically, you should start with a question and confront your theory with facts, and be ready to be surprised by the empirical material. This is not induction, nor deduction, but abduction.[8] Finally, my sociological conclusion was that while the national conflict unfolded in the rural areas, the sphere of potential cooperation was in the mixed cities. The political elites of Labor Zionism succeeded in formulating a national strategy of economic separation and geographic segregation anchored in the interests of Jewish rural workers. Conversely, the Palestinian political elites failed to formulate a shared national strategy for peasants and urban dwellers.

The research of the 1931 anti-colonial strike and its further transformation into a "national conflict" (during 1936-39) facilitated my initial insight towards understanding politics as a distinct sphere of articulation of social forces by political actors. The success of one national movement and the failure of the other were determined by the capacity of political actors to *articulate a collective identity* which mobilized the majority of the social forces and bound them through a shared claim of recognition and representation vis-à-vis the state. Chapter 2 analyzes the first anti-colonial movement of resistance against British rule in 1931, and its almost complete oblivion from history by both the Zionist and the Palestinian national discourses and political elites.

b. Split Corporatism. I started my second research program, aiming to study a "real" case of working-class struggle and mobilization that took place in 1980 discussed here in Chapter 6. After the election of a new right-wing government in 1977, it launched a liberal economic plan in order to dismantle the previous interventionist developing state, which characterized the policies of the ZLM since 1948 (Shalev, 1992; Grinberg, 1991; Maman and Rosenhek 2011). The new policies led to running inflation, which mainly affected the working class. Rank-and-file workers organized strikes and huge demonstrations, openly revolted against the *Histadrut* (the largest organization of workers and their legal representative in collective bargaining), and took the lead in the strug-

---

8   I owe this insight to a conversation with Don Handelman.

gle against government policies, shrinking salaries and mass dismissals.

Since the *Histadrut* came to play a dominant role in my research, a short clarification about its peculiar structure is in order. The *Histadrut* was established in 1920 as a quasi-state institution, providing welfare services to its members and ruled by political parties that formed a ruling coalition after elections held every four years. This structure served the political objective of creating a separate Jewish State. The *Histadrut*, however, was not representative of the workers: it imposed on the Jewish workers trade unions controlled by the ruling party. Moreover, the ZLM relied on the workers' weakness and dependency on the *Histadrut* and affiliated institutions (Shapiro, 1976; Medding, 1972; Shalev, 1992; Grinberg, 1991).

Equipped with a trendy theory of political economy, "neo-corporatism," I attempted to comprehend the workers' revolt in 1980. Corporatist theory argued that capitalism requires control of the working class, both in democratic and authoritarian regimes (Schmitter, 1974). Although there is a significant difference between these cases—one is a state imposition from above, and the other a bottom-up democratic organization—in both cases centralized trade unions bargain in the workers' name and reach political compromises with the employers and the state. Trade unions provide wage restraint and legitimacy to the regime, and in exchange they get a monopolistic position as unique representatives of the workers, and are promised continued full employment.

Rank-and-file workers, however, tend to revolt in periods of full employment and make higher demands, but in the long run they are restrained (Crouch, 1983; Pizzorno, 1978). This study involved recent events, so I used mostly interviews with working class and *Histadrut* leaders, Finance Ministers, and heads of big corporations. From the first moment it was clear that the image of a revolt against the *Histadrut* was misleading, and that there was deep hidden cooperation between the worker committees and the umbrella organization. They had to hide their coordination due to the peculiar *Histadrut* structure as provider of public services (mainly health insurance), owner of big economic enterprises, and the second-largest employer after the government. The peculiar structure of the *Histadrut* made it dependent on state subsidies and legal delegation of authority and there was a real danger that the new government might punish it for being too confrontationist. The 13 worker committees that organized in 1980 to confront the government were not the weak workers that the *Histadrut* succeeded to restrain, but those powerful workers who benefitted from their position in the primary sector of the labor market. Their wages were not restrained, and they were interested in helping the *Histadrut* maintain the political structure that facilitated their privileged position.

It became clear that neo-corporatist theory was insufficient, and I was looking for some theory able to shed light on the relation between labor market structures and worker organization. Goldthorpe (1984) provided the necessary theoretical framework, but I turned it upside down. His argument is that there are two contradictory tendencies in late capitalism: neo-corporatism when the workers are more powerful, and dual labor markets when the employers are more powerful and succeed in dividing the workers. My argument was that these were two potentially complementary models, whose combination provides the most sophisticated model of capitalist domination. (Grinberg, 1991a) Israel was a prime example. I discovered that the strong workers' resistance in 1980 unintentionally cooperated with the maintenance of a structure that divided the workers and effectively ruled them.

This research project provided important insights into the Israeli political economy: a. its labor organizations were imposed on the workers from above, similar to the authoritarian models; b. the strong workers were those who took advantage of the dual labor market structure and succeeded to organize independent struggles; c. the workers were divided according to their ethnic and national identity, as well as citizenship (Semyonov and Levin-Epstein, 1987), and had very different opportunities to organize at labor market level; d. the workers' support of political parties and trade unions are two different processes with different logics of collective action (Sturmthal, 1973); e. the power relations between trade unions and political parties are path dependent, and the sequence of events (namely, who organizes first) is crucial to understanding the form of articulation adopted by the working class (Maier, 1984).

The analysis of hyperinflation and its halting added a new concept to my previous understanding of the political sphere and the role of political actors: the potential *autonomy of the state* and its need to withstand the pressure of strong social actors as a necessary condition for controlling its resources (Skocpol, 1985). I concluded that state autonomy may be facilitated or obstructed by the actions of the political parties in power, suggesting a correction to Skocpol's theory of state autonomy:

in addition to her three conditions—crisis, professional bureaucracy and independent financial resources—I added a crucial fourth element: political facilitation by the party system and ruling coalition (Grinberg, 1991). The research revealed the differential capacities of competing political parties to mediate between state, capital, and labor. Consequently, I characterized the political sphere as a space of mediation, an arena of competition, struggle and cooperation between political actors seeking to shape state policies. Political actors represent alternative strategies of state intervention in civil society relations, and they have different capacities to coordinate civil society interests and state policies. State autonomy depends on the institutional differentiation between state apparatuses, civil society organizations, and political parties, and the ruling parties' ability to facilitate autonomous state decisions. In the Israeli case, the deep economic crisis of 1984-1985 facilitated collaboration by the two dominant parties, both of which have failed to slow down inflation in the past, thus contributing to the build-up of state autonomy.

c. *The Vicious Institutional Triangle*. The research projects of my MA studies led to the puzzle of my next research program. Why would a powerful ruling party, which had been pursuing a successful strategy of geographic and economic separation between Jews and Palestinians and established a Jewish State, be interested in expanding the borders of this state after 1967, integrating the Palestinian economy and weakening most Israeli workers? In order to comprehend this puzzle I took a step back in history to examine the sequence of events that led to the institutionalization of the split corporatist political economy. I investigated the period before 1967, starting in 1957. The fact that the ideology of the ZLM had totally rejected the option of one state and a joint economy with the Palestinians before 1947 but institutionalized it after 1967 was not only puzzling but disturbing. Equipped with the neo-corporatist and dual labor market theories and previous theoretical insights of the political sphere, I dove into archives, mainly of the *Histadrut* and the ruling party (initially called *Mapai*, and after 1968 the Labor Party).[9]

---

9   The name of the ruling party *Mapai* is the Hebrew acronym of the Eretz Israel Worker Party. In 1968, it merged with two other worker parties (*Ahdut HaAvoda* and *Rafi*) to form the Labor Party,

It soon became clear that the main concern of the leaders of *Mapai* as well as the *Histadrut* in 1960-1965 was their complete loss of control over the workers, and the fear that in the next *Histadrut* elections they would lose the majority. *Mapai* relied on the *Histadrut*'s organizational power and feared that the moment it lost the *Histadrut* elections it would also lose the Knesset (parliamentary) elections and be forced to give up its national hegemony. This is why I called the book *The Histadrut Above All* (obviously a big mistake in terms of marketing[10]): these were the words constantly repeated by the participants in internal debates.

Mapai did everything to save their hegemony in the face of working class resistance. (1) They postponed the *Histadrut* elections from 1963 to 1965; (2) they formed a new block in the run-up to the 1965 elections designed to coopt part of the revolting working class; (3) they deliberately caused the deepest recession in Israeli history after the elections aiming to weaken the workers' bargaining power; and (4) they institutionalized the economic integration of the occupied Palestinian workers after 1967, splitting the workers into different sectors of the labor markets according to their ethno-national origin. In other words, the party's powerful position and reluctance to reform the *Histadrut*'s quasi-state structure in order to open political space for democratic representation of workers was the key reason for the revision of its historic strategy of economic and political separation from Palestinians.

The theory of authoritarian state imposition of centralized trade unions was relevant here, but P. C. Schmitter's next research project also became very relevant, i.e. transition to democracy (O'Donnell and Schmitter, 1986). The challenge faced by *Mapai* and the *Histadrut* was to adjust the labor institutions to the post-1948 democratic conditions, with autonomous organized workers. Why did the institutions not accommodate to the new structural conditions of a democratic state during 1948-1967, instead preferring to reproduce the conditions that weakened the workers after 1967? Here, democratization theories were not enough and I suggested my own contribution, claiming that the dichotomy of state/civil society ignores the third distinct sphere bridging between them: the political arena (Grinberg 1993a, 2001a; see also Linz

---

which remained in power until 1977.
10   This was an ill-chosen title because the *Histadrut* was widely considered an unpopular and boring institution.

and Stepan, 1996; Collier and Collier, 1991).

My argument was that democratic regimes are based on a balance of power between civil society and state institutions, and that the tension between these two autonomous spheres opens space to the third distinct sphere of political mediation between them. I explained the failure to democratize Israel in terms of the institutional rigidity of three deeply interpenetrated and interdependent institutions: the *Histadrut*, the state, and *Mapai*. After the establishment of the Jewish State, the power of quasi-state institutions created during the British colonial era and built into the weakness of civil society was preserved. These institutions dominated the new state and formed a Vicious Triangle, extremely powerful and dominant, but also highly rigid and unable to adjust to democratic dynamics and open up space to worker representation (Shapiro, 1977; Medding, 1972; Grinberg, 1993).

The research of the full employment crisis supported the idea that successful democratic containment of social conflicts by political mediation depends on dynamic opening of the political arena to new claims, social identities, and agendas. When dominant political actors prevent representation of subordinated social forces, they cannot contain them by recourse to democratic rules of the game. This finding led to the idea of dynamic opening and closure of political space for representation as an analytical concept designed to interpret political dynamics within democratic rules of the game. I was not yet aware that within the democratic rules of the game, dominant political forces can effectively close political space to dominated populations, preventing representation. This is precisely the subject of the present research project on resistance. However, after the research on the full employment crisis, I found it necessary to devise a new, progressive research program to develop deeper understanding of the symbolic features of political space and its opposition to violent repression. To that end, Israeli-Palestinian relations seemed an appropriate field of research. It was only after comprehending the politics/violence dichotomy that I realized that political space is an analytical tool to criticize *democracy itself* (Grinberg, 2010). With this realization, I was ready to launch the present research on the sophisticated power dynamics between symbolic violence and resistance.

IV. The Political-Sociological Research Project

In July 1993 I published *The Histadrut Above All* based on my PhD. study. This was a very peculiar timing: a new Labor government was elected in 1992 seeking an agreement with the Palestinians, and a group of young leaders also sought to reform the party's relations with the *Histadrut*, which I considered, as you may recall, the core institutional obstacle to democratizing Israel. In August, one of these young leaders, also a key actor in the secret negotiations with the Palestinians—Deputy Minister of Foreign Affairs Yossi Beilin—(see Beilin, 2001) called me and suggested we meet. He had already read my book, and asked me to coordinate a think tank on turning the *Histadrut* into a democratic trade union confederation. I enthusiastically accepted the offer and spent the next four years not only facilitating discussions, but also acting as the formal strategic advisor on reforming the *Histadrut* after the election of two of the young reformist leaders as Chairs of the *Histadrut*.[11]

The story of the failure to transform the *Histadrut* into an umbrella trade union organization still waits to be written.[12] I decided, however, that I could not be both an actor and a student of the struggles I was involved in: although social sciences are not objective, to study myself proved too much for me. I had to immediately start my new research project on Israeli-Palestinian relations. A few days later a most interesting and exciting event suggested itself to me: the "peace process."

The relationship between symbolic and physical borders, military violence and democracy, which informed my political activism in the 1980s,[13] became the core theoretical insight of my progressive research project later on in the 2000s, after the violent deterioration in the Israeli-Palestinian negotiations. This project began, however, with the enthusiastic hope for peace in 1993. The period between 1982 and 1992

---

11 I was advisor of Haim Ramon during 1994-1995, and Amir Peretz during 1996-1997. For a more detailed description of the reform see Grinberg, 2007 and 2010.
12 I discontinued my advisory mission in 1997, after writing the new Histadrut Act (called Constitution) that established the principle of direct democratic elections of worker representatives. My decision to quit my advisory function was taken following my conclusion that the new democratic Act will not be implemented due to the interest of the party apparatchiks to maintain their powerful positions.
13 During the 1980s I became the speaker for reservists refusing to serve in the First Lebanon in 1982 War, and the repression of the First Intifada in 1987. The name of the movement was *Yesh Gvul* ("There is a limit/border"). The Hebrew term refers both to the symbolic, moral limit, and to the physical border of the state.

in Israel was very encouraging in terms of the strong belief that civil society organizations, mobilization and struggle could be effective in changing politics. The resistance to war (1982-1985) and occupation (1987-1992) led to the election of a new government that promised recognition for the Palestinians, negotiations, and a peace agreement. It was an ideal time to launch an investigation into the effective opening of political space.

a. Triple Democratization. On September 13, 1993 Yitzhak Rabin shook hands with Yasser Arafat on the White House lawns. This was a very moving, promising but also puzzling moment. Could mutual recognition lead to a peace agreement? I decided this would be my next research program, and some 25 highly motivated students joined my workshop to collect data and discuss the unfolding events. This workshop continued until 1997, and was renewed during 2000-2004. The material collected by the students and the discussions of current events were of incredible value to the development of my own theories.

Equipped with the idea of the Israeli-Palestinian "matrix" and the theories of transition to democracy, I formulated a preliminary theoretical framework to comprehend the type of political process we expected to witness. This initial framework was necessary in order to collect the material for the workshop; it was presented in July 1994 at the ISA Conference at Bielefeld, and was published by the *Revue Internationale de Sociologie* (Grinberg, 1994). The argument was that what we called the peace process was actually a triple transition to democracy in three distinct but interconnected political arenas without clear and recognized borders: the internal Israeli, the internal Palestinian, and the Israeli-Palestinian arenas. The democratization of the Israeli-Palestinian arena was a process of de-colonization, but could not be detached from the other two, and the main political obstacle was the need to coordinate the three arenas. I used the elitist theories of democratization in order to emphasize the crucial role of Rabin's and Arafat's leadership in coordinating and synchronizing the process in the three arenas.

After Rabin's assassination, I was shocked by the reaction of the peace supporters, who resumed the pre-1992 tribal "left-right" discourse which Rabin had worked so hard to deconstruct in order to build a majoritarian coalition in support of peace (Grinberg, 2000). This reaction facilitated the election of the most heavily criticized leader after the assassination, Benjamin Netanyahu, who led the public demonization campaign that preceded the assassination. A new question became more urgent than ever: Why does everyone keep talking about the "peace process" after it was derailed completely in 1996? Accordingly, in 1997 I took the material collected by my students and spent a sabbatical in UCLA writing the book on the failure of the "peace process." This text was never published, and as it turned out, the vicissitudes of Israeli-Palestinian relations concealed a much more complex path.

b. Imagined Democracy, Imagined Peace. When I started analyzing the material, it was clear that I had to make a significant theoretical step. Until then I had analyzed actors and interests and the conflicts among them. But now I was dealing also with people's beliefs, myths, language, and discourses. This theoretical leap to the symbolic sphere was facilitated by Benedict Anderson's concept of imagination, which I elaborated on in various directions. I began developing the idea that not only the nation is imagined, but also democracy. Moreover, the democratic political process is made possible by a double imagination: the imagination of the sovereign "people" and that of its parts represented by the parties. According to this analysis, political actors are those who manage to construct the imagined community of political supporters through shared myths, symbols, discourse and language. However, democracy "works" precisely because there is a distinction between the political actors and the social forces supporting them, and it is not only imagined but can be materialized. The democratic rules of the game create the conditions for the process of materialization of the imagined people and its parts by means of basic freedoms, separation of powers and periodic general elections. If one of these elements is significantly lacking, imagined democracy becomes an illusion, a fake (Grinberg, 1999).

Here it became clear why democratic regimes are expected to be responsive to changes in civil society; when they are non-responsive, however, we must analyze why and how social order is maintained and the democratic image is legitimized. These are crucial questions discussed also in this book, albeit in a different formulation. Israeli democracy, I concluded, is only imagined, it cannot be realized, because it denies the equal rights of a significant part of its population, mainly the Palestinians under military rule, and the Palestinian citizens not considered part of the sovereign Jewish people. The inflexible colonial political institutions created before 1948 to separate the two peoples still prevent democracy from materializing. Derailing the peace process has been a violent act against democratization, just as the negotiations towards ending the occupation have promoted peaceful democratization.

I was now equipped with the tools to explain why people believed we were still in a peace process. Not only were the nation and democracy imagined, but also peace. The imagination of peace was facilitated by the demarcation of the borders by the Intifada and the PLO's 1988 resolution to establish a state in the Occupied Territories of the West Bank and Gaza. The demarcation and recognition of its borders made it possible to imagine the Palestinian state, and the so-called two-state solution. However, it immediately opened the internal arena of social conflicts within Israel, what I call the post-conflict agendas. Thus, the imagination of peace turned these agendas into internal conflicts, based on the assumption that the external conflict with the Palestinians was already "resolved." The imagined peace helped many ignore military occupation and transformed the peace process into an illusion serving to prevent decolonization. The Israeli political arena was reshaped according to the post-conflict agendas, but was unable to coordinate the three arenas and continue the "peace process" (Grinberg, 2010).

The illusion of peace reached new and disturbing heights in 1999 when Ehud Barak was elected Prime Minister: thousands of demonstrators greeted him with shouts against the *Mizrahi* religious party *Shas* (Grinberg, 2010). It was clear that the internal struggles were much more important to Barak's supporters than negotiating with the Palestinians, and that Barak was leading Israel to a disastrous violent confrontation. My inability to convince people that peace became an illusion and we were heading towards an inevitable confrontation derailed my own research (and me too). I spent the next five years as a full time "public sociologist," writing op-eds first in Israeli newspapers, and, since Ariel Sharon replaced Barak in 2001, in international media, since no local newspaper dared publish my columns. It was only after writing a very critical op-ed that provoked threats to my life and livelihood,[14] and the government's decision to withdraw from the Gaza Strip, that I decided to write a book-length manuscript analyzing the failure of peace

---

14   http://www.haaretz.com/print-edition/opinion/academic-freedom-1.120568, http://www.haaretz.co.il/misc/1.964344

and the escalation of violence. The book was published in three different versions and languages—Arabic, Hebrew, and English (Grinberg, 2007, 2007a, 2010). The latter was the most elaborated theoretical conceptualization, and led to the present research program.

c. Politics versus Violence. If Rabin's assassination derailed the peace process and almost completely paralyzed Israeli-Palestinian negotiations, the final cut took place five years later with the violent reaction to the new Intifada that erupted in late September 2000. As opposed to the political reaction by the civil society that had criticized the violent repression of the First Intifada, in 2000 both the public and the media (Dor, 2004) were supportive of increased violence as demanded by the military elites. The military elites[15] who had rejected a military solution to the Intifada in 1988 now claimed that there was no political solution, only military. Thus, the options were either to open political space (through recognition and negotiations) or close it (by violent repression). What changed were the political context and the attitude of the military as a political actor (Grinberg, 2010, 2011, 2013).

The violent repression of the Intifada supported by both the "left" and the "right" shed light on a new question: What could cause such contradictory reactions to almost the same form of resistance? One answer was obvious: the political dramatization of the Camp David negotiations in July 2000. The summit was pre-constructed as a "moment of truth" in which Barak would discover the "real" Arafat and Israelis would be able to determine whether the Palestinians were ready for peace (Meital, 2004). If the Palestinians rejected Barak's "generous offer," so the script went, Arafat would be blamed for the failure of the peace process, and soldiers would know there was no choice but to continue fighting them (Grinberg, 2010, chapter 8). This narrative was adopted by the Israeli peace supporters even before they knew the precise content of the "generous offer."[16] The drama was consistent with the illusion of peace, which was preserved by turning a blind eye to the Palestinian suffering after

---

15 There is a debate if these are indeed the same elite (see Grinberg, 2010: part 4).
16 See a very telling interview with two intellectuals of the peace now movement ("The Ethics of Pragmatism," by Arieh Dayan, *Haaretz*, July 17, 2000). My reaction to this political construction was published as a reader's letter before the end of the summit (*Haaretz*, July 23, 2000), warning that the "left" support of Barak's alibi leads to the renewal of violence. However an op-ed article where I warn that the Prime Minister is leading consciously to a violent confrontation, I sent in August 2000 after the failure of the Camp David Summit, was not published at all.

1993, the Israeli expansion of settlements, and the fact that the new coalition formed in 1999 was opposed to any significant concession to the Palestinians.

What still was not clear to me was why the violent clashes so effectively ended all attempts to contain the vicious circle of violence by negotiations, and why the military elites succeeded so effortlessly in neutralizing the political actors and political mediation, to the point that they alone could control the level of escalation ("the height of the flames," as it was called at the time). It was clear that the military escalated violence each time a window of opportunity opened. This was evident particularly after Arafat declared a unilateral ceasefire in December 2001, which was violated by the targeted killing of Fatah leader Raed Karmi (Haaretz, January 15, 2002).

The theoretical question now was: What are the relations between violence and politics? Here Hannah Arendt's "On Violence" (1969) bailed me out. Her main argument goes against the accepted interpretation of violence as an extension of power. Rather, she argues that violence and power are two contradictory forms of domination: power is based on the rulers' legitimacy, and when they lose their legitimacy they resort to violence. One of the characteristics of violence is that it is physical, as opposed to power, which is symbolic. Moreover, in order to exert violence the soldiers must be willing to obey. Here I found the tools to explain the different attitudes of the Israeli military in 1987 and 2000: in 1987, both servicemen and officers criticized the use of excessive violence, influenced as they were by the civil society mobilization against repression (Grinberg, 2011). In 2000, public support of violence prompted soldiers to use even more violence than they were ordered to, and officers also encouraged disproportionate repressive violence (Harel and Issacharoff, 2004). The change in public opinion made the key difference: during the 1980s, significant parts of the civil society suspected that the *Likud* government was using the military power to promote its expansionist Greater Israel project and accordingly protested against the use of violence against the Palestinians. During the 1990s, however, Israel was apparently ready to end the occupation and it seemed to many that the Palestinians had rejected peaceful compromise (see Grinberg, 2010: Ch.8).

In order to explain the political dynamics in Israel/Palestine, I expanded the application of Arendt's (1969) opposition of power to violence following my previous theoretical insights. I interpreted what Arendt calls "power" as a political symbolic re-presentation of power, and "violence" as a physical presentation of power. In other words, both politics and violence are distinct and opposed forms of power. According to my theoretical conceptualization, political actors mediate social conflicts in the political arena by symbolic representation of social forces, identities, claims and agendas vis-à-vis the state. This is the peaceful, political form of power which contains social conflicts by way of dialogue. However, there is also the option of imposing the will of the powerful by violence, and this depends on the willingness of social groups mobilized by the military to exert violence. When are they ready to use violence? This is a matter of social boundaries, political context and construction of reality by political actors, civil society, and the military (Grinberg, 2011, 2012).

In order to conceptualize the opposition of political power to violence, I suggested the analytical concept of political space, believing it would contribute to an understanding of the dynamics of both peaceful containment of social conflicts and violent repression. Political space is a symbolic space of re-presentation of social forces in conflict by mediators, instead of the violent physical presentation of power. The dynamic opening of political space facilitates recognition, representation, negotiation, and compromise. Political spaces are not static, they may open or close, broaden or shrink. The fundamental precondition for opening political space is the existence of consensual and recognized borders enabling both sides to a conflict to be part of a shared political arena. When a consensual physical and symbolic border separates political arenas, violence can be contained, and while conflicts over disputed (physical or symbolic) borders are typically violent, blurred or nonexistent borders nurture a particular type of anxiety that leads social forces in conflict to support violence.

Political space is opened when, given recognized borders, some balance of power exists between dominant and dominated, and the most powerful recognize that it is better to negotiate with their moderate opponents. This is the typical process of transitions to democracy (O'Donnell and Schmitter, 1986; Przeworski, 1991). Democracy institutionalizes the rules of the game that facilitate the dynamic opening of political space, however it might prevent the opening of political space by symbolic non-recognition or misrecognition of subjugated populations (excluding them from the borders of equal citizenship, or the legitimate nation) or under conditions of imbalance of power between social forces. This is why the concept of political space is so relevant to the critique of formal democratic regimes, because it leads us to uncovering practices of exclusion, repression and denial of legitimate representation within them.

This book is dedicated to expanding the analytical framework of political space by analyzing different degrees of success and failure of various resistance movements, and uncovering symbolic violence and the repertoires of misrepresentation used by dominant political actors seeking to maintain their dominant position.

1.
INTRODUCTION: POLITICAL SPACES AND MO(VE)MENTS OF RESISTANCE

This book is about politics in Israel/Palestine. Politics, however, is too comprehensive a concept, because politics is in some sense everything and everywhere. There is politics at home, in the family, at work, among colleagues and managers. In the sports club, the homeowners association, and worker committee; on municipal, provincial, state, and national levels, as well as international forums.

Politics is not all about large-scale and complex systems. It exists wherever two or more people are part of a shared activity and a decision about that activity affects all of them. Politics refers to the process of decision making and implementation: who makes the decision? Do they take into account those affected by it? This begs the question of power relations and formal and informal decision making process. Who has power over whom? Can one person or group take a decision that affects the other unilaterally, imposing their will, or do those affected also have some power to oppose the decision and influence it? Is there a process of deliberation and dialogue, or does the decision maker have the power to ignore the interests, wishes and demands of the affected? Is the process of decision making institutionalized, namely formally regulated by consensual rules of the game? How do these rules affect the decisions made and the chances of those affected to shape the decision? How do the affected react when they are ignored? Do they accept the decision, protest or stop taking part in the shared activity, group, organization or institution?[1]

Politics is about the dynamic relations between those who make decisions and the actions and reactions of those affected by them. When some form of recognition and deliberation between the decision makers and those affected takes place formally or even informally, and the affected can influence and monitor the decision makers and change their

---

[1] On the options to accept the decision, protest or leave, see Hirshman (1970).

decisions, we can talk about an interactive deliberated decision-making process. Again, the interactivity of the political process does not depend on the size or complexity of the shared framework, or on the existence of formal rules of the game. When decisions are made while ignoring those affected we can talk about unilateral imposed processes.

Scholars who studied political processes on the nation-state level suggested a distinction between democratic and authoritarian regimes (Moore, 1965; Rustow, 1970; O'Donnell and Schmitter, 1986; Przeworski, 1991; Linz and Stepan, 1996). The theoretical framework of the research presented here attempts to go beyond the democracy/autocracy dichotomy, and comprehend dynamic political processes of change on the macro-political level of nation-states. The intention is to focus on dynamic processes of political change that exceed the scope of this schematic dichotomy, mainly in an attempt to discover the capacity of dominated social groups to mobilize, resist, and influence unilaterally imposed decisions. I investigate here dynamic political processes both with and without democratic rules of the game, and also examine the capacity of political power holders in formal democracies to ignore citizens' demands. In order to comprehend these complex political dynamics and be able to critically analyze formal democratic regimes, I have developed the concept of *political space* (Grinberg, 2010). Although my initial insights originated in my study of Israeli-Palestinian relations (Grinberg, 2010), I intend to propose here a theoretical framework of political dynamics useful for comparative analyses and critiques of a broad range of political contingencies, cases, and events.

The concept of political space refers to the peaceful containment of social conflicts by means of recognition and representation. Political space is dynamic, can be opened and closed, and was initially designed to comprehend the changing policies of recognition and rejection of Palestinian demands by the Israeli power holders in the years 1988-2006 (Grinberg, 2007, 2010, 2013a). This book is part of a new research project designed to expand the analytical framework of dynamic political processes by comparing a series of case studies of different and opposed reactions of dominant power holders to resistance by various dominated social forces, including class, ethnic, national and civil society protests. The initial concept of political space was based on the dichotomy of politics/violence, interpreting violence as the means to close political spaces, and politics as the way to open them for containing conflicts by recognition, representation, negotiation and compromise. In the present book I seek to expand the concept of dynamic political spaces by going beyond the politics/violence dichotomy, aiming to comprehend the more nuanced political dynamics occurring between instances of violent repression and vicious cycles of violence and counter-violence, on the one hand, and successful cases of containment of social conflicts by recognition, representation, negotiations and compromise on the other.

The situations and cases analyzed here focus mainly on the more subtle strategies of domination by power holders, the non-recognition or misrecognition of the needs and rights of dominated groups and the power to ignore the fundamental equality between human beings. This is not physical violence exerted on the dominated groups, but what Bourdieu (1992) has termed symbolic violence, namely the capacity of the dominant to ignore, non-recognize or misrecognize the subordinated. In order to oppose this form of domination, people who are ignored must actively demonstrate their physical presence in order to gain visibility and recognition of their needs and wills, demanding to be taken into consideration.

I suggest using the term "resistance" to refer to the proactive demonstrations of presence by subordinated social forces seeking recognition and representation in the decision-making process. The dynamics between the *symbolic* violence of the dominant and the *physical* resistance of the dominated are at the theoretical focus of this research plan. It is based on the analysis of seven different cases of resistance movements on particular political junctions in the history of Israel. The comparative research method is designed to learn about various forms of resistance mobilization, and different repertoires of struggle against dominant powers. The research is also designed to learn about the various reactions of power holders, both political actors and state institutions, and their repertoires of contention.

The Israeli case is so rich in cases of proactive resistance and reactive responses by the dominant powers that it seems an almost ideal laboratory for building social theory. I start with an anti-colonial revolt of the mixed Arab-Jewish civil society against the British Mandate in Palestine in 1931 and continue with ethnic riots (1959) and a working-class strike wave (1960-1965) during the formal democratic regime of the State of Israel in 1948-1967. During the period of the dual democratic-military regime established in Israel/Palestine after 1967, I compare four cases of resistance: ethnic riots (1971) working class mobilization (1980), national uprising against military occupation (1988-1992) and "Occupy"-style movements against neo-liberal economic policies (2011). After analyzing each case I compare them in Chapter 9, suggesting some theoretical generalizations. In this introduction I present the theoretical concept of dynamic political spaces as developed in my previous investigations, and proceed to explain how the resistance of the dominated, oppressed and non-recognized contributes to theoretical development.

II. On Politics and Violence

Hannah Arendt criticized scholars like von Clausewitz, Weber, and C.W. Mills, who assumed that violence is part and parcel of political power, an inseparable continuum (Arendt, 1969: 8, 35–6). Arendt calls "power" what I call here, for the purpose of clarity, "political power," and she clearly distinguishes between them: "Power and violence are opposites; where the one rules absolutely, the other is absent. Violence appears where power is in jeopardy" (56). According to Arendt, the main source of confusion between the two forms of domination is that they usually appear together as forms of state power. However, they differ significantly: political power is based on dialogue and consent, while violence is a unilateral imposition. Violence can destroy political power, but cannot build it, and if a ruler rules exclusively through violence without any form of political consent, the use of violence becomes intimidation—used to deter political opponents.

Political spaces of representation are opened when authoritarian ruling elites recognize their inability to continue ruling unilaterally due to the increasing violence needed in order to remain in power. When rulers opt to recognize some claims of the dominated groups and open dialogue with their representatives, the process is defined as democratization or transition to democracy (Rustow, 1970; O'Donnell and Schmitter, 1986; Przeworski, 1991; Linz and Stepan, 1996). Democratization has occurred in very different contexts and paths (Tilly, 1995), but it usually entails the institutionalized opening of political space for representation, negotiation, and compromise. However, the concept of dynamic political spaces here suggested also seeks to explain why institutionalized democracies sometimes *fail* to represent claims and opinions in civil society, and also to contain social conflicts. In these cases democracy can be fake, an illusion (O'Donnell, 1992, 1996).

Political space as a symbolic field of representation is necessary when large social groups and state apparatuses cannot be physically present in the process of decision-making, and sides in a conflict must be mediated by political actors representing them. In other words, while violence is a physical act of presentation of coercive power, politics is a symbolic act of representation of social groups and organizations. Violence can be effective only if a concrete group of people are ready to exercise it (Arendt, 1969; Mann, 2005), while politics is exercised in the absence of the social group, which is imagined and constructed by the political leaders who represent it, act on its behalf and wish to continue being its spokespersons (Bourdieu, 1992).

The crucial factor in the use of physical violence is the existence of social forces ready to use it against the other, especially when "they" are considered not part of "us." Democracy and the "nation-state" might become violent and dangerous because it excludes "internal others" and in some specific circumstances constructs them as "internal enemies," building the legitimacy to use violence against them, and the conviction of the soldiers that by obeying orders they are defending the nation (Mann, 2005).

The distinction between politics and violence helps clarify the political role of the military apparatus, namely that its action or inaction in the internal power struggle always has political implications. Tilly (1992) shows that state makers expand their territorial control and demarcate borders, extracting material and human resources from the population under their dominion. By so doing, the military defines the subjects of the state, and creates "internal" space where the state's civil apparatus can extract material resources from the "internal" population. The extraction of resources to finance the military and war forces the state's civil apparatuses to negotiate with local populations, open political space, and democratize (Tilly, 2007). In my previous work I have argued that the military elites become political actors, whatever attitude they adopt towards struggles between dominant and dominated groups. If the military uses violence against the population in support of the rulers, it closes space to political representation and mediation; if it refuses to, it creates a balance of power that facilitates the opening of political space (Grinberg, 2008, 2010, 2013a).

When the military only protects the state's external borders and avoids violence against citizens, it is considered apolitical, and when it intervenes in internal power relations or takes power directly, it is seen as a political actor.[2] In both cases, however, the military shapes the political arena, and this is the most crucial factor in creating the two fundamental preconditions for opening political space: the military demarcates the borders of the state that define the shared identity of potentially equal citizens, and facilitates a balance of power when it does not use violence against the dominated population. The contradiction between violence and politics takes the form of alternative options between military repression and the opening of political space for representation of dominated groups (Grinberg, 2013a).

III. Political Space

Although physical borders of states and symbolic boundaries of national communities are the frameworks that contain political space, they are also signals of violence. They are usually evidence of use of violence in the past—in war and colonial and imperial expansion governed by the exclusionist character of national movements—and in the present they impose limits on freedom of movement and the civil rights of individuals and groups (Balibar, 2004). At the same time, however, the existence of recognized borders facilitates the containment of conflicts within them because borders open the possibility of claims to formal equality between state subjects, the peaceful expression of demands, and the organization of dominated groups.

Whereas politics is based on recognition, representation, and dialogue, violence is based on non- or misrecognition of the Other, physical presentation of coercive power, confrontation, and unilateral dictation by the powerful. Both are forms of state power relations, but represent competing and frequently contradictory principles of conflict management.

To comprehend the tendency to use violence and historical moments when violence is perceived to be illegitimate, ineffective, or undesirable, I suggest framing the question within a dynamic concept of political

---

2 On the various forms of military-political intervention, see Stepan (2001, Ch. 4).

spaces. Usually, the meaning of the concept "political space" is taken for granted; it is used intuitively without an explicit definition or conceptualization. Political space is not a physical area but a social construct, a symbolic field of representation (Bourdieu, 1992) within a specific sphere of power relations, distinct from civil society and the state (Linz and Stepan, 1996), that frames a dynamic arena of contestation and containment of social conflicts within constantly changing opportunities (Tarrow and Tilly, 2007; Tarrow, 1996; Collier and Collier, 1991). Political spaces of representation may be opened or closed in the political arena, which is differentiated from social forces and state institutions, but is framed and determined by them. Struggles over the opening of political space take place in the political arena, mainly through the contestation of political actors, but social and state actors also take part in shaping the political arena. This book aims to expand our understanding of the dynamic opening and closure of political spaces by analyzing actions by political, social and state actors and the interactions between them.

The concept of political space suggested here is not the geographic space, or the territorial dimension of the state. The term political space, as used here, refers to the symbolic representation of social conflicts in the political arena which are mediated by political actors and framed "between" the state institutions and the civil society. The political arena (or field) is framed by the state and civil society, but is not autonomous—and its dynamic and very existence are shaped and reshaped by changes in power relations between the state and civil society.

The political arena is a symbolic field where political actors can suddenly appear and disappear, and the rules of the game can be drastically changed or revoked. Political actors may open or close political spaces claiming to be representatives of concrete social forces and speaking in their name; they seek to promote the interests of these forces, but are completely dependent on public support and the state's rules of the game that constrain their action. This lack of autonomy is a byproduct of the fact that the state and civil society are not only symbolic fields, and when social forces remove their support from specific political actors or if the state legally prevents their action, political space might close, old political actors might disappear and the political arena of mediation might be suspended by unilateral regimes. Even when the political arena is institutionalized and consolidated, political actors might be removed from their positions, and new political actors may take their place. As discussed throughout this book, the threat posed by new political actors leads incumbent actors to try to close political space to new identities, agendas, and actors. Here lies the puzzle of the present research: How can old political actors maintain their power and prevent representation within or without the democratic rules of the game.

Political actors seek to bridge tensions and conflicts at two levels: (a) between the state and its civil society, and (b) between dominant and dominated social groups within civil society. These tensions are mediated in the political arena by collective imaginations of who "we," the people, are and how the state's concrete policies are presumed to serve civil society. The political field's symbolic aspect facilitates this by imagining social forces as "groups" with shared identity and needs, as well as imagining the collective national identity of the entire civil society. Imagination is crucial in politics also in order to build visions of more desirable futures and contested interpretations of the past and present realities. In the political field, reality is constructed by symbolic means such as narratives, discourses, and myths.

IV. Political Field, Arena and Actors

Bourdieu conceives the political field as an autonomous symbolic field where competing actors vie for power. These actors' struggles are homologous of struggles in other socioeconomic fields, and by their speech and actions, political actors create the social group that cannot speak for itself. The political field appears historically as the result of the construction of bureaucratic fields of power, in tension with and differentiated from the crown.[3] The politician's power is symbolic and, by way of delegation, he can silence other group members because he speaks in their name and has a vested interest in continuing to speak for them (Bourdieu, 1992: Ch. 9).

The concept of political space suggested here shares Bourdieu's definition of the political field as a symbolic field of representations of social groups, but the most important difference concerns the assumption that the political field is autonomous. On the contrary, it is my argu-

---

3   Quoted by Wacquant (2005: 5).

ment that one of the most salient features of the political space here proposed is its lack of autonomy from other fields, because it is framed by and dependent on the state and civil society. This is also the reason for the tension with other fields and the potential absence of homology. It explains why political space can suddenly be opened and closed by critical political events. Civil society has relative autonomy and its constant dynamics shape the political field, affecting who may claim to represent it. The organization of civil society has the power to affect the political field, remove politicians who disappoint the forces they claim to represent, and support new speakers, opening political space and transforming the political arena (Cohen and Arato, 1994). In other words, it is not only the political actor who creates a social group, but social groups who are able to support or remove political actors. The dynamic interrelations between political actors and the social groups they claim to represent, and the dependence of the former on the latter, are crucial to the concept of political space and particularly to the questions raised by the present research project regarding social resistance to power.

These interrelations are also at the core of Linz and Stepan's (1996) conceptualization of "political society" as distinct from civil society, but in constant interaction with it. Political society bridges civil society and the state, and political parties have a crucial role to play in the process of democratization. The distinction between these three levels is critical to the consolidation and smooth functioning of democracy. The organization and active participation of civil society is vital to guarantee the role of political society as representative of social interests. The three levels—state, society, and politics—are distinct spheres of action: the state shapes political society and the relations within civil society, while political society mediates the conflicts within civil society and between it and the state through state apparatuses and policies. Civil society is the sphere of organization and presentation of social interests, agendas, and ideas by social actors—organizations, movements, and individuals—while politics is the sphere of political actors representing absent social groups and compromising in their name given limited state options and resources.

I refer to the political sphere, field, or arena as Linz and Stepan (1996) interpret the political society that bridges civil society and the state, which mediates conflicts between social forces. However, political society is formally organized and relatively stable when democracy is consolidated, while political spaces are in a constant dynamic: they may be closed even by the political actors in response to mass mobilizations by civil society. I argue here that the tension between civil and political societies is precisely due to the political field's lack of autonomy, and the concern of political actors for their future position and power. State and political actors can engage in conscious manipulation in an effort to demobilize civil society when they sense a threat to their power by the dynamic that helps open political spaces. This is why political spaces are dynamic and unstable, while civil society's demands might be neutralized by state and political actors seeking to maintain their power. These dynamics between civil society actors and mass movements, and the reactions of political and state actors, is the subject matter of the present research. In other words, political space is a dynamic concept: it may be opened for representation and containment of social conflicts but also closed even by consolidated democratic regimes and institutionally differentiated political societies.

The fluctuations of civil society mobilization under changing structural conditions and conjunctures have been extensively investigated by researchers of social movements who proposed the dynamic concept of political opportunities structure (POS) (Tarrow, 1998; McAdam, Tarrow and Tilly, 2001; Tarrow and Tilly, 2007). The concept of dynamic opening and closing of political spaces incorporates the idea of the constantly changing structure of opportunities. However, the POS approach focuses on opportunities open to civil society movements and organizations to mobilize social groups and shape state policies, while the focus of political space is on the political mediation between civil society and state policies and among different social groups. The analysis of dynamic political spaces focuses on political actors and their relations with civil society and state policies in changing national and international contexts. It examines the ways in which these political actors interpret and re-present social demands, or opt to ignore them due to their own interest in maintaining their power positions.[4]

The political articulation between civil society and the state and their multiple dynamics and variations has been the focus of Collier and Collier (1991) in their comparative study of the transition of Latin

---

4   This is in line with recent interest in the processes of grievance formation, which are often neglected in POS literature (Pinard, 2011).

American states from democracy to authoritarian rule and back. In their approach, political sphere is an arena of contestation, articulation, and containment of social conflicts. The greatest challenge to the capitalist regime is the democratic incorporation of the working class, while the constant dynamic of democratization and de-democratization is explained by changing global and local contexts, and the specific ways in which political parties incorporate trade unions and the working class.

The dynamic analysis of the political arena proposed by Collier and Collier (1991) is very close to my concept of dynamic opening and closing of political space, including its path-dependent aspect and the option of total elimination of the political arena by dictatorial regimes. The main difference is that according to them, civil society is mainly characterized by class conflict and politics is analyzed mainly by the party-trade union institutional links in a situation where the state's borders and national identity are *not* contested. The concepts of political arena and dynamic opening of political spaces I suggest here include other forms of social conflict precipitated by colonial and military expansion, and also conflicts between national, ethnic, and religious groups. The analytical concept of dynamic political spaces aims to include also violent repression and closure of political spaces within the multiple complexities of colonial and settler societies. However, in this book I focus on relatively contained and peaceful forms of symbolic violence by dominant elites and resistance movements of subordinated social forces.

V. Imagined Communities, Imagined Democracy, and Settler Societies

The literature of transition to democracy has emphasized citizens' shared identity as a precondition for democratization (Anderson, 1999), but the existence of frameworks of containment (sovereign states and national identities) has been taken for granted. Stepan (2001, Ch. 9) has properly commented that despite the extensive simultaneous research of transitions to democracy and the emergence of nations, these two important research projects have almost completely ignored each other. This theoretical lacuna is especially surprising because nationalism and democracy emerged almost at the same time and place—after the decay of dynastic orders and the development of capitalism in eighteenth-century Europe. Democracy is based on the idea of popular sovereignty over the state, while national communities are defined vis-à-vis state authorities, either as the sovereign people of an already established state, or a as claims of subjugated population for independence from and popular sovereignty over imposed imperial and colonial power.

Democracy institutionalizes the procedures to govern state apparatus by "the people," while the borders of the state and "the people" are taken for granted and not as a matter of contestation and conflict. As Offe correctly commented, "The people cannot decide who is the people" (1998: 116). Liberal approaches to democracy assume all citizens constitute "the people" while "organic" approaches define the nation in cultural and historical terms, and in so doing exclude a portion of the citizens. The symbolic boundaries of the people are, in several contexts, a matter of democratic struggle to open political space of representation to excluded citizens. When a subjugated group is empowered by internal or external factors, it may organize and claim its recognition and inclusion as equal citizens.

The most glorified recognized struggles for democratization are those of social groups considered part of the nation, like the struggles of the working class and suffragettes for recognition of their equal rights to vote and be represented. These were struggles demanding the opening of the political space of representation, and even when some violence was used it was a means to achieve recognition, equal citizenship and representation. However these groups were symbolically included within the boundaries of the nation, so the change demanded was only a matter of recognition of formal equality, rather than the re-imagining of the nation's boundaries. Thus, social conflict was contained by opening political space for representation, facilitated by the democratic rules of the game.

Struggles to open political space to groups defined by the national borders as *not* belonging to the nation were much more violent, and in several cases ended in ethnic cleansing and genocide. Mann (2005) shows that democratic regimes can be aggressive and brutal toward excluded social groups even more than non-democratic regimes—whether colonial, dictatorial or communist. In cases of symbolic exclusion from the nation, democracy becomes the problem: if it is "the people" who rule, and non-nationals are recognized as legitimate equal citizens, they can shape politics and state institutions and even become the rulers. In non-democratic regimes, there is no such danger because the political arena is not the bridge between the state and civil society, and there is no need for extremely violent forms of repression like ethnic cleansing. In a similar line of thought, Zakaria (1997) argues that for cultural minorities, liberalism is more crucial than democracy and a liberal dictator is preferable to an illiberal democracy. In both cases, political space for minority representation is closed, but democracy views minorities as a "threat" due to their potential claim for representation, and becomes more aggressive and repressive toward them. On the other hand, authoritarian regimes that formally prevent the political arena of mediation from becoming formally institutionalized may open other channels of mediation and dialogue with civil society, including minorities.

Democratic regimes obviously claim to be open, representative, and nonviolent; when they become violent it is justified as self-defense against an "existential threat." Elsewhere, I have emphasized the close linkage between democracy and the national community by using the term "imagined democracy" (Grinberg, 1999). Every democracy is imagined, and imagined twice: once because it imagines the national community, "the people," and again because it imagines elected political actors as if they actually represent parts or divisions and conflicts among "the people." Both "the people" and its parts are imagined and represented by parties. However, a working democracy, able to contain social conflicts by peaceful mediation and dynamic opening of political spaces of representation, is assumed to realize and materialize the imagined "ruling people" by implementing policies promised by elected officials. When these disappoint their constituencies, civil society has the potential power to make democracy real: it can mobilize, express discontent, and change the government. This is precisely the dynamic of opening political space legally framed by the democratic rules of the game. However if some group is formally or informally denied access to state power, recognition, or equal human and political rights, democracy becomes not only imagined but illusory, because it cannot be realized and cannot contain social tensions by representation. This book focuses on the Israeli imagined democracy, the obstacles to representation of various subordinated social forces, and the resistance movements that emerged claiming recognition and representation.

Israeli imaginary democracy's historic origin is the settler political project. Settler societies are the clearest cases of imaginary democracies that formally close political spaces of representation to others, in this case non-settlers. Settler societies generally established democratic regimes for European migrants, but denied equal rights to the other native and non-native populations. They occupied the "new" lands and established states that "belonged" to them. In some cases they excluded and displaced local population, killed them, or removed them to delimited areas; sometimes these populations were granted formal unequal legal status (Fredrickson, 1997; Mann, 2005). These are peculiar types of democracy because they draw a sharp line between "the people" who deserve representation and the "non-people" who are not represented and denied basic rights.

Paraphrasing Brubaker (1996), these are extreme cases of simultaneously nationalizing and de-nationalizing states: they nationalize the migrants, who otherwise would have rarely been considered "a nation," and "de-nationalize" the region's original inhabitants, who are obviously not European "national communities," but are reconstructed by the state imposed on them as an excluded and dispossessed social category. The European nation-state constantly erects internal and external borders of distinction to define who is outside the state and who are the Others inside it (Mignolo, 2000). Non-recognition of the local population in settler democracies constitutes symbolic violence, which often deteriorates into increasingly physical violence in order to maintain the regime, at the same time that the democratic institutions are improved for the recognized "nationals" (Mann, 2005).

As argued above, imagination is a vital element of politics; without it, democracy cannot work as a system of representation. However, if parts of the population are excluded from the imagined people and not recognized as equal citizens, democracy is only imagined, as it cannot contain social conflicts by the dynamic opening of political space for mediation. Exclusion and misrecognition are acts of symbolic violence, and in order to maintain the exclusion of a group, the state may use physical violence. The closure of political space to specific groups in democratic states can be achieved formally by the legal system and institutional procedures; it can also be informal, through by everyday behavior, discourse, and language. This is the major political critique suggested by the concept of political space. Chapters 2 and 7 below analyze resistance movements against the closure of political spaces by imposed colonial institutions, while Chapters 3 and 5 discuss struggles against symbolic exclusion and closure of political space to ethnic minorities. Only struggles by the working class (Chapters 4 and 6) and the "people" (the 99% in Chapter 8) were conducted to open political space to social forces given formal democratic institutions and symbolic inclusion within the boundaries of the national community.

VI. Political Actors and Democratic Closure of Political Space

Here is the dynamic feature of political spaces: given recognized borders and some balance of power between rulers and dominated groups, political spaces of representation can be opened in the political arena in order to facilitate peaceful containment of conflicts by negotiation and compromise. The political arena is framed in between the civil society and state institutions, and the political space for mediation is opened between dominant elites and dominated masses. However, the political actors must also bridge the tension between the concrete state institutions and the imagined national community. In short, political actors are mediators of multiple tensions and conflicts, they compete and in order to maintain and expand their power they may not only open political spaces for mediation, but also close them to competitors. Processes opening political space contradict the violent imposition of unilateral will.

Democratic principles, rules, and institutions are designed to consolidate the political arena as a mediator of conflicts within the state and to facilitate the dynamic opening of political spaces of representation by political actors. Securing individual freedoms of speech and association; inclusive, periodic, and open elections between competing parties; building government coalitions and protecting opposition parties (Schmitter and Karl, 1991)—all these are institutional arrangements that encourage the opening of political space to new agendas, identities, discourses, and actors. And while highly democratic constitutions and institutions may be violently eliminated by unilaterally imposed regimes, the concept of political space is designed primarily to comprehend *less* obvious closures of political space that also take place under democratic rules of the game.

The potential deterioration of formal democratic regimes into what I call "imaginary democracies" has been formulated by O'Donnell (1992, 1996) in different terms in his critique of apparently "consolidated" democracies in Latin America. The primary concern of the literature of transition to democracy was consolidation, namely long-term maintenance of democratic rules of the game, and the changing of governments by election without coups. After consolidation has been achieved, the questions focus on the failure of the newly formalized democratic regimes to contain social conflicts by means of recognition, representation, mediation, and compromise. In other words, the question is when and why political spaces for the containment of social conflicts by representation are opened, and when and how they might be closed by dominant political actors seeking to maintain their power and close the spaces for competition. These are core questions of the present research project.

The fact that democracy may not work despite the consolidation of formal rules of the game has produced a huge typology of "limited" democracies and democratic "deficits" (Collier and Levitsky, 1997). Although designed to describe specific forms that prevent the opening of political space, my interest is not in classification but in providing a tool for the analytical critique of political practices that prevent representation of social conflicts, the opening of new agendas, and the entry of new political actors. This is not a particular problem of new and deficient democratic regimes but a built-in deficiency of democracy due to its potential illusionary aspect.

Political actors often try to close political space to new competing actors precisely due to the lack of autonomy and stability that characterizes the political arena and its dependency on the support of social forces. In other words, the dynamic character of political spaces has a double meaning for political actors: the chance to increase power and the risk of losing it. Given the uncertainty built into the political arena, political actors—leaders and parties—seek to secure their positions by a wide variety of institutional and discursive means. Both are usually mutually supportive and are designed to establish durable links between political actors and the two potentially autonomous factors that determine the lack of autonomy of political society: state institutions and civil social forces. This comparative research project is also aimed to uncover both discursive and institutional means used by political actors aiming to maintain their power.

VII. Resistance Mo(ve)ments

Analyzing resistance is essential to expanding the concept of political space, because it presents the reaction of a subjugated group to the closure of political space. In order to open political space, subjugated social groups must make collective demonstrations of presence aiming at bringing to an end the hidden (symbolic) violence of their non-recognition. This is why the collective actions of subjugated groups are always acts of presence, and no matter if they are more or less violent—or even non-violent—they might provoke violent reactions by the dominant (Fredrickson, 1997: Ch. 10). However, as argued above, the use of violence is in itself a sign that the dominant group is losing political power, and it may lead either to the opening of political space or to the escalation of violence.

Resistance is the counterpart of symbolic violence. Both are mixed types of the opposite properties of violence and political power: resistance is a physical presentation of power by subordinated groups (similar to violence) seeking symbolic recognition (similar to politics), while symbolic violence is a representation of superior power of the dominant (similar to politics) used to submit a group by means of non-recognition, humiliation and degradation (similar to violence). Contrary to physical violence, symbolic violence is a more sophisticated and effective form of domination; likewise, resistance is a more sophisticated form of struggle.

The interrelations between symbolic violence and resistance are the everyday form of power relations and power struggles between dominant and dominated groups, while the opening of political space is the peaceful way to contain social conflicts. On the one hand when facing resistance the dominant can afford to ignore it, given sufficient confidence in their power; react violently when they are less confident; or recognize the subordinated and negotiate a compromise, namely open up political space having realized the ineffectiveness or immorality of violent repression. On the other hand, the subordinated cannot use symbolic violence because they cannot ignore the power used against them by the dominant. After presenting their power in the public sphere they may empower their representatives to speak in their name upon recognition, or may intensify their resistance.

The most extreme cases of resistance occur when organized violence is escalated by both sides, taking the form of a "war" where the victory of one is the other's defeat. When the dominant group succeeds, this could mean authoritarian rule at best, and displacement, mass murder, or genocide at worst (Mann, 2005). Complete victory by the subordinated group means violent takeover and removal of the previous rulers. Such scenarios include civil society revolutions installing democracy instead of the authoritarian regime, national liberation revolutions installing local leadership instead of colonial rule, and class revolutions replacing the dominant class (Tilly, 1993; Skocpol, 1980). The intention here is to investigate instances of resistance that *do not* lead to escalation of violence, war, and unilateral victory, but to varied degrees of recognition and representation by opening political spaces to subordinated social forces.

My suggested definition of resistance is the attempt to open political space through physical presentation of power by subordinated social forces seeking recognition and representation. This resistance can be understood as a movement because it mobilizes social forces over a long period, creating a relation between the timeframe and collective action which constitutes the *mo(ve)ment*. The elements of the theoretical framework of dynamic political spaces developed from one research project to the other, as described in the Prologue, and led to the questions at the core of the present project: What are the social forces involved in resistance? What do they resist and why? What are the differential effects of resistance movements? What are their immediate and long-term achievements and failures? The investigation of resistance also led to the most critical question: What are the *repertoires of subjugation* used by the dominant political actors aiming at neutralizing resistance?

Movements and moments are intertwined, hence the term *mo(ve) ment*. The moment refers to the timeframe between the initial intrusion into the public sphere, when the movement mobilizes collective action and succeeds in making the group visible. At that point in time, collective identity and claims are defined and publicly discussed by social activists, opinion leaders and political actors. In principle, the moment of resistance can be short or prolonged; in the cases analyzed here, the timeframes range from one month of ethnic riots (April 1959) to five years of working class strikes (1960-1965) and Palestinian national revolt (1987-1992). The moment ends when the movement, its agendas, claims and ideas no longer attract public interest after the problem is considered to have been solved, with the group legitimately represented or successfully marginalized by political or state actors.

In what follows, each chapter is dedicated to a particular resistance mo(ve)ment, following the same analytical framework. I start with a background description and analysis of the construction of dominant power and subjugation of a specific social group, aiming to understand the mo(ve)ment's context. The analysis of the initial intrusion into the public sphere is important in order to understand how dominant groups react to it—by recognition or repression or some combination of both. The dynamics of recognition or repression, success or failure, will help us understand the sources of power wielded by the dominant compared to the dominated social groups.

The analysis of each mo(ve)ment's duration will help us understand the autonomous sources of power of the resisting social groups, and also the threat they present to the rulers. Public dissolution of the mo(ve)ment does not necessarily spell its political end, and I discuss why specific movements lost momentum, became marginalized and eventually disappeared. I then analyze their aftermath, in which powerful groups react to the movement in what I term *counter-mo(ve)ment*.

Similarly to the movement, the timeframe of the counter-mo(ve)ment varies from a few months to several years. In all cases, it is an attempt by dominant groups and rulers to reestablish their powerful position by redefining agendas, discourses, institutions and structures. The counter-mo(ve)ment, however, is never a return to the status quo ante but a re-accommodation of the political arena by either attempting to shrink the space opened by the mo(ve)ment (never to become totally closed ever again), coopting its leaders or taking other steps to regain control over the now open political space. The goal of the counter-mo(ve)ment is to prevent future eruption of a new resistance mo(ve)ment. It does not always succeed, and when it does, its success is often partial. Accordingly, each chapter will present the historical background of the resistance mo(ve)ment, its lifecycle and counter-mo(ve)ment.

VIII. Between Social Actors and Social Movements

The concept of *mo(ve)ments* refers to the peculiar intersection of the *movement* and *moment* of mass mobilization, and is designed to distinguish these movements both from the best known concepts of social movement research—"cycles of protest" (Tarrow, 1989) and "political opportunities structure" (Eisinger, 1973; Tilly, 1978; McAdam, 1996). This book discusses the time framing (moment) of resistance movements, aiming to comprehend the historical contingencies that empower specific social identities and explore why political opportunities are opened, and what caused the weakening of the dominant powers, aiming to analyze the linkage between the moment and movement.

Mo(ve)ments of resistance differ from social movements in several aspects. The moment does not occur in the middle of the "curve" between closed and open political opportunities (Eisinger, 1973; Tilly, 1978; McAdam, 1996); it is rather a matter of almost complete closure of legitimate channels of representation. The "political" aspect of the opportunity is not just a matter of structural, institutional or formal politics, but also a matter of symbolic repression of identities, narratives, discourses and agendas. This is the reason why we must study and comprehend the local conditions of the specific case (Kriesi et al., 1995), the social conflicts and tools used by the dominant groups to maintain their power, and the sequence of events that provoke the political dynamics of protest, including the influence of international factors.

Movements of resistance seek to gain recognition and representation of their claims, and protest against the dominant power, as well as against the entire political system, including the opposition, for failing to represent the claims of the oppressed (Snow, 2004). The mo(ve)ment of resistance is not necessarily the culmination of any long-term action by social activists and organizers but a volcanic eruption of repressed discontent that suddenly finds a way up to the public surface. It is not a cycle (Tarrow, 1989), however, because when the moment ends the institutionalized political actors threatened by the movement react to prevent a new cycle. I call this reaction counter-mo(ve)ment because the resistance mo(ve)ment has always some effect—whether in the short, middle or long term—which does not necessarily represent its original claims; it rather has unintended consequences, provoking in some cases the completely opposite reaction. Here my analysis departs from the social movement literature that usually assumes various positive outcomes, including the institutionalization of social protest and actors, and even actual change in government policies (Tarrow, 1998; McAdam, 1996; Meyer, 2004).

Although the concept of resistance movements suggested here differs from social movements, there is some overlap. Both types of movements are framed by significant historical moments of beginning and ending, and both mobilize social forces. While resistance movements are physical presentations of power in the absence of political space for recognition and representation of a specific group, social movements may represent agendas and issues with no necessary mass mobilization supporting them, and often tend to institutionalize and establish links with political actors.

The overlapping occurs when social and resistance movements have both features: as resistance movements they physically express the power of misrepresented subordinated social groups; and as social movements they also have clear identities and names decided by social actors who formally set forth who they are and what they want. I discuss two such cases in this book: the Israeli Black Panthers (1971-1973) and Forum/13 (1980). The interesting common denominator of the overlapping cases is that the social actors continued arguing that the *movement* was still alive after the *moment* of resistance had passed, and when they had lost the capacity to mobilize their constituencies.

In cases of resistance without a social movement, the memory of the event takes on a dual meaning. On the one hand, formal narratives tend to marginalize or even neglect these events. On the other hand, the ideas and agendas invoked in those mo(ve)ments often reemerge in the future. Thus, the 1959 Wadi Salib riots inspired the Black Panthers in 1971; the working class revolt in 1960-65 inspired Forum/13; and the Intifada of 1987-92 inspired the Second Intifada in 2000. The next Chapter focuses on the peculiar phenomenon of "historical amnesia," questioning exactly why there is absolutely no memory or legacy of the successful 1931 Jewish-Arab anti-colonial strike.

IX. Conclusion

This book proposes a theoretical framework designed to uncover, analyze and criticize the repression of subordinated social forces under either military or colonial rule, and also within legitimate democratic rules of the game. The historical chapters analyze the context of political domination and exclusion that facilitates the emergence of the mo(ve)ment of resistance. In the concluding chapter, I suggest some generalizations related to the various forms of resistance and their success in

CHAPTER ONE

opening political space, as well as to the repertoire of options available to the dominant groups seeking to shrink the political space of subordinated masses and roll back their achievements in the aftermath.

Each chapter attempts to solve a crucial historical puzzle through the analysis of a mo(ve)ment of resistance, no matter how marginal and short-lived. The most telling in this sense is Chapter 2, which seeks to comprehend the ethno-national conflict between Jews and Arabs and its tragic deterioration into the forced migration of Palestinians in 1948 by analyzing a joint anti-colonial strike that succeeded in reducing government transportation levies in 1931. Chapter 3 seeks to fathom the strange phenomenon of a so-called Labor party which actually represented the *Ashkenazi* (European Jewish) middle classes by analyzing the repression of *Mizrahi* (Middle-Eastern Jewish) ethnic riots of 1959. Next, Chapter 4 analyzes the working-class revolt during the period of full employment (1960-1965) in an attempt to explain why the Labor Party institutionalized the occupation of the West Bank and Gaza Strip and the integration of the Palestinians into Israeli economy as a captive market under military rule. Chapter 5 analyzes the Israeli Black Panthers movement, looking for the sources of ethno-class mobilization of the "left" against the "right" among the Israeli electorate, and the complete sweeping of all socioeconomic, cultural, and political issues under the tribal carpet. Chapter 6 conceptualizes the political economy of hyperinflation and its management through the imposition of neo-liberal policies and structures by analyzing the struggle of powerful workers to protect their privileged status. The following chapter analyzes Israel's ability to maintain its military control over the Palestinians by looking into the Intifada resistance mo(ve)ment (1987-1993) and its relative limited success in establishing the Palestinian Authority (PA) under continued Israeli domination. Finally, Chapter 8 discusses the unprecedented mass mobilization of civil society against the capital-state linkage in the name of "the people" and uses previous conceptualizations of political repertoires of distortion to analyze the 2013 electoral campaign.

On the whole, the book discusses the tremendous obstacles of the Israeli polity, preventing the opening of political space to the representation of the working class, *Mizrahi* Jews and Palestinians. The comprehensive analysis offered below suggests that Israel is an *imaginary* or *illusionary democracy*, namely a regime that effectively closes political space to subordinated groups. It is effective precisely owing to its success in legitimizing itself as a democracy, both locally and internationally. The repressive features of Israeli democracy, however, are not unique. They occur in various forms in all democratic regimes, enabling them to close political space to subordinated groups, as witnessed in the 2011 Occupy movements in Europe, Latin America, Israel and the US, that followed the Arab Spring. The Israeli case, however, stands out in terms of its variety of forms and cases, helping me formulate, elaborate, and expand the theoretical framework of dynamic political spaces.

2.
1931 — An Arab-Jewish Civil Society Struggle against the British Colonial Government

I. Introduction

This chapter analyzes a marginal mo(ve)ment of resistance in the history of Jews and Arabs during the period when Palestine was ruled by the British Empire. It presents the political and economic context of this resistance in historical perspective. Rather than attempting to present the entire period, it focuses on the construction of the political organizations and institutions that ultimately came to govern the State of Israel, starting with the formation of the first Zionist political parties in 1905. In doing so, it clearly distinguishes between nation-building and state-building efforts: it analyzes the strategies of political actors aiming to define the boundaries, shared values and goals of the national community (nation building), as well as its efforts to build political organizations and institutions able to achieve these goals (state building).

The purpose here is to explain why the British colonial rule has concluded with an ethnic war leading to the dislocation and dispossession of Palestinian Arabs and to the establishment of an ethno-national Jewish State. In order to do so, I will analyze an exceptional case of a joint anti-colonial struggle by Arab-Jewish civil society against arbitrary taxes levied by the British government in 1931. This chapter will discuss why such a strike took place and what ensured its immediate success, but also why it was subsequently completely ignored and erased from both national memories. It will show how, within five years, popular mobilization was redirected to the Arab Revolt against the British and ethnic clashes between Arabs and Jews, which later deteriorated into internal Palestinian clashes and national disintegration during 1938-39.

The analysis of the 1931 joint strike, its immediate economic success and longer term failure to open a shared political space for the Jewish-Arab civil society, will help us to understand the broader political process that eventually led to the Zionist victory and Palestinian defeat in 1948. It will also help us conceptualize the tension between the political institutions created before 1948 and the new state's democratic rules of the game, and the resulting failure to open political space and contain social conflicts through representation, which will be discussed in following chapters.

II. THE JEWISH SETTLEMENT OF PALESTINE

Jewish immigration to Palestine in the last two decades of the nineteenth century, then under the control of the Ottoman Empire, was supported by Jewish capital transfers in the form of philanthropic donations designed to help the Jewish settlers buy land and agricultural equipment. Due to the country's limited arable land area, however, and its relatively high population density (Kimmerling, 1983), Jewish purchase of Arab lands significantly increased Arab labor supply. By the early twentieth century it was fairly clear that Jews would not be able to become agricultural workers, due to the large number of Arab workers who were naturally far more skilled than Jews emigrating from Eastern Europe (Shafir, 1989). Moreover, the Arab workers were ready to work for lower wages, for two main reasons: their lower standard of living compared to the Jews (whose benchmark was Eastern European towns), and the availability of small holdings in Arab villages as a basic source of income.

Jewish officials had admitted the failure of employing Jewish manual workers in Jewish-owned settlements before the start of a new Jewish immigration wave in 1904, pushed mainly by the deteriorating conditions in Tzarist Russia. The large majority of Jews migrated in these years to the West, mainly North and South America, but an ideologically motivated minority migrated to Palestine, later known as the *Second Aliyah* (literally, ascent) (Shafir, 1989).[1] Members of this new migration wave founded the political institutions that ruled Zionism and Israel from 1933 to 1977, therefore the comprehension of their behavior, or-

---

1   In the years 1904-1914, 1,200,000 Jews immigrated to the U.S., compared to only 35,000 Jews who immigrated to Palestine; in the years 1880-1914, 300,000 Jews immigrated to England, 100,000 to Argentina, 80,000 to France, 60,000 to Canada, and 50,000 to South Africa (Elroi, 2004: 11-13).

ganization, and strategies is so crucial to the political analysis of Israel (Eizenstadt, 1967; Shapiro, 1976, 1977; Horowitz and Lissak, 1978, Kimmerling, 1983; Shafir, 1989). In socioeconomic terms, this migration wave was different than that of the first colonizers: these were not families attempting to work in their own properties, but youngsters organized in groups, willing to be employed as the Jewish landowners' salaried workers, and adhering to a Zionist-socialist ideology. These youngsters were called "workers," not because they came from working-class background, but because they did not have enough cash to buy properties of their own and become "farmers"[2]; they were ideologically committed to become agricultural workers and saw themselves as pioneers (*Chalutzim*) building a new socialist society for those Jews that will migrate in the future Eretz Israel, the Land of Jewish yearning (Eizenstadt, 1967; Kimmerling, 1983).

The *Second Aliyah* youngsters quickly found out that realizing the lofty ideal of working for the Jewish colonists involved conflict both with the Jewish employers and with the Arab workers. The pioneers of the Jewish "working class" were helpless against those two groups (Shafir 1989). In principle, the economic weakness of workers in the labor market pushes them to take political action claiming state intervention against free market principles (Sturmthal, 1973; Bonacich, 1972, 1979). However, in the Israeli/Palestinian case this type of claim was irrelevant, because neither Jews nor Arabs controlled state institutions which regulated the labor market. The weakness of the Ottoman Empire and the absence of state institutions able to regulate markets is the most important feature of the political context that framed the Socialist-Zionist strategy before the establishment of the British Mandate.

Immediately after their arrival to Palestine in 1905, these youngsters formed two parties, based on organizational affiliations in pre-immigration Zionist youth movements: *Hapoel Hatzair* (the Young Worker) and *Poaley Zion* (the Workers of Zion) (Shapiro 1976). These parties supported their members economically through saving funds and joint kitchens, and also represented them politically in the World Zionist Organization (WZO). The pioneer "worker's" parties sought to design institutions and political strategy that will enable their members to settle in the Land of Israel and find employment, despite extremely difficult circumstances

---

2 The Hebrew term in Hebrew is *Ikarim*.

that weakened Jewish workers. These parties' initial strategies included attempts to lower Jewish workers' salaries to compete with Arab labor, appeals to the Jewish farmers' ethnic solidarity despite profit motives, and attempts to import cheaper Jewish workers such as Yemenite Jews. All of these strategies failed (Shafir, 1989).

Only when the workers' parties and the WZO formulated a joint strategy for settling the new migrants could real progress be attained. This strategy was called "constructive socialism," meaning that socialism in Palestine will not be the product of class struggle against capitalism, but of political control of markets and cooperative institutions co-existing with private capital. The highest value in its ideological jargon was Hebrew Labor (*avodá ivrit*), which completely rejected the capitalist class interest to hire Arab workers. Constructive socialism (or "constructivism") was a peculiar blend of meticulous colonization planning,[3] and spontaneous colonization practices invented with the aim of overcoming the employment obstacles the Jewish immigrants faced. This strategy represented a merger of two key Zionist elements: the flow of young immigrants from Eastern Europe motivated by Zionist and Socialist ideologies and the mobilization of West European Zionist capitalists to support Jewish victims of modern East European anti-Semitism in their attempt to resettle in Israel/Palestine.

The vision of the winning Labor Zionist strategy during the pre-1948 period was a Jewish economy segregated from the Arab economy, which must be achieved by a costly long-term effort to buy lands and keep them out of the free market by national institutions designed to secure employment exclusively to Jewish workers (Kimmerling, 1983). This strategy was supported not only by socialist parties in Palestine but also by the liberal bourgeoisie in Western Europe led by the General Zionists party and WZO Chair Haim Weizmann, who coined the slogan "another goat and another acre"… The West-European philanthropists' public investment strategy required a local organization of the migrant future workers—these were the Hebrew workers' parties. These parties were interested in channeling Zionist funds to the absorption of their members in Palestine, but their strategy required an additional, decisive factor: the money will be transferred to economic endeavors dictated

---

3   The cooperative colonization planning was formulated by German economist Franz Oppenheimer (1864-1943) in the European context.

not by capitalist profit maximization but by political institutions controlled by Labor Zionist parties (Shapiro, 1976).

This is one of the most crucial keys to understanding the political economy in Palestine and Jewish/Arab relations. From its very beginning, Zionism was a political project opposed to the free-market logic: from a purely economic perspective, it made no sense to buy costly Arab lands or employ costly Jewish workers (Shapiro, 1976; Kimmerling, 1982, 1983; Shafir, 1989; Shalev, 1992). Labor Zionist political economy meant political control of the main economic factors: land, labor, and capital. The first settlement form created according to this political principle was the farming cooperative (*Kibbutz* and *Moshav*[4]), designed to reduce labor costs thanks to internal cooperative labor organization, and at the same time maintain the Hebrew Labor principle by ensuring land ownership by Zionist institutions (such as the Jewish National Fund (JNF), or *Keren Kayemet*), and preventing the employment of Arabs with the support of Zionist public funds (such as the United Israel Appeal, or *Keren Hayesod*). Giving up on the profit motive obviated the need to employ cheap labor (Shafir, 1989). In other words, Labor Zionism sought to displace Arabs from lands and markets, namely geographic and economic segregation.

The *Kibbutz* was founded as an egalitarian society for its members, but was at the same time highly exclusive and closed to other social identities. Although its strategic goal was to exclude Palestinian Arabs from Jewish economy, its selection mechanisms also operated to exclude others, including Oriental and religious Jews. This exclusion exacerbated in the long range the internal ethnic conflict between the dominant European Jews and the Oriental Jews.

All the Labor Zionist political and economic institutions obviously ran directly counter to the free market logic which dictated, in this context, a dual colonialist regime of Jewish employers and Arab workers. The Zionist political intervention against the free market was motivated by the desire to ensure the economic survival of the poorer new Jewish immigrants. Given this Zionist goal, the workers' parties succeeded in maximizing their political clout through control of both public capital

---

4   The *Moshav* was less collectivist than the *Kibbutz*, and also less exclusive. Although until the establishment of the state there were no significant numbers of religious and Oriental Jews in the *Moshavim* (Hebrew plural of *Moshav*), after 1948 the state settled many of them in *Moshavim*.

and the immigrants, who became completely dependent on the parties' resources and services (Shapiro, 1976; Shalev, 1992). This segregationist strategy was crucial in preventing the formation of a joint civil society vis-à-vis the British State. It constructed Jewish-Arab relations as a violent conflict which could not be contained by the opening of political space for representation and negotiation. Britain's support of the Zionist endeavor was a key factor in closing political space for conflict containment, in that it rejected the Arab demand to establish a joint parliamentary Council based on proportional representative elections. Given the struggle over borders, democracy was not deemed the solution to the conflict, but rather the problem.

III. THE *HISTADRUT*: A JEWISH (QUASI-)WELFARE STATE

The cooperative organization was designed for agricultural production and rural settlements and proved highly suitable to them given their relatively small size and social cohesion, as well as relative geographic isolation and common belief in the constructive socialist ideology. However, in the towns it proved far less suitable. The rapid development of Tel Aviv—the first segregated Jewish City—after the First World War (Biger, 1984; LeVine, 1998), and the contemporaneous establishment of the British Mandate, the government required a reorganization of Labor Zionism in new institutional frameworks. The new Labor institutions were designed to establish a viable Jewish economy subject to political supervision and to mobilize political support by the new immigrants who—much to the dismay of the Zionist elite—tended to prefer towns over rural areas. This is the political and economic context of the establishment in 1920 of the General Federation of Hebrew Workers in the Land of Israel (*Hahistadrut Haclalit shel haovdim haivrim beeretz Israel*), or in short, the *Histadrut* ("Federation") (Shapiro, 1976; Shalev, 1992; Grinberg, 1991).

In addition to the agricultural cooperatives, the *Histadrut* created another type of economic organization, the "institutional enterprise" (*Meshek Mosadi*), under the direct control of the *Histadrut* holding company, the Workers' Society (*Hevrat Haovdim*—hereafter, WS). The institutional enterprises were large economic corporations owned, managed and controlled by the *Histadrut* political apparatchiks, and usually funded by the WZO, designed to create jobs for Jewish immigrants (called Hebrew Labor) and prevent the employment of Arabs. In the institutional enterprises managed by the WS the profit motive played a secondary role, and was subordinated to the Zionist colonization objectives. The economic viability of these corporations required an ongoing capital influx. The first institutional enterprises controlled by the WS were (1) *Bank Hapoalim*, a Bank founded following WZO's decision to allocate £50,000 to funding cooperative workers' activities; (2) *Solel Boneh*, a construction company established by the merger of *Hapoel Hatzair* and *Poaley Zion*'s Construction Chambers who had competed for British construction contracts prior to the establishment of the *Histadrut*; (3) *Hamashbir Hamerkazi*, a nationwide marketing corporation; and (4) *Tnuva*, an agricultural produce marketer and dairy products manufacturer (Greenberg, 1984).

In addition to its economic roles and settlement activities, the *Histadrut* undertook almost all the government functions and public services which were lacking in the absence of a Jewish state, mainly education and health. The *Histadrut* established a very sophisticated and exclusive Jewish welfare quasi-state: it provided housing, education and health insurance to all classes, not only the working class. The nature of *Histadrut* membership was very much akin to state "citizenship": members received welfare services and had voting rights. The *Histadrut*'s governance structure was also state-like: multi-party proportional elections to a "parliament" (*Vaad Hapoel*, Executive Committee), which in turn appointed a "government" (*Vaadá Merakezet*, Central Committee), composed of proportionally representative coalition faction members. The *Histadrut*'s executive was dominated by a majority coalition of parties whose political power relied on the welfare services provided to their constituencies (Shalev, 1992; Grinberg, 1991, 1993).

The *Histadrut* was the key institutional apparatus of the Jewish state-building process. In 1920 it founded and commanded the *Haganah*, the military organization of the *Yishuv*[5] and forerunner of the Israeli Defense Forces (IDF), and later on funded and controlled the *Palmach* elite underground militia (Horowitz and Lissak, 1978; Ben Eliezer, 1998). As the very well documented research of Shafir (1989) shows, the military

---

5 The Hebrew term *Yishuv* literally means settlement, but is used here (as elsewhere) to refer to the entire Jewish pre-statehood community in Israel/Palestine.

approach was encouraged by political leaders of the Jewish workers, who came to the conclusion that ethnic hostility can help achieve the goal of excluding the Arab peasants from the labor market. Ethno-national hostility became, therefore, a key element in the economic strategy of the organized Jewish working ethno-class in the rural areas.

In contrast to the situation in the isolated rural areas, in the mixed towns, it proved more difficult to secure exclusive employment for Jews, and institutional initiatives to control the labor market were far more complex. To promote this goal, the *Histadrut* created employment exchange bureaus which allocated jobs exclusively to *Histadrut* members (Tokatli, 1979). The *Histadrut* pressured employers to hire workers only through these offices. This was a hotly contested issue between the *Histadrut* and private employers on the one hand, and on the other with Jewish groups opposed to the *Histadrut*'s labor monopoly, mainly the right-wing Revisionists led by Ze'ev Jabotinsky (Shapira, 1977).

Control of the labor market designed to ensure Jewish employment was thus directly exercised by employing Jews in the WS corporations, and indirectly through the employment exchange bureaus. The *Histadrut*'s labor policy was focused on concern with reducing Jewish unemployment and ensuring their economic absorption, much more than on concern with the salaries or working conditions of those already employed (Zusman, 1974; Shapira, 1978). This policy implicated an inherent conflict between the *Histadrut*'s political-Zionist considerations and its considerations as a large-scale employer on the one hand, and the workers' class interests and motivation to form (bona fide) labor unions for class struggle purposes on the other (Shalev, 1992; Grinberg, 1993). Representative and democratic trade union organization was a threat to the *Histadrut*, as it could lead to the establishment of unions whose members would not necessarily be *Histadrut* members, including joint Jewish-Arab unions. In dealing with this inherent conflict, the *Histadrut* and the Zionist Labor Movement as a whole consistently prioritized ethno-national considerations (Sternhell, 1995; Lockman, 1996; Bernstein, 2000).

The *Histadrut* institutions were founded on the principles of the Zionist worker settlements in rural areas, as they were designed to promote the political goal of economic segregation which was opposed to the liberal free-market integrative logic. Therefore, the *Histadrut* did not form representative trade unions, but rather political-bureaucratic apparatuses designed to control workers and labor markets. At both the national and local levels trade unions were politically controlled by the *Histadrut*'s ruling party and subordinated to bureaucratic non-representative organs (Grinberg, 1991; Shalev, 1992; Bernstein, 2000). In order to maintain control over the Jewish employees, the *Histadrut* preferred them to be party members, even if this meant members of opposition parties, rather than belong to independent trade unions. Zionist worker parties cooperated in the construction of a political arena that closed the space to direct worker representation.

IV. Zionist Labor: The Build-up of Settler Nationalism

The *Histadrut* was an extremely powerful quasi-state which benefitted from the Zionist movement's cooperation with the British State. It was not only an instrument of the institutional state-building process, but also a nation-building tool carving out the community's symbolic borders (Bernstein, 2000). Beyond its strictly economic and political functions, the Histadrut dominated all levels of communal life. It established its own cultural institutions, theaters and artist groups, and employed writers, poets and popular singers. It had its own daily newspaper, in addition to the party organs, and organized the major national sport association (*Hapoel*). Its national educational institutions were both formal and informal, including the workers' school system (*Zerem Haovdim*) and almost all youth movements; the latter played a crucial role in political and military mobilization (Ben Eliezer, 1998). These functions were considered no less important than economic enterprises.

As I mentioned above, the overarching goal of subordinating any independent social force and particular interest to political control was typical of the entire Zionist project. However, it is important to emphasize here that it was the Jewish workers' parties which invented, designed and established the institutional framework and adapted it to the Jewish workers' employment needs. These institutions ensured that the *Histadrut* and its ruling parties (the ZLM[6]) remain dominant among

---

6   The parties of the Zionist Labor Movement included the ruling party *Mapai* (a union of *Hapoel Hatzair* and *Achdut Haavoda* in 1930) and other small parties that united and split, and changed their names, including *Hashomer Hatzair, Poalei Tzion Smol, Achdut Havoda* and *Mapam*.

Jews loyal to the Zionist ideology (Horowitz and Lissak, 1978). ZLM became the hegemonic power of the *Yishuv* because it had the ability to subject every particular and individual interest to the political principles of Zionist constructivism. There were two main reasons for that. First, even non-working class Jews were interested in Hebrew Labor. Clerks, professionals, and merchants all benefitted from the expansion of Jewish employment opportunities and their de facto subsidization by the WZO; only a minority of private landowners and industrialists who employed (cheaper) Arab workers opposed the Hebrew Labor strategy (Horowitz 1948; Shapira 1977). Second, the *Histadrut's* welfare-state services were made available to all the Jews (except private employers), not only salaried workers, hence its popularity among middle-class Jews who could not afford them on a private basis.

The ZLM dominant status in the *Yishuv* was not maintained easily, and was affected by crises in different periods and the ability of its leadership to reformulate and redesign appropriate strategies. These strategies defined Zionism's political aims, the social coalition that could potentially support them, and the institutional frameworks required for achieving them, which were also designed to serve the constituents' interests (Shapiro, 1976). These strategy building processes will hereafter be collectively referred to as Nation Building, when referring to defining the national boundaries and objectives, and State Building, in reference to the institutional framework working towards those objectives and maintaining political control.

From its very beginning, the Zionist movement implemented a policy of demarcating a clear political boundary separating the Jewish settlers from the Arab locals, and gradually and quietly excluding the Arabs from lands and labor markets, so as to eventually create a segregated political *and* economical geographical entity. This process was promoted by the two main political forces in the WZO, albeit to a different degree: it was mainly supported by the ZLM parties and accepted by the liberal General Zionist European politicians. Increasingly, the difference between them caused the former to gradually, though consistently, overpower the latter. The success of the ZLM political parties was achieved thanks to its sophisticated, creative and innovative responses to challenges and impressive ability to overcome crises. We have hitherto referred to the cooperative settlement strategy (the *Kibbutz*) of dealing with the crisis of competition with cheaper Arab labor, and the Jewish emerging welfare quasi-state (the *Histadrut*) in response to the establishment of the British Mandate, and the subsequent accelerated urban development of Palestine. Two additional elements in the state building strategy were (1) the establishment of a unified party representing the two central ideological currents of constructivist Zionism (*Mapai*, Hebrew acronym for *Eretz Israel* Workers Party *Mifleget Poalei Eretz Israel*) in 1930, which became the ruling party in the WZO in 1933 (Shapiro, 1976); and (2) creating a national military organization (*Haganah*) and shaping a relative moderate policy of restraint in the Jewish-Arab context[7] until the hostilities at the decisive stage of territorial segregation and physical displacement in 1947-48 (Ben Eliezer, 1998).

The establishment of *Mapai* had wide-ranging national implications. It began with the economic failure of assimilating the Fourth *Aliyah* comprised of Polish Jews who immigrated in 1924-1926 and settled mainly in towns. These were mostly families with some economic resources, whose arrival initially generated an economic boom, mainly in the construction sector, only to be followed by a deep recession two years later (Giladi, 1973). One of the consequences of this downturn was the bankruptcy of *Solel Boneh* and growing discontent of urban workers against the *Histadrut* who could not provide their most basic necessity—employment (Dan, 1963).

The two-year depression also deeply affected the Arab population, making it increasingly hostile to Jewish immigration, with anti-Jewish violence erupting in mixed towns in 1929 following a dispute over the Wailing Wall in Jerusalem. Muslim worshipers exited the Mosques on Friday and attacked religious Jews in their four sacred towns—Jerusalem, Hebron, Safed and Tiberias—despite the fact that these Jews were not settlers and had been living there as peaceful neighbors for centuries. The clashes claimed the lives of 133 Jews as well as 116 Arabs, killed in self-defense or retaliation (Naor and Giladi, 1990, 187-8; Kimmerling and Migdal, 2003).

Following the clashes, the Mandate Government established a commission of inquiry, which concluded that the economic crisis had been the main reason for Arab despair, and attributed both land dispossession and unemployment among the Arab population directly to Zionist

---

7   This restraint is relative compared to the terrorist acts by the right wing underground militias Irgun (*Etzel*) and Stern Gang (*Lehi*).

segregationist strategies (Shaw, 1930).[8]

The ZLM leaders also concluded that the economic crisis required a strategic shift, but in the opposite direction; not ending the segregationist policies, but enhancing them. From then on, their objective would be to dominate the entire Zionist Movement, not only the *Histadrut* and its affiliated institutions. To do so, *Mapai*, the party established in 1930, would vie for control of the WZO, and through it dictate a national strategy of political control of market economy.

Ben Gurion called this strategic shift "from class to nation," while Berl Katzenelson[9] coined the term "working nation" (Ben Gurion, 1974; Shapiro, 1976; Shapira, 1977; Horowitz and Lissak, 1978). Both concepts and the new strategy were compatible with the original discourse and ideology of socialist constructivism that sought to build a new society without class struggle.

The core of the new strategy was that the ZLM would no longer be a "subcontractor" of the WZO, but will lead Zionism by itself. The WZO would continue the financial support to private capitalists, but only to those of them who will cooperate with the *Histadrut* and accept the Hebrew Labor principle—in that case they will be recognized as "Zionists" (Shapira, 1978). When the Great Arab Strike of 1936 broke out, as we will see later in this chapter, the national institutions were already dominated by the ZLM, enabling it to deepen the segregation still further, while at the same time providing economic assistance to capitalists as well (Shapira, 1978; Kimmerling, 1983b). This way, the ZLM used its material resources to rally the Jewish capitalists to the cause of economic segregation.

However, on the eve of the new era of Zionism, dominated by the segregationist strategy of the ZLM, an event on the opposite direction took place during 1931: a joint organization of Jews and Arabs struggling together against British taxation of motor transportation. On the basis of middle class common economic interests of trucks and buses

---

[8] The Shaw Report (1930) was officially titled Report of the commission on the Palestine disturbances of August 1929.

[9] David Ben-Gurion (1886-1973) served as the *Histadrut*'s secretary general from 1921-1935, led *Mapai* from 1930-1963, and was Israel's first prime minister and minister of defense in 1948-1953 and 1955-1963. Aharonson (1999) discusses his ideological agendas; Bar-Zohar (1986) provides a more complete biography. Berl Katzenelson (1887-1944) is considered by many to be ZLM's most prominent intellectual. He was the founder and chief editor of *Davar*, the *Histadrut*'s official daily newspaper between 1925 and 1944. See Shapira (1980) for a comprehensive biography.

owners, spontaneously organized a strike that succeeded to mobilize the support of the whole population, Jews and Arabs, to a typical civil society anti-colonial struggle against the taxes imposed by an arbitrary state. The next section describes and analyzes the peculiar mo(ve)ment of resistance that went against the dominant current of Jewish/Arab ethno-nationalist clashes.

V. The Drivers' Strike: Civil Society Resistance to Arbitrary Colonial Taxation[10]

The joint Arab-Jewish drivers' strike challenged the pattern of political economic control during the British Mandate period—in which the Zionist economic segregation policy succeeded to displace Arab peasants from their Lands and disarticulate Palestinian national solidarity. I will describe and analyze here the joint Arab-Jewish drivers' strike as an example of the "impossible path," the alternative history of what could have happened but did not happen, in the relationship between Jews and Arabs, aiming to comprehend the further hostile dynamics. Five years after the joint strike, the same drivers that cooperated against the British, were at the front of ethnic clashes between two national movements, the Palestinian Arabs drivers as leading strikers of the six month general strike declared in April 1936, and Jewish drivers as strike breakers. In 1936 a joint struggle against the British was already unthinkable.

In 1931, Jewish and Arab truck and bus drivers went on a joint strike in protest against taxes levied by the British government. For all intents and purposes, the strike may be viewed as an anti-colonial uprising: an external colonial regime unilaterally levies taxes on the local population, while they have no legitimate political representation able to affect the decision making process of a government imposed on them from the outside. The typical anti-colonial claim "no taxation without representation" could not be raised in the Israel/Palestine context due to the political disagreement between Zionists and Palestinian Arabs about building the political space for representation, both during the British Mandate and after. However, in 1931 the entire civil society, Arabs and Jews alike, organized on the basis of a common economic interest, which could

---

10   For a more detailed description and analysis of the strike, see Grinberg (2003).

have lead to broader cooperation against the British rule. This struggle was lead by the Jewish and Arab urban bourgeoisie which was politically marginalized and defeated by ZLM later on. To better understand the subsequent predominance of the ethno-national conflict, I suggest we first analyze the temporary success of Jewish-Arab civil society cooperation against the colonial state, and then analyze why the successful joint strike subsequently failed to open up political space for containment of ethno-national conflict by means of representation, mediation, and compromise.

The strikers' joint organization included (1) private companies owned by wealthy Arab bourgeois offering public transportation as well as tourism services; (2) public transportation cooperatives owned by individual middle class Jews affiliated to the *Histadrut*'s Department for Cooperatives; and (3) private Jewish and Arabs owners of only one truck or bus, mainly for delivery purposes, called the "singles," who represented the majority of the drivers in both communities, but were not organized. During the strike, bus and truck drivers were joined by the owners of private cars, who represented less than a quarter of all vehicles in Palestine (400 cars from a total of 2400 vehicles, Census of Palestine 1931).

Within the context of the British financial crisis after 1929, the attempt to levy taxes and customs duties on motor transportation was motivated by the budget deficit of the Mandate government in Palestine, caused by the failure of the state owned train company. While the government deficit in 1931 was 100,000 pounds sterling, the deficit of the train company was larger, 150,000 pounds sterling. From 1918 onwards, the British developed the transportation infrastructures in Palestine in order to boost economic activity that will increase tax returns. This included mainly road and railway building (Metzer, 1991). However, due to Palestine's small size, motor transportation proved more economic, and most of the population, as well as the merchants, preferred buses and trucks to the government-owned trains.

The increased taxes and customs duties made public transportation and delivery services, as well as private transportation, very expensive. This led to the formation of a broad-based front against government policy, which included both the merchants, who suffered from the increased costs of transportation and the individual users of public transportation services. The drivers' strike was general, suspended all transportation in the entire country, and went on for ten days. At the end, the government caved in, fearing that the strike might expand to include all merchants—Jews and Arabs—within days. During the strike, joint demonstrations were held in the mixed cities, serving to further emphasize the entire population's shared attitude against the British government (*Palestine Post*, November 1931).

The increased taxes and customs duties were designed to make motor transportation more expensive, but since they were higher than those levied in neighboring countries such as Egypt and Syria, they met with growing resentment. The first to reach the conclusion that an organized response is required were the owners of the Arab bus companies, who hired a young lawyer educated in London, Hasan Sidqi el-Dajani, to negotiate with the government the reduction of oil taxes. However, once the attempt to negotiate with the government failed, el-Dajani realized that in order to organize an effective strike it is necessary to mobilize the support of the singles and Jewish cooperatives too (*Davar*, August 20, 1931). In other words, in order to protect the interests of big Arab companies against the government it was required to mobilize the entire transportation sector, including Jews. This was exactly what the ZLM sought to prevent by promoting economic segregation and creating separate Jewish cooperatives. However, given the equal non-discriminated damage caused by the taxes to the singles, the big companies and the cooperatives, they had a common interest to go to strike, and organized together.

The struggle began with an almost spontaneous 24-hour warning strike on August 7, 1931. Although the *Histadrut* made an effort to prevent the strike and thwart the joint organization, when it failed to do so it demanded the establishment of a joint central committee based on parity representation of Jews and Arabs. The demand for parity was consistent with the Zionist objection to opening up political space as long as the Jews were a minority in Palestine, and was usually rejected by the Arabs for the same reason. However, at this juncture it was accepted. Consequently, the manager of the *Histadrut*'s cooperative department, Shraga Gorochowsky,[11] was nominated as el-Dajani's deputy, and a central committee of the joint motor transportation organization, composed of 16 Arabs and 16 Jews, was established (Grinberg, 2003).

---

11 Shraga Gorochowsky later changed his name to Shraga Goren and became an important WS manager.

Despite various attempts by the *Histadrut* to postpone the strike in order to gain enough time to persuade the British to give in without a strike, the popularity of the struggle grew and they failed to prevent it. The decision not to compromise was made by the British Treasury in London under the impact of the economic crisis in Britain despite the warning of the local government that the strike might be successful and its recommendation to cancel the new taxes.[12]

The general strike followed the government's rejection of the recommendations suggested by a commission of inquiry it formed after the warning strike together with representatives of the drivers and chambers of commerce, to reduce the taxes. The strike gained enormous popularity. It totally paralyzed motorized transportation, affecting tourism, imports, exports, commerce, marketing of agricultural products, and more. Joint Jewish-Arab demonstrations in mixed cities caused tremendous excitement precisely because they took place only two years after the 1929 clashes. Suddenly, out of the blue, people could easily imagine inter-ethnic economic cooperation and daily coexistence. For example, Haim Arlosoroff, Head of the Jewish Agency's Political Department, wrote:

> This is an exceptional conjuncture in the development of Arab affairs ... and if we do not allow it to pass by unused, it may be in a certain sense a turning point in the development of Arab-Jewish relations ...We could, within a comparatively short period, establish a network of daily relations between our settlements and the Arab villages surrounding them, along the lines of the joint Railwaymen's Club and the combined action of the car-drivers during the recent months, and the commission of inquiry set up by the Government. I do not want to expand any further in describing the possibilities, which are so strongly evident that I almost seem to touch them with my hands every day...[13]

After ten days of strike and no sign of government readiness to com-

---

12 National Archives, file Co 814/27, Executive Council decisions (minutes), meeting 426, July 1, 1931, and meeting 428, July 27, 1931.
13 Haim Arlosoroff letter to Pinchas Ruttenberg, ZA file S/25-3061 (November 22, 1931).

promise, some merchants started their own commerce strike in solidarity with the drivers, and called others to start a general commerce strike (*Davar*, September 11, 1931). At this moment of spontaneous degeneration of the struggle into a total anti-colonial uprising, the Zionist leadership succeeded to persuade the government to give up and compromise, in order to prevent the expansion of the strike and the total loss of political control of the events.[14] One of the most striking features of the transportation strike was the complete absence of violence despite the *Histadrut* warnings that the strike might deteriorate into ethnic clashes.

In a meeting of the *Histadrut* Central Committee before the strike Secretary General Ben Gurion expressed his concerns regarding the strike: he argued that it might endanger isolated settlements that could be attacked, but also expressed his fear of the political implications in the aftermath of a successful strike.[15] Indeed, the strike's success ran counter the ZLM strategy of segregation, because it demonstrated that free markets can foster shared interests, cooperation, and joint organization, enabling workers of both ethnic origins to overcome the unilateral imposition of the colonial state. Since the end of the strike, the *Histadrut*, and particularly Ben Gurion, worked hard to underplay the enthusiasm and hopes ignited by the joint struggle and reinforce the segregation strategy. The success of this strategy and the resulting closure of political space to bi-national representation, however, cannot be explained only in terms of individual efforts by political actors. It was the complex matrix of Jewish-Arab class and ethnic relations and political articulation that ultimately spelled the doom of inter-ethnic collaboration.

VI. Political Developments after the Strike: Reinforcing Segregation

The analysis of the strike's aftermath is critical to understanding the segregationist strategy's success and the ensuing violent confrontation between two ethno-national communities in Palestine. Having said that, we must also bear in mind two critical international factors affecting lo-

---

14 National Committee Protocols, Zionist Archives file J1/7243 (June 29, 1931); Histadrut Central Committee Protocols, LA file M-17 (November 9, 1931)
15 Lavon Archives, Executive Committee Minutes, M-17, August 3, 1931.

cal politics: (1) Hitler's rise to power in Germany and the resulting wave of Jewish immigrants to Israel/Palestine; and (2) British cooperation with the Zionist encouragement of Jewish immigration in this crucial timing. Given these conditions Zionist pressures designed to prevent inter-ethnic cooperation eventually gained the upper hand.

Invigorated by the success of the strike, the drivers' union leader, Advocate Hassan Sidqi el-Dajani, approached ZLM leaders in order to expand Arab-Jewish cooperation to other sectors, including joint unionization of various occupations and professions. His proposals included the request to provide *Histadrut* welfare services to the Arab population in order to demonstrate the potential benefits to the Arabs from Jewish immigration to and investment in Palestine. He also suggested devising a model for economic assimilation of Jewish immigrants that will not adversely affect Arab employment.[16]

Although some moderate Zionist labor leaders (including Shertok[17] and Arlosoroff) responded favorably and started negotiating with el-Dajani, after more than one year it became clear that the *Histadrut* headed by Ben Gurion is not interested in cooperation, and in fact rejected his proposals (Grinberg, 2003). The goal of the ZLM leadership was precisely the opposite: to prevent the expansion of bi-national cooperation that might lead to political negotiations on the future of Jewish-Arab relationships.[18] This was exactly what el-Dajani was proposing to discuss, but not only his initiative was discouraged, even the limited cooperation in the transportation sector was terminated by the *Histadrut* with the creation of a separate and comprehensive Jewish transportation cooperative called *Egged* in 1933, following a merger of the Jewish cooperatives and "singles" which took part in the joint strike (*Davar*, February 2, 1933).

At the same time that the post-strike negotiations were being held, a crucial political change ended the historical moment of the joint Jewish-Arab resistance movement: the ZLM led by *Mapai* was assuming a leading role in the WZO and the imposition of its segregationist strategy. As

---

16   Dov Hoz letters, Zionist Archives file S/25-2961 (January 22, 1932, January 20, 1932).
17   Moshe Shertok (later Sharett) (1994-1965) edited *Davar* in 1925-31. In 1933-1948, he headed the Jewish Agency's political department. He served as Israel's first foreign minister until 1956. In 1953-55 he also served as Israel's second prime minister.
18   The attitude of the Zionist leadership was not unified against cooperation. A few leaders supported an agreement and cooperation with el-Dajani, the most salient was Haim Arlosoroff. However, he was isolated, and in 1933 was killed by an anonymous assassin.

mentioned above, the most crucial political change during the British Mandate period was the shift of ZLM strategy from being a subcontractor of the Zionist movement to leading it (Horowitz and Lissak, 1978; Shapiro, 1976). In 1933 *Mapai*[19] won the elections with 44% of the votes to the WZO Congress, compared to 29% in 1931. It was even more powerful among the Jewish voters in Palestine, where it won 68%. In 1935, *Mapai* won 48.8% of the votes, and 69.5% in Palestine (Horowitz and Lissak, 1978). By 1935 the strategic shift was complete, and the Secretary General of the *Histadrut*, David Ben Gurion, was elected Chairman of the Executive of the Jewish Agency, namely the WZO Government in Palestine.

During 1933-1935, the Palestinian demographic and socioeconomic situation changed radically. A new wave of immigrants fleeing from Hitler's Germany and other countries where anti-Semitism was on the rise almost doubled the Jewish population.[20] Many of these new immigrants were wealthy, and their arrival and investments stimulated economic growth and ensured full employment in the *Yishuv*. They settled in the big mixed cities, Jaffa-Tel Aviv[21], Haifa, and Jerusalem, transforming them into metropolitan centers with significant Jewish majorities (Naor and Giladi; 1990; Horowitz and Lissak, 1978).[22] Although the Arab middle and upper classes also benefited from the economic prosperity, they realized that they were losing economic and political power.[23]

Given the complete absence of political dialogue with the Zionist leadership, and the British cooperation with Jewish immigration, the Arab Higher Committee in Palestine declared a general Arab strike in April 1936. The strike, involving mainly the commerce and transporta-

---

19   Mapai did not participate as a separate party but was the majority party in an electoral union of all ZLM parties.
20   More than 130,000 Jews immigrated to Palestine in the years 1933-1936, increasing the Jewish population by about 80% (Kochavi, 1998).
21   Despite the attempts of Tel Aviv founders to separate it from the larger and older Arab Jaffa, it remained as part of the Jaffa municipality until 1936, and it remained extremely connected to Jaffa after the municipal separation (LeVine, 1998).
22   In Haifa the number of Jews increased from 16,000 in 1931 to over 50,000 in 1936; by 1938, they became the largest ethnic community. In Tel-Aviv, their number tripled from about 45,000 in 1931, to over 145,000 by 1936. In Jerusalem, the Jews were already a majority in 1931 and by 1936 their number increased from 54,000 to 74,000 (compared to 39,000 non-Jews) (Horowitz and Lissak, 1978).
23   This concern of the Arab middle classes in the cities were expressed mainly with relation to the municipal elections in Haifa and Jerusalem (*Haaretz*, November 29, 1933, June 7, 1934, October 3, 1934).

tion sectors, was partially joined by urban workers and some agricultural salaried workers. It was the onset of what would later be termed the Arab Revolt.[24]

The strikers demanded suspension of Jewish immigration and land sales to Jews. Although during its six months there were violent attacks against both British and Jews, the most significant element of the revolt at this stage was the strike, which continued—under pressure by the radical groups—despite the economic damages it caused to the strikers. The strike ended when the Mandate government agreed to appoint a commission of inquiry to suggest a solution to the ethnic conflict. This was the Peel Commission, which submitted its recommendations in 1937. It came to the conclusion that the partition of Palestine into two nation-states with some territorial contiguity would be the best solution to the conflict.[25] This conclusion was rejected by the Arabs, as well as some Jews, and failed to contain the escalation of the revolt. After 1937 the struggle was no longer a politically regulated strike but rather a decentralized armed struggle that became increasingly violent, and was aggressively repressed by the British (Hughes, 2010). Finally, the armed struggle deteriorated into internal violence against "traitors," or Arabs suspected of willingness to compromise and collaborate with the Jews (Porath, 1976; Sayigh, 1979; Cohen, 2008). These included el-Dajani, who was also a leading figure in the 1936 strike: he was assassinated in 1938.[26]

The Arab strike led to an economic recession in Palestine, but the big difference compared to the 1927-28 recession was that now the ZLM parties controlled the Zionist funds and took a completely different attitude towards the crisis. *Mapai* was established in 1930 exactly with this purpose in mind: to lead Zionism before another economic crisis could occur. The idea was to use Zionist funds not to rescue small private businesses but Jewish employment and *Histadrut* enterprises. The Arab strike unintentionally created the opportunity to accomplish the ZLM's segregationist goals, mainly because Jewish workers were now able to replace the striking Arabs. This was most evident in the Haifa

---

24 In collective Palestinian memory the leaders, activists and fighters of this revolt are called revolutionaries (Kassem, 2011).
25 Formally known as the Palestine Royal Commission, the commission of inquiry which operated in Palestine in 1936-37 was chaired by the Earl Peel (Naor and Giladi, 1990, 287-290).
26 The question about who killed him has remained open since then, with different speculations.

port, but also in some *Moshavot*[27] (Shapira, 1977; Kimmerling, 1982). In addition, the Jewish Agency used its funds to subsidize Jewish capitalists committed to the employment of Jews. This was the meaning of the slogans "from class to nation" and the "working nation": "nation" meant economic ethno-national segregation, and all Jewish ethno-classes and individuals supporting this strategy were considered legitimate Zionists (Shapira, 1977). According to the ZLM political construction of reality, class struggle was ethno-national, against the employment of Arab workers and against the purchase of Arab products. The strike did most damage to the strikers, so they did not continue after the disappointing decision by the Peel Commission. However, the struggle continued in a much more violent form and provided additional justification for the ZLM's separatist strategy.

Already by the beginning of the Arab Revolt in 1936, it was clear that the constructivist strategy of purchasing lands had exhausted its benefits (Kimmerling, 1983). Since then, the security dangers of isolated Jewish settlements provoked the gradual replacement of the constructivist strategy by a military expansionist strategy, including operations such as "Tower and Stockade"[28] and offensive military actions. The military strategies prepared the *Yishuv*'s armed forces for the imminent breakout of general hostilities upon the declaration of a Jewish State (Horowitz and Lissak, 1978; Ben Eliezer, 1998). Finally, the Arab Revolt was brutally repressed by the British, with almost 4,000 revolutionaries killed and almost 15,000 wounded (Hughes, 2009); more than 15,000 activists and leaders were arrested (Kimmerling and Migdal, 2003).[29]

VII. Analyzing the Matrix: The Dynamic of Zionist Nation-

---

27 *Moshavot* is the Hebrew term for colonies. The first segregated Zionist settlements outside the mixed cities were called *Moshavot*.
28 "Tower and stockade" (*Homa UMigdal*) was a strategy used by Zionist settlers during the Arab Revolt, when the establishment of new Jewish settlements was restricted by the Mandatory authorities. During the course of this campaign, 52 new Jewish settlements were established throughout the country (Naor and Giladi, 1990).
29 The brutality of the British repression was salient also in the eyes of the Jews. In 1988, when he was Minister of Security and the IDF was criticized for the brutality of the repression of Palestinians, Rabin argued that it is very moderate compared to the brutality of the British against the Arab Revolt.

Building and Palestinian Disintegration

The Arab Strike of 1936 ended with a great victory for the ZLM and its segregation policy in particular. However, the ZLM segregationist strategy had territorial implications: the Jews would have to give up parts of Israel/Palestine's lands in order to ensure that the future Jewish State would have a significant Jewish majority (Shafir 1989). This willingness for territorial "compromise" was explicitly stated by some pragmatist *Mapai*'s leadership during the Peel Commission's discussions, and mainly in 1947 when the UN General Assembly debated Resolution 181: Palestine Partition Plan.

The drivers' strike test case sheds a sobering light on the crucial influence of the interests of Jewish rural workers on ZLM's segregationist nation-building strategy. Other Jewish class interests such as those represented by merchants, industrial and agricultural private employers could also benefit from free market integration. These were the "market forces" that pushed towards a mixed economy. Urban, particularly skilled workers, employed by a single employer, also had an interest in inter-ethnic unionization (Lockman, 1996; Berstein, 2000).[30] Other salaried urban workers, such as teachers and clerks, also had no particular interest in segregation because they were not competing with Arab workers. The ZLM thus acted against the integrationist push of market forces and the social classes associated with them in mixed cities in order to promote the interests of Jewish rural workers. This operated against the opening of political space to joint organizations and segregated the populations as part of the drive for a separate Jewish State.

This segregationist strategy resulted not only in the nation building of a separate Jewish community, but also in the internal political disintegration of the Palestinian-Arab community. This path transformed the colonial encounter between Jewish settlers and indigenous Arabs into a national conflict over political domination. The construction of the Jewish-Arab encounter as a national conflict prevented the two cultural communities from political negotiation of a shared future based on common interests and common markets in a shared homeland and

---

30 A relatively small group (less than 100) of skilled workers employed by the British train company unionized jointly (Lockman, 1996). This case was exalted by the *Histadrut* and its partisan historians as attesting to the international spirit in the unionization of Jewish workers, but I still consider it an exception that prooves the segregationist rule.

state. The joint drivers' strike proved both the potential for social and economic cooperation and the inability of the Jewish and Arab urban bourgeoisies and petite bourgeoisies to have their common economic interests represented in the political arena, which would promote mediation and compromise able to contain the ethno-national tensions provoked by Zionist immigration.[31]

The political weakness of both bourgeois ethno-classes lies at the core of my explanation of the inability to transform the Arab-Jewish urban cooperation into a vision of coexistence in a shared state. The political weakness of Jewish merchants, employers and self employed workers, and their failure to promote their class interests in the political arena, meant that they had to accept the ZLM leadership and its segregationist strategy. Conversely, the political fragility of the Arab economic elites was due to their inability to define a shared national goal able to protect the Palestinian peasants from land dispossession and worker displacement from the labor markets. The Palestinian collective identity was shaped by the territorial boundaries established by the British mandate in Palestine and by the struggle against displacement from their lands by the Zionist colonization. The class interest of the Palestinian bourgeoisie to benefit from capital flux and economic expansion caused by Jewish immigration prevented them from consolidating a coherent national strategy together with the peasants opposing Zionist colonization. The internal class contradictions between the Palestinian peasants and urban bourgeoisie became all too obvious during the Arab Revolt and ultimately led to the total collapse of Palestinian organizations, ending in mass dispossession and dislocation in 1948 (Nakba).

Although the segregationist nation- and state-building strategy was facilitated by the ZLM's dominant position in Zionist institutions, this did not mean that there were no alternative Zionist visions of the future. Socio-economic groups and political organizations ranging from workers to capitalists, liberals to socialists, did not see the need for economic or political separation (Shumsky, 2010; Hattis, 1970; Shafir, 2011). However, all the non-segregationist strategies proved politically ineffective due to their inability to deal with the peculiar dynamics of the Arab-Jewish matrix, which weakened the moderate elements and

---

31 Shafir (2011) describes an interesting attempt by a group of leading Jewish capitalists in 1936 to suggest a plan to resolve the economic difficulties caused to the Arabs by Jewish immigration.

strengthened the extremists who led the Jewish Zionists to supremacy, and the Palestinian Arabs to self-destruction. This dynamic deserves particular attention because it ultimately led to the failure to form a unified national movement of Palestinian Arabs, and also to the perpetuation of violent ethno-national clashes within the framework of a sovereign Jewish State that imposes Jewish supremacy.

The Arab population of British Mandate Palestine was mostly rural, albeit with a substantial urban minority of some 30%, concentrated in several large cities, most of them living in mixed cities with a growing Jewish population (mainly Jerusalem, Haifa and Jaffa). These cities were integrated in the global market economy even before the Zionist colonization. There were several sectors characterized by common Arab-Jewish economic interests in these cities, particularly among the merchants, who all profited from the Zionist economic boom, but also big landowners who usually preferred living in cities and not in their rural properties.

Conversely, the rural areas were adversely affected by the socialist Zionist settlements. The main conflict in the rural areas was not caused by the Zionists' efforts to buy Arab lands, but by the ZLM effort to prevent Arabs from working in the lands purchased with Zionist funds, mainly by the organization of exclusivist cooperatives (Shaw Report, 1930). In other words, the problem was not necessarily the sale transaction (in which the Arab seller usually made a considerable profit), but in the exclusion of Arab workers, in lands settled in cooperative forms as *Kibbutzim* and *Moshavim*. Unlike them, the lands privately owned by Jewish farmers in the *Moshavot* continued to employ Arab labor (Shapira, 1977; Shafir, 1989).

In the mixed towns, commercial exchanges served to blur national boundaries and promoted cooperation. For example, mixed municipal chambers of commerce existed until the 1929 hostilities, and as a matter of fact they continued to cooperate even after the clashes.[32] This Jewish-Arab urban bourgeoisie that could potentially develop a joint strategy was neutralized by the salience of the conflicts over land ownership and employment in the rural areas. The most important aspect of the rural conflict was its opposite effect on the two emerging ethno-national communities: it made the Jewish community more cohesive while dividing

---

32 For instance, the mixed chamber in Jerusalem (*Davar*, January 27, 1930).

the Arab community between landowners who sold real estate to Jews at a premium, and the peasants who remained unemployed. Among the Jews, the bourgeoisie was politically de-legitimized, because its interest in employing and trading with Arabs ran counter to the ZLM segregationist agenda that came to dominate the national movement (Shapira, 1977). Among the Arabs, the urban bourgeoisie which benefited from exchanges with the Jewish settlers failed to protect the interests of the rural majority, and it was de-legitimized and unable to lead a cohesive national movement (Cohen, 2008).

While the constructivist Zionist strategy managed to enforce its segregationist policy using the violent conflict to consolidate its institutional control, the Arab national movement collapsed as a result. The key political achievement of the ZLM leadership was transforming the particular economic interests of Jewish rural workers into a national political interest in economic separation and Jewish employment. The Arab urban elites were unable to transform their particular interests in trading with the Jews, and thereby benefitting from the economic development in the cities, into a national political interest and failed to protect the peasants. As we have already seen, el-Dajani's very creative proposals to formulate an integrationist national strategy for the Palestinians failed miserably.

Hence, unlike the process of Jewish military buildup, subject to political supervision and aided by the British (Ben Eliezer, 1998), the Palestinian Arabs responded with spontaneous and disorganized violence, mainly by peasants (Sayigh, 1979).[33] It is my argument that this lack of a stable power hierarchy resulted from the lack of a consensual Palestinian strategy of dealing with Jewish colonization, manifested by constant internal conflicts among Palestinian factions, with the rural factions supporting uncompromising struggle against Zionism and attacking the urban bourgeoisie for its moderate approach (Cohen, 2008; Khalidi, 2006). The Palestinian national disintegration and the Zionist nation building are two sides of the same coin. It is evident in the deterioration of the 1936 strike into internecine strife in 1938-1939 and culminated in the total leadership void of 1948, when masses of Palestinians fled or were forcibly deported from both towns and villages

---

33   Fanon (1965) explains the various tools of anti-colonial struggles between the peasants and the Europeanized urban classes.

(Morris, 2008; Pappe, 2006).

The Jewish-Arab encounter in Israel/Palestine includes several types of class relations and political processes, but it is their combination which makes the Zionist-Palestinian case so peculiar. The Jewish settler's economic, political, organizational, administrative, military and diplomatic advantages were to be expected, due to the huge gaps between Europe and the Middle East and the colonial experience of European colonialism. These gaps were exacerbated by the financial and diplomatic support of the international Zionist Movement and the British Mandate government backing of the Zionist project. However, it was not only these predictable advantages, but also the decisive strategic victory of segregationist Labor Zionism and the subsequent subjugation of the Palestinians that made this case so peculiar. This dual dynamics—constructing Zionist nationalism while destroying Palestinian nationalism—is the key sociological clue to understanding the peculiar process.

The matrix of Jewish-Arab relations involves internal socioeconomic and political conflicts between ethno-classes over the attitude of each towards the other ethno-national community. The political (in)ability to articulate the national interest and mobilize all classes to promote a unified strategy was the critical factor that determined the course of history. The internal struggle among the Jewish ethno-classes concerned the issue of economic segregation. The ZLM political elites succeeded in articulating the economic interest of the rural workers in the political sphere and turning it into the victorious strategy of Zionism by subordinating and mobilizing all other ethno-classes to support it.

The internal struggle among Palestinian Arab ethno-classes was between the urban elites who benefited from Jewish immigration and market expansion and the peasants who lost their lands and jobs to Zionist settlers. This political inability to design a coherent national strategy led to internal disintegration during the 1936-1939 revolt and to total disaster in 1948. The Arab encounter with the Jewish settlers defined both the boundaries and content of the Palestinians' national identity but also destroyed them as a national community because of the resulting class contradictions.

VIII. Conclusion

CHAPTER TWO

The pre-1948 period was characterized by coexistence, competition and conflicts between various Jewish and Arab ethno-classes within the framework of external rule, first by the Turkish Ottomans, and from 1918 onwards, the British Mandate. During this period, the overarching Zionist aim of establishing a National Home for the Jews in Israel/Palestine encountered the opposition of an indigenous Arab majority already integrated in the world market economy with skilled urban elites. This was a significant difference compared to other cases of European settler societies, which were characterized either by vast lands available for settlement and weak indigenous populations (the Americas and Australia), by the absence of local urban elites (South Africa) or by the strong support of a colonial state (North Africa).

The joint strike mo(ve)ment of resistance took place in a critical juncture of an interim period, between the economic crisis that started in 1927 and the renewed economic expansion following the new migration wave in 1933. The 1927 crisis led to significant shrinking of Jewish immigration and deteriorated into violent ethnic clashes in 1929 that uncovered the tensions between segregated Zionist colonization and the displaced Arab peasants. The clashes were perceived as a warning that Jewish-Arab relations might deteriorate irreversibly. The conclusion of the Mandate government was that the ZLM strategy of segregated settlement and the displacement of Arab peasants from their lands was the reason for the discontent, and that the displaced peasants should be reallocated new lands for cultivation (Shaw, 1930).

It was only after Hitler's rise to power and the ensuing wave of Jewish immigration that the economic atmosphere changed, and within three years the Jewish population was doubled. In the mixed cities Jews even became the majority (Horowitz and Lissak, 1978), provoking the reaction of the Arab bourgeoisie and political parties in 1936. In the meantime, in 1933-1935, ZLM managed to occupy a leading position in WZO which subsequently enabled it to take advantage of the 1936 Arab Revolt to reinforce its segregationist strategy.

The British policy was critical in shaping the opportunities of both parties to the conflict. When it discriminated between them it encouraged ethnic hostilities, and when treated equally it facilitated the construction of a joint civil society. This is the logic of divide and rule: when the state treats citizen identities differently, they relate differently to the state and to the other. The mo(ve)ment of resistance took place when, under the impact of the global economic crisis, the British Government demanded from the Mandate Government in Palestine to extract more money from the local population. In that instance, the local Government treated all citizens equally, as the new transportation tax affected both Jews and Arabs.

The resulting joint Jewish-Arab anti-colonial strike of 1931—this historic "slip of the tongue" (Grinberg, 2003)—is an important exception to the general rule in the colonial encounter. The foregoing analysis of a potential alternative history provides better understanding of the forces that eventually imposed their worldviews, strategies and interests on others. The story of the joint strike has been forgotten because it fits neither the Zionist nor the Palestinian national narratives. It does not fit the former, which assumes that all Palestinians totally rejected Jewish immigration and fought against it despite the Zionists' peaceful intentions, and it contradicts the latter, which claims that Zionism was all about displacing the Palestinians.

The urban economic elites' inability to neutralize the conflict over lands and jobs in the rural areas and to build on their common interests in the cities to formulate a political strategy to mobilize all Jews and Arabs is at the core of the discontinuity between the joint strike and its violent aftermath. The drivers' organization and their coalition with chambers of commerce in 1931 paved the way to the organization of the six-month separate Arab strike in 1936; however, this was the counter-mo(ve)ment. The 1936 General Strike and the violent clashes it involved closed the political space to bi-national cooperation of the civil society and led to the appointment of the Peel Commission, which proposed the partition of Palestine. In turn, the partition plan facilitated the imagination of the Labor Zionist vision of the future, but became the Palestinian Arab nightmare in that it led to the internal struggles of 1938-1939 due to the lack of a collective national strategy.

The concept of political space helps us understand why the violent ethno-national clashes closed the shared Jewish-Arab space for representation that had been opened by the joint strike. The mo(ve)ment of resistance was extremely successful in its direct goal of reducing the transportation taxes levied by the government thanks to its ability to completely disrupt transportation, as well as to popular support of their demands. Immediately after November 1931, Hassan Sidqi el-Dajani opened negotiations with Labor Zionist leaders seeking to continue the moment of the movement. His proposal was to expand the autonomous organization of civil society modeled on the successful joint Jewish-Arab strike. Such coordination and cooperation were necessary in order to establish a joint state and rule Israel/Palestine after the British have left.

The ZLM leaders rejected the idea of a shared civil society organization that might lead to continued confrontation with the British Government due to two main reasons: (1) the Zionist settlement in Palestine depended on the Government for continued economic and political support, including migration permits; and (2) the concept of joint organizations ran counter to the ZLM's segregationist strategy.

Thus, the counter-mo(ve)ment to the successful resistance united two forces against it: the ZLM segregationist leadership and the anti-Zionist Arab revolt. In this sense, the Arab revolt unintentionally helped ZLM leaders neutralize the civil society that had begun to emerge during the 1931 resistant mo(ve)ment. The ethno-national confrontation and violent clashes were the most effective counter-mo(ve)ment to neutralize the emerging bi-national civil society, closing political space for mutual recognition and compromise.

The Zionist segregationist strategy succeeded in carving out the symbolic borders of the nation in preparation for the physical borders of the state. The failure of the Palestinian elites is explained by their ambivalence between integration and separation. For the Palestinians, separation meant giving up their sovereignty in many towns and villages, while integration meant creating a shared political arena. The Palestinians as a nation could not come to terms with either option.

To conclude, the Jewish political and economic pre-1948 colonial institutions operated against the free market trends inherent to the mixed cities, which pushed for an integrated Jewish-Arab economy. The ZLM succeeded in creating a reality that was opposed to those trends. This is perhaps the most salient phenomenon of that period. As we shall see in the following chapters, however, the free market push for integration did not disappear with the establishment of the Jewish State. Tensions between the free market and the ZLM political institutions continued to haunt Israeli/Palestinian history in very peculiar ways. The partition of Israel/Palestine in 1948 and the ensuing forced migration of Palestinians (*Nakba*) were the result of the political articulation of the Jewish community by the ZLM institutions and the aspiration to establish a Jewish State with a democratic regime. The partition was facilitated by the strategy of segregated settlements, however without their migration and prevention of return the Palestinians within the 1949 ceasefire borders would have represented 60% of the population (900,000 compared to 600,000 Jews). Ethnic segregation and forced migration were preconditions for establishing democratic rules of the game in a state with Jewish majority (see Mann, 2005). Moreover, although the remaining Palestinians were given individual citizenship and voting rights, they were subjected to military administration until 1966.

Although the Zionist political arena was based on democratic rules of the game, its institutions and organizations were not broadly representative but designed to control or exclude non-Jewish minorities. After 1948, this non-representative political arena spawned the mo(ve)ments of resistance described in the chapters that follow. Chapters 3-4 show how ZLM institutions were unable to adapt to free-market conditions and democratic rules of the game, and how their failure to open political space to broader ethnic and working-class representation led to the expansion of the state to the pre-1948 borders. Next, Chapters 5-8 analyze the dual military democratic regime established after this territorial expansion, its inability to open space to broader representation, and the anti-colonial Palestinian uprising.

3.
1959 — Wadi Salib Riots:
Culminating a Decade of Ethnic Discrimination

This chapter discusses the first decade of the Jewish State, characterized by significant demographic changes and the establishment of the ethnic hierarchy of Israeli society by means of physical segregation and socioeconomic discrimination. Ethnic distinctions were made not only between Jews and Arabs, but also between European and Oriental or Middle-Eastern Jews (hereafter, *Ashkenazim* and *Mizrahim*, respectively). These were founded on the dominant Orientalist discourse as well as the political and economic power of the veteran *Ashkenazi* elites and Zionist pioneers. This period ends with the Wadi Salib Riots of North-African Jews in 1959, analyzed below as the mo(ve)ment of resistance that uncovers the construction of the tools of political economical domination in the new state, built on ethnic discrimination and cultural division of labor (Swirski and Bernstein, 1980).

Sparked by an incident in the Wadi Salib neighborhood Haifa, the ethnic riots of North African Jews spread all over the country and lasted four weeks. These events took place at the end of a large period of unemployment, precisely when the industrialization policy sponsored by the developing state succeeded in creating full employment (Halevi and Klinov-Malul, 1968). For this reason, these events are usually considered to have had no significant impact, although they are related to a much more influential wave of ethnic riots later on in 1971-1973 (see chapter 5). However, I will argue here that despite the fact that full employment encouraged a new wave of class struggles and mobilization (discussed in chapter 4), the strong linkage between class and ethnicity became one of the most salient features of Israeli political parties since 1959. The ethnic aspect of the riots and of their repression shaped the parliamentary elections held six months after the riots, in November 1959. In the longer term, it also created a pattern of ethnic misrepresentation and tribal channeling of ethnic fears into the political arena.

As we shall see in Chapter 5, the prolonged and influential Black Panther riots during 1971-1973 failed to end this distortion; on the contrary, the latter mo(ve)ment was used to reinforce the prevailing pattern. In what follows, as well as in Chapter 5, I show how ethnic tensions, an issue seldom discussed in election campaigns, became a key factor in political mobilization, despite—or more accurately because of—having no legitimate political space for autonomous representation.

The following analysis of ethnic resistance will further develop and expand the concept of political space, further distinguishing it from alternative concepts such as political field (Bourdieu, 1992) society (Linz and Stepan, 1996) or arena (Collier and Collier, 1991). All these concepts treat the political as a sphere of struggle between political actors, assuming homology, representation or articulation of civil society interests. In my discussion of ethnic resistance I seek to show how political actors prevent opening a space of representation by new actors, expanding our knowledge of the repertoire of political distortions and misrepresentation.

I. Background

The first years after the establishment of the state of Israel were a period of fundamental and significant transformations. First, in terms of population, an estimated 700,000 Palestinian refugees fled the country[1] and little less than 700,000 Jews immigrated to Israel within five years, 45% of them *Mizrahim* (Eyal, 2005: 70).[2] Second, the Jewish State became a viable and powerful entity. It suddenly came to own large-scale property: it controlled capital imports and appropriated all of the real estate left behind by the Palestinian refugees. This appropriation was enabled by a series of regulations and laws, most importantly the Absentee Property Law of 1950, which secured the Jewish state's control over all

---

1   The number of Palestinian refugees is controversial, ranging between the official Israeli estimate of 520,000 and Abu-Sitta's evaluation of 935,000 (Abu-Sitta, 2004). Morris (1987) estimates it at around 700,000. Between 1948 and 1953, about 25,000 refugees managed to return to their homeland, and eventually receive Israeli citizenship (Cohen, 2006: 92).
2   Between May 1948 and December 1953, 309,567 immigrants came to Israel from Communist Eastern Europe (including the USSR); 25,503 from Western Europe; 243,836 from the Middle East and other parts of Asia; 107,867 from North and South Africa; and 24,769 were listed as having an "unknown" origin (Hacohen, 2003).

CHAPTER THREE

"abandoned" Arab lands (Benziman and Mansour, 1992).[3] Among other things, this newly gained economic power was used to implement the young state's ideological commitment to the absorption of the massive wave of Jewish immigrants.

The absorption of the new immigrants was not a difficult challenge for the old, pre-independence institutions[4]—above all, the Jewish Agency, the *Histadrut* and the *Mapai* ruling party—that were very well prepared to deal with it. It required administration of huge populations, feeding them and providing them with housing. The new government also had to provide them with jobs, health, education and other services. All these needs had already been successfully met by the ZLM and the Jewish Agency under the British Mandate rule, and their quasi-state institutions were therefore both politically and administratively prepared for the emergency. The new immigrants were totally dependent on the state and quasi-state institutions, both ruled by *Mapai*. The pre-state institutions were not only well equipped to solve the immigrants' problems, but also to control them politically through services provided to the new needy citizens, which ensured their dependence for years to come. In other words, the institutions established before 1948 in order to control the markets and the Jewish immigrants who arrived during that period and sought to carve out the symbolic and physical borders of the Jewish State were later used to control the new immigrants and close the political space for their representation.

This period was characterized by the unequal encounter between the already settled Jewish population of Israel—mostly of *Ashkenazi* (East-European) descent—who controlled the economy, politics, administration, culture, education and military, and the new immigrants from Arab countries (*Mizrahim*). Consequently, the assimilation of immigrants was controlled by the established *Ashkenazi* leadership. The tendency was to

---

3   After the 1948 War, Israel issued a series of ordinances aimed at legitimizing its control of the occupied Arab territories. The legal basis for this expropriation was reinforced in several stages, beginning with the Absentee Property law of 1950 and the Land Acquisition Law of 1953. These laws gave power over the lands to a custodian who was legally forbidden to sell them to anybody but the state's development authority (Khamaisi, 2003: 431). The process was completed in 1959-1960 with the creation of a new legal category called "Israel lands" (Forman and Kedar, 2004).

4   Note that the focus is on the institutional capacities, rather than on the difficulties faced by individual public workers when encountering the immigrants. The archives are full of individual reports about the immigrants' difficult living conditions, their suffering, and also the difficulties experienced by the public workers. For a detailed description see Eliav (1972).

settle the *Mizrahim* in segregated peripheral settlements designed to fill the geographic and economic vacuum left by the Palestinian refugees, functioning as a buffer to prevent their return. The *Ashkenazi* migrants (mostly Holocaust survivors) who were also assimilated during these years were better equipped, with language (*Yiddish*) and contacts (family and friends) helping most of them avoid being settled in the peripheral areas.

The uneven encounter between the veteran *Ashkenazi* community and the immigrants from Arab countries constructed the *Mizrahim* as an ethnic community, despite the significant cultural and language differences among their various countries of origin, such as Morocco, Iraq, Yemen, and Tunisia. The Orientalist approach that developed during the pre-1948 period viewed all Arabs as culturally inferior, and for some *Ashkenazi* veterans the Jews coming from Arab countries were even "less developed" than the local Arabs.[5] The economic gap between these two newly "ethnicized" Jewish communities only widened during that period and in the following years owing to the large-scale German reparation payments transferred to individual *Ashkenazi* Holocaust victims. In addition, the bulk reparations paid directly to the State of Israel further strengthened *Mapai*'s stronghold over the state and *Histadrut*, which in turn controlled the funds allocated to the social groups that supported the ruling party, facilitating the mobility of veteran *Ashkenazi* workers to the managerial and professional middle classes (Carmi and Rosenfeld, 1989; Swirski and Bernstein, 1980). This fundamental inequality and the policies of physical segregation and economic discrimination constructed a hierarchic society with two ethno-classes: the *Mizrahi* lower classes and the *Ashkenazi* middle classes.

The Palestinian Arabs who remained within the borders of the new state—usually called the "minorities" or "Israeli Arabs"—were significantly more marginalized. Until 1966, they were subjected to martial law (Lustick, 1980; Zureik, 1979). By constructing the Arab citizens as an "enemy," controlling their movements and restricting their employment through permits, the military managed to gain control of the labor market and to allocate the new jobs to the immigrant Jews, in cooperation with the Histadrut (Porat, 1966; Ratner, 1956, Lustick, 1980). The

---

5   For a detailed description of how *Ashkenazi* veterans treated new *Mizrahi* immigrants, see Segev (1986).

establishment of the Jewish State provoked a radical transformation of economic relations between Jews and Arabs, with unprecedented political control of Jewish institutions over labor, land and capital markets from 1948 onwards. This is due to the fact that since then not only did the ZLM and the Jewish Agency continue acting to protect and promote the economic interests of the Jews vis-à-vis the Arabs, but now they were joined by a powerful state apparatus and the military which were able to control the markets and discriminate social groups according to their location in the hierarchy ladder (Shafir and Peled, 2002).

The period discussed in this chapter is characterized by tight administrative control over the economy through state institutions, the military, and the *Histadrut*—all of them controlled by the ruling party *Mapai* (Medding, 1972; Shapiro, 1977). This control was used to carry out unprecedented large-scale national tasks such as feeding the entire population, providing affordable housing and investing in industrial development (Halevi and Klinov-Malul, 1968).

II. Physical Segregation, National Security and Politics

During the Second World War, the Palestinian economy boomed thanks to the British Mandate's protectionist policy and the increased demands due to the geopolitical needs of the Empire at war (Metzer 1998). Following inflationary pressures, Jewish urban workers became disgruntled and began unionizing and acting against *Mapai*'s leadership in the *Histadrut* and Jewish Agency. Consequently, towards the *Histadrut* elections in 1965 the leadership of the United Kibbutz Movement (*HaKibbutz HaMeuhad*) split from *Mapai* to form a new party (*Achdut Haavoda*), which managed to mobilize significant numbers of urban workers. *Mapai* eventually won these elections thanks to the *Histadrut*'s efficient political apparatus and the support of the urban middle class, but the rural opposition—which also relied on resistant urban workers and youth movement activists—gained considerable strength (Yishai, 1978; Horowitz and Lissak, 1978).[6]

---

6   *Ahdut Haavoda* won 17.7% of the votes and became the second-largest party in the *Histadrut* after *Mapai*. The three Zionist labor parties opposing *Mapai* (including *Hashomer Hatzair* and *Poalei Tzion Smol*) got 38% of the votes (Yizhar, 2005: 45).

The Second World War accelerated two processes in the *Yishuv*. The first was the military preparation for fighting the British rule after the war and for the expected war with the Arabs (Ben Eliezer, 1998). The second was the formation of a substantial political force with militant positions on political issues, which defined itself as "leftist," mainly in reference to its pro-working class platform and identification with the Soviet Union (Margalit, 1991). In 1948, *Achdut Haavoda* and *Hashomer Hatzair* merged to become the United Workers Party, better known in acronym form as *Mapam*. *Mapam* immediately gained a dominant position in the *Kibbutz* movement, in the largest underground militia (*Palmach*), and among urban workers and youth movements. Despite its recognition of the legitimate authority of the new State institutions and the *Histadrut*, *Mapam* represented a real threat to the dominant position of *Mapai* during Israel's early years. In the first *Knesset* elections it was the second largest party (with 19 out of 120 Knesset members), and in the Histadrut elections it won 34% of the votes (Horowitz and Lissak, 1978; Yishai, 1978; Ben Eliezer, 1998).

This so-called "leftist" party was opposed to *Mapai*'s tendency for territorial compromise that was based on the assumption that the establishment of a Jewish State is more important than the expansion of its borders. *Mapai*'s position was supported by many salaried workers, the urban middle class and the *Histadrut* bureaucracy, who also controlled the larger militia, *Haganah*. During the 1948 war, *Mapai* managed to consolidate its control of the new state by subjecting all underground military organizations to the IDF General Staff (Ben Eliezer, 1998). This policy was called "statism," and emphasized the consolidation of legitimacy and sovereign power of the new state institutions vis-à-vis the power of partisan organizations which held powerful positions during the British mandate period. The contingencies of war enabled the emerging national institutions to take over, particularly thanks to the dominant position of *Mapai* in the *Histadrut* (Medding, 1972; Shapiro, 1977; Horowitz and Lissak, 1978).

Despite the disputes regarding the territorial compromise, which was finally decided by *Mapai*'s preference of partition, one issue was never seriously contested—ethnic segregation. During the pre-1948 period's settlement activity—characterized as we have seen by a trend for both labor market and territorial segregation from the Arabs—a basic consensus took hold: it was clear that the future State of Israel should include a minimal number of Arabs. The ZLM political and military elites took this for granted. This delicate issue was not often talked of openly, much less discussed in writing, but it required the readiness of soldiers and officers to perpetuate the cleansing.

The demographic result of the 1947-1948 armed struggles was that only some 160,000 Arabs were left within the borders of the State of Israel, while the big majority escaped or were forced to leave their homes and became refugees (Cohen, 2006; Morris, 1987). The abandoned houses in mixed and Arab towns were appropriated by state housing companies and repopulated by Jews, while many villages were largely flattened by bulldozers, their lands settled later by Jewish immigrants but remaining under state ownership.[7] The so-called "absentee" Arabs who remained outside the new state's borders were denied the right to return to their homes, and thus became refugees, despite UN General Assembly Resolution 194: Right of Return. In the long range the Right of Return became one of the constitutive Palestinian national myths. However, at first it was a concrete reality, since immediately after the 1949 armistice agreements thousands attempted to cross the borders (called in Hebrew *mistanenim*, literally: infiltrators),[8] whether to resettle their homes, to take property left in a rush, to pick fruits and vegetables left to rot or tend to their herds (Morris, 1993). Some of them succeeded to penetrate the borders and stay inside the country as "internal refugees" (Cohen, 2003).

These attempts to return across the borders from the Gaza Strip, West Bank and Lebanon, and the IDF's efforts to prevent them, shaped the violent relationship between the new state and the land's former inhabitants, but just as important, defined the political status of those who remained. The Arabs who did not stay outside the borders as refugees—although formally attributed citizenship—were actually second-class citizens at best and considered potential collaborators with the enemy attempting to return. They were not controlled in democratic ways, but subjected to military administration. Despite the fact that they had suffrage rights to vote and be elected every four years, they were depen-

---

7   The lands owned by refugees were nationalized according to the 1950 Absentee Property Law.
8   This term has different meaning depending who uses it. The Israeli government, politicians and media used it to describe the danger of hostile penetration of the borders, while Palestinians use the same Hebrew term to describe the hero that succeeded to return to his country (Kassem, 2011)

dent on their local military commander for work permits, permission to leave their villages, and other citizen rights that became "privileges" of the Jews (Lustick, 1980; Zureik, 1979; Cohen, 2003)

The IDF thus had a key role to play, not only vis-à-vis Israel's "external" enemies, but also vis-à-vis the (potential) enemies from within. Not only did the country's Arab citizens remain under martial law, but they were excluded from the legitimate national community by not being summoned for mandatory military service, like the country's Jewish citizens. This policy proved a success because the Arab population accepted it and felt alienated towards the new state, its leadership, and its objectives. The only exception was the Israeli Communist Party, which demanded complete equality in both rights and duties, including military service (Lustick, 1980). The very definition of the new entity as a Jewish State, symbolically manifested in its national symbols such as the flag and anthem, also served to exclude the Arabs. Finally, and crucially for our purposes, the pre-statehood effort to take over their lands and marginalize them from the labor market continued unabated, both through policies of land expropriation and budgetary discrimination (Forman and Kedar, 2004), and through the military's supervision of the labor market, which was coordinated with the *Histadrut*'s employment exchanges (Lustick, 1980; Zureik, 1979; Cohen, 2006).

As argued above, military institutions may function as democratic actors only when they protect the citizens from external threats and control the borders. By doing so, the military frames the potential political space by demarcating the borders of the state where citizens enjoy civil rights and their claims are considered legitimate and worthy of representation. However, when the military is used by rulers against parts of the citizenry, democracy cannot be realized, the political space of the citizens is violently closed, and it cannot function as a container of social conflicts. Thus, both the second-class citizenship of the so-called Israeli Arabs and the military's role institutionalized the limitations of Israeli democracy from the very beginning of the Jewish State. The IDF became an ethno-national military and a political actor involved in shaping "national" (Jewish) policy towards the Arab citizens. The fact that the main struggle was waged over natural resources (land and water) transformed Arab resistance into an ethno-national conflict with the state, rather than merely a struggle against ethnic discrimination.

Moreover, the problematic political action of the IDF was beyond the question of the control of Arab citizens; it was related to the absence of clear institutional boundaries between the military and the political apparatus of the ruling party. After the establishment of the state, *Mapai* continued its pre-1948 effort to dominate the military and promote officers according to party affiliation, mainly in order to prevent *Mapam* supporters from reaching top positions. The party had a Recruited Members Committee for this purpose, and senior officers were often summoned to its political meetings (Medding, 1972; Shapiro, 1977; Peri, 1983, 2006).

In this sense, *Mapai*'s "statism" was misleading: it demanded all the other partisan organizations and power bases to disarm and disband in 1948, aiming to consolidate and legitimize the authority of the new state institutions. However, its own powerful partisan apparatus was not similarly disbanded after the establishment of the new state, and it continued to control state and quasi-state institutions such as government ministries, the IDF, the *Histadrut* and the Jewish Agency (Shapiro, 1977). This lack of clear institutional boundaries between state security and politics, so typical of the pre-1948 period, remained one of the most salient anti-democratic features of the period discussed in this chapter, with martial law being only one of its most sinister manifestations. The strong political control of State institutions and civil society after 1948 could no longer be attributed to the struggle against British colonial rule. The blurred boundaries of the political field and its expansion to the state and civil society became the most salient feature of the new, formally democratic state, which continued to control markets and rule populations unilaterally without representation.

According to this colonial logic, the ruling party used the military administration to control the Arab population and promote its objectives. This is the main reason why most opposition, but also coalition parties other than *Mapai*, supported the abolition of martial law, claiming that under the security pretext it was actually designed to protect *Mapai*'s rule by securing Arab votes in return for selective allocation of permits (Lustick, 1980; Peri, 1983).

Significantly, the IDF's relationship with *Mapai* was not unilateral. It was not that the military was used by the ruling party for its political aims, but rather a political quid pro quo. The IDF benefited from this interpenetrated relationship with state institutions and the ruling party, in the form of freedom for operating beyond Israel's borders (Morris,

1993). In other words, in return for their political loyalty, the young officers who just won a great victory in the 1948 War were awarded with a free hand to act against the Arab-Palestinian population. This refers not only to the martial law but also to the struggle against the refugees across the borders. As documented by Israel's Foreign Minister, and later Prime Minister Moshe Sharet, in the first years after the establishment of the state, it seems the government had little control over such military initiatives (Sharet, 1978). In other words, the ruling party used its strong ties with the military to control the Arab population, but in exchange gave up its authority to control military violence against the Palestinians, either within or beyond the borders. It was precisely after the opposition parties succeeded in abolishing martial law within Israel (in 1966) that the military began pressuring for expansion of the borders, and managed to maintain its powerful position as political actor thanks to that expansion in the 1967 War.[9]

III. The Post-Colonial "Anti-Democratic Catch": The Labor Institutional Complex

The question of demarcating the institutional boundaries separating the new state apparatuses from the military sheds light on a broader issue typical of postcolonial regimes—the problematic distinction between new state institutions and pre-state political organizations. This is a general problem that characterizes struggles for independence waged against colonial regimes: the political actors that organize and mobilize civil society fighting for independence are those which eventually design and dominate the new state's institutions. The establishment of the new institutions is guided mainly by the desire to maintain and even expand the power of the new rulers, while limiting the relative autonomy of state institutions and civil society vis-à-vis the ruling political elites. The state building process in postcolonial regimes is thus necessarily problematic in terms of democracy, as it is characterized by blurred institutional boundaries. This "anti-democratic catch" in postcolonial regimes

---

9   The political role of the military in Israel is a very important subject, and it was studied by many scholars from various perspectives (Kimmerling, 1993; Peri, 1983, 2006; Ben Eliezer, 1998; Helman, 1999; Levy, 2003, 2007). I presented my own view in Grinberg (2008, 2010, Part 4).

results from the inability to open up a political space for democratic representation and mediation, due to the absence of the necessary balance of power between state and society.

Mapai's statism was strongly trapped by the postcolonial "anti-democratic catch," but the problem was exacerbated due to the extensive power held by the pre-state institutions (the Jewish Agency and *Histadrut*) and the armed conflict with the Palestinians and Arab countries, which were effectively used to legitimize the military control of Arab citizens and retaliation operations beyond the borders. The path-dependent transition from British Mandatory rule to a Jewish State was further complicated by the peculiar features of the Israeli case. Before 1948, state institutions were well established, but split. Some of them were British (including legislation, law enforcement, economy, utilities, and border control). Others were run by the Jewish Agency (foreign affairs, capital raising, immigration, settlement, education, and militia) that represented the Jewish people and continued to operate after 1948.[10] Still others were run by the *Histadrut* (health, education, welfare, housing, employment, industry and commerce, and transportation) (Shapiro, 1976; Shalev, 1992; Grinberg, 1991, 1993).

The new State of Israel inherited not only populations and lands thanks to its military victory, but also the British state institutions. Nevertheless, the Jewish Agency continued its involvement in settlement and immigration activities, while the *Histadrut* continued most of its economic and welfare-state activities apart from education, which was taken over by the state. This institutional continuity played a key role in shaping the structure of power and control in Israeli society (Horowitz and Lissak, 1978); however, it blurred the boundaries between the state and the ruling party. Until 1948, *Mapai* controlled Jewish society through the *Histadrut* and Jewish Agency. Afterwards, the new state and quasi-state apparatuses expanded their functions also to the areas previously controlled by the British Government, and became more sophisticated and complex, with the introduction of new state institutions into the old *Mapai* structure of control over civil society (Medding, 1972; Shapiro, 1977; Grinberg, 1993).

---

10 The continued role of the WZO and the Jewish Agency in the State of Israel after 1948 is not at all obvious, and is very problematic. David Ben Gurion, the new Prime Minister and former Chair of the Jewish Agency, strongly supported dismantling the governmental functions of the Jewish Agency but was overruled.

Importantly, this institutional continuity—interpreted by some functionalist researchers as a positive sign of stability (Horowitz and Lissak, 1978)—is interpreted here as the main source of tensions and conflicts in Israeli society, as well as the main barrier to the democratic opening of political space to subordinated social groups. Therefore the tension between the *Yishuv* institutions and the post-1948 structural and institutional developments inevitably generated mo(ve)ments of resistance. This book seeks to explain some of these conflicts within the framework of Israel's unique combination of the universal phenomenon of problematic transition from a colonial to an independent and democratic society, and the peculiarities of the Jewish State. The power of state institutions to close political space to subordinated social groups and the capacity of political actors to use state power and take advantage of civil society's weakness to reproduce their dominant position is at the core of all the mo(ve)ments of resistance analyzed here.

Mapai successfully managed to enhance its dominant position by retaining and reinforcing the *Yishuv* institutions under its control. This enabled it to delegate state functions to the *Histadrut* and avoid handing them over to the new state. Thus, for example, the continued role as a provider of public health services enabled it to recruit an ongoing stream of new members, who had no other option of receiving those services and were forced to affiliate as *Histadrut* members (what I have called "citizens" that deserve welfare services and have voting rights). *Mapai* also allocated considerable state funds to the *Histadrut*, both in order to build new clinics and to support the WS (Workers Society—*Hevrat Haovdim*) enterprises and the cooperative settlements (Medding, 1972; Shalev, 1992; Grinberg, 1993).

Although these moves did have some Zionist (nation building) and socialist (building an economy under political control) ideological justifications, it seems that *Mapai* was mainly interested in increasing the *Histadrut*'s political and economic power in order to consolidate its hegemony as the ruling party by making the Jewish population dependent on the *Histadrut*. After 1948, both Jews and Arabs became dependent on quasi-state institutions, the *Histadrut* and the military, but in different ways. The difference was that while the Arabs were dependent on the military for travel and employment permits and on the *Histadrut* employment exchange, the Jews relied only on the *Histadrut* for employment and public services, conditioned on pseudo-voluntary membership. This dependency regime naturally ran counter to the citizenship principle: it was not enough to be a citizen to have free movement, free access to labor markets and to receive public services, something extra was required. Jews were required to be *Histadrut* members, while Arabs had to collaborate with the military ruler (Lustick, 1980; Shalev, 1992; Cohen, 2006). This Israeli quasi-citizenship was largely exacerbated after 1967; it is the flip side of the postcolonial "anti-democratic catch."

Maintaining the *Histadrut*'s pre-state structure after 1948 created a unique institutional setting: a triangle of interdependence between the new State of Israel, the *Histadrut*, and *Mapai* (Grinberg, 1993, 1993a). *Mapai* needed to maintain the *Histadrut* institutions in order to mobilize members and voters, secure jobs for supporters, and provide financial and organizational resources for party activities. In turn, the party provided the *Histadrut* with ideologically and organizationally committed activists, leadership cadre, and the coordination required for continued state collaboration. Finally, the state provided the *Histadrut* with a legal framework to continue doing its quasi-state activities as well as considerable funding, while the *Histadrut* reciprocated by controlling the labor market and investing in economic development. However, the triangular nature of this relationship was a source of endless friction and conflicts between the three partners. Instead of normal political exchanges where each partner can demand return for its services, the relationships were based on mutual interdependency without any ability to change it. This Vicious Triangle is what prevented the necessary institutional flexibility so painfully lacking in the three organizations in order to face the dramatic socioeconomic transformations occurring around them (Grinberg, 1993).

One of the major implications of this Vicious Triangle was an imbalance of powers. Although the state formally held top authority, among the three it was *Mapai* who controlled both the state and the *Histadrut*, and mediated conflicts between the two. It was often the case that *Mapai* delegates in the government and *Histadrut* clashed within party organs, conflicts that were usually resolved by party dictates. It was also quite common for senior state officials to cross the state-party divide and participate in internal *Mapai* debates (Medding, 1972; Shapiro, 1977).

However, *Mapai*'s dominance was not unlimited. Although it dictated state policies and controlled the *Histadrut*, it was powerless in the critical area of delegation of state functions to the *Histadrut* due to its dependency on the latter. The reason is that all *Mapai* members, activists and officials were affiliated with the *Histadrut* apparatus in one way or another. In other words, the party's abilities to delegate state functions and resources to the *Histadrut* were subject to its dependence on the *Histadrut* and the power of its officials within *Mapai*. In short, the Vicious Triangle thus maintained the *Histadrut*'s power vis-à-vis the state, thanks to *Mapai*'s interest in maintaining control over the state.[11] Many of the political struggles and transformations during this period were directly affected by the implications of this retention of the pre-state institutional structure, finally broken up only in 1995.[12] I have termed elsewhere the complex ties between the *Histadrut* apparatus and its ruling party "Labor Institutional Complex" (LIC). The LIC complex ties— which prevented institutional change and opening space to new ideas, interests, identities and actors—were maintained even after the labor party lost the elections in 1977 (Grinberg, 1991).

That having been said, we must remember that the Vicious Triangle was formed under circumstances in which the joint challenge of the three forces was the economic and political assimilation of a huge immigration wave and appropriation of the enormous assets left behind by Palestinian refugees. In this sense, the policy of maintaining the pre-state structure was very effective. Just as in the formative period, Zionism's guiding principle was not citizenship per se, but rather Jewish institutional and economic buildup. The goal was not to empower the citizens but rather to maintain institutional control of the economy and the citizens, both Jews and Arabs, in their own particular ways.

---

[11] My book *Histadrut above all* (Grinberg, 1993) focuses on this vicious triangle, the institutional inflexibility of the state and the ruling party, and the final reconstruction of neo-colonial structural conditions after 1967 fitting the needs of Labor Zionist institutions.

[12] In 1994, a group of young reformists split from the Labor party and won the *Histadrut* elections aiming to break the party's institutional dependency on the *Histadrut* apparatus. In order to do so they supported a new national health insurance bill (1995) that separated health services from *Histadrut* membership. For the sake of transparency, note that the author was employed by the *Histadrut* as an advisor on institutional reforms.

IV. Assimilating the Massive Immigration Wave

Even before the 1948 hostilities ended, a huge wave of Jewish immigrants began pouring into the young state, mainly holocaust survivors from Europe and entire Jewish communities from Arab countries.[13] Within four years, the veteran Jewish population which arrived before the Second World War became a minority, and the state was required to provide quick solutions for urgent housing, nutrition, employment, health, and education needs. Hundreds of thousands of immigrants were first housed in tents, later in transition camps (*Maabarot*) and finally in permanent residences, mostly public housing, or Arab houses left empty in the cities (such as Jerusalem, Haifa, Jaffa, Acre, Ramla and Lod).[14] Health services were provided mainly by the *Histadrut*'s health maintenance organization, which monopolized medical care in most of the new settlements (Zalmanowitz, 1981). Public education was mainly provided by the state.

The main difficulty in the state's early years was to feed the entire population, since a significant part of the arable lands were abandoned by their rural Arab owners and their return was prevented. The main economic effort was to settle the Jewish immigrants on lands owned by Arab villages legally defined as "abandoned," after their destruction. This effort was intended to serve a dual purpose: politically, to gain control of the land and prevent the refugees from returning, and economically, to produce food for the growing urban population. For the first time, Jews from Arab countries were required to work in agriculture, as opposed to the pre-state socialist settlement period when the national ideology served to mobilize European Jews but neglected the option of *Mizrahi* rural workers (Shafir, 1989). These new immigrants, most of whom had been urban dwellers, were settled without any affiliation to pre-state ideological settlement movements. This led to the development of two types of non-kibbutz cooperative settlements: the old *Moshavim* (agricultural cooperatives) settled by *Ashkenazi* Jews with well-developed connections in the Labor Movement, and the new *Moshavim* settled by *Mizrahi* immigrants who found it difficult to establish themselves eco-

---

13 See Hacohen (1994).
14 At the beginning this took place in a very chaotic way, and immigrants took the initiative and occupied empty Arab houses, while running away from the governmental *maabarot* (Lewin-Epstein, Elmelech, and Semyonov, 1997).

nomically due to their lack of political connections (Schwartz, 1995).

The process of dismantling the *Maabarot* and transference of the population to peripheral and isolated areas of abandoned Arab Lands discriminated against the *Mizrahim* and ran counter to the formal Zionist ideology of creating one unified nation through a melting pot of all Jewish immigrants (Cohen, 1969). The official discourse was of formal equality between Jews, the formal policy was to make no distinctions among Jews, and the Zionist project was supposedly aimed at creating a "new Jew" in the Land of Israel. However, the new state's settlement policy actually created two separate ethnic categories: the veteran *Ashkenazi* Jews with political, administrative and military power bases and connections, and the *Mizrahi* new immigrants positioned peripherally in both socioeconomic and geographic terms (Swirski and Bernstein, 1980; Yiftachel, 2006). The new immigrants in the frontier settlements were mostly *Mizrahim*, while most of the European or *Ashkenazi* new immigrants—who had family and cultural relations with the veteran Jews—managed to steer clear of the periphery and find housing in the central cities.

This trend of settling the *Mizrahi* immigrants along the new state's frontiers, with hardly any *Ashkenazi* population (except the *Kibbutzim*), became exacerbated with the later immigration from North Africa, particularly Morocco. This second post-1948 immigration wave, which followed the weakening of French colonialism from 1956 onwards, was directed to new peripheral townships as a continuation of the population dispersion policy, but not for agricultural purposes. These new settlements were called "development towns" (*Ayarot Pituach*), a name which represented the government's intention to encourage capital investments in them, but proved out of touch with realities: the dependency on the established rural settlements, the huge difficulty attracting capital to peripheral areas and the compensating tendency to invest in low-skilled, low-pay and low-standard small industries. These ethnically homogeneous and dependent development towns became a structural factor which only increased the education and employment gap in the Jewish population, which government discrimination policies constructed as two ethno-classes: *Ashkenazi* middle classes and *Mizrahi* peripheral lower classes (Swirski and Bernstein, 1982; Grinberg, 1989).

This settlement pattern, motivated as it was by Zionist colonization goals, shaped a peculiar structure of town-village relationships.

CHAPTER THREE

Towns usually tend to develop as centers of services, commerce, and employment for surrounding rural areas and attract rural population to the cities. In the case of Zionist colonization, this was hardly the case. Agricultural settlements, established by national-political rather than economic considerations, always represented a numerical minority, but had a decisive political influence on the political institutions. The established rural settlement were also well organized to provide their own cultural, educational, health, marketing and financial services.

This meant that the veteran rural settlements—*Kibbutzim* and *Moshavim*—did not need the new development towns as centers of services. This is the context that reversed the rural-town dependency relationship, as the new *Mizrahi* immigrants in the development towns depended on the veteran *Ashkenazi* cooperative settlements for employment. This was true first for work in agriculture, and later also in construction, manufacturing, and private services (Razin, 1984). These inverse relationships in Israeli society shaped a sociopolitical reality of far-reaching historical implications. These may be understood only within an analytical framework which identifies the Zionist colonization process for what it was: a process motivated by political rather than economic considerations. In this context it is clear how the veteran settlers—with their political connections and national prestige—became dominant in the peripheral areas. On the other hand, as we shall see below, the resulting legacy of envy and hatred of *Mizrahi* peripheral workers towards their *Ashkenazi* "socialist" employers sowed the seeds for a future political whirlwind.

To conclude, the process of settling the new immigrants during Israel's first decade created three clearly distinguished and highly segregated ethnic groups, whose identity was shaped by their economic, geographic, and political status: (1) The veteran and dominant *Ashkenazi* Jewish elites; (2) The Arab second-class citizens under martial law; and (3) The new *Mizrahi* immigrants designated to replace the Palestinian refugees—to occupy the physical space and their economic functions in agriculture, construction and services.

The *Mizrahi* immigrants were situated as a buffer between the dominant *Ashkenazi* veterans and the subjugated local Arab citizens. They were "in-between" on all levels: geographic, socioeconomic, cultural, and political. As we shall see in what follows, within this conflictual construction of three ethno-classes, the *Mizrahim* faced extremely adverse conditions for collective action. This difficult position, combined with the military control of the Palestinians, constitute the fundamental shortcomings of the Israeli political field, limiting the possibility of opening up political space for the containment of social conflicts. The absence of political space is the fuel of resistance movements; however, it is not a sufficient condition: social groups must have also additional sources of power in order to revolt.

V. Industrialization and Unionization of the Powerful Workers[15]

Following the initial effort to settle the so-called "abandoned" Arab lands and increase agricultural production to feed the new immigrants, the Israeli government initiated a massive industrialization campaign starting in 1954. The "development towns" were actually part of a much broader centralized planning move designed to create jobs for the unemployed immigrants.

This industrialization policy, personified by the relentless Minister of Commerce and Industry Pinhas Sapir,[16] relied on several basic factors: (1) the existence of a large unemployed workforce creating the investment incentive of low-cost production; (2) a huge flux of capital from Germany to individuals and the Government, increasing local demand and government investment resources; and (3) a government initiative to encourage industrialization, including legislation and substantial subsidization of investment (Kleinman, 1967).

Sapir's centralized industrialization policy resulted in a local economic miracle, with average annual growth of 10%. This growth resulted more from capital and workforce inflows and less from technological development, increased productivity, and capital accumulation (Halevi and Klinov-Malul, 1968). This fact is critical for understanding the subsequent recession. The sector which led the substantial growth in the 1950s and early 1960s was construction (and construction-related industries), which was needed to provide housing for the immigrants. The sector was largely financed by government subsidies. Accordingly,

---

15 For a detailed discussion of the *Histadrut* structure and various forms of workers' organization, see Grinberg (1991).
16 See Greenberg (2011) for a biography.

it should come as no surprise that the construction companies owned by the *Histadrut* WS holding company also enjoyed impressive growth (Dan, 1963).

The government was keenly interested in promoting investments in construction and industrializing the periphery, and the economic enterprises administered by the WS were more than willing to take part in this national endeavor. In return, however, they demanded affordable loans and guarantees. The government therefore agreed to allocate a considerable part of the capital accumulated in pension funds owned by the *Histadrut* to provide large-scale credit to WS. This gave the WS subsidiaries an advantage in the competition with the privately owned companies, but also considerable political power. WS often negotiated with the government for state resource allocation instead of investing out of its own pocket; these negotiations were mediated by *Mapai*, which controlled both the government and the *Histadrut* under the Vicious Triangle discussed above (Grinberg, 1993).

The public figure most identified with the *Histadrut*'s political power was its Secretary General Pinhas Lavon. Formerly Minister of Security, Lavon was considered (together with Minister of Treasury Levi Eshkol), a leading candidate to succeed Ben Gurion as *Mapai* party leader and Prime Minister. A miserable security fiasco (codenamed the Unfortunate Affair—*Essek Habish*), however, forced him to resign from the ministry and overshadowed his prestige (Yanay, 1969). Lavon united the managers of WS under his leadership, and successfully negotiated with the government for the allocation of no less than half of the capital accumulated by the *Histadrut*-run pension funds[17] to the WS holding company. This move secured substantial autonomy for the *Histadrut* vis-à-vis the government, and later for the WS management vis-à-vis the *Histadrut*, since this financial arrangement was multi-annual and independent of the annual state budget discussions (Grinberg, 1991, 1993). Later on, I will elaborate on the role played by this arrangement ("the WS Financial Plan") in key political and economic developments, particularly hyperinflation (Chapter 6).

Lavon did not only control WS under his centralized leadership, but

---

17   Cumulative pension funds were created and managed by the *Histadrut* in private-sector and *Histadrut*-owned enterprises, as opposed to budgetary pension agreements for the state employees.

also pushed to consolidate trade union control of workers under the *Histadrut*. Indeed, during the 1950s most employees depended on the *Histadrut* for jobs, pay and social benefits. High unemployment weakened the employees' bargaining power, and the huge immigration acted to reduce wages (Baharal, 1965). Under these objective conditions, the *Histadrut* could reinforce its political structure, which controlled the employees and kept them dependent, without a democratic need to represent them.

Not all workers, however, were powerless. Every group of workers which had some potential of causing economic damage by threatening to strike began unionizing independently of the *Histadrut* and *Mapai*. In fact, the initial act of every such group was to liberate itself from *Mapai* control, in order to gain real achievements for the workers (Grinberg, 1991, 1996). This liberation meant either organizing a completely independent trade union or gaining autonomy within the *Histadrut* and organizing elections directly representative of the workers and not controlled by parties. During this decade several powerful worker organizations became "independent" or "autonomous." Their degree of independence was affected by three factors: the employer's identity, their pre-state organization, and power relations with the *Histadrut*.

The first groups to liberate themselves of the *Histadrut* were the professional employees, who were not threatened by competition with the new immigrants. These included the engineers, academics, physicians, university professors and high-school teachers. Large worker committees such as the Electric Corporation Committee also began operating autonomously (Tokatli, 1979). In sectors where the employees were exposed to competition with unemployed immigrants, they were powerless and virtually unable to unionize and act autonomously, increasing their dependence on the *Histadrut* and *Mapai*.

The well-organized and powerful professional groups that managed to unionize were mostly composed of veteran European Jews, and succeeded in maintaining high wages, better working conditions and social benefits. This served to widen the gap between the two Jewish ethno-classes, and also perpetuated a dual labor market,[18] as they came to be identified with skilled and unskilled workers respectively (Baharal,

---

18 For a discussion of the concepts of dual and split labor market, see (Grinberg, 1991).

1965).[19] This trend was further perpetuated by the government's education policy, which created two distinct programs with different social mobility tracks, which eventually created two ethno-classes. In order to quickly prepare the immigrants for the labor market, "occupational" high-schools directed students to low-level blue-collar technical training, most of them *Mizrahim*. This was opposed to the academic preparatory high-schools for the middle and upper classes, where most students were *Ashkenazi* (Nahon, 1993a; Yona and Saporta, 2004). The special educational track for *Mizrahi* widened the educational gap between the ethno-classes in the next generation and prevented higher education from *Mizrahi* children educated in Israel.[20]

Beyond the capital accumulated by its WS enterprises and pension funds, the *Histadrut* attempted to control the entire labor market. To do so, it often had to crush independent labor unions. This was true of the seamen[21] and also of the professionals, some of whom eventually remained outside the *Histadrut* organizational roof as a result of this policy, including the high-school teachers, the physicians and the university professors (Tokatli, 1979).

Despite the *Histadrut*'s formal policy of acting to minimize wage gaps, the stronger workers' independent unionization resulted in the exact opposite. The *Histadrut*'s intimate ties with the government and WS economic interests on the one hand, and the growing strengths of the professionals' union on the other alienated the *Histadrut* from the weak and underemployed *Mizrahi* immigrants, who became a marginalized and dependent ethno-working class.

---

19 The term dual refers to different technical skills and wages (Piore, 1971) while split refers to ethnic hostility (Bonacich, 1972). I have suggested elsewhere (Grinberg, 1991) that these are not necessarily contradictory terms.
20 As Nahon's (1993a) research demonstrated, those who arrived in Israel after graduating from high school in their original country were able to bypass the educational barrier of the "occupational" track.
21 An exceptional attempt to overcome competition with the unemployed workers in order to maintain pre-immigration salary levels was the strike called the Seamen's Revolt in 1951. This struggle was exceptionally intense, and the young state's leadership acted decisively, including the use of military force, to counteract the threat of independent unionization. Although the strike was crushed, the seamen managed to form an autonomous trade union within the *Histadrut* (Eshel, 1994).

VI. THE WADI SALIB RIOTS: RESISTING ETHNIC DISCRIMINATION

At the end of the decade, when the industrialization economic policy started to produce the expected outcome of full employment, a momentous event took place, which shook the Israeli public for several years, and came to be registered in its collective memory as the first *Mizrahi* uprising (Chetrit, 2004). Wadi Salib was an inner city Arab neighborhood in Haifa, emptied during 1948 and then inhabited by new immigrants from North Africa. Around 15,000 citizens lived there in miserable housing conditions and economic deprivation, very near to the prosperous commercial area Hadar, of the *Ashkenazi* middle class, on one side, and to the Arab neighborhood of Wadi Nisnass on the other side. As we will see these specific geographic, social, and economic conditions were very similar to those that characterized the Musrara neighborhood of Jerusalem, where the next ethnic uprising started (of the Black Panthers, 1971-73; see Chapter 5).

The riots broke out on the eve of the 1959 Knesset elections and generated heated public discussions, which ended in the greatest ever electoral victory for *Mapai*. Most of the literature on Israeli elections has tended to ignore its' ethnic background and attributed the ruling party's landslide to the victorious 1956 war with Egypt, as well as a brilliant campaign centered on the elderly and charismatic Ben Gurion as a safe bet (Bar-Zohar, 1977; Yanay 1969). Although these factors had doubtless been important, it seems that the decisive contribution of the Wadi Salib events was forgotten, hence the analysis proposed below. This test case will be analyzed in order to shed light on the political implications of the new social structure in Israel based on the ethnic hierarchy constructed during the 1950s. The different reactions to the Wadi Salib riots in the political arena reflected the increasing tension within ruling circles between those identified with the new state apparati ("statism") versus those identified with the pre-state *Histadrut* and party organizations ("movementism"), and between them and the opposition parties.

The spark that lit the fire was a relatively minor incident between neighborhood dwellers and the police, following the shooting of a local drunk by policemen and the rumors that he died in the hospital. The locals reacted with rage, and police used excessive force to maintain order. The violent response only made things worse when the demonstrators marched to the close Hadar neighborhood and turned ever more violent, burning cars and breaking the windows of fancy shops the next day (Dahan-Kalev, 1991).

The demonstrators claimed that North African immigrants were discriminated against by the state and the ruling party. In response the dominant Mayor of the city, Aba Hushi,[22] compared the violence to the Nazi Kristallnacht or Crystal Night ("Leil Abdulach"), the demonstrators were portrayed as hooligans and criminals by the ruling elites, delegitimizing their demands and mobilizing the fear and hate of the *Ashkenazi* population (Chetrit, 2004; Cohen, 2009). Haifa was very well known by the dominant position of the ruling party and its local Worker Council since 1936, when it succeeded in occupying vacant jobs in the harbor and developing a very efficient and profitable company of port services. Due to the strength of *Mapai* and the *Histadrut* in the city, and its relative autonomy vis-à-vis the central authorities of the party and the *Histadrut*, the city gained the name of "Red Haifa." The strongman in the repression of the rioters was Secretary of the Haifa Workers Council Joseph Almogi, whose "success" later earned him the positions of chair of the electoral campaign (in 1959), and party secretary (in 1960).

The first target of the Wadi Salib demonstrators was the powerful ruling party and its electoral meetings, claiming their responsibility for discrimination. The demonstrations were led by a local organization of North Africans (*Likud Iotzei Tzfon Africa*) that initially called to demonstrate the day after the shooting incident. The violent demonstrations, however, quickly spread to several towns inhabited by North African immigrants. The most visible form of protest was the attack and burning down of the *Mapai* or *Histadrut* local office, quite correctly perceived as a symbol of the state. Over the next month, similar riots and demonstrations took place in different towns as Acco, Tel Hanan, Beer Sheba, Kiriat Shmona, and Migdal Haemek. In other places—like Jerusalem, Ramla and Lod—the government succeeded to prevent the initiatives to demonstrate (Dahan-Kalev, 1991; Chetrit 2004).

The claim that North African immigrants are suffering very difficult housing and economic conditions, and that there is a big gap between them and the *Ashkenazi* population was not in dispute. This was almost a consensus among all parties in the Knesset debate, including some *Mapai* members (Knesset Protocols, July 13, 1959). The debate was re-

---

22 For a non-critical personal biography, see Eshel (2002).

lated to the question who incited the population, if there were criminal elements involved, and mainly if the government was doing enough to solve the miseries of the population. This is the reason that the Government immediately decided to form an Inquiry Committee to investigate the Wadi Salib events (Etziony Committee); however, it refused the initiative of the opposition to expand the investigation to the riots in other cities, and to investigate the social conditions that led to the violent demonstrations (Knesset Protocols, July 29, 1959).

Although the government recognized the claims, it did not recognize the claimers, who were de-legitimized, criminalized, repressed, and sentenced to jail (Shitrit, 2004). The different organs of *Mapai*, both within the government and the *Histadrut*, mobilized all the forces at their disposal (except the military) to crush the uprising. This included the police, but also the paramilitary Worker Troops (*Plugot Hapoel*) organized by the local Workers Councils of the *Histadrut*. *Mapai* claimed that the demonstrations were not spontaneous, and that partisan agitators attempted to reap political gain out of the ethnic strife. Obviously, on the eve of the Knesset elections this was not a completely groundless assertion. However, it is hardly likely that opposition parties initiated the uprising, but rather that they used the spontaneous outburst for their own purposes.

Despite the tense atmosphere, attempts to crush the uprising and the concurrent electoral campaign exposed a profound disagreement within *Mapai* itself. The *Mapai* electoral campaign headquarters tried to draw voter attention not only to the elderly leader Ben Gurion, but also to new party members with military backgrounds. The most prominent of these was Moshe Dayan, IDF Chief of Staff during the 1956 Sinai campaign. Dayan was Ben Gurion's protégé in the security establishment, and represented the younger *Mapai* generation. The day after *Mapai*'s electoral meeting in Wadi Salib was cancelled due to threats by local demonstrators, Ben Gurion and Dayan decided to visit the neighborhood and talked with the people in the streets. The purpose of this visit was to show that Ben Gurion and Dayan were not the target of popular rage and anger, and to make a clear distinction between their personal popularity and the protest against the party, the *Histadrut*, and workers council apparatchiks (*Davar*, July 27, 1959).

While the demonstrations were being suppressed by the police and the *Histadrut*'s militia, Moshe Dayan was sent to appear before *Mizrahi*

CHAPTER THREE

immigrants in the peripheral new development towns. It was assumed that no one would dare raise a hand against this war hero, a complete different type of leader compared to the veteran *Ashkenazi* apparatchiks. Indeed, Dayan was much better received by North African immigrants than other *Mapai* and *Histadrut* officials. Moreover, he himself expressed understanding of the alienation felt by his audiences against the party-*Histadrut* apparatus, and legitimized in his speeches the bitterness and protest against the ruling party, indirectly supporting an anti-*Mapai* vote. Dayan's message was simple: although *Mapai* and the *Histadrut* are powerful establishments which are alienated from you, Ben Gurion and youngsters such as Dayan truly want to revitalize the party with new policies and young leaders (Grinberg, 1993).

These messages were of course fully backed by Ben Gurion, but enraged senior *Mapai* and *Histadrut* officials, creating tension which only increased after the elections. Ultimately, however, Dayan proved his political effectiveness in crushing the uprising. Ben Gurion and Dayan's military-statist credentials, together with the violent suppression on the ground, ensured *Mapai*'s landslide. Although the opposition parties broadened their support among the *Mizrahi* poor, *Mapai* more than compensated for that among the urban *Ashkenazi* middle-class, and it was its greatest electoral victory ever (Smith, 1969).

One salient result was the relative parliamentary success of the local initiative to form an ethnic party of North African immigrants and their further disappearance. According to various reports, the leaders of the Wadi Salib revolt have organized previously, apparently aiming to participate in the approaching Knesset elections (Dahan Kalev, 1991; Chetrit, 2004). They called their party North African Immigrants Union (*Likud Iotzei Tzfon Africa*), and the initial intention was to join the ruling party, but they apparently felt insulted by the humiliating treatment and the attempt to use them as "voting contractors" instead of legitimate representatives of their neighborhood (Bernstein, 1975; Dahan Kalev, 1991; Chetrit 2004).

The previous existence of this local organization and the electoral context helped to transform the incident of the policemen shooting into ethnic riots. David Ben Harush, the most salient figure of the party, was arrested after a big demonstration on July 31, 1959. He was tried and sentenced for two years prison. During the elections, the leaders of the party were in jail, and with almost no money and no national organization they succeeded to mobilize 8,200 votes, that is 0.8% of the electorate (Shitrit, 2004). This was a relative success given the lack of organization and the incarceration of the leaders, but it failed to enter the Knesset due to the minimum 1 percent vote, and there was no significant continuity after the elections. The public impact, however, remained lodged in the memory of the *Mizrahi* ethno-class, and only twelve years after Wadi Salib riots a new and stronger ethnic mo(ve)ment of *Mizrahi* resistance finally succeeded in gaining recognition of their legitimate claims, although no political space for representation was opened.

VII. THE COUNTER-MO(VE)MENT: CLOSURE OF POLITICAL SPACE TO MIZRAHI ACTORS

Three main facts related to the riots are significant to the analysis of the ethnic content of the resistance movement: (1) it took place at the heart of a large city and spread to other areas including isolated development towns; (2) the demonstrators protested the discrimination of North-African immigrants, rather than *Mizrahi* Jews in general; (3) it took place in a mixed Jewish-Arab city, where North African immigrants lived near *Ashkenazi* upper and middle class and discriminated Arabs.

North African immigrants were mainly settled all over the country in the frontier buffer zone evacuated by Palestinians, most of them in the new development towns, and a minority living in houses formerly owned by Palestinians in the big mixed cities. Their problem was different than that of the immigrants from Yemen and Iraq, who also settled partly in the periphery but also near the major population centers. The latter assimilated quicker in the economy and administration, they could identify and be integrated by the previous immigrants of their land of origin who had arrived before 1948 (Grinberg, 1989). Conversely, the vast majority of North African Jews immigrated in the mid-1950s. They were settled in frontier townships and had nobody to speak in their name in the political sphere, even as a co-opted leader (Grinberg, 1989). Their exposure and cultural similarity to the Arab "enemy" population only served to underscore their marginal status within Jewish society. As we have observed, the dominant Orientalist discourse assumed that all Jews coming from Arab countries belonged to same category, so there was no need for North African representation or even cooptation, and the presence of Knesset members and a minister from Iraq and Yemen was sufficient.

Despite the fertile ground for discontent, the North African Jews failed to become a political force or even a social movement with recognized leaders speaking in their name. In order to open political space for recognition and build political force able to represent them, it was needed: first, social actors able to establish connections between people living in different cities and towns; second, to be able to speak the legitimate language of power and articulate general demands from the state; and third, to design a joint strategy, establishing a joint organization on the basis of a sense of ethnic solidarity. The new migrants, lacking the cultural capital of the dominant language and the political discourse, the rules of the game, and media contacts, were unable to transform the spontaneous expression of rage into a collective actor.

The organizers of the riots were aware of the need to enter the political arena. They have organized their own group called *Likud Iotzei Tzfon Africa* (North African Immigrants Union) and attempted to act within the ruling party, but, as mentioned, felt humiliated by their treatment. This humiliating attitude by the owners of symbolic power is precisely the symbolic violence that provokes the physical violence of the repressed. They find themselves forced to use violence due to their misrecognition and the lack of cultural power. Despite their failure to enter the political arena as actors who can represent the group, they succeeded to gain recognition of their discrimination following the power struggles provoked by the riots within the ruling party.

The parties competing with *Mapai* were encouraged by potential electoral gains in the approaching elections, and attempted to give voice to the North African immigrants by emphasizing the legitimacy of their claims, but not of their leaders. The most earnest in these attempts was *Herut* (led by Menachem Begin), followed by *Achdut Haavoda* and the National Religious Party. Note, however, that these attempts to gain votes did not lead to representation of North African agendas or identities. The parties involved did not improve the living conditions of the protesting immigrants, formulate a collective strategy or establish any organizations for or with the North African community.

The activity of some established opposition parties prevented the development of an independent leadership representative of the North

African immigrants. *Mizrahi* leaders and representatives could only advance within the framework of existing parties, with organizations, discourses, agendas and goals shaped during the pre-1948 period. In the literature, this is called "cooptation." In the Israeli case, this process represents also a subtle form of cooperation, albeit not necessarily intentional or coordinated, between all the pre-1948 *Ashkenazi* established parties that effectively closed political space to the demands and agendas of the Jewish migrants that were collectively marked as *Mizrahim*. This is how political parties can become anti-democratic without breaking the democratic rules of the game. The reason for such cooperation was simple: independent representation would have undoubtedly come at the expense of all parties involved (see Grinberg, 2010: Part 3 for a more detailed discussion of *Mizrahi* misrepresentation).

The way to close the political space to ethnic claims was to delegitimize *Mizrahi* collective claims, presenting them as an essential negation of the Zionist melting pot ideal, and at the same time delegitimize their autonomous organization and struggles, portraying them as "the ethnic demon" (Herzog, 1986). The sophisticated cooperation between *Mapai* and *Herut* (and later Labor party and *Likud*, respectively) was designed to mobilize the ethnic identities in indirect and latent ways (Shapiro, 1991), without opening political space for articulation and discussion of these identities. The complete delegitimization of *Mizrahi* representation was the most important long-term historical result of the Wadi Salib Riots.

While some opposition parties tried to gain from this anti-*Mapai* protest, the ruling party gained much more (among the *Ashkenazi* constituency) from proving its ability to "pacify" the new immigrants and suppress the uprising. The suppression of the Wadi Salib riots enabled the ruling party and some competing parties to make electoral gains, but, most importantly, it created a long-term pattern of distorted ethnic mobilization which countered the movement of *Mizrahi* resistance and prevented direct representation. Those parties who supported the uprising attempted to gain voters from among the underprivileged, while *Mapai* sought to gain more votes from the *Ashkenazi* middle class fears of *Mizrahi* riots and claims. *Mapai*'s aggressive response allayed these fears, proving that someone was in control of the situation and will not let the North Africans run wild. According to this interpretation, *Mapai*'s above-mentioned landslide became the counter-mo(ve)ment of the Wadi Salib ethnic riots. In the 1959 elections, *Mapai* was transformed into the "political protector" of the *Ashkenazi* veteran population: it did not necessarily represent *Ashkenazi* interests or identities, but "protected" them, expressed their fears and established new dependent relations between the party and its supporters.

I suggest here that the Wadi Salib resistant mo(ve)ment had a crucial historical significance, in that it heralded the birth of a new repertoire of ethnic misrepresentation through tribal channeling of collective feelings of fear, hostility and vengefulness. These feelings were mobilized in the run-up to the elections in a very subtle and manipulative way aiming to prevent direct political debate on ethnic claims, identities and conflicts. Thanks to this new repertoire of distortion and misrepresentation *Mapai* mobilized the great majority of *Ashkenazi* voters in the 1959 elections. As we shall see in Chapter 5, this peculiar pattern of tribal channeling of fear and closure of political space to ethnic representation was further refined and expanded after the second mo(ve)ment of ethnic resistance in 1971-73.

The previous "statism-versus-movementism" conflict found during the Wadi Salib uprising its practical expression in the different approaches suggested to coopting the *Mizrahim* in the establishment. While *Mapai* and the *Histadrut* formed committees to advance *Mizrahi* officials (mainly Iraqi and Yemenite [Grinberg, 1989]), Ben Gurion coined the slogan (which remained quite catchy even decades later) that the *Mizrahi* Jews will really be assimilated when the first Yemenite Chief of Staff is appointed. The two approaches suggested different mechanisms for assimilating and controlling the new immigrants and cooptation of their leaders. *Mapai* and the *Histadrut* sought to rely on their dependence on their services on the one hand, and on their institutional ability to secure jobs for them on the other, as effective means of control. Conversely, the statists believed that identifying with the state and being promoted in military ranks will legitimize the existing social order. These two strategies differed not only with regard to the required modus operandi, but above all in the perceived timeframe: while the *Histadrut's* approach provided an immediate solution to the control problem, the statist offered a long-term solution. However, neither the latter nor the former had much time to spare, and both lost a considerable degree of their control as Israeli economy approached virtual full employment.

VIII. Conclusion

The period in question saw the most significant transformations in Israeli society with the establishment of an ethnically segregated Jewish State. The Zionist Labor Movement organizations created during the formative period of the British Mandate successfully overcame momentous challenges, such as the 1948 War and the assimilation of an unprecedented immigration wave. They also figured out how to overcome the free market tendency of preferring low-cost labor which threatened Jewish employment by using government budgets to create jobs, and martial law to prevent free market competition with Arab citizens. Nevertheless, the successful transition from the *Yishuv* organization to the institutionalization of the Jewish State and the realization of the imagined nation concealed a profound crisis that would only be revealed in full in the second decade discussed in the next chapter.

What I have elsewhere called the crisis of statehood (Grinberg, 1993a) was related to the tension between the powerful political institutions established during the formative colonial period on the one hand, and the new democratic rules of the game and state borders framing civil society on the other. The new state represented the fundamental precondition for the democratic opening of political space to new agendas and identities. However, the strength of the ruling political institutions and the weakness of civil society prevented effective action by the political opposition (Shapiro, 1977). Instead of opening political space for representation, the combined weakness of civil society and the electoral competition with opposition parties led to the manipulative channeling of tribal ethnic hostility and cooptation.[23]

The analysis of the ethnic resistance mo(ve)ment provides three important insights that expand the concept of political space. The first is related to the difference between the recognition of the identity of a social group and non-recognition of representative political actors. In the absence of representation there is no further opening of political space, namely no mediation, no negotiation and no compromise. While the recognition of collective identity is an important step in the process of opening political space, neglecting direct representation may constitute an efficient means of closing the space by misrecognition of agendas and

---

23   On Mapai's cooptation efforts after Wadi Salib, see Chetrit (2010).

claims and the complete absence of negotiations.

The second insight is related to the struggles among the legitimate actors in the political arena and their competition for public support. As suggested by the structure of political opportunities theory (Tarrow, 1998), resistance movements may achieve social recognition when some political actors recognize the potential to mobilize ethnic protest in order to gain votes. When there are also internal divisions among the ruling elites, any type of resistance has a better chance to be recognized. In our case, such internal divisions opened the space both for the recognition of legitimate *Mizrahi* claims (Dayan's speeches) and for their repression, designed to allay *Ashkenazi* fears (mainly represented by Abba Hushi's comparison of the Wadi Salib riots to Kristallnacht).

The third insight is related to the manipulation of symbols in the political arena. When the identity of the resistant social group is recognized but its autonomous representation is rejected, cooptation of its leaders is often an effective tool for shrinking political space to new identities and agendas. Cooptation is possible in the political arena precisely because it is a symbolic field of representations, different from the actual social actors' claim of representation. Cooptation may appear only when a social group is recognized but its distinct collective interests are not legitimized. This occurs when legitimate political actors seek to mobilize the citizen's votes by manipulating their identity without, however, resolving the social conflicts and tensions underlying its hostility.

Discrimination and ethnic claims may be contained by cooptation when the discriminated social groups have no power base: no economic power of organized workers, educated middle classes or capitalists; no symbolic power able to legitimize their claims; and no cultural power, as group members do not speak the language of political power that legitimizes the authority of the state itself. I will discuss the distinction between symbolic power and the languages of state power in Chapters 5 and 9, where the differences became more evident.

The closure of political space and the dominant position of the ruling party were evident above all with regard to the Arab citizens subjected to martial law, who voted under the pressure of military agents for the party that was repressing them. The closure of political space also affected the recently arrived Jewish immigrants from Arab countries who depended on state institutions for all their needs. Paradoxically, the only force which could support democratization was the free market, and the empowerment of private capital, middle and working classes vis-à-vis the state. However, the empowerment of free market forces facing the strong political apparatus designed to rule them (during the colonial period) created such a threat to the ruling institutions that it was not likely to transpire. This provoked a new resistance mo(ve)ment, discussed in the next chapter.

4.
1960-1965 — The Action Committees' Revolt: Full Employment Crisis, Failed Democratization and State Expansion[1]

I. Introduction

This chapter discusses the most significant structural change in the Israeli history—the de-facto annexation of the West Bank and Gaza Strip and the unequal integration of the Palestinian population. This institutional change was not a necessary result of the 1967 War, but rather a political decision made after the war, supported by a meticulous institutional design of economic dependency and military subjugation. The puzzle analyzed here is why the Zionist Labor Movement abandoned its pre-1948 nation-building strategy (see Chapter 2) of geographic and economic separation from the Palestinians. Why did it return to the British Mandate borders and impose colonial domination after having accepted partition? In order to comprehend this sudden historical development, I analyze the crisis of statehood that preceded the war, in an attempt to explain why the ZLM intentionally adjusted itself so effectively to the new structural situation of expanded state borders.

The beginning of this period was characterized, for the first time in Israel's history, by full employment. Within a few years, Israeli economy moved from deep unemployment to labor shortage, mainly in the metropolitan areas, with only some unemployment pockets remaining in peripheral areas inhabited by *Mizrahi* ethno-classes. Under these conditions, military control of the Arab labor force gradually weakened due to increasing pressure by the employers, until Arab workers were practically allowed free movement by 1962. The process of integrating Arab workers in the Israeli market was accompanied by the gradual equalization of salaries between Jewish and Arab, *Ashkenazi* and *Mizrahi* workers (Ben Porat, 1966). During the full employment period, Arab and *Mizrahi* ethno-classes became part of a process of working class homogenization.

---

1 This chapter is based on an archive study published in Hebrew in book format (Grinberg, 1993).

The decade is thus characterized by the increased bargaining power of industrial workers, following a period when they had been extremely dependent on the *Histadrut*. Beginning in the early 1960s, semi- and unskilled workers began unionizing with relative autonomy from the *Histadrut* apparatus, demanding higher wages and going out on widespread strikes; the latter were labeled "wildcat" because they ran against *Histadrut* policies. This process took place despite the *Histadrut*'s reluctance to support the strikers, because by that time it had almost completely lost control of the labor market. As real wages rose steadily in 1960-1965, it became clear that the economic and political elites, as well as their established institutions, were completely unable either to undermine worker resistance or restrain their demands (Bar-El and Michael, 1977).

Mapai lost control of the workers precisely when it was trying to steer a new economic policy design to adjust Israeli prices to world level in order to improve its trading balance. This policy, announced in 1962, focused on a large one-time devaluation of the local currency followed by the determination of a uniform formal exchange rate (as opposed to the previous subsidization system consisting of varying sector-based rates). This move was designed to limit state intervention in determining exchange rates, but also sought to cut the budget by reducing real wages and capital subsidization. The result of the devaluation was precisely the opposite, however, due to the workers' reaction: they demanded pay raises and obtained an average wage increase of 30% in real terms (Halevi and Klinov-Malul, 1968: 224). Subsequently, the industrialists demanded government subsidies to avoid raising their prices. Thus, the *Histadrut*'s inability to represent or at least control the workers' resistance movement sabotaged the government's economic policy, leading to increased subsidies and fiscal deficit, and greater local demand, which led in turn to greater deficit and so on.

Paradoxically, whereas during Israel's early years labor movement institutions were well-prepared for the challenges of assimilating and settling the new immigrants, providing for their basic needs and employing them, the new conditions of full employment produced a profound economic and political crisis. At the beginning the crisis led to increased institutional tension between state and *Histadrut* leaders (called "statism versus movementism" in contemporary jargon). This tension erupted in the form of direct confrontation between Prime Minister

David Ben Gurion and *Histadrut* Secretary General Pinhas Lavon, under the guise of an old security fiasco (the so-called Lavon Affair; see Tevet, 1992; Bar Zohar, 1977). This initial confrontation revolved essentially around the government's authority to make autonomous economic and political decisions (Grinberg, 1993).

Following Lavon's dismissal as a result of the first confrontation, it became evident that even when the *Histadrut* and *Mapai* cooperated with the government they were able to control the economy only when the population depended on them for its everyday needs. However, under full employment and rapid growth which empower broader social groups, the old-fashioned institutions established during the colonial era proved ineffective. In a formal democracy under full employment conditions, the previous dependency of workers had disappeared, and they were able to unionize freely and even threaten to form their own party. Full employment thus posed a real threat to the ruling political institutions in the form of classes empowered by the free market, be it the working class or the middle class and private employers. From a broader perspective, structural free market and democratic transition clashed with the old colonial political institutions, which attempted to continue imposing their control of the markets and state.

The ZLM's political and economic institutions were designed mainly to serve the political power elite and ensure its control over the economy and civil society with the objective of separating Jews from Arabs and establishing a Jewish nation-state. Having accomplished this objective, the ZLM institutions were deeply involved in the labor, capital, and product markets, supporting expanded state investment in promoting industrial development (Shalev, 1992; Halevi and Klinov-Malul, 1968; Maman and Rosenhek, 2011). Facing the threats of full employment, *Mapai* and the *Histadrut* made an effort to maintain control over various interest groups empowered by rapid growth, including the industrialists, the private employers, the prospering middle class, and the workers, who now wielded greater bargaining power (Rosenfeld and Carmi, 1979; Grinberg, 1993; Bar-El and Michael, 1977; Brauer, 1989).

The resistant mo(ve)ment pressured the *Histadrut* and the three "working class" parties which controlled it (*Mapai*, *Ahdut Haavoda*, and *Mapam*) to adjust to the new situation. Each party responded differently to the challenge, as worker protests and strikes fuelled disagreements both among and within them. Whereas the *Histadrut* and *Mapai* sought to restrain the workers, *Ahdut Haavoda* and *Mapam* tended to support rank-and-file demands. However, all *Histadrut* factions, including *Mapai* members, were in conflict with *Mapai*'s pro-government control advocates, or "statists," who wished to weaken the *Histadrut*, which was supported by the "movementists." All these internal struggles were shaped by the challenge presented by the working class mo(ve)ment of resistance.

II. The Lavon Affair

Immediately after his 1959 landslide, Ben Gurion and his "statist" supporters began pushing for institutional reforms designed to adjust the *Histadrut* and *Mapai* to the new structural conditions created by the establishment of the State of Israel and subsequent economic developments (Yanay, 1969). The "statist" reformers aimed at radical weakening of the *Histadrut* and other pre-1948 colonial institutions, partly through the (failed) Public Health Bill designed to deny the *Histadrut* its main welfare-state service and its basis for mass membership.[2] Another failed initiative was a radical revision of the electoral system by switching from national and proportional elections of Knesset members to regional elections. This initiative was designed to deny party apparati centralized control of *Knesset* member appointments and to empower popular leaders at the expense of grey apparatchiks. The "statist" reformers sought to use state institutions to mobilize political support and enhance their position, and their main obstacle was the non-representative and anti-democratic structure of the pre-1948 labor institutions. The closure of political space to middle and working classes and *Mizrahi* representatives was the background of the internal struggles within the party.

Towards the end of 1960, Israel found itself experiencing one of the most confusing and dramatic confrontations within the ruling party, which left its mark on the national collective memory. The Lavon Affair was so dramatic and significant that for many years it would be known simply as "The Affair." The emotional storm raged all the more as this was a top-secret affair, whose facts were hidden from the public. In a

---

2   The Public Health Bill was rejected, and only in 1995 did a new initiative succeed in passing a similar bill (see Chapter 7).

manner that was to characterize similar future affairs, the press was not allowed to report the goings-on behind the scenes, and editors carefully phrased their headlines using codenames understandable only to those "in the know," quoting the "senior officer," his "secretary," the "third man," etc.

In later years, many researchers saw the internal clash within *Mapai* which accompanied this affair as indicative of the struggle between the "juniors" and the "old guard," "statists" vs. "movementists," or Ben Gurion's juniors (*Tzeirei* Ben Gurion) vs. the oligarchic heads of the party apparatus (Tevet, 1992; Hassin and Horowitz, 1961; Yanay, 1969; Bar Zohar, 1977). The Lavon Affair was indeed related to all these aspects, above all the Vicious Triangle discussed in the previous chapter (government, *Histadrut* and *Mapai*). Indeed, this was a turning point that broke the spell and facilitated the reshaping of political coalitions.

Pinhas Lavon, *Histadrut* General Secretary since 1956, was considered one of Ben Gurion's potential heirs (the second potential Minister of Treasury Levi Eshkol). Previously, when Ben Gurion had resigned from his dual office of Prime Minister and Security Minister (1953), and according to his recommendation, Moshe Sharet (previously Foreign Minister) was appointed Prime Minister and Lavon Security Minister. In 1954, during Lavon's yearlong tenure, Israeli intelligence attempted to embroil Egypt's new government under Nasser in a conflict with the US government. An Israeli spy network operating in Egypt planned and even executed amateurish terrorist attacks against US-related targets, designed to seem as though carried out by anti-American Egyptian extremists. The agents were caught, their leaders executed and others sentenced to long prison terms. Following these events, quite euphemistically codenamed "the Unfortunate Affair" a two-member examination committee was appointed to find out who was to blame for this failure[3] (Hassin and Horowitz, 1961). The Olshan-Dori Committee failed to arrive at definitive conclusions, but the main suspects, who did not manage to completely clear their names, were Lavon and Military Intelligence Chief Binyamin Jibli. Following the committee's conclusions, Lavon decided to resign and accepted the appointment of *Histadrut* Secretary General, but remained embittered towards certain members of

---

3   In popular discourse, the question was: "Who gave the order?" It continued to echo in collective memory and popular culture for decades.

the security establishment.[4]

The affair returned to the headlines in 1960, this time in an entirely different context. Since 1957, *Mapai* has been fraught with conflicts between *Histadrut* officials and Ben Gurion and his "juniors." These became exacerbated with the 1959 elections, when the opposing sides competed over the nomination of party candidates before the elections, and even more intensively over the composition of the new government. The next year was particularly tense, with the conflict centering on *Histadrut* General Secretary Lavon and Treasury Minister Levi Eshkol, who wished to minimize the former's authority to intervene in macroeconomic issues such as taxation and budgeting. Backed by *Mapam* and *Ahdut Haavoda*, the *Histadrut* leader demanded to take part in such decisions to prevent policies deemed contrary to working class interests, and asserted that if not consulted, he could no longer restrain workers' salary demands (Grinberg, 1993).

The government found itself helpless and powerless, with the party in danger of splitting between "statists" and "movementists." Paradoxically, full employment—which usually strengthens social-democratic parties—was the fundamental cause of this crisis. *Mapai*, however, was not a bona fide social-democratic party, as it was not geared to represent the workers, but rather to control them by forcing them to depend on it due to their weakness in the labor market. The 1959 general elections, as mentioned, were a landslide victory for Ben-Gurion and the "statists"; however, this achievement proved ineffective, since the "movementists" held the majority in the *Histadrut*, the party HQ, and other key bodies (Yanay, 1969; Medding, 1972). It was then that they stumbled upon the old security affair.

In September 1960 the press ran a story about a belated court hearing in the matter of one of the key players in the "Unfortunate Affair."[5] This

---

4   These included the Director General of the Ministry of Security Shimon Peres, Chief of General Staff Moshe Dayan, and their patron, Ben Gurion, who allegedly conspired against Lavon. For further details on this complex and highly controversial affair, see Tevet (1992); Hassin and Horowitz (1961); Yanay (1969); and Bar Zohar (1977). The question of responsibility for the debacle is still a matter for investigations and debates (for example, a TV program in 2008 still debated it: http://www.flix.co.il/tapuz/showVideo.asp?m=2887117).

5   This person—Avri Elad—was codenamed the Third Man (marking his location in the chain of command); he was tried belatedly due to years-long absence from Israel. The trial supposedly brought to light new evidence regarding to the eternal question of who gave the order, and Lavon saw it as an opportunity to publicly clear his name (Shaham, 1998: 192-3).

piece of news brought an unresolved issue, forgotten by most politicians and almost unknown to most citizens, back to the public agenda. The intensity of the renewed affair can only be understood on the background of the earlier strife among *Mapai* leaders regarding the *Histadrut*'s powers. *Mapai* leaders feared that the combination of a personal conflict between Lavon and Ben Gurion and the existing tension around the *Histadrut* question could spell the electoral end of the party. Therefore, everyone accepted the rules of the game suggested by the new Party Secretary Joseph Almogi.[6] He suggested to all the *Mapai* members involved in the party debates to abstain from publicly discussing any possible linkage between the security affair and the power struggle between the government and the *Histadrut*. The fact that Ben Gurion and Eshkol, on the one hand, and Lavon, on the other, were involved in another, parallel conflict was deliberately hidden from the public (Grinberg, 1993: 98).

When the new trial began in 1960, Lavon demanded public rehabilitation, while Ben Gurion wanted to investigate the entire affair in court or in a national inquiry commission. Whereas Lavon sought a party decision in his favor and relied on the movementists' support, Ben Gurion sought a decision by state institutions (assuming the decision would not clear Lavon) in order to emphasize the government's superior authority. The renewed Lavon Affair conflict continued for more than four months, until it finally concluded in a way which did not reflect either of these positions, when the Party Central Committee resolved to dismiss Lavon from his office as *Histadrut* General Secretary. The fact that Lavon's dismissal ended the confrontation makes clear that the conflict did not actually revolve around the 1954 fiasco, but rather around the power relations between the *Histadrut* and the government in 1960.

The dismissal did not reflect Ben Gurion's "statist" position, and certainly not Lavon's wishes, but another interest which gradually came to dominate *Mapai*'s agenda: the ruling party's desire to maintain the power of the LIC, albeit with increased party control by the *Histadrut*, a desire represented above all by Eshkol (for both institutional and personal considerations). It was through the Lavon affair that Eshkol consolidated his leadership in *Mapai* vis-à-vis the two older leaders who fought one another and damaged the party (Grinberg, 1993).

---

6 Almogi, as you may recall, had played a key role in suppressing the *Wadi Salib* Riots as Secretary of the Haifa Workers Council.

The Lavon Affair enabled Eshkol to define the crisis and confrontation—between the pre-state colonial institutions on the one side and the market economy and democratic state on the other—in partisan terms: no to Ben Gurion's "statism," which risked *Mapai*'s dominant position in the state, but also no to Lavon's "movementism," which undermined the party rule of the *Histadrut* and risked undercutting the government's authority over the markets. He therefore moved to dismiss Lavon, but did so without accepting Ben Gurion's demand to weaken both the *Histadrut* and *Mapai*. This proved quite complicated, since Lavon enjoyed broad support by the *Histadrut* apparatus, the workers, *Mapai*'s coalition partners both in the government and *Histadrut* (*Mapam* and *Ahdut Haavoda*), and the opposition parties, each for its own reasons. Having successfully navigated the party between "statism" and "movementism," Eshkol became its undeclared leader, although Ben Gurion remained Prime Minister for two more years. It was Eshkol who negotiated the formation of the next government after the elections had been moved forward to 1961 due to the Lavon Affair fallout.[7] Eshkol also cultivated close cooperation between the government and newly appointed *Histadrut* leaders. Above all, it was Eshkol who formulated *Mapai*'s political strategy for surviving the full employment crisis while retaining the pre-state institutions, by allying with the *Ahdut Haavoda* Party (as we shall see below).

The Lavon Affair was typical of struggles characterizing the initial full employment period. The delicate balance among the three sides of the Vicious Triangle was shattered due to loss of control over the workers, forcing *Mapai* to decide which actor of the triangle would dominate in the future. Eshkol chose the party over the government and *Histadrut*. This meant that government and *Histadrut* representatives met under party auspices to reach compromises in economic policy questions. This was deemed necessary in order to overcome the crisis while maintaining the *Histadrut*'s quasi-welfare state structure and *Mapai*'s control over it, thus retaining the party's hegemonic position in the state. The result was that the *Histadrut* should continue acting not as a trade union

---

7   In the Israeli system, the president (a titular figurehead) asks the leader of the strongest parliamentary faction to form the government after the elections. Although this representative is usually also the designated prime minister, this is not legally binding. Thus, in 1961, *Mapai* decided to ask Eshkol to form Ben Gurion's new government, since most other parties were at odds with him, while Eshkol maintained cordial working relationships with them throughout the Lavon crisis.

representing the workers but as a centralist federation with Mapai's interests in mind, which literally translated to forcing wage restraint on weak and dependent workers. The problem left unresolved by Eshkol's political maneuvers was the empowerment of the working class under full employment. In order to neutralize the workers' power, it was necessary to prevent their representation in the political sphere, namely to close political space. To do so, Eshkol sought to form a new political coalition towards the 1965 elections. After winning the elections, a structural solution to weaken the workers became necessary.

III. The Action Committees' Working Class Revolt: The Histadrut Challenged by Resistance

During 1960-1965, *Histadrut* leaders observed with concern how workers' councils and trade unions begin to establish themselves and initiate worker struggles against their authority. The *Histadrut*'s control began to crumble, as an increasing number of workers declared "wildcat" strikes,[8] with rising prices, as well as standards of living, workers' pay rose regardless of official decisions of the *Histadrut* trade unions division against their strikes. The inability of the political institutions to negotiate collective agreements with the workers' direct representatives meant the government's economic policy became ineffective, with a growing balance-of-payment deficit (Bar-El and Michael, 1977; Shalev, 1992; Greenwald, 1972).

Following Lavon's overthrow and *Mapai*'s renewed control of the *Histadrut*, the newly appointed *Histadrut* leaders drastically changed the attitude towards the workers, and initiated an open and active policy of containing rank and file spontaneous struggles. The new *Histadrut* leadership under Secretary General Aaron Becker and Trade Union Department Chairman Yeruham Meshel tried to aggressively crush any strike declared without their approval. Nevertheless, the "wildcat" strikes multiplied, as the workers came to believe they would gain more without the *Histadrut*'s mediation services (Bar-El and Michael, 1977; Friedman, 1963).

---

8   According to the Law and Histadrut constitution strikes must be declared by the Trade Union division, otherwise there are considered illegal, or "wildcat" in workers slang.

Although the *Histadrut* did not serve the interests of the weaker workers in Lavon's time as well, it supported them to a certain degree. To do so, it intervened with the government's economic policies, protesting against rising prices, increased taxation, and any policy contrary to working class interests, while at the same time agreeing to freeze workers' wages. Thanks to this double-edged policy, it managed to maintain its status both with the workers dependent on it and with the government. The change since 1961 was due to two parallel factors. First, the workers became less dependent on the *Histadrut* thanks to full employment. Second, the new *Histadrut* leadership changed its confrontationist attitude within the Vicious Triangle by cooperating in planning the government's cost-cutting effort, and agreeing to continued wage restraint in a period of economic growth. Consequently, it was often forced into conflict with rank-and-file workers, and in fact stopped relying on its control of the workers to empower itself vis-à-vis the employers, thus becoming weaker than ever.

From 1960 onwards, as the government's industrialization policy began to make itself felt, the industrial workers' unionization problem became increasingly severe. Industrial worker councils represented relatively small groups of workers in isolated factories, as opposed to the professional trade unions with thousands of members nationwide, or national and powerful public sector worker councils in services such as the Electric Corporation, ports, airports, railways, post and customs. The industrial workers had no independent unions and relied on unions directly controlled by *Histadrut* officials, who were usually *Mapai* members (Tokatli, 1979).

Thanks to full employment, workers' councils directly elected at the plant level began operating independently of the *Histadrut*, regardless of party affiliations. To compete for the workers' support, council activists tried to prove that they were loyal to the workers more than to their parties. Full employment thus created a class mobilization atmosphere that pushed rank and file workers' leaders to disengage from their partisan affiliations. Under this radicalization dynamic, no matter which party held the majority, elected workers' councils were radicalized by the more radical minorities. This situation became very common, as leftist minority activists created non-official representative bodies known as "action committees" to compete with the worker councils, which were still controlled—at least formally—by *Mapai* (Grinberg, 1993).

The fundamental cause of this process was full employment combined with attempts by both the government and *Histadrut* to restrain the workers' wage demands. This situation embroiled *Ahdut Haavoda* in a particular type of internal contradiction[9]: its activists were highly visible in the action committees and industrial labor strife, while their party leaders were partners with *Mapai* in both the government and *Histadrut* coalitions' anti-worker decisions. The party's leaders tried to escape this contradiction by blaming *Mapai* for not involving them in the most important economic decisions. In other words, they did not claim to open political space and recognize the legitimate workers' demands and representatives, but pretended to speak in their name instead. However, the contradiction between the employers' interests and those of the workers became exacerbated after Lavon's dismissal and the tightened cooperation between the *Histadrut* and the *Mapai*-led government. The previous conflict between the *Histadrut* (Lavon) and the government (Ben Gurion) was transformed, after Lavon, to an inter-party conflict (*Mapai* versus *Ahdut Haavoda*) as well as an intra-party conflict between worker activists and party representatives in the government.

From *Mapai*'s perspective, the burning issue was its loss of control over action committees, even those established and led by *Mapai* activists, as they had to respond to rank-and-file pressures. The action committees organized activities to demonstrate solidarity with striking workers, initiated protests and organized general strikes, supported by *Mapam* and *Ahdut Haavoda* activists, as well as opposition parties from the left—the Communist Party—and right-wing *Herut*. The action committees were the most direct manifestation of worker resistance to the *Histadrut*'s policies of dependency rather than representation and its quasi-state structure. Action committees became the nemesis of *Mapai* leaders in the government and *Histadrut*, to such an extent that when striking, even the professional trade unions used the deterring name of "action committee" for their strike headquarters.

The action committees' uprising was the most visible manifestation

---

[9] This double face of *Ahdut HaAvoda* might be confusing. Its economic interests were determined by the *kibbutz* movement, which was an employer (since 1948) with its own industries, and was dependent on state subsidies. However, the majority of its voters were urban workers and activists in the action committees. These opposed interests were articulated inside the party, thanks to the loyalty of activists and leaders to their shared partisan interests.

of the new structural reality created by full employment, a reality the pre-state colonial LIC could not direct or control. The pressure for reforming the LIC came from classes which began to organize and to erode *Mapai*'s electoral powerbase. Not only did the workers begin to act independently, but the private industrialists also increased their pressure on the government (Shalev, 1984). As seen below, the solution to the Labor Movement's crisis was formulated in two stages: a political solution of cooptation towards the 1965 elections and an economic solution thereafter. As we shall see next, *Mapai* discovered a more fundamental solution, involving far-reaching structural transformation of the state and economy, following the occupation of the West Bank and Gaza Strip in June 1967.

IV. Counter-Mo(ve)ment I: The Political Reaction to Resistance— The Alignment of *Mapai* and *Ahdut Haavoda*

The bi-partisan structure of the Israeli political field that survived until the 1999 elections[10] was finally consolidated towards the 1965 elections with the formation of the *Mapai-Ahdut Haavoda* alignment (hereafter, the Alignment) and the right-wing block of *Herut*-Liberals.[11] As mentioned above, before the elections *Mapai* was threatened both by the workers' increasing power and the action committees' revolt, but it was also threatened by the rising power of an emerging urban middle class and private capital industrialists, which were represented by the Liberal Party. At the same time, the worker parties were considering the formation of a big front of workers' parties based on *Mapam* and *Ahdut Haavoda* and headed by Pinhas Lavon, who threatened to split from *Mapai* with his followers. Within the *Histadrut*, the situation was even more dangerous, because all parties started cooperating against *Mapai*'s hegemonic power, and even Menachem Begin's right-wing *Herut* decided to

---

10   For an analysis of the breakdown of the bi-partisan polarized mobilization, see Grinberg (2010: Ch. 6-8).

11   Until 1961, *Mapai* was the dominant ruling party (Shapiro, 1977; Medding, 1973). In 1965, a new right-wing party block was formed which managed to gain almost a quarter of the votes, and began presenting itself as a real alternative. This dual structure persisted until 1996. In the next elections, in 1999, the two largest parties managed to win only a third of the votes combined (Grinberg, 2010).

compete in the *Histadrut* elections for the first time.[12] Begin confessed that most *Herut* voters had joined the *Histadrut* for its health services, and believed that *Mapai*'s hegemonic position in the State could only be crushed by breaking its hold over the *Histadrut*. The political danger for *Mapai* was that if all non-*Mapai* parties would cooperate on the streets and support the action committees' revolt, such a front could also be formed within the *Histadrut* (Shapiro, 1991; Grinberg, 1993). This threat became manifest in the Knesset, where the workers' parties and the right wing had already cooperated on several issues aiming to erode *Mapai*'s hegemony.[13]

Mapai's leadership took all those threats very seriously. From the Lavon Affair onwards, Eshkol's leadership was based among other things on an understanding within *Mapai*'s elites that the radical worker parties had to be neutralized, especially when their threat to form a workers' front only grew whenever Ben Gurion talked about his plans to weaken the *Histadrut*. This is why, after saving the party from disaster during the Lavon Affair, Eshkol focused on neutralizing the demands of Ben Gurion and his supporters. These demands were designed to produce a radical change of the pre-state colonial LIC, adjusting it to the new structural conditions of formal democracy and free markets.

In order to maintain party hegemony, Eshkol first had to ensure *Mapai*'s continued control of the *Histadrut*, and through it, close the political space to the working class. This task was far from simple in the run-up to the 1965 elections, when worker councils and trade unions demanded wage increases. One way to regain control of the workers was to weaken them by reversing the full employment policy, but such an unpopular reversal was problematic so close to the expected *Histadrut* and *Knesset* elections. Thus it was clear that some economic solution could only be found after the elections. The question remained how to maintain *Mapai*'s control of the *Histadrut* at a time when its popularity among the workers was at an all-time low.

Eshkol's answer was to cooperate with veteran *Mapai* and *Histadrut* leaders (as opposed to Ben Gurion and his "juniors") and design a strategic move to align with *Ahdut Haavoda* in the upcoming *Knesset* and

---

12 *Herut* did so after failing in its attempt to create an alternative National Workers Federation.
13 This right-left coalition against *Mapai* in the *Knesset* was dubbed the "Nir Coalition" following the symbolic election of the Knesset Speaker by that name rather than *Mapai*'s candidate.

Histadrut elections. This strategy aimed at gaining legitimacy in the eyes of the uprising workers, thanks to *Ahdut Haavoda*'s open support of the action committees' revolt and the involvement of its members in worker struggles. This was a very effective form of indirect cooptation, because worker leaders were not even coopted to the power structures or elites—it was the party that penetrated the working class, supported its struggles and gained legitimacy among the workers. An electoral block with *Ahdut Haavoda* was highly expedient, because despite its pro-labor image, it was very loyal to *Mapai*'s economic policy, due to the economic interests of its predominant *kibbutz* movement. It was the senior partner in both the government and *Histadrut* coalitions and despite its rhetoric support of the workers, in practice it contributed to implementing policies designed to keep them under control. *Ahdut Haavoda*, however, was able to succeed where *Mapai* had failed under conditions of full employment: retaining the employees' trust. The Alignment was thus designed to reflect both *Mapai*'s policy of wage restraint in the government and *Ahdut Haavoda*'s pro-worker policy in the action committees (Grinberg, 1993).

The formation of the new Alignment was seen by *Mapai*'s leaders as a critical move to ensure absolute majority in the *Histadrut*.[14] As expected, Ben Gurion and his supporters opposed it for the very reasons it was supported so enthusiastically by the great majority of *Mapai* activists and *Histadrut* apparatchiks. Ben Gurion's opposition to the Alignment reopened the old Lavon Affair wounds in the run-up to the elections. Now, however, Ben Gurion no longer attacked Lavon—who had by then been neutralized by Eshkol—but Eshkol himself. Ben Gurion realized that the structural changes he was trying to promote were doomed to fail under an Alignment which would control both the *Histadrut* and the government. His struggle inside the party failed, however, and he decided to split and form a party of his own, *Rafi* (acronym for List of Israeli Workers *Reshimat Poalei Israel*) (Yanay, 1969; Bar Zohar, 1977). Given the action committees' revolt, the threat of Ben Gurion's new party was seen by *Mapai*'s leaders as far less dangerous than the formation of a new workers party based on *Ahdut Haavoda*, *Mapam*, and *Mapai* followers of Lavon. This was precisely the political decision taken by the ruling party: to marginalize Ben Gurion rather than risk the formation

---

14   Which proved to be the case in retrospect, with 50.88% of the votes.

of an autonomous worker front against *Mapai* designed to open political space for working class representation.

The political right was also concerned by the Alignment. Private industrialists feared it would lead *Mapai* to adopt more socialist economic policies under the influence of *Ahdut Haavoda*. For the same reason, the Liberal Party feared it would no longer be a potential coalition member. It did not trust the new Treasury Minister Pinhas Sapir's[15] promises that the goal of the new Alignment was better control of the working class. Therefore, in response to the Alignment, the liberals joined forces with *Herut* in a right-wing block (*Gahal*), with active involvement and support by the private industrialists (Shapiro, 1991).

The difference between the two blocks lays in the power and status of their various constituents vis-à-vis the establishment and its resources. They had in common the fact that neither represented a pure class interest, but a mixture of contradictory class interests. The Alignment represented the large government- and *Histadrut*-owned corporations, the powerful and unionized public sector employees, and the bureaucratic, state-dependent middle class. On the other hand, *Gahal* represented the private capitalists, the self-employed bourgeoisie not supported by the state, and the peripheral and non-unionized *Mizrahi* workers. Both gave up on representing a specific class interest group for a general and loosely defined image of "right" and "left," competing for the definition of the common good. Consequently, the immediate result of the formation of two multi-class blocks was the closure of political space for the representation of class interests and agendas.[16] Both blocks preferred to hide the class conflicts and contain them within the party, without open political debate on economic policies, values and ideas. Following Gil Eyal (2003: 140), I suggest using the term "condensation" to refer to this repertoire of political misrepresentation aiming to conceal distinct class agendas and interests within one party. This repertoire does not represent a clear social interest but takes several groups and merges them within a single collective identity.

Eshkol's strategy in the run-up to the 1965 elections succeeded in retaining the *Histadrut* pre-state colonial multi-class structure as a provider

---

15 After Ben Gurion's resignation in 1963, Eshkol was appointed as Prime Minister and Sapir as Treasury Minister.
16 The only parties which remained loyal to a distinct social group were *Mapam*, the Communists, the Independent Liberals and the religious parties.

of welfare-state services, as opposed to a bona fide trade union federation. This success constructed the entire political arena in the image and form of the *Histadrut*: two large, multi-class blocks with opposing views on how to allocate state resources—one designed to control the *Histadrut* and through it the public, and the other opposing the ruling party's hegemonic power in the *Histadrut* and state. As we shall see in the next chapter, however, the political meaning of "left" and "right" in Israel came to be radically redefined after 1967, when class and ethnicity merged.

V. Counter-Mo(ve)ment II: The Economic Reaction—Breaking the Workers' Powerbase by Recession Policies (1966-67)

After the new Alignment had won both the national and the *Histadrut* elections,[17] the new government returned to deal with the economic crisis caused by the increased power of the workers and the inflationary pressures resulting from pay increases and the employers' demands for government subsidies. Its solution was a new recessionary economic policy. For many years, private industrialists had been threatening the government that without product subsidization they would be forced to raise prices. The government became accustomed to respond by allocating subsidies, because wage increases for workers in the entire economy would have proved much more costly (Grinberg, 1993). In any case, it was clear that this policy, coupled with the previously mentioned wage struggles, effectively meant that the government and *Histadrut* lost control over macroeconomic developments, as both wages and prices rose wildly (Shalev, 1984).

The wage increases in 1960-1965 were perceived as dangerous to the economy not only because of their inflationary consequences, but also due to their balance-of-payment effects. While production grew significantly, expanded local demand (thanks to the wage increases but also to the reparation payments from Germany and government investments) significantly increased the commercial deficit.

The government's recession policy reduced local demand significantly

---

17   In the 1965 Knesset elections, the Alignment obtained 36.7% of the votes and became the largest party, followed by *Gahal*'s 25.1% (Smith, 1969). In the Histadrut elections, the Alignment obtained 50.88% of the votes, followed by *Gahal*'s 15.2% (*Davar*, October 5, 1965).

through painful cuts in the government's development budgets and capital subsidies. Thanks to this policy, imports were reduced and exports grew (Klinov and Halevi, 1968). This policy's timing—late 1965—made sense in several respects. First, it was initiated right after the elections and expected to immediately affect salaried workers and many manufacturers (who would naturally resent it), while reaping benefits only years later. In the run-up to the elections, the government continued its expansive policy, exacerbating inflationary pressures thereby. In addition, the government faced a deadline in 1967, when the reparation payments from Germany were to stop (Greenwald, 1972: 25).[18] For about ten years, until 1967, the government financed its import surplus with unilateral Mark-denominated transfers. After that deadline, a serious economic crisis was bound to occur should the balance of payments not improve significantly (Arnon, 1979).

Beside this macroeconomic rationale, the government also had internal political reasons for the recession policy, as it wanted to change the power relations between it and the private employers and workers (Shalev, 1984). After the *Histadrut* had lost control over its workers due to full employment, and the government could not withstand the pressures of the public sector employees and private sector employers, *Mapai* chose to expand government expenses in both directions in the run-up to the elections. This "political business cycle" was very costly in 1965. After the elections, however, with dwindling financial resources, it was time for a different solution (Ben-Porath, 1975).

The need for economic restraint was also due to the fact that the Alignment provided a solution only to the political power question of maintaining control over the government and *Histadrut*, but not to the key economic actors—namely, workers and industrialists. The post-election recession policy was the economic complementation of the political attempt to regain control of the workers after the success of the pre-election political move. It served the government's interest in reducing its expenses and fiscal deficit, and the *Histadrut*'s interest in the re-subjugation of the workers. This was not the private employers' preferred solution to the problem; their demand was to import non-unionized low-cost workers in order to allow the economy to keep grow-

---

18 It is important to emphasize here that the reparation payments to the government were discontinued, but the individual indemnization payments continued.

ing and weaken the local unionized workers.[19] However, the government was opposed to the private employers' demand, because it would not solve the commercial and fiscal deficit problems.

The recession policy was initiated by the government and coordinated with the *Histadrut* new leaders (Becker, 1982; Grinberg, 1993). It affected employer and employee groups differentially, with the main impact felt by the economic peripheries. Since the policy included drastic development budget cuts, the construction sector and related industries were most severely affected. For the first time since the absorption of the great immigration waves, unemployment crossed the 100,000 mark, or up to 12.5% of the labor force (Shalev, 1984). Public reaction was intense, with extensive warning strikes and massive anti-government demonstrations.[20] Immigration was reduced to a trickle and emigration rose alarmingly.[21] This was the first time an Israeli government abandoned the policy of securing full employment for Jews out of economic considerations, and also the first time Israel had a negative immigration balance (Shalev, 1984).

The recession's economic rationale was cutting government spending to reduce demand, in order to force capital to become more efficient and competitive internationally. This naturally meant reducing labor costs and channeling production to export markets following the reduced local demand. The entire working class was in danger: in the labor market, competition with the unemployed caused the employed workers' wages to shrink, while in the product market, reduced demand threatened continued production and employment.

The employers were also affected by reduced demand. The most powerful organization uniquely affected by the recession policy were the Workers Society (WS) companies owned by the *Histadrut*, since most of its enterprises were related to construction and depended on governmental subsidies. Moreover, while the private sector (as well as the *kibbutzim*) could operate flexibly in the labor market and dismiss work-

---

19 They borrowed the idea from Germany, which started to import workers from Turkey. In the Israeli case the private employers suggested importing workers from Cyprus and Greece (*Yediot Aharonot*, March 13, 1964).

20 Bar-El and Michael (1977: 50) document 284 strikes in 1965 and 276 in 1966, compared to an average of just 140 each year between 1960 and 1964.

21 In the years 1961-1964, 215,000 Jews immigrated to Israel; in 1964-1967, only 70,000 (Mendeltzweig and Magor, 1984: 16-17). After almost a decade of constant decline, emigration from Israel rose from 4 emigrants per 1,000 citizens in 1965, to 5.5 in 1966-7 (Lamdani, 1989).

ers or worsen their social conditions, the *Histadrut*-owned economy was more severely affected due to its own trade union policy which made it difficult to dismiss employees. The WS also suffered from the increased cost of money, as its extensive debt—largely in the form of government bonds—became more expensive than free loans in the private sector coming from low bank credit.[22]

Although the Alignment government was well aware of the difficulties involved in its new policy, Treasury Minister Pinhas Sapir—the recession policy's architect—refused the WS' demands for subsidized loans.[23] The government's ability to reject such pressures was historically remarkable. The policy of ensuring full employment for Jews (Hebrew Labor), which had characterized Zionism from the formative period through the post-1948 immigration waves, became a liability in a sovereign state at a time of full employment. It was then revealed that the state had little ability to make decisions detrimental to the interests of strong social groups under ordinary circumstances. Indeed, state autonomy can often be asserted only in times of crisis (Skocpol, 1985). This reasoning is expressed by the practical recommendations of the "Washington Concensus" (from hereon WC) partners (IMF, WB, and US Treasury) to dramatize the depth of a crisis before introducing austerity measures (Williamson, 1994). Only during the recession did the government make a sincere attempt to lead an autonomous policy, dictated by its independent institutional needs and considerations, and only after the 1965 elections did it have a chance to succeed despite the pressures by workers, private employers, and WS managers.[24]

VI. Counter-Mo(ve)ment III: Structural Adjustment by Colonial Institutions—The Dual Regime

The main problem with the recession policy was that the popular discontent it provoked endangered *Mapai*'s hegemony in the run-up to

---

22 Discussions between Sapir and WS managers (2.3.1966 and 8.7.1966; Lavon Institute, IV-204-4-1337).
23 I would like to express my personal gratitude to Aaron Becker, the former *Histadrut* Secretary General, for giving me access to his private archive, where I discovered the precious debates between Sapir and the WS managers during 1966-1967 (Lavon Institute, file IV-204-4-1337).
24 See Skocpol (1985) for a discussion of state autonomy.

the 1969 elections. In the last pre-war meeting between the Treasury Minister and managers of WS enterprises at the end of April 1967, two revealing comments indicate why *Mapai* accommodated so easily to the occupation of the West Bank and Gaza. During the meeting, Sapir expressed the state's strong autonomous position and rejected demands to subsidize the WS companies with non-indexed loans. One WS manager explained that the problem was the shrinking of the market and reduced demand combined with their inability to dismiss workers and reduce excess production. However, he argued, if there was a new migration wave of one million Jews, WS will be able to solve its overproduction problem by selling them products now stored in warehouses. Sapir replied that the government would not renew the old policy of subsidizing inefficient industries, but gave the *Histadrut* managers an insider's "tip": there would be new government subsidies for military industries, so they could start investing there. However, he could not promise that war would continue forever, and if peace prevailed they might lose the money.[25]

A few weeks after this meeting, the occupation of the West Bank, Gaza Strip, Golan Heights, and Sinai Peninsula solved all economic problems and facilitated the construction of a new, dual structure of political economic domination. Within 10 days after the June 1967 War, WS managers met with military officers (instead of Sapir) in order to plan the marketing of products in the "Occupied Areas" (*ezorei hakibush* in Hebrew).[26] A captive market of one-and-a-half million Palestinians was forced to buy Israeli products, and the state began heavily subsidizing the military industry (Mintz and Ward, 1988; Berglas, 1989). Note that I do not argue that the war was driven by political or economic considerations. Most of the evidence shows that the security establishment was the force pushing for war, largely by the sense of threat manufactured by general mobilization and the manipulation of public pressure to nominate the popular general Moshe Dayan as Security Minister (Gluska, 2004; Peri, 2006). My argument is that after the war, with the *Histadrut* organs in crisis, both the WS and the Trade Unions Department rapidly designed a new structure of political economic domination

---

25   Discussions between Sapir and WS managers (24.4,1967; Lavon Institute, IV-204-4-1337).
26   The meeting between WS managers and IDF officers to plan "product marketing in the Occupied Areas" took place on June 26, 1967 (Lavon Institute, IV-204-5-64).

in an attempt to solve their prewar crisis, and that they cooperated with the military administration of the Occupied Territories (OT) to that end (Grinberg, 1993: Chs. 8-9). The new structures ended the recession and renewed prosperity, creating a very positive and enthusiastic political atmosphere in the run-up to the 1969 elections. The long term political, economic, and moral implications of the military occupation of Palestinians and their integration in the Israeli economy were ignored. The new colonial structure divided and weakened the working class and recreated the pre-1948 dependence of Israeli workers on the *Histadrut*.

One of the most intriguing questions regarding the Israeli labor movement is why it abandoned its original state-building Zionist ideology of a separated economy in favor of an integrated Israeli-Palestinian economy after 1967. This was not a single ideological resolution, nor the product of secret collusion among self-interested actors. The historical shift of ZLM's state- and nation-building strategies was inadvertent, a byproduct of a sequence of events associated with the bureaucratic adjustment to the new postwar structural conditions, rather than the well thought-out product of political discussions and long-term decision-making. Moreover, postwar government and *Histadrut* adjustment policies had been characterized by short-term bureaucratic thinking, without any ability or willingness to come to terms with long-term consequences (Gazit, 1985; Beilin, 1985; Grinberg, 1993).

Since the ruling party was unable to make significant long-term decisions, the question that preoccupied the state and *Histadrut* bureaucracies in the meantime was how to manage the Palestinian economy until the time in which such decisions would be made (Gazit, 1985; Grinberg, 1993a). This policy was euphemized as "maintaining the status-quo." Soon it was realized that this would be impossible, since any decision meant transforming the so-called "status-quo" and shaping a new relationship between Israel and the Palestinians now under its control. In addition to the *Histadrut*'s institutional interest in the occupation, there were major political forces that pushed for integrating the non-citizen Palestinians in the Israeli economy—a process publicly called "economic integration." These forces were two political parties in government, *Rafi* and *Ahdut Haavoda*, that immediately after the war merged with *Mapai* to form the Labor Party that remained in power until 1977 (Beilin, 1985). Even within *Mapai* itself, which was then considered moderate relatively to the annexationist positions of *Rafi* and *Ahdut Haavoda*, voices were heard in support of continued occupation, but these emphasized the distinction between their territorial aspirations and unwillingness to govern the population. This ambivalent stand was expressed in a discussion between Eshkol and his successor Golda Meir. In response to a famous saying by Eshkol ("I like the dowry [Palestinians lands] but dislike the bride [their inhabitants]"), Meir said it was impossible to "have the dowry without the bride" (Gazit, 1985).[27]

The security establishment was put in charge of the Palestinian population. These grew significantly, both in budgetary terms and in their power to shape future economic relations with the Palestinians thanks to their sovereignty over the Territories and authority over the movement of people, goods and capital. From the military's bureaucratic point of view, the priority was to appease the population as soon as possible. This appeasement included both ensuring employment for the Palestinians and improving the Israelis' standard of living (Gazit, 1985). In other words, the security establishment occupied the political sphere of mediation between civil society and state, controlling the markets and legitimizing the new regime. To do so, it had to minimize the damages of the occupation to the Israeli population and maximize its benefits. Exactly as in the pre-1948 period, certain groups of Israelis felt threatened by the free-market principles requiring open flow of workers, goods and capital between sovereign Israel and the OT. The political objectives of "economic integration" were thus very similar to those faced prior to 1948 by the ZLM quasi-state institutions and the British colonial government: regulating markets so as to protect Jewish employers and workers on the one hand, and allowing the Palestinians to subsist economically on the other. However now it was not the responsibility of the British Mandate government, but of the Israeli military and its civilian government.

The urgent issues requiring resolution in order to ensure the viability of the occupation were economic: how to market Palestinian produce and provide employment to Palestinian workers. These issues were temporarily resolved in ways that satisfied the interests of Israeli economic elites and damaged mainly the lower *Mizrahi* ethno-classes and the unity of the working class, while institutionalizing the Palestinians'

---

27 See Grinberg (2009) on the complex significance of this duality in a regime founded on those two contradictory premises—including the land but excluding the inhabitants.

structural dependency on the Israeli economy. In the long run, these "pragmatic" solutions prevented the alternative two-state solution from being adopted. The military and labor movement were both responsible for this development, as they deliberately undermined the ZLM's historic national strategy designed to control markets through economic and territorial separation. Since 1967, the national strategy was to control the market by militarily regulating economic exchanges and controlling the external borders between Israel/Palestine and its neighbors, as well as the internal ones between "Israel" and the "Territories." This was now possible, since the Jewish State could use the military to control both the territory and its inhabitants; this control was considered legitimate because it was defined as apolitical and reduced to a simple matter of "security." Security became the legitimizing myth of this dual regime, concealing the political role of the military and depoliticizing the debate on the future relations with the Palestinians (Grinberg, 2010).

As previously mentioned, the immediate priority was to market Israeli goods in the OT by turning the occupied Palestinian population into a captive market for high-priced Israeli goods. In order to do so, Israel closed the borders with Jordan (the West Bank) and Egypt (Gaza), where Palestinians could buy goods for better prices, and imposed the higher prices of Israeli products and Israeli customs (a policy strictly maintained until and beyond the writing of this book). Israeli manufacturers benefitted from this decision, particularly those who had stockpiled goods during the recession rather than downsizing, such as the WS factories. These managed to empty their warehouses rather quickly and then expand production in the aftermath of the recession (Grinberg, 1993).

A more thorny issue was how to market the Palestinians' agricultural produce. Israeli farmers stood to lose from free competition with low-cost Palestinian produce. After several months of indecision, a formula was worked out which satisfied both Israeli and Palestinian farmers without requiring that they compete. This formula was called the "Open Bridges Policy," and it basically meant that Palestinian farm goods would be exported to Jordan (across the eponymous river) but were prevented from entering Israeli markets (Gazit, 1985). Here, too, the guiding principle was to protect Israeli farmers' interests while forcing the Palestinian farmers to become dependent on the military government for export licenses.

Another critical issue was finding employment for unemployed Palestinian workers. From a military-bureaucratic point of view, the challenge was to provide jobs to keep the men busy as well as satisfied. The idea was to prevent unemployment, which was seen as conducive to resistance to the occupation. Militarily speaking, the question where these workers will be employed was secondary, and it was decided by other powerful actors. The Israeli employers sought to have them work in Israel, particularly in sectors abandoned by their Israeli workers during the recession and in the immediate postwar period, such as construction and agriculture (Grinberg, 1993). However, this ran counter to the interests of Israeli workers, whose competition with non-unionized workers without any social rights could leave them jobless or underpaid. This issue was discussed formally only from mid-1968 onward, despite the fact that Palestinians were smuggled to work on *kibbutz* agriculture and construction in Jerusalem shortly after the war.[28] This delay helped resolve the conflict of interest, since the threat of unemployment receded as the postwar boom ensured full employment.[29]

The full employment of Jews prevented direct competition; however, there was still the question of labor costs. The *Histadrut* was mainly interested in preventing the entry of cheap labor by avoiding paying social rights and pension allowances, mainly due to the danger to its own pension funds, threatened as they were by this non-unionized labor force. The agreement with the government included both the direct deduction of pension payments by the employers and also union taxes from non-citizen Palestinian workers, without providing them with any representation.[30] In addition, the WS enterprises benefitted as employers, because they were interested in employing dependent and non-unionized workers. And finally, as a centralized and monopolistic trade union, the *Histadrut* benefitted from the resulting weakening of unskilled Israeli workers, as this enabled it to regain its control over them and the ability to "represent" them in negotiations with the business sector, an ability which it had lost in the early 1960s. Only workers not threatened

---

28 Finance Minister Sapir commented on this pioneering role of the *kibbutzim* in a government meeting as the security cabinet on October 15, 1967 (Lavon Institute IV-104 15-2-2).
29 In the years 1965-1967, the monthly average of job seekers almost doubled, rising from 27,980 to over 55,000; however, in 1969 this average declined back to 27,174, and in 1971 to 19,451 (Keisar, 1973).
30 See Lavon Institute Archives, file IV-212-2-419, 17.11.1968 and 3.12.1968.

by non-organized Palestinian competition were empowered by the new structures. These were the professional unions and workers employed by the state and state owned companies. As shown in Chapter 6, the new dual structure empowered strong workers and capital and weakened not only peripheral and unskilled workers but also state autonomy, eventually leading to hyperinflation, a deep economic crisis and renewed workers' resistance.

The formula of protecting strong Israeli interests while ensuring Palestinian dependency worked here as well. The least protected were the unskilled Israeli workers who could potentially compete for jobs with the Palestinians, as the employers, the *Histadrut*, the IDF and the Ministry of Treasury preferred the employment of Palestinians, each for its own reasons. The potentially damaged Israeli workers were peripheral unskilled *Mizrahim* or Palestinian citizens, usually employed in construction, agriculture, low-tech industry, and personal services.

The dual political economy of Israel/Palestine institutionalized after June 1967 readjusted state structures to the pre-1948 ZLM institutions. At the core of these institutions were the *Histadrut* welfare quasi-state organs and the parties of its ruling coalition (collectively, the LIC), which were now built on the structural weakness of the workers and civil society due to the competition with Palestinians in the markets. This market competition facilitated the construction of institutions that created dependency of workers without direct representation. As in the pre-1948 period, there were no mechanisms or channels of democratic opening of political space and representation of workers. During that period, the legitimacy of the ZLM was ensured by its provision of welfare services policies designed to create a separate economy and state. When this goal was achieved in 1948, the workers were empowered and threatened the pre-1948 labor colonial institutions.

After the 1967 War, ZLM leaders recognized that the structural conditions of potential replacement of the Israeli workers were necessary in order to retain the power of the LIC. The new conditions closed political space to worker representation, and maintained ZLM's non-democratic and non-representative institutions. However, in order to protect the Israeli economy against open competition, it had to build a very complex economic and military regime of domination. This dual regime was based on the distinction between two types of territories: those dominated and controlled by the military, and Israel "proper," where citizens enjoyed formal democratic rights and institutions. In this regime, the military played a critical political role presented as apolitical: protecting Israelis against the Palestinians. This role was called security, and it legitimized the repression of Palestinian resistance and the direct intervention of the IDF in political decisions. Thus, ever since 1967, "security" largely means protecting powerful Israeli groups against competition with Palestinians and extraction of the latter's resources. To maintain security, the IDF has been transformed into the most important regulator of a (very) political economy.[31]

Two non-democratic, quasi-state institutions occupied the political sphere and closed the political space for democratic representation of interests, agendas and ideas: the *Histadrut* and the IDF. As soon as they found a way to cooperate in controlling the Palestinians after 1967, a dual regime of democratic-military rule was put in place: democratic rules of the game for the Israelis, military rule for the Palestinians. However, the dual regime closed political space to subordinated groups on both sides of the Israel-Palestine hyphen. This was because two fundamental conditions for the opening up of political space were no longer there: recognized borders either including or excluding the Palestinians, and a balance of power between the dominated and dominant social groups. In other words, the fundamental conditions that endangered the colonial institutions of the LIC by opening up political space during 1948-1967 were abolished by the territorial expansion and the institutionalization of a new colonial regime able to divide and rule both populations. This was precisely the goal of the LIC before 1948; it could only be achieved by returning to the British Mandate borders and incorporating the Palestinians without granting them citizenship.

VII. Conclusion

Israel's second decade exposed the contradiction between pre-state, non-democratic and non-representative labor institutions, and democratic pressures to open political space to the autonomous civil society—workers, middle classes, and employers empowered by full employment and economic expansion—given the existence of state borders. The

---

31   The term (very) political economy was coined by Brynen (2000).

pre-state colonial institutions relied on political intervention against free-market competition aiming to achieve the national objectives of full employment for Jews and assimilation of new Jewish immigrants. This institutional design ensured the dependence of broad social groups on the political organs responsible for resource allocation.

The Zionist policy of protecting Jewish workers enabled both *Mapai* and the *Histadrut* to remain in power without actually representing them. However, in the early 1960s, full employment considerably weakened the working class's dependence on the LIC, and the democratic legal framework created the opportunity to balance the power of the state and *Histadrut*. Under these conditions, a new rank-and-file leadership emerged, representing autonomous class interests and claiming recognition, namely, opening up political space for the working class. The working class struggle was waged mainly in the big industrial areas of Tel Aviv and Haifa, while the peripheral *Mizrahi* ethno-classes in the development towns remained discriminated against, weak, and dependent on the LIC. In the cities, *Mizrahi* workers became part of the working class strike movement facilitated by the homogenization of labor during industrialization and full employment.

This working class resistance mo(ve)ment lasted five years and secured significant economic achievements, mainly in terms of wages and unionization. However, given the political parties' penetration of worker action committees, most worker leaders were co-opted by the parties. With the exception of the Communist Party and *Herut* activists, most worker activists were affiliated with one of the ZLM parties. Many heads of the Histadrut Worker Councils in the cities were *kibbutz* members who were older and more experienced than most workers. These had a vested interest in maintaining the *Histadrut*'s quasi-state structure as it served the economic interests of their respective *kibbutz* movements, and enabled them to share in the bureaucratic power of both the *Histadrut* and the state (Shapiro, 1977). One concrete way to open political space for working class representation was to form a front of worker parties representing the new power of the workers against the rigid and inaccessible Vicious Triangle of *Histadrut-Mapai*-State. This was precisely the threat represented by Lavon and his followers: to split from *Mapai* and form a worker's front with *Ahdut Haavoda* and *Mapam* towards the 1965 elections.

In order to close political space to working class autonomous representation, *Mapai* coordinated a triple counter-mo(ve)ment: (1) political, towards the 1965 elections: (2) economic, after the elections; and (3) structural, reorganizing the political economy after 1967. The political step of the counter-mo(ve)ment was designed to prevent the formation of a working class political front. To do so, *Mapai* formed the Alignment with *Ahdut Haavoda* in the run-up to the 1965 elections. The Alignment was a clear case of "condensation" (Eyal, 2003) of class interests within one party, in addition to the repertoire of "tribal channeling" of ethnic fears previously used to prevent ethnic political representation (Chapter 3). Although successful in closing political space for working class representation in the political field, "condensation" did not prevent the workers' continued resistance in the economic field.

In its attempt to weaken the working class in the economic field, the new post-1965 Alignment government initiated the second counter-mo(ve)ment by pursuing an aggressive policy of state-induced recession, breaking away with the old Zionist tradition of full employment for Jews, as well as with the developmental state policy (Shalev, 1984). However, widespread opposition threatened to undermine the power of the ruling political institutions before the 1969 elections.

The expected loss of political hegemony was prevented in 1967 by the structural transformation which forged a new link between economy, state, and politics. This was the final cut of the third counter-mo(ve)ment. The new dual political economy reestablished colonial domination of Palestinians in the OT combined with dependency of weak workers on the *Histadrut-Mapai* LIC that maintained Zionist Labor's non-democratic institutions' ability to control both the workers and the labor markets.

This unintended consequence of the 1967 War and the resultant peculiar reshaping of the state had three crucial elements: (1) blurring state borders by the integration of the Palestinian captive market and non-organized workers; (2) maintaining the borders between the sovereign state and the OT for legal and political purposes, preventing joint organization of workers, segmenting the labor market and weakening the working class as a whole; and (3) concealing the mediating role of politics by using the word "security" to refer to the military's role in protecting the interests of powerful economic groups within the sovereign State.

The theoretical framework of political space is necessary to understand why the first two counter-mo(ve)ments—the political Alignment and state-induced recession—were not enough to crush the working class mo(ve)ment of resistance, and why the third, structural factor was so necessary. Without a restructuring of the political economy and establishment of a dual regime of domination, the effects of the working class resistance threatened to destroy the power of ruling institutions. However, within the dual economy some working-class groups still occupied strong positions in the labor market. Chapter 6 will describe and analyze the last mo(ve)ment of class resistance in 1980, preceded by Chapter 5's analysis of the *Mizrahi* lower ethno-classes' reaction to the new structure of dual political economy.

5.
1971 — THE BLACK PANTHERS MOVEMENT: ETHNIC TENSIONS AND "LEFT-RIGHT" TRIBAL POLARIZATION

I. INTRODUCTION

With the general mobilization of military reserves in May 1967, unemployment figures became irrelevant and all economic and political processes took a new turn. *Rafi* and *Gahal*[1] joined the government and *Rafi*'s new leader,[2] Moshe Dayan, was appointed Minister of Security. The stunning military victory that followed the anxious "waiting period," culminating in the occupation of the Old City of Jerusalem, helped Israeli society forget the prewar economic crises and conflicts that preoccupied it less than three months before.

The heady sense of victory in the June 1967 War and its continuation as the War of Attrition with Egypt facilitated the establishment of a broad-based coalition government and heralded a relatively long period of industrial peace that lasted until 1970. During those years, no new collective agreements or cost-of-living allowances were signed, as part of the process of adjusting wages to the new labor market structure. As described in Chapter 4, the war caused tremendous structural changes by opening the labor market to the entrance of unorganized workers from the recently occupied Palestinian areas. The war also expanded the local consumer market by creating a Palestinian captive market for Israeli goods, in addition to the renewal of Jewish immigration and capital imports. The economy resumed its growth in 1967, with the GNP increasing by 10% (Yoran, 1989: 371), matching the high levels of the first half of the decade. However, the rise in security spending affected the balance of payments and national debt continued to rise (Berglas, 1989).

---

1   In Chapter 4 I described the formation of these two parties in the run-up to the 1965 elections, *Rafi* as a splinter of *Mapai* led by Ben Gurion, and *Gahal* as a block of hawkish *Herut* and the Liberal Party.
2   Ben Gurion retired from politics after realizing that *Rafi* was not strong enough electorally to prevent the formation of any coalition without it.

CHAPTER FIVE

The most remarkable structural change took place in the labor market, as the economy moved from deep unemployment to full employment. This period saw the most significant segmentation of the labor market,[3] with long-term economic and political implications. Masses of previously unemployed Jewish workers returned to the labor market, but not necessarily in the same peripheral sectors—construction, agriculture, or light industry—where they had been employed prior to the 1966 recession. Some of them advanced to the primary sectors of public service and advanced industries, particularly the security industry. These two sectors were blocked to competing Palestinian workers (both citizens and non-citizens) for a variety of reasons, mainly security considerations, but also their lack of requisite technological skills (Grinberg, 1991). Accordingly, the Palestinian workers were employed in the secondary sector, freeing up Jewish workforce for jobs requiring technical expertise or managerial positions.

Apparently, this segmentation occurred almost without any direct competition for jobs, but in a process of gradual adjustment of supply and demand, in which unemployed Jews entered the more stable labor market while their Palestinian counterparts settled for the remains. Thus it was "market forces" that funneled the non-citizen residents of the OT into the unstable and lower paying sectors. However, the state had a crucial role in maintaining the subjugated status of Palestinian workers by denying their civil rights and subjecting them to military rule (Shalev, 1992; Semyonov and Lewin-Epstein, 1987).

The most remarkable political economic phenomenon of the post-1967 years was the intimate linkage between market segments and ethnic origins, which crystallized ethno-class identities and fuelled struggles for the opening up of political space to new social actors,

---

3   For a full description of the restructuration of the Israeli labor market after 1967, see Semyonov and Lewin-Epstein (1987). I use here the terms segmentation and segmented labor market as a general theory of divided markets, and not as the implementation of the segmented labor market theory (Gordon et al 1982). There are three different explanations to the division between types of labor markets and types of workers, and in my view each of them described some specific phenomena, meaning they are not mutually exclusive. Dual labor market refers to a technical adaptation between types of employers and workers, without necessary direct competition between them (Piore and Dorenberg, 1971). Split labor market refers to workers with different labor price and direct competition that leads to ethnic hostility (Bonacich, 1972). Segmented labor market theory refers to the interest of the employers to divide and rule the workers (Gordon et al., 1982). I assume that all these processes were at work at different levels, places and sectors, so I prefer to use "segmented" as a general term and not as a specific theory.

agendas and discourses on ethnic disadvantage—the same space that had been shut down in the violent repression of the 1959 Wadi Salib riots. The "moment" of the Black Panther resistance movement sparked six months after the cease fire agreement with Egypt that ended the War of Attrition, and it ended when the 1973 War disabled the movement's capacity to mobilize masses. This mo(ve)ment of resistance represented a reaction to the new structuring of the dual Israeli/Palestinian political economy, which had created four completely distinct ethno-classes. The Black Panthers protested against their discrimination as *Mizrahim* despite the fact they were also Jews. They succeeded in gaining recognition and improving the economic situation of their constituencies, although they failed in their attempt to accomplish political representation and mediate their collective interests. In 2013, the *Mizrahi* collective identity is arguably still the forbidden identity in Israel. I will discuss this fascinating phenomenon in the conclusion of this chapter, as well as in Chapters 8 and 9.

The post-1967 structure of the Israeli political economy was composed of at least four ethno-classes with different levels of civil rights, cultural capital, and positioning in the labor market (Nahon, 1993a; Semyonov and Lewin-Epstein, 1987; Grinberg, 1991; Shafir and Peled, 2002):

1. *European Ashkenazi Jews* largely controlled the economy, the state, and the political apparatuses. They were highly educated and employed in the stable segments characterized by higher salaries and guaranteed social rights (Grinberg, 1991). These groups were represented by strong and autonomous trade unions within the *Histadrut* or were fully independent of it.[4] Their main advantage over the other groups was their cultural capital as members of the dominant ethno-class and their privileged "republican" citizen rights (Shafir and Peled, 2002).

2. *Mizrahi Jews* from Arab countries were economically and politically weaker, and their children found it harder to advance in the formal education system (Nahon, 1993a). They were settled in Israel's peripheral areas and employed in relatively unstable segments with lower pay

---

4   As we may recall from Chapter 3 the most powerful professional workers gained a fully independent position from the *Histadrut*. These were the physicians, the university professors and the high school teachers.

and no guaranteed social rights (Semyonov and Lewin-Epstein, 1987; Shafir and Peled, 2002). These workers were represented by relatively weak unions controlled by *Mapai* and the *Histadrut* and were dependent on them for their economic conditions (Grinberg, 1991). Their advantage over the two remaining groups was their Jewish identity, which entitled them to ethno-national citizenship, which (at least formally) legitimized their demand for full equality with the first group given Israel's definition as a Jewish State (Shafir and Peled, 2002).

3. *Palestinian citizens of Israel* were disadvantaged compared to the first two groups in terms of labor market segments and union representation. Their basic advantage compared to the last group (which became more significant as the years went by) was their citizenship, which enabled them to achieve significant, albeit limited, improvement through legitimate political bodies (Semyonov and Lewin-Epstein, 1987; Shafir and Peled, 2002; Smooha, 2002).

4. *Palestinians under military control* in the OT had no civil rights, including the right of free association (for either economic or political purposes), were economically dependent on the state, and were forced to seek temporary employment in sovereign Israel, regardless of their skills or education.

The segmentation of the labor market is interpreted here as an unintended consequence of the 1967 War. However, it became a structural solution for the problem faced by *Mapai* and the *Histadrut* during the previous period of full employment. The new segmented labor market structure split the workers according to levels of citizenship, cultural capital and unionization power. Once the labor market homogenization process had thus been reversed, the *Histadrut*'s pre-1967 difficulty to restrain the workers disappeared.

The new dual political economic structure provided a long term solution to the challenge presented by working class resistance and limited state control of the workforce, as opposed to the temporary prewar recession policy which threatened the ruling party with electoral failure in 1969. After 1967, many Jewish workers benefitted from the segmented labor market, and only those who remained unemployed or employed in secondary sectors continued to threaten *Mapai*'s electoral position. The protest against the discrimination of the *Mizrahi* lower ethno-classes was voiced by the Black Panthers resistance mo(ve)ment during 1971-1973 and was later on channeled to the right wing nationalist party since the 1973 elections.

Full employment in the primary sector created a new economic problem due to the workers' empowerment, and the resulting difficulty of restraining their demands. However, this resulted mainly in budgetary pressures which did not seem too acute when the dual regime of domination was institutionalized. The government felt confident thanks to the influx of capital from the US and the income from the oil in occupied Sinai, which enabled it to finance its fiscal and trade-balance deficits (Grinberg, 1991, 1993; Shalev, 1992). It was only after the liberalization of the economy by the new *Likud* Government that inflation spiraled out of control. The implementation of neoliberal economic policies and the resultant hyperinflation will be discussed in the next Chapter.

II. Perpetuating the Control of Non-Citizen Palestinians

The array of decisions related to regulating the economic relations with the non-citizen Palestinians produced a complex pattern of both political and economic control, in which the military played a key role in protecting the interests of Israeli power groups. This pattern was characterized by the military control of movement through borders, including the movement of Palestinian workers into the areas of pre-1967 Israel;[5] marketing of costly Israeli goods in the OT while preventing the entrance of cheaper imports from Jordan and Egypt; and marketing Palestinian farming goods in Jordan at a low price, without allowing its sale in sovereign Israel. The Palestinian economy enjoyed very little capital investment, and the considerable taxes collected from Palestinian workers were pocketed by state bureaucracies. Economically, the main beneficiaries of this arrangement were Israeli employers, producers, and the Ministry of Treasure; but the Palestinians also benefitted from the growth of the entire Israeli/Palestinian economy, particularly those who traded with and worked in Israel. The Palestinian economy became dependent on Israel and its markets captive, but the postwar

---

5   I will refer hereon to the areas of Israel before 1967 also as sovereign Israel, or simply Israel. The occupied territories will be called also territories, West Bank and Gaza or simply OT.

boom ensured years of stability and relative peace, despite the denial of the Palestinians' civil, political and national rights.

The dependency relations were manifested mainly in the lack of technological development and industrialization: the manufacturing sector's contribution to the Palestinian economy remained below 20% (compared to 30% in Israel) and the factories themselves were relatively small, with an average of 4 workers per factory (compared to 28 in Israel) (Sagi, Sheinin and Perlman, 1992). However, the boom did raise standards of living: during the first years the economic boom was unprecedented, with annual GNP growth of 20% during the first years of occupation (Arnon and Weinblatt, 2001). Between 1971 and 1987, the Palestinian economy grew by 4.8% annually, compared to 2.6% in Jordan and Egypt and 3.9% in Syria (Sagi, Sheinin and Perlman, 1992). However, as theorists of dependency have shown, development is not an issue of economic growth; rather, it is about industrialization and spread of new technologies (Cardoso and Faletto, 1979). On the Israeli side, the postwar period saw greater economic development, but this time it was not construction that led the economy but rather security, as we shall see below.

The Palestinians in the Territories initially responded to the occupation with resistance, but as economic integration raised their standards of living, violent opposition and terrorism were not embraced by the masses, and instead became the sporadic actions of clandestine groups, mainly of refugees penetrating the borders from Lebanon and Jordan. Palestinian merchants and workers found integration with Israel to be lucrative enough to mollify their frustration, while their continued prosperity was dependent on obtaining military government permits.

The Palestinians' limited resistance, and the few violent attacks that captured the headlines, failed to undermine Israeli control, and in fact reinforced it: the IDF and the General Security Service (*Shabak*) could easily handle the terrorists while their actions enabled the politicians to avoid the recognition of Palestinian suffering and legitimate claims. The Jewish citizens supported the military repression almost unanimously, and had no doubt that fighting terrorism required continued control over the Palestinians, at least "temporarily." This reinforced sense of shared destiny in the face of terrorism, together with the imagined "temporary" nature of occupation, almost completely stymied any

Israeli reservations regarding its actual perpetuation (see Azoulay and Ophir, 2013).

This definition of temporary occupation was called in those days "maintenance of the status-quo." According to this discourse, a future return to the 1967 borders would occur when the Arabs would be ready and willing to recognize Israel and coexist in peace. This discourse of legitimizing control over the Palestinians—which I have elsewhere called the "security myth" (Grinberg, 2010: Ch. 10)—presented the military as an apolitical institution. The IDF repression was constructed as essential for Israel's security, including its efforts to disadvantage the Palestinians and perpetuate the occupation. Palestinian violent resistance only reinforced the security myth and helped close political space to potential negotiations and mutual recognition. The security myth relied on the assumption that Israel has no need nor interest in controlling the Territories or their inhabitants, and that once a partner would recognize Israel he could be entrusted with both.[6]

Regulating the joint economy and perpetuating Palestinian dependency represented a radical break with the original objectives of the Israeli labor movement, which had always sought to create a separate Jewish economy over Jewish-controlled territory (see chapter 2). However, it is important to understand that the pre-1948 nation-building strategy of separation was motivated by the lack of state institutions able to protect Jewish interests against free-market competition with the Arab economy in Mandatory Palestine. Such state institutions facilitated economic integration after having been developed and refined during the Military Government of Israel's Palestinian citizens in 1948-1966. During this period, the IDF and *Histadrut* specialized in controlling civilian populations while protecting Jewish economic interests (Lustick, 1980; Ratner, 1956; Ben Porat, 1966).

Faced with the threat to the *Histadrut*'s economic and bureaucratic power in 1960-1967, the Labor Movement adjusted its ideology to the new structural situation. As we have seen in Chapter 4, the dual political economy created as a result of the 1967 war enabled the *Histadrut* to reestablish its dominant position by regaining control over

---

6 This is why the security myth began to shatter only following the PLO's recognition of Israel in 1988, and was reconstructed after the Second Intifada. For a detailed analysis, see Grinberg (2010: Part 4).

the weakened Israeli workers who depended on it for employment and wage raises. Under such conditions, it was difficult to convince the supporters of the new strategy that *Mapai* and the *Histadrut* should avoid this temptation and stick to the "outdated" principles of Hebrew Labor and a separate Jewish State (such arguments were raised by the "old guard" leaders, particularly David Ben Gurion and Pinhas Lavon).

However, as we shall see below, strengthening the ruling party was a short-term consideration which proved much more temporary than other consequences of perpetuating control over the Palestinians, which became an integral part of the structure of Israeli political economy. By abandoning its unique strategy, ZLM lost its legitimacy and historical role and was removed from power within a decade. In fact, it bought time in power with the hard currency of transforming the state structure into a dual democratic/military regime over the whole area of Israel/Palestine, a regime that combined military rule of Palestinians with democracy for Jews (Grinberg, 2008). The security myth, repression of the Palestinians and counter-violence closed political space and prevented serious public discussion of the political problems involved in the occupation and containment of social conflicts. Two large party blocks were formed which mobilized support using national myths designed to justify the need to continue the occupation while misrepresenting socioeconomic and cultural conflicts within the Israeli population and constructing mutual hostility. The new dichotomy of "left"-and "right"-wing national myths legitimizing the occupation institutionalized polarized tribal politics of mutual incitement against the Other. Thus, the military-democratic regime closed democratic political space to parties representing different interests and identities, and offering real options, rather than mythical political ones, to the public (Shapiro, 1996; Grinberg, 1999, 2010).

III. "Security" as the Organizing Principle of the Dual Political Economy

In the years 1950-1965, economic growth was fuelled by capital transfers—mainly coming from German compensation payments—and the expansion of the consumer and labor markets as a result of the flux of massive Jewish immigration. All these were pushed forward by the construction industry significantly subsidized by the government, which also started large-scale projects such as National Water Carrier and the deep seaport at Ashdod. In 1967-1973, however, the leading and most subsidized industry was security. Capital flowed mainly from the US (for weapons imports).[7] The consumer and labor markets were expanded by the integration of Palestinian workers and captive consumers, but just as importantly by a renewed immigration wave that followed the world Jewry's identification with Israel following the 1967 victory.

Under these circumstances, the industries serving the IDF—mostly publicly owned (either by the government or the *Histadrut*)—became highly lucrative (Bichler, 1991: 162). The importance of the security industry for Israeli exports grew both in proportion and in absolute numbers,[8] as Israel gradually became one of the biggest weapons exporters in the world. As was suggested by Sapir in April 1967,[9] the WS invested mainly in the security industry and profited considerably from deep subsidization. This success was ensured both by political connections with the ruling party and by the Society's policy of recruiting executives from among high-ranking military veterans, who had very good connections with the IDF senior commanders (Maman, 1997; Peri and Neubach, 1984). The security industry came to lead technological development in Israel, with defense exports riding on the wave of the IDF's victorious reputation (Blumenthal, 1984; Peri, 1983).

The economic and political developments after 1967 quickly destabilized the shaky prewar balance between the organs of the Vicious Triangle: *Histadrut-Mapai*-State. The Ministry of Security emerged as a rich source of funds for subsidizing factories and workers, controlling huge resources autonomously of the Ministry of Treasury. In fact, the dual structure of domination also divided state bureaucracy: the Ministry of Security became an autonomous actor vis-à-vis the Ministry of Treasury, not only by virtue of its sovereignty over the OT, but also by virtue of its control of an increasing portion of the state budget, which

---

[7] From 1970 the US has been subsidizing its own defense industry by helping Israel buy its products (Bichler, 1991: 225-36).

[8] In 1972, security exports represented 5% of total exports, and were worth 50 million dollars; by 1982, they represented 18% of total exports, and were worth 800 million dollars (Peri and Neubach, 1984: 53).

[9] Discussions between Sapir and Workers Society's officials, 24.4,1967, Lavon Institute, IV-204-4-1337.

allowed it to play a central role in expanding economic activity and subsidizing both capital and labor in security industries. As discussed above, the Ministry of Security was also responsible for regulating the movement of goods and labor across the so-called Green Line separating sovereign Israel from the Territories, protecting the key power groups of Jewish capitalists and farmers within Israel. This second role ensured it broad-based legitimacy.

The internal division of state actors and power struggles between the Security and Treasury Ministries came to a head rather quickly—within months after the war. Unlike the recession period, when the Ministry of Treasury enjoyed considerable autonomy and was able to control state resources and direct economic processes despite pressures by various key stakeholders, the Ministry of Security now became a virtually independent resource allocation apparatus. As opposed to the prewar recession policy under which the Treasury Ministry managed to control security spending, the Ministry of Security began funneling funds on a massive scale, with its "clients" (managers and workers) covertly collaborating in pressuring the government to expand their subsidization (Aharoni, 1992). In other words, the recession's objective of transforming the power relations between employers and employees on the one hand, and the State on the other, restraining their claims through budget cuts, was reverted immediately after the war. However, while prior to 1967 the government was under the threat that German funding would soon end, after the war it turned to reliable US aid focused on the country's security needs (Arnon, 1981). This fact provided extra support to the demands of the security establishment for greater budgets and its autonomous power to allocate resources.

The change in the internal power balance and the struggle between the two agencies was clearly manifested in a secret government meeting held in October 1967 to discuss the 1968 security budget (Lavon Institute October 15, 1967, IV-104 15-2-2).[10] The main conflict was between Treasury Minister Pinhas Sapir and Security Minister Moshe Dayan. In response to Dayan's demands for a budget increase, Sapir suggested that the prewar budgetary restraint—the so called "recession policy"—must be continued. He argued that the war changed

---

10 I am indebted to the then Secretary General of the *Histadrut*, Mr. Aaron Becker, for letting me access the minutes of this meeting in his private archive.

nothing, and that "Israel hasn't found any oil yet" to finance its deficit. Prime Minister Levi Eshkol, who supported Dayan's demands of budgetary increase, corrected him. According to Eshkol, after the war Israel's financial situation has improved significantly and the "recession policy" must be discontinued. Although Israel found oil in the recently occupied Sinai desert rather than in its own territory, it had oil wells that could finance the increased security spending for the next five years. Eshkol also believed that the war changed the economic "atmosphere" for the better and that with the economy's expansion, there was no sense in proceeding with the recession policy. Sapir's demand to continue pursuing the prewar policy actually represented his ministry's political desire to retain its dominant position in managing the budget rather than allowing the Ministry of Security to autonomously allocate its budget. After 1967 the balance of power would not shift again for a long time,[11] and the state's autonomous position, vis-à-vis powerful economic interests temporally established during 1966-67, was now lost again due to the internal rift between two competing actors.

In addition to the shifting balance of power among government ministries and their splitting, and the state's weakening ability to prevent the expansion of subsidization, the ruling coalition was torn also by a strategic debate. Here, too, the conflict pitted Dayan—*Rafi*'s leader after Ben Gurion's retirement—against *Mapai*'s Sapir, hitherto considered Eshkol's consensual successor. The postwar period was characterized not only by giddy enthusiasm, but also by economic prosperity, strengthening of the ruling parties identified with the ZLM, and close cooperation between the *Histadrut* and the IDF. Leaders in the different labor parties came to the conclusion that the conditions were ripe for reuniting the movement by having *Rafi* rejoin *Mapai*. Accordingly, negotiations began in 1967 for the establishment of an integrated "alignment" of all so-called "workers' parties," initially by uniting *Mapai*, *Ahdut Haavoda*, and *Rafi* as the Labor Party. Subsequently, prior to the elections, *Mapam* also joined in, and the new block was called the Alignment (*Ma'arach*), after the *Mapai-Ahdut Haavoda* block in 1965 elections. These developments only deepened the conflict between Dayan and Sapir, who represented not only two ministries and two political

---

[11] The Finance Ministry regained its autonomous position only after halting hyperinflation in 1985 (see Chapter 6 and Grinberg, 1991).

parties, but also two opposing strategies regarding the future of Israeli occupation of the Territories. Although the debates were still interpreted using prewar discourse—between "statism" and "movementism"[12]—they now revolved around the Israeli political economy's realignment after the economic integration of the OT and the newly autonomous status of Dayan's Ministry of Security (Grinberg, 1993; Beilin, 1985).

The new dual regime spawned new patterns of control, and hence new alliances and coalitions, making the "statist-movementist" debate obsolete. In the aftermath of the war, the "statist" security establishment was only too happy to cooperate with the *Histadrut*, the quasi-state core institution of "movementism." The *Histadrut* supported the military government in controlling the OT's Palestinian workers, while WS became one of the main benefactors of Security Ministry subsidy allocations. Workers in the security industry also benefited from relatively high wages made possible by the fact that their employers did not operate on a profit basis, but rather on a "cost-plus" basis, in which the government financed the manufacturing costs plus a constant profit rate, ridding the management of the need to worry about cutting labor costs (Barkai, 1987; Peri, 1983). In other words the expanded security budget subsidized both firms and workers, transforming them into the Security Ministry "clients" and political supporters.

Mapai stood to lose the most, as both the "statist" and "movementist" bureaucracies got along very well without it, thanks to the economic prosperity, US capital inflows and the Palestinian captive market. Under these new structural conditions occurred the most significant institutional change of Israel's political economy: the *Histadrut* and the security establishment's relative autonomy made the ruling party virtually redundant as a source of legitimacy and domination of populations and resources. Recruiting new members and resources and giving jobs to activists continued without *Mapai*'s mediation. Moreover, the younger leaders Moshe Dayan (*Rafi*) and Yigal Alon (*Ahdut Haavoda*) were more able to understand and act in the new situation in the Alignment, and could take advantage of *Mapai* and their leaders. They were the ones who formulated plans for the future control of the OT while expanding the state's borders, and they were the ones widely seen as Eshkol's potential successors. Most *Mapai* officials in state and

---

12   See chapters 3 and 4.

Histadrut bureaucracies began splitting into *Rafi* versus *Ahdut Haavoda* supporters, as their own party began fading away as a political entity with its own distinct strategy (Beilin, 1985). The far-reaching implication was the complete abandonment of the original strategy of establishing a separate Jewish politico-economic entity. In practical terms, *Mapai* was forced to reorganize itself as the Labor Party, electing the relatively lackluster Golda Meir as its new leader after Eshkol's demise in 1969. The election of Meir rather than the more dominant Sapir was a compromise between *Rafi* and *Ahdut Haavoda*, demonstrating the fact that *Mapai* had already begun its decline.

Under these circumstances, *Mapai*'s only source of real power was its continued control of the Treasury Ministry, albeit restricted by the inflow of new resources directly to the autonomous Ministry of Security. In 1968, the Treasury Minister invented a new capital injection system, aiming to secure political allies while maintaining control over the allocation of capital. This new system was to be one of the main sources of inflationary pressure later on (see Chapter 6), and eventually led to the *Histadrut*'s downfall in the longer run. The new allocation system was invented in the context of the institutionalization of the Security Minister autonomous allocation system, and in response to pressures by WS managers to obtain state subsidies, dating back to the recession period (see Chapter 4). Thus, precisely when the Israeli economy was pulling out of the recession and WS managed to market its produce as well as receive generous subsidies from the Ministry of Security, Treasury Minister Sapir decided to grant the WS non-indexed loans. This arrangement was called "indexing insurance," and it allowed the transfer of half the funds accumulated by the *Histadrut* pension funds as non-indexed loans to the firms owned by the *Histadrut* (an arrangement called "the WS Financial Plan": see also chapter 3) (Grinberg, 1991, 1993).

This agreement, signed by Treasury Minister, WS and Bank Hapoalim, was the first in a series of capital subsidization arrangements. From 1968 onwards, the Ministry of Treasury began subsidizing additional groups using non-indexed loans, such as mortgage borrowers and private capital investors. However, the difference between the WS Financial Plan subsidies by "indexing insurance" and the subsidies provided to private investors lay in the political transparency and public control. The Financial Plan was a an agreement that allowed for government subsidization without public scrutiny, while the other forms were legal governmental decisions subject to Parliamentary controls. Many of the internal conflicts within the newly constituted Labor Party, including those publicized after 1973 as "corruption affairs," were related to the difficulties in supervising allocation of the subsidies transferred to the WS through the Financial Plan (Yadlin, 1980). The Treasury Ministry's undertaking to subsidize loans by not linking them to the CPI meant that borrowers benefitted from the growing inflation, including all *Histadrut* firms and the aforementioned mortgagors and private capital investments. This became the main source of the government's swelling internal debt in the 1970s, leading to a deep fiscal crisis (State Comptroller Report, 1977: 111-2; 1980: 50; see also Chapter 6).

The hyperinflation crisis analyzed in the next chapter was an indirect result of the split between the Ministries of Security and Treasury, reflecting the dual regime, which undermined state autonomy and weakened its ability to restrain subsidies after 1967. The split of the state's control apparatuses was adjusted to the dual regime of democratic/military domination, dividing state bureaucracies between the administrators of sovereign Israel (Treasury Ministry) and the OT (Security Ministry). These ministries vied for resources and subsidization powers. No wonder that private and public managers of companies, which benefitted from these subsidies, spent more time fostering political connections with party officials than actually managing their companies (Aharoni, 1992).

IV. The First Package Deal

Not only the industrialists and the government, but also the labor markets and worker organizations began to split, adjusting themselves to the new dual political economic structure. Under increasing labor market segmentation, those workers unthreatened by potential competition with the Palestinian workforce began formulating independent strategies. Large-scale worker strikes in the private sector became a thing of the past, and most struggles focused on the state-owned companies: the air and sea ports, merchant navy, national air carriers and utilities. Beyond their ownership structure, all these companies were characterized by their formal designation as "security enterprises" not allowed to employ Palestinians, be they citizens or non-citizens (Grinberg, 1991).

In 1969, Yitzhak Ben-Aharon was appointed Secretary General of the *Histadrut*. Ben-Aharon was a key leader in *Ahdut Haavoda* and one of the main forces behind the initiative to form the first Alignment towards 1965 elections.[13] He supported the struggles of the powerful worker committees, most notably the Ashdod longshoremen struggle, and therefore the Alignment ended his appointment in the next *Histadrut* elections (1973) (Tokatli, 1979; Osnat, 2004). Nevertheless, the longshoremen, as well as other strong workers represented by the big committees that gained in power after 1967, were public workers paid by the state. This structural positioning allowed them to accumulate power and influence, manifested in their ability to strike and improve their wages in isolated struggles since 1967, and collectively organize to oppose government policies in 1979 (as discussed in Chapter 6). However, the workers employed in the business sector (a new term that includes both the *Histadrut* and WS owned companies and private sector employers)[14] became weakened due to competition with non-unionized Palestinian workers. After the war, the *Histadrut* followed a double-edged policy: on the one hand, it helped the Ministry of Security control the entry of non-citizen Palestinian workers and signed restrained collective wage agreements in the business sector; on the other, it backed the powerful employees in the public sectors when they demanded higher pay. In other words, in its incarnation as employer in the business sector it helped restrain the workers, but where the state footed the bill it did not try or did not succeed in doing so (Grinberg, 1991). Despite this, the *Histadrut* managed to maintain its pro-worker image thanks to the rhetoric of the charismatic leadership of Ben-Aharon, who was vocal in favor of worker rights and in

---

13 Ben Aharon's article (*Davar*, January 11, 1963) is considered the catalyst to the negotiations that led to the alignment.

14 The concept of business sector (*sector iski*), and the collective wage agreements of the business sector appeared in 1967. Until then, there were three types of employers: private, government and *Histadrut*. The business sector includes both private and *Histadrut* employers, and it represents the radical change of the *Histadrut* and its orientation towards increased profits and wage restraint. This orientation was the result of Sapir's success, during the 1966-7 recession, in forcing WS managers to implement private sector practices, oriented towards profit. The public sector includes all workers employed directly by the government or companies and services owned and provided by the State.

attacking both the private and state employers.

In the 1969 elections, the new Alignment (which now included *Rafi* and *Mapam* in addition to *Mapai* and *Ahdut Haavoda*) won by a landslide, thanks to the military victory and subsequent economic prosperity; it rose from 45 Knesset members in 1965 (53 including *Mapam*'s 8) to 56 in 1969. *Gahal*, which had joined the national union coalition in the run-up to the 1967 War and failed to act as an effective opposition, did not gain in strength, remaining with 26 members (Arian, 1973). Under these circumstances, the *Histadrut* also sought to reassert its power over the workers and held elections in 28 trade unions, following a long period without any elections. Among all the weak worker groups, the elections were general and proportional, as in the elections to the Knesset—and the Alignment scored an impressive victory. On the other hand, among most professional unions where the *Histadrut* had far less clout the elections were direct (without party control) and federations such as the engineers' and academics' even managed to gain budgetary autonomy in 1969 (Tokatli, 1979).

Unlike the growing democratization of professional unions, which gained in strength following the labor market segmentation in 1967, the unskilled workers became weaker and under-represented at the union level. They were controlled by unions closely supervised by the *Histadrut* and the ruling party, and did not enjoy direct representation (elected in the workplace) in the union or *Histadrut* organs. Thanks to the close correlation between weakness in the labor market and the non-representative structure of the unions controlling the workers, the *Histadrut* managed to restrain their wages. In the public sector, characterized by more independent unions and powerful committees, this proved to be much more difficult (Grinberg, 1991).[15]

This difficulty was borne out by the first tripartite negotiations between the *Histadrut*, the government, and the private employers over a National Package Deal that was to govern pay, prices and taxes (Taub and Galin, 1971; Grinberg, 1991). The government was interested in such a deal, both as a large employer in the public sector, with its increasingly vocal demands for wage increases, and as the entity respon-

---

15 For a detailed description and analysis of the correlation between labor market structures and different trade unions election systems see Chapter 3 in my book *Split corporatism in Israel* (Grinberg, 1991) .

sible for the economy as a whole, aiming at reducing demand (and the resulting imports) and restraining the inflation. The private employers were interested in a uniform collective wage agreement in order to prevent competition for labor force among themselves, which pushed the workers' wages upwards. Finally, the *Histadrut* sought to regain its status as the representative of all workers in a national negotiation, rather than the factory-level struggles of the previous years.

The outcome was a 4% pay raise, with an additional 4% to be paid in bonds over the next five years. Three joint tripartite committees were formed to supervise the agreement's implementation. The government undertook to keep tax raises to a minimum, and the private employers agreed to avoid price hikes. Despite these parties' demand that this agreement would put an end to employee demands, it was agreed—as the *Histadrut* had demanded—to initiate industry- and factory-level negotiations on other employment terms than wages. In doing so, the *Histadrut* sought to avoid direct confrontation with the powerful worker committees, which had the advantage of an agreed-upon framework for differential bargaining (Taub and Galin, 1971; Tokatli, 1979; Grinberg, 1991).

The Package Deal was the first in a series of similar tripartite collective agreements with peculiar, neo-corporatist features. Although it managed to restrain wage increases in various sectors where the workers became weaker, most powerful worker groups initiated labor disputes and achieved higher wage raises. In the middle of 1970, a series of industrial conflicts broke out, turning it into what was then a peak year in terms of strikes and lost workdays, mostly in the public sector (Tokatli, 1979).[16] The Package Deal thus became a sort of "floor" which protected all workers whose wages would have been continually eroded by the high inflation had it not been for the *Histadrut*'s efforts.

In order to halt the decline in the foreign exchange reserves, the government began raising overseas funds in an increasing scale, mainly from the US. This exposed a structural flaw of the Israeli economy that was to plague it increasingly as security spending grew: the high rates of foreign aid and the import surplus increased the demand for services

---

16 The number of lost workdays grew by 280% compared to 1969, reaching 390,344 lost workdays in 163 strikes (Survey by the department of Industrial relations, 1972, in *Labour and national insurance*, 24[7], Ministry of Labour [Hebrew]).

and non-tradable commodities, leading to the development of an inflated service sector. It was precisely this structure which increased the bargaining power of state employees (Gross, 1983; Zakai and Zussman, 1983; Shalev, 1992).

However, following further agreements signed by the *Histadrut* in order to limit pay raises to 14% over the years 1972-1974, another wave of strikes broke out. This allowed the engineers to secure 35% pay raises for the next two years, followed by the other academics, journalists and teachers. The Ashdod longshoremen received 40%, followed by the nurses (42%) and the doctors (45%) (Tokatli, 1979). These pressures were the result of spiraling inflation, which averaged 12%-20% annually in 1971-1973. Its main victims were the employees who were unable to bargain independently and depended on the *Histadrut* for their modest wage raises.

Without independent bargaining power in the labor market, the weaker workers had no reason to support the Labor Party, which began to pay the price for the labor market segmentation and the resulting weakening of *Mizrahi* Oriental Jews in peripheral areas in the 1973 elections (Peres and Shemer, 1984; Diskin, 1988). In the run-up to these elections, *Gahal* mobilized the support of several groups and leaders and changed its name to *Likud*. The literal meaning of *Likud* is "consolidation," but it was also reminiscent of the Wadi Salib riots, which led to the formation of a party called *Likud Yotzei Tzfon Africa*, whose leader, David Ben Harush, joined the "new" *Likud* (Dahan Kalev, 1991). The new party gained almost 50% in strength and became the only true alternative to the Labor Party. Although the development of two multi-class party blocks, each representing both salaried and professional workers, began in 1965, it was not until 1973 that *Gahal-Likud* managed to become a true threat to the ruling party. The Labor Party held on to power for just another four years. This change of the political arena took place after a new wave of *Mizrahi* resistant mo(ve)ment, much broader and more prolonged than the Wadi Salib riots, provoked by the discrimination against the *Mizrahim* in the segmented labor market of the dual regime.

V. THE BLACK PANTHERS MO(VE)MENT: *MIZRAHI* ETHNO-CLASS PROTEST[17]

The most significant indication of organized social unrest within the borders of sovereign Israel after 1967 was a new protest movement of *Mizrahi* Jews that organized in 1971 under the name Black Panthers (inspired by the eponymous US movement). Its young leaders (mostly in their early 20s) came from a poor neighborhood in Jerusalem, and protested mainly against their discrimination compared to new immigrants from western countries and particularly the Soviet Union, which let some Jews go during the détente. The new immigrants received generous government aid, with large discounts in buying apartments and cars, while the young *Mizrahi* and their parents were still living in ramshackle housing projects, *Maabarot*[18] and abandoned Arab houses. In West Jerusalem, most of the empty Arab houses had belonged to wealthy families in neighborhoods like Katamon, Bak'a, Talbiya and Musrara. The Israeli government expropriated all of them to provide housing for migrants; the big houses were divided into smaller units so that each family occupied one room and shared the bathroom and kitchen with the others.

The Black Panthers claimed that *Mizrahim* were discriminated against because of their Oriental origin and dark skin. Beginning in March 1971, they organized mass demonstrations in Jerusalem that deteriorated into violent clashes with the police and shocked the entire country (Bernstein, 1976; Dahan Kalev, 1991; Chetrit, 2010; Lev and Shenhav, 2009). Apparently, it was only then that the Labor Party leadership fully realized that hidden beneath the surface of the Israeli-Arab conflict was a mass of alienated Jews who could threaten its hegemonic power. Therefore, one of its reactions was to significantly expand the state transfer payments and to institutionalize a more universal welfare state instead of the previous regime of state subsidies for the poor (Hofnung, 2006). This huge budget expansion was one of the three most important factors in the inflationary process (that

---

[17] This section is based on Bernstein (1976), Dahan Kalev (1991), and Chetrit (2010), but also on my own involvement, experiences and conversations with movement leaders and activists.

[18] The Hebrew term connotes a transition period. *Maabarot* were precarious small houses built by the government to provide provisional housing to immigrants. The original intention was to destroy these houses in the near future, but this turned out to be a very lengthy process.

provoked the class resistance movement discussed in Ch. 6), after the capital subsidies through "indexing insurance" and the increase in security expenditure.[19]

It seems that it was no coincidence that the resistant movement broke out in Jerusalem, of all places. Jerusalem was extremely diverse in terms of its population, aggravating social gaps and tensions. After the occupation of East Jerusalem in 1967, the government invested huge funds within a very short period to build new Jewish neighborhoods in the occupied areas, aiming to tighten its control of the Palestinian parts of the city, as many believed Israel could retain East Jerusalem even if forced to withdraw from the rest of the West Bank. The expansionist policy—not only territorial but also economic—was diametrically opposed to the prewar recession policy, which was singularly detrimental to workers in the secondary market segments (mostly *Mizrahim*). However, the new neighborhoods were built for the new immigrants who came in droves after the war, most of them *Ashkenazim*, and not for the veteran *Mizrahi* citizens. In addition, the city's economic integration meant that many Palestinians began to work in the construction industry and private services, taking jobs away from *Mizrahi* workers in the secondary segment and keeping wages down. All this happened in the Jerusalem boiling pot within just three years, in an area of one square kilometer. What gave birth to the mo(ve)ment of resistance was that the *Mizrahim* experienced tangible discrimination in housing, education, and the job market, as well as the government's tendency to ignore their claims and demands. Instead of the regular career path of *Ashkenazi* youth (high-school, military service, university, skilled job market), many *Mizrahi* youngsters had minimal primary education, were incarcerated before 18 for misdemeanors, and were not recruited by the military because they were expected to be trouble makers. In their interviews and public meetings, the Black Panthers' leaders were very effective in describing their personal path and transforming it into a collective narrative with clear political demands (Bernstein, forthcoming).[20]

---

19 For an insightful political economic analysis of the inflationary effects of the opening of political space to lower status groups, see Goldthorpe (1978).
20 For a very lively description of *Mizrahi* life-courses, see the protocol of the Black Panthers' meeting with the Prime Minister Golda Meir on April 13, 1971. http://www.golda.gov.il/archive/home/he/1/1150633350/1199352757/panterim-_part1.PDF.pdf.

The leadership nucleus of the Israeli Black Panthers came from the Musrara neighborhood. Prior to 1948, Musrara had been an affluent Arab neighborhood. After the war, its houses were allotted to new Jewish immigrants, mainly from Morocco, who lived in overcrowded conditions in Arab houses and several other housing projects built in the 1950s, notorious for their low standards. Until 1967, Musrara bordered on Jordanian East Jerusalem—nudged right between the two parts of the city. After Israel occupied East Jerusalem that year, Palestinian workers began crossing the neighborhood on their way to Western Jerusalem. Musrara was also right next to Ramat Eshkol, the first new neighborhood built in the occupied areas of Jerusalem, populated by new *Ashkenazi* immigrants. This meant that the leaders of the emerging protest movement lived right where the major structural injustices of the postwar political economy were most evident.

The first riots erupted in March 1971, a few months after the cease fire agreement that ended the post-1967 War of Attrition between Israel and Egypt. The riots came after almost four years of complete closure of the political space to socioeconomic agendas, due to the euphoria provoked by the 1967 victory, and the depression of the protracted War of Attrition. The moment of resistance was framed by the cease fire agreement coupled with Anwar Saadat's call to negotiate a peace agreement (Shafir, 1999a) on the one hand, and the October 1973 War on the other.

The Black Panthers' young leaders[21] received help and advice on how to organize and formulate their demands from three municipality employees working with teenagers at risk, and a few activists from *Matzpen*, a radical anti-Zionist political group inspired by the new left in the US and Western Europe; the latter tended to frame the struggle within a Marxist class analysis and language that were foreign to the *Mizrahi* population (Lev and Shenhav, 2009). The Black Panthers organized the first demonstration on March 3, 1971, despite the fact that the police did not give them official permit. The very name "Black Panthers" and their claim that there was racist discrimination in Israel had a tremendous impact on the Israeli public opinion. They succeeded in attracting immediate attention, and also police repression, including arrests and infiltration into their ranks (Chetrit, 2010; Lev and Shenhav, 2010).

---

21 The most prominent were Saadia Marciano, Charlie Bitton, Reuven Abargil, and Cochabi Shemesh.

Similar to the Wadi Salib events, the attempt to close political space for recognition focused on the leaders' "criminal" background—indeed, most of them had been jailed in the past. However, despite initial police repression and government attacks, the movement's impact on public opinion and the support it gained among *Mizrahim* led to a meeting between the Prime Minister and the movement leaders one month after the first demonstration.[22] This was a very important meeting where the Black Panthers and their claims were publicly recognized, despite the apparent failure of the dialogue due to the government's rejection of the Black Panthers' authority to represent *Mizrahi* claims. During the meeting a real process of negotiations started, but it ended with a big rift and a very famous statement by Prime Minister Meir that "they are not nice guys" (Chetrit, 2010; Bernstein, forthcoming).

On May 18, a new demonstration without a police permit mobilized thousands from all over the country, but mainly Jerusalem's poor neighborhoods. This demonstration deteriorated into violent clashes with the police, with demonstrators throwing stones and Molotov cocktails, resulting in dozens of casualties on both sides (*Haaretz* and *Yediot Ahronot*, May 19, 1971). The government soon decided to appoint a commission of inquiry into the socioeconomic situation of the at-risk youth chaired by Dr. Israel Katz (the Prime Minister Commission on Children and Youth in Distress, or less formally, the Katz Commission). Indeed, the commission confirmed that the *Mizrahim* suffered from economic hardship and recommended changes in state policies, primarily complementary income payments to low-income families and investment in education in the periphery. An education system reform was designed to prevent *Mizrahi* children from dropping out before high school. These reforms, however, failed to change the basic conditions that reproduced the social structure by the education system and even expanded original gaps (Nahon, 1993a).

The Black Panthers started organizing in the run-up to the 1973 elections, both in the *Histadrut* (scheduled for September) and the Knesset (October). They teamed with Shalom Cohen, a journalist born in Egypt, who was a Knesset member for a small radical party (*Haolam Haze*) that sympathized with the movement, and asked him to lead the

---

22 See Protocol of the meeting in Golda Meir's archive. http://www.golda.gov.il/archive/home/he/1/1150633350/1199352757/panterim-_part1.PDF.pdf.

new party. In the *Histadrut* elections they had a relatively significant success (2.2%) (Bernstein, 1976).²³ However, the Knesset elections were postponed due to the 1973 War, and when they were finally held in December, the Black Panthers had already lost their momentum and failed to mobilize the minimum 1% of the vote required to nominate a Knesset member. The *Likud* succeeded in mobilizing the great majority of *Mizrahi* votes (Peres and Shemer, 1984), thanks to its effective use of the *Mizrahi* claims against their discrimination by the Labor movement.

The Black Panthers mo(ve)ment of resistance was incredibly successful in opening political space to the recognition of the agenda, claims, and identity of the *Mizrahi* lower ethno-class. However, it failed to open space for stable representation, negotiation, and compromise; namely, they failed to establish themselves as an independent political actor. Due to this failure, they continued working as a typical social movement, with a clear name and identity, organizational structure, formal demands and relations with the formal political parties. However when the moment passed after the October 1973 War their decay was quick and painfully evident: they failed to mobilize mass demonstrations, organized only few public acts with less than thirty participants, and finally split, coopted by leftist parties in the run-up to the 1977 elections.²⁴

The most salient success of the Black Panthers was the recognition of *Mizrahi* claims, manifested by the allocation of state resources and the educational reform, which significantly improved the living conditions of Israel's *Mizrahi* citizens in the long term (Hofnung, 2006). The failure to organize as a political actor able to represent the *Mizrahi* ethno-class interests and claims was due not only to the individual abilities of the Panthers' young leaders, but also to the power structure of the dual democratic/military regime of domination, and the cooperation and concerted efforts by legitimate political actors to delegitimize autonomous *Mizrahi* representation.

---

23   I met the Black Panthers' leaders for the first time in the *Histadrut Vaad Hapoel* (parliamentary body) when I, too, became a member.
24   My own participation was during the 1974-1977 period, which was characterized by few symbolic activities, and the later split and cooptation. In retrospect I realized that I had been one of the agents of Saadia Marciano's pre-election cooptation to the socialist-Zionist *Sheli* block.

VI. The Counter-Mo(ve)ment: Denying Representation by Tribal Channeling

Unlike the 1959 Wadi Salib riots analyzed in Chapter 3, which erupted during an electorate campaign and were quickly suppressed, this time the protest continued on-and-off until the 1973 War. The Black Panthers became a social movement, with a distinct identity, recognized leadership, and sustained organization, although fragile and poorly financed. They succeeded in opening political space for the recognition of *Mizrahi* discrimination and a legitimate claim for equal rights. After Wadi Salib, the main form of social activism was worker "action committees" and strikes, thanks to full employment which empowered rank-and-file workers and unified *Mizrahi* and *Ashkenazi* workers in metropolitan centers. In the peripheral development towns populated mainly by the *Mizrahi* lower ethno-class, however, unemployment and dependency on the *Histadrut* and state continued. After 1967, industrial workers in the private sector were no longer able to fight for better conditions because the labor market structure divided and weakened them (Semyonov and Lewin-Epstein, 1987; Grinberg, 1991). The *Mizrahim* were now in a structural position that facilitated the formation of a distinct and collective *Mizrahi* identity based on their common discrimination. On the one hand, they saw how the standard of living of the middle class, largely composed of *Ashkenazim*, was rapidly rising, and on the other they saw how the Palestinian population was subjected to military rule and becoming hopelessly dependent on the Israeli economy. The *Mizrahim* were positioned in-between: even those of them who managed to secure stable jobs always had an *Ashkenazi* "above" them and a Palestinian "below" them. Under these conditions of ethnic stratification and state privileges for Jews, they preferred to emphasize their ethno-national Jewish identity in demanding equality to the *Ashkenazi* upper classes, instead of their "inferior" image as Oriental or Arab Jews. This was the core symbolic weakness of the Black Panthers' demand for *Mizrahi* autonomous representation, and the *Likud*'s significant advantage.

Mizrahi activists seeking to gain political power through the mainstream ruling parties rather than through the Black Panthers failed to do so, and usually found their way to the *Likud* opposition party. The *Likud* opened its doors to young *Mizrahi* activists mainly in the lower party ranks and municipal elections in the development towns, effectively co-opting them (Grinberg, 1989). Its leader and future Prime Minister Menachem Begin eloquently articulated the two basic sentiments of the *Mizrahi* population: resentment of the *Ashkenazi* discrimination identified with the Zionist Labor Movement, and the ethno-nationalist demand for equal privileges to all Jews, particularly as brothers in arms (Shapiro, 1991; Peled, 1992). This strategy emphasized both ethno-national solidarity and national hostility towards the Palestinians: equality with those above them (the *Ashkenazim*) and economic integration of those below them (the Palestinians) under continued discrimination guaranteed by the military rule. Thus, citizenship, as a basis of equal rights, became a completely empty concept since the institutionalization of the dual democratic/military regime in 1967 (Shafir and Peled, 2002; Grinberg, 2008).

The most significant electoral turning point in terms of *Mizrahi* support for the *Likud* occurred as early as 1973 (Peres and Shemer, 1984; Diskin, 1988). My argument here is that the main factors behind the electoral change in 1973 were the labor market segmentation after 1967, the shock of the 1973 war, and the effect of the *Mizrahi* resistance mo(ve)ment ignited by the Black Panthers. Menachem Begin, remarkably, framed all these events within a discourse that sought to reclaim the lost dignity of *Mizrahi* soldiers and the peripheral *Mizrahi* lower classes through the national myth and biblical promise of Greater Israel, materialized by the 1967 conquests (Shapiro, 1991).

Begin was able to speak the two most legitimate languages of state power: the Jewish superior position vis-à-vis the Palestinians, and the religious legitimacy of controlling the occupied West Bank, Biblically named "Judea and Samaria." Neither the young *Mizrahi* leaders of the Black Panthers nor the elder Member of Knesset Shalom Cohen were willing or able to speak these languages of power, and openly supported the recognition of the Palestinian rights. However, Begin's discourse was very effective in mobilizing *Mizrahi* voters after 1967, and particularly after 1973, because it channeled their feelings of revenge against the *Ashkenazi* elites using the religious myth of the Promised Land. However it offered no direct solution to the social discrimination of *Mizrahim*, as this resulted from their peripheral position in the segmented labor market, the education system and segregated neighborhoods and settlements.

CHAPTER FIVE

The political meaning of the Greater Israel myth was the perpetuation of the dual democratic/military regime, including not only subjugation of the Palestinians but also maintanance of the *Mizrahi* inferior status. When this national myth turned into political reality after 1967, it could be articulated by the *Likud* as incitement against the disadvantaging Other, without opening up political space for *Mizrahi* representation. Instead, the *Likud* could at best offer cooptation of some *Mizrahi* leaders who had emerged mainly in local elections in the peripheral development towns (Grinberg, 1989), and at worst a sophisticated repertoire of misrepresentation at the national level by tribal channeling of anger, rage, and hate towards the *Ashkenazi* upper classes and the Palestinian lower classes.

As the parliamentary elections were held right after the 1973 War, social issues were pushed aside. This meant that although ethnicity and discrimination were the motivation for the *Mizrahi* vote, they found themselves unable to discuss discrimination directly and open political space for their authentic representation. In other words, although 1967 represents a key structural turning point in terms of the distinct *Mizrahi* socioeconomic position, they failed to open political space and remained marginalized in the new political economy as well. While the Black Panthers' protest was crucial to the recognition of ethnic discrimination and the legitimacy of *Mizrahi* claims for equality, they also could not open political space for their autonomous representation, mediation, and compromise. Their inability to articulate a coherent alternative to the dual regime and the subjugation of the Palestinians led to the empowering of the *Likud*, which channeled *Mizrahi* feelings against the "*Ashkenazi* Left" and the Palestinian "enemy," thereby closing political space for their representation.

Inadvertently, the Black Panther mo(ve)ment of resistance contributed significantly to bipartisan tribal mobilization in that it delegitimized the ruling party due to its discrimination against the *Mizrahim*. Although this opened space for *Mizrahi* recognition and liberation from the ruling party, the Panthers proved unable to mobilize their constituencies against the dual political economic regime of domination over Israel/Palestine that maintained the *Mizrahi* marginal position in the ethnic hierarchy. The *Likud* ethno-national rhetoric of national unity and formal equality among Jews, coupled with the maintenance of Palestinian subjugation, appeared a much more realistic strategy to most *Mizrahi* voters. The nationalist sentiments after the 1973 War facilitated the integration of *Mizrahim*, without giving them autonomous voice, and criticism of the government's security failures could easily channel the *Mizrahi* anti-government feelings.

VII. Conclusion

As we shall see in the next Chapter, in 1977 the Alignment lost the elections and collapsed as a ruling party. Its loss of a third of its former electoral power resulted mainly from discrete decisions which affected one social group or the other. This campaign was not lost due to minor changes in the support of certain constituencies—it represented the total collapse of a party and political movement which had led the nation-state building project for more than forty years. The 1977 elections showed that most of the Israeli public, including party activists, lost faith in the Alignment's ability to cope with the problems created by the new dual democratic/military regime, whether socioeconomic or political.

The success of the segregationist project in 1948 with the establishment of a separate Jewish State uncovered the tension between the ZLM's means and goals on the one hand, and democracy and autonomous civil society on the other. These contradictions provoked the crisis of statehood discussed in Chapter 4 and the almost complete loss of control over the workers during 1960-1965, leading to the threat of losing the 1969 elections due to the enduring recession. The 1967 occupation ran counter to ZLM's segregationist strategies, but succeeded in establishing a dual regime able to contain the contradictions referred to above. In the dual democratic/military political economic regime, Jews and Palestinians were integrated in a single economy, without full citizenship rights or free markets for the latter. The dual regime defined the territory within the pre-1967 borders as areas of democracy and free markets, and the rest as militarily occupied territories whose subjugated populations were denied those freedoms. Although the contradictions were contained by the dual regime, the Zionist Labor Movement could no longer legitimize its actions. If indeed the occupation was legitimate, the *Likud* and its support of Jewish supremacy over the entire "Greater Israel" was ideally suitable as a ruling party.

In addition to the crisis of legitimacy, the new dual regime provoked a social crisis due to the restructuring of society by the economic integration of the Palestinians. The Black Panthers resistance mo(ve)ment reflects the reaction of *Mizrahi* citizens to their new location in between the *Ashkenazi* elites and the subjugated Palestinians in the OT. The location of the Musrara neighborhood between the Palestinian areas of Jerusalem and the center of the Israeli city resembles the concrete social location of the *Mizrahi* Jews.

Since 1967, citizenship has not been the basis for claiming equal rights. In the Jewish State that discriminates against Palestinian Arabs in both sides of the green line, being a Jew guarantees rights more than being a citizen. Although the Black Panthers protested against the discrimination of the "Black," they could not speak for oppressed Palestinians and continue representing the entire *Mizrahi* electorate. They also could not represent their identity as Jewish-Arabs, as some intellectuals suggested (Shohat, 1988; Chetrit, 2010; Shenhav, 2006) because the Jewish ethno-national identity was defined by the hostility to the Arab nation and state privileges for ethnic Jews. As a matter of fact, the leaders of the Black Panthers movement came to the conclusion that they must also identify with the rights of the Palestinians. This attitude caused their almost total marginalization, as the Black Panthers leaders split and joined two parties identified with the claim for a two-state solution and negotiations with the PLO in 1977. I would like to emphasize that only the leaders joined the anti-occupation parties, and the *Mizrahi* masses voted for *Likud*.

The Black Panther resistant mo(ve)ment opened the political space for the recognition of *Mizrahi* claims and the critics of the regime, but only Begin and the *Likud* were able to benefit from this opening, with their ethno-national discourse claiming Jewish solidarity and equality (Shapiro, 1991). This channeling of *Mizrahi* rage against the *Ashkenazi* elites and against the subjugated Arabs mobilized *Mizrahi* votes, but blocked their autonomous representation and ignored their distinct concrete demands.

If the political aftermath of the Wadi Salib riots was the transformation of *Mapai* into the party that mobilized the fears of the *Ashkenazi* middle classes and prevented open debate over ethno-class relations, the Black Panther mo(ve)ment of resistance provoked the parallel process of *Mizrahi* mobilization by the *Likud*. This repertoire of distortion of ethno-class agendas and interests by tribal channeling of the fears and anger of social groups without open debate almost hermetically closed political space to representation of both socioeconomic and ethnic agendas and demands.

Since the 1981 elections everything was channeled to a tribal mobilization of "left" and "right." This tribal mobilization was dichotomous: people were mobilized not by their political ideas on how the state should cope with class conflict or ethnic discrimination, but by channeling a sense of belonging to the tribe combined with hatred and fear of the Other. The "left-right" tribal polarization condensed all the conflicts within it: class, ethnicity and religion, which were mobilized by tribal symbols, language and myths. The "left" tribe mobilized mainly *Ashkenazi* secular middle classes while the "right" mobilized religious and traditionalist Jews, as well as *Mizrahi* lower classes.

This phenomenon of dichotomous tribal channeling shrinks political space and denies access to new political actors and identities in a sophisticated way, because political leaders and actors are constrained by a polarized dichotomy: you are either "left" or "right," friend or foe. Arian (1998) calls this tacit cooperation between competing parties to close political space to new actors a "cartel." Thus, "dichotomous polarization" and "cartel cooperation" are two repertoires operating in addition to "condensation" and "tribal channeling," which have been analyzed in the previous chapters.

The *Mizrahi* collective identity remained delegitimized and "forbidden," unable to speak the ethno-national language that legitimized subjugation of the "inferior" Arabs. A new party representing Black Panther supporters emerged only after the *Likud* administration continued to discriminate against the *Mizrahi* lower ethno-class, once it became apparent that its economic policies only exacerbated inequality. The new party, *Shas* (see Dayan, 1999; Chetrit, 2010), which first competed in the 1984 national elections,[25] was able to reconcile the *Mizrahi* collective identity and a legitimate language of power, the Jewish religion. Only when the slogan was a call to return to the ancient tradition of Sephardic Jews, legitimizing the dual regime that privileged the Jews, did *Mizrahi* identity find legitimate political space for its representation. A long and convoluted way took them from the Black Panthers

---

25 *Shas* was founded in the run-up to the local elections in Jerusalem in 1983.

resistance mo(ve)ment through the *Likud* to *Shas*. This was definitely not a process of political representation, but rather misrepresentation, given the power structure of the dual democratic/military regime in Israel/Palestine.

However, the 1977 electoral defeat of Labor was due not only to the disaffection of the peripheral social sectors (who had already begun supporting the *Likud* in 1973), but also to the desire of those who benefitted from the government's economic policy to find a way out of the crisis in the labor movement, such as *Dash* voters and leaders. Victory fell to those who had found clear ideological justification for the dual regime. As we shall see in the next chapter, however, since the crisis was not only ideological but more profoundly politico-economic—due to the inability of the dual state to control its resources—the *Likud*'s rise to power exacerbated Israel's urgent difficulties, rather than solving them.

6.
1980 — FORUM/13 POWERFUL WORKERS: HYPERINFLATION AND THE CHALLENGE TO STATE AUTONOMY[1]

I. INTRODUCTION

The May 1977 election results were a continuation of the existing trend of *Mizrahi* lower classes shifting their support from the Alignment to the *Likud*, primarily in the peripheral development towns. The *Mizrahi* protest initiated by the Black Panthers in 1971 culminated with the *Likud*'s rise to power in 1977, albeit this was a far cry from the original intentions of the movement's leaders, who joined two small left-wing parties that were part of the 1977 elections, as mentioned above.

The creation of a new party called *Dash*, most of whose members and voters had been formerly associated with the Labor Movement, and the widespread corruption within the Alignment's ranks were two external manifestations of a deeper phenomenon everyone had been aware of ever since 1967: the Labor Movement had lost its way. *Dash* attracted many votes of all ideological shades from among the upper and middle class, mainly *Ashkenazis* in the big cities (Diskin, 1988). However, its attempt to become the power broker failed, since the Alignment's downfall was such that no coalition government could be formed under its leadership (Rubinstein, 1982). After its electoral defeat, the Alignment leadership mobilized to save its control of the *Histadrut*. Thanks to a huge organizational effort, most *Histadrut* members, including many who had voted for the *Likud* in the parliamentary elections, were persuaded to vote for the Alignment in the *Histadrut* elections. The argument was that if the main opposition party in the Knesset continues controlling the *Histadrut*, the working class would benefit in its struggle

---

[1] This chapter is based on my MA research thesis (Grinberg, 1985), which was later published as the book *Split corporatism in Israel* (Grinberg, 1991). Some of the interviews quoted here were published only in 1991, others only in 1985.

against the new anti-labor economic policy only to be expected of a liberal Minister of Treasury. This campaign proved a surprising success: for the first time, the Alignment received more votes in the *Histadrut* elections than in the Knesset elections: 523,000 against 430,000 (Bahat, 1979). As in the aftermath of the 1960s crisis, the *Histadrut* proved its survival skills under difficult conditions. However, as we shall see below, the long-term implication of the Alignment's electoral defeat in the Knesset was a weakening of the *Histadrut*'s huge economic power.

Thus, the path towards the decline of the Zionist Labor Movement passed through two main historical moments: (1) the loss of the hegemonic ideological position it had held since 1967 following the institutionalization of a dual democratic/military regime over all Israel/Palestine; and (2) the loss of power in 1977 to the *Likud*, which was equipped with an ideology able to legitimize the new political realities institutionalized by the ZLM. Ever since 1977, the labor movement progressively deteriorated organizationally, ideologically and economically. Even the attempt to breathe new life into the movement in 1992-1995 (discussed in the next chapter) by changing the agenda and the order of priorities, putting an end to the occupation and reforming the *Histadrut*, eventually failed on both counts.

The *Likud*'s rise to power made many Israelis fear that, with its new political alliance with *Mafdal* (the pro-settlement National Religious Party), it would follow a strategy of exacerbating the Israeli-Arab conflict. This fear led almost immediately to the establishment of the Peace Now protest movement (T. Reshef, 1996). On the other hand, many others, even members of the labor movement, expected the new liberal economic policy to overcome the crisis provoked by the Alignment's over-interventionist approach (Grinberg, 1991).

However, right at the beginning of Begin's first term as Prime Minister, these two widely held expectations—economic success and external national conflict escalation—failed to materialize; on the contrary, the opposite was true. While the new government's economic policy quickly drove the economy into unprecedented three-figure inflation, Begin surprised everyone with a historic peace treaty with Egypt.

This chapter discusses the forces that pushed towards inflation, the threat posed by liberal policies to weak and strong workers, and the organized reaction of the most powerful 13 worker committees in a mo(ve)ment of resistance to the government's economic policy. I will argue that the class struggle against the liberal economic policies succeeded in the short term to prevent direct damage to the powerful workers, but that later on, the counter-mo(ve)ment led to the imposition of a radical neo-liberal policy—designed according to the principles of the Washington Consensus (WC)[2]—aiming to halt hyperinflation and weaken all organized labor. The question discussed below is why and how the powerful workers' organization and resistance mo(ve)ment ended up in the implementation of the neo-liberal economic plan in 1985, a historic turning point that structurally dismantled worker power.

II. Background: Economic Crisis, Wage Restraint, Capital Subsidies and Political Turnabout

After the 1973 elections, it became clear that two large party blocks were now fighting for power, both with a socioeconomically condensed electoral basis. This melted the tribal dichotomy of the political arena, which, as we have seen in Chapter 4, emerged towards 1965, removed the class conflicts from the partisan competition, and channeled them into the parties themselves. Disagreements regarding the country's economic policy split the parties from within rather than one from the other. The phenomenon of a party representing class interests, identities and demands—the prime examples being *Mapam* and the Liberal Party in the 1960s—became obsolete. In the context of the dual regime that institutionalized the ethno-class hierarchies, even a party with a salient class ideology, such as the Communist Party, became mainly the representative party of the ethno-national minority of Palestinian citizens, after most Jewish voters had abandoned it.

While the Alignment was troubled by incessant debates both within its own ranks and between the government and *Histadrut* during 1974-1977, the *Likud* was able to evade its internal contradictions and benefitted from being in the opposition. As a melting multi-class opposition party, which mobilized both private capital economic elites and *Mizrahi* low ethno-class, it managed to attack the government both from the economic right and left at the same time. From the right, the members

---

2 See Williamson (1989) for a detailed description of the principles of the Washington Consensus and their political logic.

of its constituent Liberal Party demanded a more liberal economic policy; and from the left by its *Mizrahi* coopted figures, particularly David Levi, head of its *Histadrut* faction, which opposed cancelling subsidies of basic goods and the commodification of welfare services and supported workers' wage demands. As we shall see below, once the *Likud* came into power, it implemented its multi-class contradictory economic policies, causing inflation to soar.

The 1973 *Yom-Kippur* War spelled the end of rapid growth and accelerated the negative economic processes that had begun already in 1967. The balance of payments was worsened, while security expenses, capital imports, and loans required to replenish military equipment spiraled.[3] At the same time, the structural problem of the increasing share of the public sector in the economy and national product only deepened. Inflation reached an annual level of 30-40%, this time due to increased public spending. Another factor that exacerbated this situation was the decrease in Jewish immigration, which, together with the world energy crisis, brought growth to a halt. Capital imports for the US could only be used to buy specific military supplies in the US, making it extremely difficult to fund public and civil services.

In order to continue providing its services at their current level, the government responded by raising taxes (Shalev, 1992; Ben Porat, 1986; Berglass, 1986). At the same time, it began to cut its subsidization of basic goods such as bread and milk. Even more important in terms of social consequences was the new exchange rate policy called "crawling devaluation,"[4] designed to promote exports and reduce private consumption. The inflation that resulted from the currency devaluation significantly increased the extent of capital subsidization in the form of non-indexed loans (see Chapter 5), providing the private employers and the WS with government aid above and beyond what they had already been enjoying in the form of salary erosion due to inflation. Finally, the government supported the employers by its policy of wage restraint, implemented mainly at the expense of the weak and peripheral workers.

---

3   During 1970-1975, the import surplus more than tripled, from 1,262 to 4,050 million dollars. Security related imports rose from about 490 million dollars in 1972 to 1.25 billion after the 1973 War and reached a peak of 1.85 billion dollars in 1975. Loans (from the US—the main source—the Jewish Diaspora, Germany, and other sources) grew from 475 million dollars in 1970 to 1.473 billion (Arnon, 1981: 82-6).

4   The "crawling devaluation" was a policy of slow devaluation controlled by the government.

All these developments forced rank-and-file workers into the defensive, and 1974 saw a sharp fall in the frequency of wage raises and industrial conflicts. The rank and file worker councils demanded that the *Histadrut* lead the struggle against the government's policy. Accordingly, the *Histadrut* tried to organize protests in order to suggest that the policy led by the Alignment could cause its representatives in the *Histadrut* to lose the workers' trust. This was a thinly veiled threat to the employers (should the *Histadrut* lose all control over the workers).

Despite its public protests, however, the *Histadrut* leadership collaborated with the government's economic policy, and in August 1975 it signed a new four-year pay cost-of-living allowance agreement with the private employers, according to which the compensation for inflation will be paid out twice a year at a reduced rate of 70% of the rise in the consumer price index. This "underpayment" of the cost-of-living allowance was an additional refinement of the mechanism designed to reduce the general wage levels in order to neutralize the achievement of the more powerful worker groups. Due to the "underpayment" mechanism of the cost-of-living allowance agreement, the higher the inflation, the greater the income gaps between the powerful and weak worker groups (Leviatan, 1982).

One of the most salient labor conflicts initiated by powerful worker groups was the El-Al airlines general strike in 1975. Towards the end of the year, the worker councils in El Al convened other worker councils to protest the economic situation, hoping to mobilize them in the future. This convention was designed to warn both the *Histadrut* and the government that their economic policy of wage restraint might push other worker councils to coordinated independent struggles, similar to the "action committees" of the early 1960s. However, the convention's organizers reached the conclusion that their initiative was bound to fail, as the workers in the private sector were too weak and dependent on the *Histadrut* to rebel against it (Interview with Eli Ben-Menachem, Grinberg, 1985).

The workers' growing unrest pushed the *Histadrut* to present economic demands to the labor government, despite its leaders' intention to support the policy of wage restraint. Frequent conflicts around various issues between the *Histadrut* and the government turned the Alignment block—which controlled both—into an arena of class conflict. In order to mediate between the two positions and shape a unified policy, the ruling party formed a "resolution committee" composed of 7 representatives each from the government, *Histadrut* and the Labor Party (Y. Reshef, 1981).

As the government and *Histadrut* struggled to restrain wage raises in the public sector through a centralized policy, the employees themselves began to bypass the economy-wide policy of wage restraint by what was called "wage crawl,"[5] achieved by industry- department- and place of work-level agreements. The wage crawl, which increased significantly from 1974 onwards, widened the gap between the strong and weak workers even further (Zussman and Zakai, 1983).

In 1976, taxes were raised further, public and private consumption was down, and investments shrank, but so did the import surplus. Two months before the collective wage agreements in the business sector were to expire, the *Histadrut* and private employers signed a collective wage agreement which provided for a pay raise ceiling of 3% for 1976, and another 3% for 1977. In the public sector, however, the demands were much higher and could be restrained only with great difficulty in the run-up to the 1977 elections, and more generous sector-level agreements were signed with various worker groups (Tokatli, 1979).

In early 1977, the government proposed a "mandatory mediation bill" that threatened the interests of all organized workers, and weakened the status of the *Histadrut* as their representative. This move led to a severe conflict between the government and the *Histadrut* and proved that the latter was no longer capable of restraining the workers, while the ruling party could no longer act as a political mediator. Under this threat, Prime Minister Yitzhak Rabin and *Histadrut* Secretary General Yeruham Meshel signed a Package Deal which froze all prices, profits, taxes and wages, but they were unable to implement it (Y. Reshef, 1981).

The economic and political crisis was accompanied not only by constant bickering within the ruling party and its government and *Histadrut* representatives, but also by unprecedented corruption affairs of Alignment officials in *Histadrut* firms and government ministries, culminating in the suicide of Housing Minister Abraham Offer following a police investigation on corruption. Eventually, even Rabin had to resign after it had been revealed that his wife kept an illegal bank account in the US.

---

5   The concept of "wage crawl" refers to raising salaries by promoting workers within the plant's ranks, thus bypassing the official wage restraint provided for in the collective agreements.

The crisis in the Alignment, and consequent loss of voters from the low-income salaried class to the *Likud*, convinced several leaders formerly affiliated with the ZLM to form a new party in order to remain in power at all costs (Yadlin, 1980). These were members of the security establishment, executives from private and *Histadrut* corporations, university professors, and professionals. The new central party was called the Democratic Movement for Change, known in its Hebrew acronym as *Dash*. This party's objective was to keep its members in power whatever the election results would be, in the hope of gaining a decisive axis position as power broker between the two blocks to their right and left—assumed to be of equal power, and none of the blocks can form a 61 KMs coalition without *Dash*—and therefore being able to dictate the terms of the coalition. However, despite having won an impressive 15 (out of 120) seats in the 1977 Knesset, *Dash* could not prevent a *Likud* government from being formed because the Alignment lost many more votes than expected, and the *Likud* was able to form a 61 KMs coalition without *Dash*.[6]

III. The Economic Turnabout: Liberalization Deepens the Crisis

After the establishment of the new coalition government headed by the *Likud*, the new Treasury Minister Simcha Ehrlich announced an "economic turnabout" in November 1977. The new "liberal" policy included eliminating the government's control of the exchange rate that had formerly characterized the Alignment's interventionist economy. This announcement was met by protests by the workers, particularly those aligned with the *Histadrut* leadership. Prior to the renewal of the Framework Agreements in the spring of 1978, the *Histadrut* called upon the trade union leaders to avoid a "catch-as-you-can" policy. In that, it attempted to signal that even if the *Likud* controlled the state, the *Histadrut* still sought economic stability and would not let the stronger

---

6   The 61-member coalition initially included the *Likud*, with 45 Knesset members (KMs); two religious parties—the *Mafdal* (12 KMs) and *Agudat Israel* (4). It was later joined by Moshe Dayan as an independent member (having left the Labor Party), and *Dash* (15 KMs). The Alignment secured only 32 KMs. The other opposition parties were *Hadash* (5), *Sheli* (2); and *Ra'am, Agudat Israel Workers, Ratz*, the *Independent Liberals* and Plato Sharon's party, with 1 KM each (from the Knesset Website: http://www.knesset.gov.il/history/heb/heb_hist9_s.htm).

employees loose, even though it was clear that it could achieve much more than the expressed demands (Y. Reshef, 1981). This became the key question during the period discussed in this chapter: if the *Histadrut* did not share in state power, why did it still try to restrain the wages of the more powerful employees in the public sector?

In March 1978, the Framework Agreement in the business sector[7] was signed, providing for 12.5% wage raises on October 1978 and April 1979 (Grinberg, 1991: 77),[8] in an attempt to protect the real wages against the rising inflation rate. However, the main difficulty was with the public sector, and in order to curtail the employees' demands, *Histadrut* secretary general Yeruham Meshel and Simcha Ehrlich tried to negotiate directly and formulated a series of agreements. These agreements eventually failed to mitigate the pressures for wage raises proportional to the rising inflation. The attempt to jointly manage the employees' wages raises came to an end in March 1979, when Ehrlich signed a separate agreement with the Engineers' Association[9] without consulting the *Histadrut*. Under these conditions, the *Histadrut* was no longer willing to restrain the employees and announced that the Treasury Ministry was responsible for the negotiations' failure (Y. Reshef, 1981).

These events shed light on the *Histadrut*'s interest in restraining wage demands in the public sector as well. The government's agreement with the engineers also required the firms of the business sector to raise the engineers' wages, leading to pressures for across-the-board wage raises in both sectors. Given the fact that the *Histadrut* was still the biggest employer in the business sector, the government signature of the engineers' agreement caused financial damage to all firms owned by the Worker's Society. The Ministry of Treasury continued to sign separate wage agreements in the public sector, bypassing the *Histadrut* and undermining its role as monopolistic centralized trade union. In January-March 1979, inflation accelerated significantly, reaching a 56.1% annual rate in March (Arnon, 1981: 69), thus eroding real wages even more. Given the increasing discontent among the workers, the *Histadrut* declared a four-hour warning general strike. Almost all workers responded

---

7 On the meaning of the business sector, see Chapter 5, footnote 14.
8 To be adjusted according to inflation.
9 This agreement included a new wage scale and wage increases of about 30% (23% basic increase and additional compensations). See *Haaretz*, March 29, 1977.

favorably, with many calling outspokenly for Ehrlich's resignation. However, the *Histadrut* failed in its attempts to calm the workers' unrest and distrust (Tokatli, 1979; Y. Reshef, 1981).

Facing these inflationary pressures, the government adopted a classic restraint policy. Aiming to cut its spending, it cancelled some of the capital subsidies, announcing on May 1979 that the non-indexed loans allocated to private capital investors and mortgage borrowers would be linked to the Consumer Price Index (CPI). Thus it eliminated the "indexing insurance" system of capital subsidies policy adopted by the Labor government in 1968 (see Chapter 5). The exception to this was the WS Financial Plan, which was a bilateral agreement with the *Histadrut* rather than an autonomous government resolution, signed every five years (expected to expire on October 1980). Hence, capital subsidies to WS companies continued to flow. The cutting of capital subsidies, however, more than restraining inflation, created a new problem: sharp reduction in investments in the private sector (Razin, 1979).

Precisely when the wages and prices crisis took another turn for the worse, the *Histadrut* allied itself with the employers' association—the Economic Organizations' Coordination Bureau (EOCB)—in an attempt to bypass the government and try to manage the economy and subsidize capital and wages independently of the Ministry of Treasury. To prevent wage erosion as a result of the running inflation, the private employers and the *Histadrut* agreed to make several down payments on the cost-of-living allowance (COLA) during January-October 1979, forcing the government to pay the public employees. The COLA agreement was part of a huge political-economic deal that also included the allocation of Financial Plan non-indexed loans to private employers. During these months, the credit shortage worsened due to the halt of capital subsidies made by Ehrlich. To overcome this shortage, the Manufacturers' Association negotiated a macro-economic deal with the *Histadrut*'s pension funds and *Bank Hapoalim*. They signed a comprehensive pension agreement aiming to increase the pension funds' capital accumulation and to share the benefits from the non-indexed loans provided in the WS Financial Plan with private employers. In June 1979, the comprehensive pension agreement was signed, significantly expanding the Financial Plan's resources, with all firms represented in the Manufacturers' Association's undertaking to insure their employees in the new fund. In return, *Bank Hapoalim* extended non-indexed loans to these firms, guaranteed and subsidized by the government's "indexing insurance" agreement, signed with the *Histadrut* in 1968 (Grinberg, 1991).[10]

The 1979 comprehensive pension agreement was actually a politico-economic package deal based on the *Histadrut*'s and industrialists' joint interest in the continuation of an expansive inflationary policy, while allocating small wage raises to prevent the total collapse of wage agreements and loss of *Histadrut* control of the workers. The *Histadrut* and the private employers demonstrated their ability to prevent such a collapse and restrain wages against the government's financial policy by expanding the government's capital subsidies allocated by the WS Financial Plan. Despite the agreement, however, recession began creeping in while inflation kept rising, to an annual rate of 130% in the third quarter of 1979. Unemployment also rose beginning in September, particularly in the manufacturing sector. Rising inflation required increased down payments on the COLA, as well as raising their rate from 70% to 80% of the CPI from October (Leviatan, 1982). Using this coordinated policy, the *Histadrut* and the employers sought to avoid a general collapse. However, they attempted to do it bypassing the third key player in the economy—the government.

After two and a half years of a currency liberalization policy, Israeli economy was in deep crisis: inflation rose from an annual rate of 30% in 1976 to almost 170% in the last quarter of 1979. The financial market boomed, but production slowed, real wages dropped, unemployment began to soar and it became increasingly difficult to raise industrial loans. Abraham Shavit, Chairman of the Manufacturers' Association and the EOCB, called for a general employers' lockout, and *Histadrut* leader Yeruham Meshel announced that he would be forced to declare a general strike if inflation was not halted (Grinberg, 1991). In other words, the EOCB-*Histadrut* cooperation against the government represented multi-class civil society rejection of government policies.

Treasury Minister Simcha Ehrlich had little option but to resign, and was replaced by Yigal Horowitz. The new minister acted to reduce the public sector's size and government spending, and to align them with the slow-down in the private sector, since their non-alignment made

---

10   Since 1970 this agreement was a five years agreement, and was renewed in 1975. The government was expected to renew it in October 1980, and, as we will see, this renewal was at the core of re-organizing the Government-*Histadrut*-business sector power relations.

the economic crisis particularly severe: demand rose together with imports and private consumption, while investments ground to a halt. The entire business sector—both private and *Histadrut*-owned—had a vested interest in restraining wage raises and the extent of employment in the public sector. The government realized that its current policy in the public sector was bound to lead to an even deeper crisis. In order to align the economic processes with the state budget, the new minister acted to reduce government spending as well as private consumption by freezing credit and minimizing basic product subsidies—two moves which caused the recession to deepen. To complete his plan, he had to restore good relations with the *Histadrut* and employers in order to restrain demands for higher wages, in order to reduce government spending and raise the profitability of Israeli exports that suffered greatly over the past months (Interview with Horowitz, in Grinberg, 1985, 1991).

Note that the political economic analysis offered here diverges from traditional economic theories of inflation. Classic economists tend to focus on budgetary deficits ("monetarist" theory) and rising demands ("cost-push" theory). These factors were indeed at work in 1970s Israel, but more than anything else, they reflected a broader politico-economic phenomenon: the uneven balance of power among crucial economic actors—mainly the weakness of the state vis-à-vis private and WS capital, but also strong organized labor among public-sector and professional workers. The government lacked autonomy due to the internal division of state apparatuses between security and treasury under the dual regime, and the interdependency of the *Histadrut-Mapai*-State Vicious Triangle. The political economic conceptualization of inflation suggested here differs from economic theories that explain it in terms of the actor that causes it, be it the government (monetarist) or the workers (cost-push) (Goldthorpe, 1978). The explanation here focuses on the power relations between the state, capital and organized workers, and the extent of the state's autonomous capacity to restrain pressures to increase subsidies, raise wages, and control the value of local currency. Accordingly, like its causes, the solution to inflation is political, and there is no single prescription for carrying it out.[11] It is within this

---

11   Elsewhere (Grinberg, 1999a) I have analyzed the economic stabilization plan in Argentina (1986), which was very similar to the Israeli plan (1985). The difference between the failure in Argentina

context that the *Histadrut*'s actions serve to explain the rising inflation rates since 1967, a process exacerbated by the *Likud*'s rise to power; only when the government secured the *Histadrut*'s cooperation could inflation be halted.[12]

Since 1967, the WS and private corporations (jointly, the business sector) were both interested in higher inflation rates because of the subsidization of capital in the form of non-indexed government loans. It also managed to buttress its position as the employees' representative only among the less powerful sectors of the labor market, while the more powerful employees, organized in national worker councils and professional associations, managed to act independently. This increased the pressures on government spending (capital subsidization and wage increases) without the government reaping the benefits of cooperation by the *Histadrut* or the private employers. This situation was evident even before the *Likud*'s rise to power, during the Alignment government of 1974-1977. As we have seen, these years were characterized by constant internal rifts between the *Histadrut* and government, and the difficulties of the ruling party in both institutions in mediating between them (Harel and Galin, 1978).

When the *Likud* won the elections the *Histadrut* became even less committed to political and economic restraint of inflationary pressures, since it no longer felt responsible for running the state and the national economy, and there was no political space to mediate between them. In addition, it still had the ability to allocate non-indexed loans to business sector employers, not only to the WS firms but also to the private sector. The political economic implications of the *Histadrut*'s peculiar structure—as both workers' representative and big capital owner—and its quasi-state powers vis-à-vis the government and private employers

---

and the success in Israel, I argued, is related to the different political power of the state vis-à-vis crucial economic actors.

[12] This was a crucial insight revealed to me by Professor Michael Bruno in a very sincere interview I had with him, together with my MA supervisor Professor Michael Shalev (Grinberg, 1991). Bruno explained that the failure of *Likud* governments to halt inflation lay in their misunderstanding of the important role of the *Histadrut*, and also that the negotiations with the *Histadrut* were crucial to the success of the economic stabilization program. This explanation is political, and cannot be part of the economic discourse that dissociates markets from politics. In my opinion, the deep understanding of political forces and the conscious attempt to present their actions as professional and a-political is one of the key factors in the incredible success of economists in politics; see John Williamson's "In search for a manual for technopols" (1994). For a sociological analysis of the historical construction of the a-political image of economists, see Fourcade (2009).

is central to understanding hyperinflation in Israel and the political changes from 1980 onwards (Grinberg, 1991).

IV. Powerful Resistance: The 13 Strong Worker Committees

Yigal Horowitz, the new Treasury Minister, shared his plans with the Manufacturers Association and secured their support. To do so, he appointed its chairman, Abraham (Buma) Shavit, as Chairman of the El-Al Board, with the explicit intention of restraining wages and employment in the national carrier. Horowitz announced that El-Al employees were the "compass" to which the rest of the public sector employees were aligned. He planned to threaten El-Al with closure, showing the entire public sector labor force who was the boss. By doing so, he sought to ally himself with the leaders of the public sector in their struggle against high wages that spilled over also into the business sector (interviews with Shavit and Horowitz, in Grinberg, 1985, 1991).

In mid-November 1979 the recession deepened, and factories ran into credit shortage. The Israel Aviation Industries (IAI) announced the impending dismissal of 1,500 workers, while the El-Al Chairman suspended the negotiations for a new collective agreement. At the same time, Horowitz called a press conference to present his new economic plan: eliminating basic product subsidies, freezing up industrial credit, budget cuts, and absolutely no wage increases. This policy was designed to reduce Israel's trade deficit, encourage employees to move from the service to the manufacturing sector, and slow down the inflation (*Yediot Ahronot*, November 4, 18, 19, and 20, 1979). Following the Finance Minister's announcement, basic product prices increased sharply and it was feared that unemployment would reach unsustainable levels. The public reacted with rage, with wild protests in Jerusalem's inner city neighborhoods populated by staunch *Likud* supporters. The demonstrators demanded "money for the poor neighborhoods and not for the settlements."[13] Under huge pressure from the worker committees, particularly in the manufacturing sector, the *Histadrut* leadership de-

---

[13] The reason for these calls was that while the government was cutting its subsidies, it kept expanding its investments in building Jewish settlements in the Occupied Territories (*Yediot Aharonot*, November 20, 1979).

cided to call a general 24-hour strike on November 27 (*Yediot Ahronot*, November 26, 1979). This decision ran counter to the *Histadrut*'s relatively moderate policies, as well as to the interests of the WS. The two other large employers, the government and the private industrialists, immediately joined forces to prevent the strike.

The *Histadrut* found itself trapped in its internal structural contradiction. On the one hand, the disgruntled workers pressured for a general strike, which would probably be a success, while cancelling it could lead to independent protests on the ground coupled with unrest against the *Histadrut*. On the other hand, during the months leading up to the announcement of the strike, the *Histadrut* had managed to forge an alliance with the private industrialists and it expected the new Treasury Minister to renew the government's cooperation with them. A strike under these circumstances was liable to undermine the *Histadrut*'s relationship with both parties.

Under pressure by the government, which blamed the *Histadrut* for planning a "political strike" to serve the opposition, and following an appeal by the industrialists to the Labor Court charging that the *Histadrut* had not declared a labor dispute as required by law, the *Histadrut* backed off (*Yediot Ahronot*, November 27, 1979). The immediate result was that the most powerful worker committees joined forces in what came to be called the "13 Strong Worker Committees Forum" (henceforth, Forum/13) (Grinberg, 1985).

The forces that led the *Histadrut* to announce the strike and later recoil point to its three main structural weaknesses. First, the *Histadrut* became alienated from ordinary workers. It called the strike only after sensing their resentment, and called it off without their consent. The Secretary General cancelled the strike himself, without discussing it in any *Histadrut* elected forum—even the Coordinating Committee was forced to ratify this decision retroactively.

Second, workers were not represented in the *Histadrut* organs. It was ruled by parties, which lent much credence to the claim that this was a partisan strike designed to weaken the *Likud* Government. Delegates to the *Histadrut* Parliament (*Ha'Vaad Hapoel*) and bureaucratic apparatuses were elected on a partisan basis and the Coordinating Committee (its executive body) was run by a coalition of political parties. The *Histadrut* was indeed dominated by the Alignment, with the *Likud* in the opposition, and had no way of refuting the allegation to imply that the *Likud* delegates were against the strike. This was despite the fact that some of the worker councils deeply disappointed by the cancellation of the strike were dominated by *Likud* supporters.

Finally, the Workers' Society's economic interests as an employer made them oppose the strike, at least tacitly, while the two other main employers, the government and the private industrialists were outspoken in their opposition.

In the past, the *Histadrut* usually managed to overcome these inherent contradictions by various methods. However, at the end of 1979 it could no longer do so. All major employers, including WS, wanted to restrain wage increases, while the workers were firmly opposed to that. The source of the *Histadrut*'s historic power was its Achilles' heel in late 1979: the fact that it was the employees' representative and a large employer at the same time.

Unable to mediate between the employees and the employers, the *Histadrut* lost power and control. Its General Secretary, Yeruham Meshel, realized that only a group of employees acting on its own behalf and under its own responsibility could fill the newly created vacuum and represent worker interests (Interview with Yeruham Meshel, in Grinberg, 1991). The heads of the powerful worker committees realized that the *Histadrut* was unable to confront the government and the employers directly as it feared losing state subsidies and undermining its position as the formal representative of all employees in Israel. They also realized that the *Histadrut* feared that the strike would damage WS companies and was not even certain that the employees would go on strike (Interview with Eli Ben-Menahem, in Grinberg, 1985).

The *Histadrut*'s weakness undermined the power of the entire working class. While in the past workers were able to form unions able to open up some political space for representing the workers and negotiating in their name, this space was now in danger of shrinking. The only way to prevent the employees from losing their power was through an independent organization that would counterbalance state power and force it to open up political space for negotiations. This organization would have to represent the employees directly, irrespective of their partisan affiliations, and therefore include committees controlled by both big parties. Finally, in order to focus the struggle against the government, rather than dilute it by combatting all employers across the board, it was important that the organization would be based on worker committees of state-owned firms, rather than on *Histadrut*-owned or private firms. This would appease the *Histadrut* and fill in the vacuum its structure had created by misrepresenting the workers.

Until 1979, the *Histadrut* signed two types of collective wage agreements, one for the business sector and the second for the public sectors. These agreements served a dual purpose, as they provided for wage increases for all employees—including Forum/13 members—while allowing the powerful worker groups to obtain additional industry- and factory-level allowances. In this sense, the Forum spoke for the entire working class, which had a vested interest in empowering the *Histadrut* vis-à-vis the employers. These would ensure minimal wage increases for the weaker employees, but also would enable the stronger workers to gain more. At the end of 1979, the *Histadrut*'s weakness threatened the "compass"—the more powerful worker councils—with downsizing expected in IAI, El-Al and *Histadrut*-owned firms. At the same time, all sectors were threatened with even worse workforce reductions due to the deepening recession.

In addition to unemployment, employees feared wage reductions, not only in the form of erosion caused by inflation, but also in the form of nominal cuts. Israel Electric Corporation (IEC), for example, decided to eliminate its employees' exemption from electricity bills. In response, the employees declared a labor dispute and the government threatened to issue a restraining order to prevent the strike. However, the most prominent arena of worker strife was El-Al: under pressure by the new chairman, the pilots agreed to a 15% wage cut, and Shavit gave the ground crews an ultimatum: they must sign a similar agreement by December 31, or the company would be closed. Several hours before this ultimatum was to expire, the El-Al worker committee convened the heads of most powerful committees, who announced the foundation of a joint Forum to ensure mutual support in future labor disputes. All powerful committees in the public sectors feared that the Finance Minister would deal with them as Shavit was dealing with El-Al. The other committees viewed the labor agreement in El-Al, signed by the pilots, as a bad omen. The threat of dismissal unless an agreement was signed according to the employer's terms could be made in any of other state-owned companies, all the more so since it was Horowitz who had encouraged Shavit to be inflexible (Grinberg, 1991).

The fear of Horowitz's aggressive policy was one of the main motivators for convening Forum/13. Its members were as follows: IAI, IEC, El-Al ground crews, Post-Engineering (the Post and Communication Ministry's telecom department), Israel Broadcasting Authority (IBA), Dead Sea Works (DSW), Airports Authority, Merchant Fleet Officers Union, Longshoremen Union, Israel Ports, Israel Association of General Aviation, and the Israeli Radiographers Union. They deliberately decided to exclude the private industry and *Histadrut* employees, as these were too dependent on the *Histadrut*.

The thirteen members of the forum share the following characteristics:

1. They all represent government employees, mostly in state-owned firms, apart from the radiologists and telecom engineers employed directly by government ministries (Health and Post and Communication, respectively).

2. Most represent manufacturing industries and blue-collar workers, apart from the radiologists and IBA workers. In addition, most are related to central services provided by the government to export industries, including forms of international transportation, utilities such as electricity and telecom, and two large state-owned manufacturing plants—IAI and DSW.

3. Most have industry-level privileged status in wage negotiations, apart from the telecom employees included in the *Histadrut*-government employees' agreement. This means that after signing the public sector Framework Agreement, they have no trade union above them to negotiate wages on their behalf. The committee itself, even when it is a local one, is in charge of industry- and factory-level negotiations. Some of the forum committees are not even included in the Framework Agreements, including the aviators and the two mariner committees.

4. All committees are elected directly rather than on a partisan basis. Six forum committees are local, four are national (IEC, IBA, telecom, and Airports Authority) and three are trade unions (the two mariner councils and the radiologists).

5. Committee members' party affiliation is diverse. Some of them are predominantly Alignment members (IEC, Longshoremen Union), some are *Likud* members (DSW, Airports Authority, and aviators), some are mixed (El-Al, IAI) and others are non-partisan (radiologists and IBA).

6. The employees' wages are average to high. The forum does not represent lower-paid employees such as blue-collar manufacturing or con-

struction workers, but does represent workers with average incomes, such as lower-level longshoremen, telecom engineers and El-Al employees. Finally, IEC and IAI engineers, high-level telecom technicians and merchant fleet officers are among the higher-paid employees in Israel.

7. Because they are employed in government firms, most employee groups represented in the forum have security clearance, and are therefore necessarily Jewish citizens. This acts against the employer's ability to restrain wage demands using the threat of hiring unorganized labor.

Forum/13 main's source of power was the fact that they were essential to local manufacturing and export. This enabled them to threaten the main three employers—the government, private industrialists, and WS. As long as the forum did not challenge the *Histadrut* monopoly as the employees' representative and the economic situation unified the employers in the effort to restrain wage increases, this organization played an invaluable role that the *Histadrut* was no longer able to, which helped to strengthen it indirectly.

According to interviews with Forum/13 leaders and Meshel, despite their image as revolting against the *Histadrut* authority, behind the curtains Meshel supported the Forum and was very proud to claim that he had encouraged them (Interview with Yeruham Meshel, in Grinberg, 1991). The reasons are obvious: Forum/13 resolved the *Histadrut*'s inherent contradictions without having to transform its structure: on the one hand, it provided support of directly elected rank- and-file workers against government policies without requiring changes in the *Histadrut*'s non-representative partisan structure; on the other hand, the *Histadrut* would not have to publicly endorse labor's militant positions. The worker committees were in direct contact with their members and were not committed to the economic interests of WS. Thus, they enabled the *Histadrut* to continue functioning as an organization accountable to the entire economy—above all to WS—as well as the central representative organization of all employees, and was expected to continue cooperating with the government.

In January 1980, when growing resentment in the business sector firms threatened to force the *Histadrut*'s hand again, the Forum came to its rescue: it went on a 24-hour strike in the name of the entire working class in the business sector. Its demands were identical to the *Histadrut*'s: opening up the two Collective Framework Agreements in April 1980, updating the graduated tax scales (to compensate for inflation), maintaining real wage levels, and preventing mass unemployment. However, the Forum's methods were distinctly different: the strike immobilized exports by cutting Israel off from the rest of the world. Forum leaders rejected the *Histadrut*'s appeal to strike one council at a time, each on a different day, so as to leave the *Histadrut* in control of the situation. The Forum strike was very different, and keenly felt. However, it was not designed to achieve any immediate economic objectives, but a political goal: to gain recognition of the Forum as the workers' representative, their independence and power. Indeed, this strike was so effective that the Forum was never required to call another one—threatening to strike sufficed to force the employers to the negotiating table.

The Forum/13 collective action constitutes a very peculiar resistant mo(ve)ment: it did not organize the entire working class, but it balanced the power of the state and employers. The Forum did not demand any institutional changes in the *Histadrut* in order to resolve the structural weaknesses that closed political space to worker representation. Its action empowered the *Histadrut* as a representative of the workers, preventing its traditional tendency to undermine workers' interests. The balancing of the employers' power vis-à-vis the workers and neutralizing the WS interests as employers within the *Histadrut* enabled its leadership to reject the Treasury Minister's wage-freezing policy. In July 1980, new Collective Framework Agreements in the business and public sectors were signed. Two months before, the workers' backing of the *Histadrut* in its confrontation against the employers' and the government's attempt to restrain their wages was manifested in the largest demonstration ever in Israel, when hundreds of thousands of workers thronged the streets of Tel Aviv on May 1, 1980, in a *Histadrut*-organized protest against the government's inflationary policy and intention to restrain wages (*Davar*, May 2, 1980).

V. Elections under Hyperinflation

Forum/13 supported the *Histadrut's* wage demands from the employers, until the signing of the public and business sector Framework Agreements in July 1980. From that point onwards, the forum began seeking improved agreements for its own members, clashed directly with Treasury Minister Horowitz and thwarted a wage restraining Package Deal between the *Histadrut* and the government. When Horowitz saw the *Histadrut*'s inability to control the public sector employees, and realized that his policy of shrinking that sector was going to fail, he attacked the main source of cheap credit for the entire business sector by putting an end to the WS Financial Plan. In October 1980, he revoked the special agreement providing for non-indexed loans from the *Histadrut*'s pension funds—the material basis for the *Histadrut*'s vested interest in inflation (Grinberg, 1991).[14]

Eliminating the non-indexed loans was a crucial political-economic event, a profound structural transformation of state-*Histadrut* relations. In the long run, it was a key factor in the financial collapse of most *Histadrut*-owned firms and organizations dependent on the WS Financial Plan, including *Kupat Holim Clalit* (the *Histadrut*'s HMO), the *Solel Bone* construction giant, the *Koor* conglomerate, and almost all the agricultural settlements. In the short run, the result was Horowitz's dismissal in the run-up to the elections. Once he had made that momentous decision, the *Histadrut* and the private industrialists stopped cooperating with the Treasury Ministry, Forum/13 intensified its wage pressures, and both inflation and recession deepened. Under these circumstances, the ministers in charge of social affairs, headed by David Levi, demanded that Begin dismiss Horowitz before the elections in June 1981, or the *Likud* would be doomed to fail.

It is important to emphasize here that the *Likud*'s major electoral power base was the low *Mizrahi* ethno-class, which had been severely affected by the *Likud* government's economic policy. Despite the government's impressive achievement of signing a peace treaty with Egypt in 1979, enthusiastically supported by the large majority of the population, its opinion poll results were dismal due to its economic policy. The *Histadrut*'s image as a staunch opponent of the *Likud*'s liberal economic policy attracted huge support, and reflected favorably on the Alignment. According to February 1981 opinion polls, the Alignment was expected to win 34 KMs and the *Likud* only 13 (*Yediot Ahronot*, February 27, 1981).

---

14 In a very revealing interview (Grinberg, 1991), Horowitz explained why he cancelled the subsidization of the *Histadrut*'s financial plan. As a matter fact, he argued, he was not Israel's Treasury Minister; the real minister was Yaakov Levinson (the powerful CEO of *Bank Hapoalim*), who allocated the Plan's non-indexed loans. While Horowitz attempted to shrink available credit he was unable to control the subsidized credit allocated by Bank Hapoalim and subsidized by the state.

It was only a matter of time before Horowitz would lose his job. Every ruling party needs a Treasury Minister aware of its need to be reelected, but what made this particular new appointment unique was the short time remaining before the elections, and the complete volte-face demanded of the new minister. Horowitz would forever be remembered as "Yigal—I'm broke," while the new minister, Yoram Aridor, would forever be remembered for having sharply reduced the customs charges, enabling practically every household to afford hitherto expensive electric appliances, including the new Israeli fad—color TV. Forum/13 members and public sector employees as a whole enjoyed a high wage increase. Soon enough, opinion poll trends reversed, and the *Likud* caught up with the Alignment; by June, both parties were expected to win 42 KMs in the next Knesset elections (*Yediot Ahronot*, June 28, 1981). In fact, the Forum/13 resistance movement ended at the moment that Yigal Horowitz was replaced, and the strong public workers were no longer targeted as the "problem" of the economy. In short, high wages were not considered a problem anymore, and the weakness of the business sector workers no longer affected the powerful workers' achievements.

The 1981 elections were salient in Israeli history because of the tribal ethnic hostility between "left" and "right" supporters, and also the expansionist economic policy towards the elections. Apparently, not only was the *Likud*'s economic policy one of the main causes of the running inflation, but it was nigh impossible to bring it to a halt without the Alignment's support. This was due to the *Likud*'s institutional disconnection from the most powerful employers and workers, unlike the Alignment's direct bureaucratic access to both groups through the *Histadrut*. The 1981 elections made these facts clear through the government's unprecedented unilateral capital transfers to the public (to ensure reelection) as well as its incapacity to recollect the money following its slim electoral victory.

Every electoral economy (usually called "political business cycle") assumes that the pre-election expansion would be followed by post-election downsizing, also directed by the government (Ben Porat, 1975; Temkin and Ben Hanan, 1986). However, under the circumstances of the 1981 campaign, the new Treasury Minister could not reverse the financial expansion trend nor frustrate the high expectations for the continuation of his expansive policy. Aridor could find no partners for a restraining wage policy and his package deal suggestions were rejected.

It seemed that the *Histadrut*, the employers, and the powerful workers sought to benefit from the Treasury Ministry's generosity before the elections and refused to help it bring the economy under control later on. Instead of standing its ground, the ministry responded by continuing the expansive policy and backed the banks in their share rigging scheme to keep the stock market booming.

After the *Likud* succeeded to be reelected,[15] the inflation ran amok as a result of the lack of cooperation by the *Histadrut* and the employers, as well as the general public's expectation that nothing would be able to halt it at that point. The government lost all control over prices and wages, and to make matters worse, the economy's shrinkage that was supposed to occur in the aftermath of the elections in a well-planned and graduated manner came abruptly with the crash of bank shares in October 1983. The result of the crash, in addition to Aridor's replacement, was further public mistrust of the government's ability to control the economy: inflation reached a historic high of 466% in 1984.

However, the crisis that characterized the *Likud*'s second term was even broader, including a political crisis that led to Begin's resignation only one month before the stock market crash. Several weeks after completing its evacuation of the Sinai Peninsula as stipulated in its peace accord with Egypt, the government started in June 1982 what would become a prolonged and unsuccessful war in Lebanon. The government did not manage to pull out the troops, and continued casualties were met by mounting protests. Begin finally abdicated a few months after a commission of investigation into the massacre in the Sabra and Shatila refugee camps determined that his Security Minister, Ariel Sharon, would have to resign.[16] The *Likud* nominated as its new Prime Minister the seemingly lackluster Yitzhak Shamir, aiming to block the other, more popular would-be successors: Ariel Sharon, due to his role in the War, and David Levi, the most prominent coopted *Mizrahi* leader.

Despite all the circumstances that played against a *Likud* victory—the economic crisis, the fiasco in Lebanon, and the loss of Begin's

---

15 The results of 1981 Knesset elections were *Likud* 48 seats, Labor 47, National Religious Party 6, *Agudat Israel* 4, *Hadash* 4, *Tehia* 3, *Tami* 3, *Telem* 2, *Shinui* 2, *Ratz* 1.

16 See Schiff and Yaari (1984) or Shiffer (1984) for a detailed account of the war's progression and the Sabra and Shatila massacre. The reader "Lebanon war: Between protest and compliance" provides a more comprehensive review, including sociological, philosophical, and international perspectives (Rosen, 1983).

charismatic leadership—the Alignment failed to win the majority in the 1984 elections. This failure indicates that even after seven years in opposition, the labor movement failed to reassess its historic role, redefine its goals and correct its mistakes. The main reasons for that were the continued centrality of the *Histadrut* and its control of the Alignment on the one hand, and the depth of the *Histadrut*'s economic and organizational crisis due to the *Likud*'s policies on the other. The *Histadrut* was already on a downward slope, it could no longer stand up to the Treasury Ministry as in the previous term, and the ministry's populist policies exposed its inherent contradiction between its role as a labor representative and its economic interests as an employer. It was the weakest workers, most severely hit by the inflation, who were not sufficiently protected by the *Histadrut*. These workers, however, voted for the *Likud*, incited by the tribal hostility that channeled the *Mizrahi* ethno-class against ZLM institutions. Both parties cooperated to close political space to the representation of class and ethnic claims, interests, and identities: the *Histadrut* and the Labor Party by preventing worker representation and both parties by channeling ethno-class tensions to hostile tribal mobilization.

The 1984 elections ended in a stalemate, which was perhaps disappointing for the Alignment but augured well for halting inflation. Neither of the two big parties was able to form a coalition government without the support of two small parties that positioned themselves in between the two big blocks, headed by two former *Likud* ministers who had split from the party after confrontations with its leadership: Yigal Horowitz, ex-Treasury Minister, and Ezer Weitzman, ex-Security Minister. Both parties conditioned their participation in the next coalition on the formation of a national unity government in order to halt inflation and pull out of Lebanon. Having failed as Treasury Minister, Horowitz had long ago concluded that without the *Histadrut*'s help, the economy could not be brought under control. To ensure the *Histadrut*'s cooperation, the Alignment had to be included in the government (Interview with Horowitz, in Grinberg, 1985, 1991).

However, the Alignment's presence in the government still did not ensure the *Histadrut*'s control over the employees. The main threat to any new economic plan was workers' resistance undermining the government's ability to implement it. In order to overcome the expected worker resistance the *Histadrut*'s cooperation was vital (Interview with

Michael Bruno, in Grinberg, 1991). As you may recall, the *Histadrut* did not represent the workers directly, and its officials were elected every four years on a partisan basis. Its collaboration with the government in restraining workers' demands in a period of hyperinflation would have endangered the Alignment's historic control of the *Histadrut*. Therefore, although Shamir and Alignment leader Shimon Peres did form a national unity government in September 1984,[17] it took them another ten months to implement an economic stabilization plan. The waiting period until after the *Histadrut* elections in May 1985 was characterized by tripartite (Government-*Histadrut*-EOCB) cooperation in signing and implementing package deals freezing prices and wages, with no budget cuts or exchange rate freezing. Although these deals demonstrated the ability of the three major players to cooperate in controlling prices and wages, they also demonstrated that without the additional monetary and fiscal steps required, inflation would run even wilder after the freezing periods expired. Only after the reelection and legitimization of the *Histadrut* leadership, could the Economic Plan be implemented. This historical fact—the ten-month delay in implementing the plan, despite its urgency—emphasizes the deterrent power of worker collective action, and the central role of the *Histadrut*'s cooperation in restraining workers resistance. In 1980, Forum/13 prevented the *Histadrut*'s leadership from cooperating with Yigal Horowitz; now he demanded a government with the Labor Party in order to secure the *Histadrut*'s cooperation. This was the meaning, purpose, and content of the National Unity Government.

VI. Counter-Mo(ve)ment: The Economic Stabilization Plan

The National Unity Government (hereafter NUG) was formed as a coalition between the "left" and "right," with the Labor Party and *Likud* at the center, together with other, smaller parties, that altogether represented 105 KMs.[18] The agreement was unique due to the even election results:

---

17   According to the rotation agreement between the parties, Peres would be Prime Minister during the first two years of the term, and replaced by Shamir in 1986.
18   The rotation agreement was signed between Labor and *Likud* parties, each of the representing a block of parties: the Labor block included Labor (44 seats), *Shinui* (3), *Yahad* (3) and *Ometz* (1), the *Likud* block included *Likud* (41) *Shas* (4) National Religious Party (4) *Tami* (1) *Agudat Israel* (2) and

the offices of Prime Minister and Minister of Foreign Affairs were to be rotative, with Shimon Peres at Prime Minister Yitzhak Shamir as Minister of Foreign Affairs in the first two years, and vice versa during 1986-1988. The Ministry of Security will be headed by Yitzhak Rabin (Labor) and the Ministry of Treasury Yitzhak Modai (*Likud*).

The NUG, headed by Shimon Peres (1984-1986), had two major achievements: pulling the IDF out of Lebanon[19] and reducing the inflation rate from an annual level of 466% in July 1985 to 25% in March the next year. This was achieved thanks to the government's resoluteness and success in forcing both the workers and employers to accept the plan. Further accomplishments of the Emergency Economic Stabilization Plan (EESP) were significant reduction of the trade balance deficit and the creation of a budgetary surplus. EESP built upon the package deals which, although failing to stop the inflation, created favorable conditions to halt inflation later on. In addition to freezing wages and prices, the government decided to devalue the local currency, which eroded the real wages and reduced the budgetary deficit.

In mid-May 1985—the very day the elections to the *Histadrut* were held, and this was no coincidence—a government team convened to work out EESP's operational details. The team, headed by General Director of the Ministry of Treasury Immanuel Sharon, included the renowned Professors Michael Bruno and Ethan Berglas, the Prime Minister's advisor Amnon Neubach, and Mordechai Frenkel of the Bank of Israel's research department (Patinkin, 1993). Before completing its work, the team initiated a series of preliminary restraining steps, which shortly paved the way for more drastic moves. Less than a week after the team started working, the government increased the VAT (Value Added Tax) by 2%, doubled the foreign travel tax from 150 to 300 dollars, and also raised several purchase taxes. In addition, the government restrained its own budget by freezing employee recruitment and new contracts in the government service, and denying credit (*Yediot Ahronot*, May 20, 1985(. A week later, the government raised the price of petrol and of basic products by eliminating its subsidies (*Yediot Ahronot*, May 28, 1985).

Morasha (2). In the opposition remained the leftist *Hadash* (4) and *Ratz* (3), the Progressive list for Peace (2), and the extreme right *Tehia-Tzomet* (5) and Kahana (1).

19 The withdrawal of the IDF from Lebanon was not complete, because it still maintained its control of the south through a pro-Israeli local militia called the Army of South Lebanon. It was only in May 2000 that a complete withdrawal took place.

The prices of all other products, which had been frozen for two months by the March 1985 Package Deal, were raised by 14% on a single day. In June, it almost seemed as though the entire economic system—prices, labor agreements and government fiscals—was on the verge of collapse.

The private employers, briefed by Immanuel Sharon on the government's intention to implement a comprehensive plan, announced their retreat from the package deals and began pressuring for further price increases in order to enter the plan period under better conditions. This was achieved after the extreme step of calling a lockout strike in the food industry (*Yediot Ahronot*, June 2, 3, 16, 17, 20, 21, and 25, 1985).Two days into the strike that paralyzed production the government caved in and agreed to raise food prices, and four days later, it began to authorize price increases for other industrial goods.

The country's fiscal condition was also critical. Its foreign exchange reserves, after having dwindled over a period of several months, fell by 25% in June, to a mere $1.5 billion.[20] Due to the running inflation, the taxation system also crumbled, worsening the budgetary deficit. From the government's point of view, this was the right time to act.

The EESP team was united in its view that the plan must solve the two fundamental problems, inflation and the balance of payment, together. To do so, the state budget had to be cut, combined with a large one-time devaluation, immediately followed by freezing the main relative prices—wages, exchange rate, goods, and the interest rate. The salaried workers would have to be compensated, but their compensation would be at a relatively low rate, so that wages would become stabilized at a level lower than they had been, providing the industrialists and exporters with extra incentive in addition to the devaluation and price increases. The planned wage erosion level was 10% compared to July 1985, a level which was already quite low, but in fact the wage erosion turned out to be deeper (Grinberg, 1991; Bruno, 1986).

One of the main disputes within the EESP team revolved around the exchange rate stabilization issue. Those who supported an exchange

---

20 These figures were considered a real danger to the state due to Israel's dependency on foreign currency for the import of crucial raw materials as oil. However, there is evidence that the economic team consciously manipulated the figures aiming to exaggerate the crisis and force the political echelons to adopt their plan (Interview with Michael Bruno, in Grinberg, 1991).The need to fabricate a crisis in order to convince the politicians later became one of the consensual suggestions to technopols (see Williamson, 1994: 20)

rate freeze—headed by Professor Bruno, whose victory became clear to all in 1986, when he was appointed Bank of Israel governor—believed the government should stop using devaluation to protect the private employers against the employees' wage increases, as it was too costly for the country. In other words, part of the plan to halt inflation was to force the employers to confront employee demands or pay the price out of their own pocket. The opponents of absolute exchange rate freeze wanted to assure the employers that, should wages rise, the exchange rate would be adjusted by 5%. They believed that an absolute freeze would reduce export profitability too sharply, deepening the recession, and the country would be better off if it continued protecting the employers against their workers.

However, the government prepared to confront the workers by itself. Prior to its decision to adopt the EESP on July 1, 1985, Prime Minister Peres and *Likud* Minister of Finance Yitzhak Modai held a series of meetings with the leaders of the *Histadrut* after their reelection, but failed to secure their agreement to the plan. In order to force it on the *Histadrut*, and particularly the employees, Modai decided to let it be known that the government intended to enforce the plan using emergency decrees. When this became known, the decrees themselves became the focus of the dispute with the *Histadrut*, and the details of the EESP itself were largely forgotten, as we shall see below.

These were the principles of the EESP as presented to the government before it made its final decision on June 30, 1985:[21]

a) *Timescale*. The program was to last one year, with an initial emergency period of three months.

b) *Goals*. Rapid reduction of inflation, increase in foreign currency reserves, and improvement of the balance of payments. This would lay the foundations for renewed economic growth and restructuring.

c) *Measures*. A 20%, devaluation, cuts in subsidies of basic products and the budget, coupled with freezing of wages, prices, and exchange and interest rates.

d) *Financing*. A budget cut of 750 million dollars, reduction of manpower in the public sector, and of subsidies on production and capital.

e) *Rate of Exchange*. Should wages rise beyond the desired level, the

---

21 This is Neucbach's (1986) version of the plan.

exchange rate would be adjusted proportionally. Exchange rate insurance for exporters will be suspended.

f) *Wages.* Real wages will be eroded by 10%. Compensation for inflation will be arranged with the *Histadrut*. COLA will be suspended during the stabilization period. Wages of public sector workers will be reduced by 3%.

g) *Prices.* Permission will be granted to raise prices by 15-20%, followed by a freeze.

h) *Capital market reform.* Gradually, non-negotiable bonds would become negotiable. To begin with, this principle would be applied to career advancement funds and savings programs. No more non-negotiable bonds would be issued and bonds issued in the future would be index-linked for a period of two years only.

i) *Interest.* The Bank of Israel would intervene only in the second month, should interest rates exceed 25% per month.

j) *Dynamics.* In the first stage, fixing the nominal wages should ensure a steady rate of exchange and halt inflation. That would contribute to the budget and make it possible to reduce taxes. This move would help stabilize real wages and the transition to an economy without price control.

k) *Evaluation.* The real test would be the curbing of inflation and growth of foreign currency reserves in the coming three months. This stabilization would be a precondition for renewal of growth, which would require a gradual disengagement of the government from the capital market.

The government's operative decisions contained several revisions compared to the original plan submitted by the team. The capital market reform is not mentioned in the government's resolutions, nor is the suspension of the exchange rate insurance arrangement. The formal devaluation rate was indeed 18.8%, but considering the fluctuations over the last preceding days, it was actually 25%.

The EESP was met with severe criticism from within the government and opposed by most *Likud* ministers. Its most outspoken critic was David Levi, who argued that the government had no moral authority to decide on such a plan. Minister Levi's position reinforced the opposition in the *Histadrut*, where a cross-party coalition was formed against the plan. However, it seems that the very fact that the *Likud* was in the government contributed to preventing a much more virulent opposition to the plan, since popular resentment had no significant representation in the opposition capable of threatening the government. The *Histadrut* did express some of that resentment, but also played a key role in the plan's success, precisely because it criticized it while at the same time cooperating with the government. The employees had good reasons to oppose the EESP: their wages had already been eroded, and further erosion was to be expected due to the elimination of basic product subsidies, with compensation already promised to be low.

Before the government ended its deliberations, the *Histadrut* leaders convened its parliament (*Va'ad hapoel*) and called to convene an extraordinary meeting of the central committee to fight the EESP. When the committee met, the *Histadrut* leaders were already well aware of EESP's serious implications for the employees, but still tried to keep matters calm by passing a moderate resolution: to prepare all the worker committees for the struggle over the next few days, and convene them on July 4. This moderate resolution was taken despite widespread calls for an immediate general strike. The Chairman of the powerful IEC Workers Committee promised the disgruntled workers that "the strong committees will fight for the weak"; in other words, he wanted to remind them that in the past the very threat by Forum/13 to strike was enough to resist any anti-labor government policies. However, the resentment was so intense that pressure from below forced the *Histadrut* to call a general strike immediately following the government's formal announcement of the plan. The result was that the entire economy went on strike on July 2—the largest strike in Israel's history (*Haaretz*, July 3, 1985). Having failed to prevent it, the *Histadrut* leaders pretended they had initiated it.

The general strike and continued threats by the worker councils placed the *Histadrut* in a strong starting position for negotiating with the government. General Secretary Israel Keisar made a series of sophisticated moves designed to channel the workers' rage instead of allowing the emergence of a resistance movement that could develop into a revolt against his cooperative attitude. One of his original stratagems to avoid de-legitimization of the *Histadrut* due to its other hat as an employer was his announcement that the WS would pay the cost-of-living allowance subject to the wage agreement, and as stipulated in the EESP. He also renewed the alliance with the heads of the powerful workers committees, but this time they were to collaborate in the open, directly with Keisar, neutralizing the Forum/13 independent organization. Thus for example, the IEC Committee (the one most committed to the Labor and *Histadrut* leadership and the one which benefitted most from their differential power) declared a labor dispute and immediately went on a slowdown strike, helping to subordinate the other powerful committees to the *Histadrut*'s central committee and to prevent a general strike of Forum/13. Following this move, the *Histadrut* ordered the IBA workers to shut down Israel's public TV channel (the only one broadcasting at that time) on the very day and hour when Prime Minister Peres was to go on air and present EESP to the public. Thus, following the July 2 one-day strike forced upon the *Histadrut* from below, it quickly managed to regain central control of the workers by way of open cooperation with the powerful worker committees, which went on separate strikes, whether independently of or by direct orders from the anti-EESP *Histadrut* Central Committee.

An additional factor that contributed to the *Histadrut*'s ability to contain worker resistance and remain in control of the situation was its old partner, the Manufacturers Association. The latter attacked the government's policy of enforcing EESP with emergency decrees and publicly supported the *Histadrut*'s demands that EESP be revised by way of negotiation and the revocation of emergency decrees. They began discussing joint proposals with the *Histadrut* and agreements on compensating the workers for their wage erosion in the private sector. In other words, by 1985 the employers and powerful worker committees—the *Histadrut*'s main partners since 1977—were still its main allies against the government. The only thing that changed was their weakening vis-à-vis the government due to the cancellation of the WS Financial Plan in 1980, and the broad NUG coalition backing the program.

Due to the severe fiscal and monetary crisis, the government acted autonomously, regardless of potential backlash affecting the main powerful groups.[22] The state's autonomy was made possible thanks to the availability of the professional and authoritative team of planners headed by Immanuel Sharon, the broad bipartisan political backing of the government, and the financial support by the US government. The latter collaborated with Sharon's team by pressuring the government to adopt the EESP and by granting it a one-time gift of $1.5 billion—called

---

22   For a discussion of the concept of State autonomy see Skocpol, Rueschmeier and Evans (1985).

a "safety net"—to enable it to avoid devaluation under pressure by the exporters (Interview with Michael Bruno, in Grinberg, 1991; Maman and Rosenhek, 2011). Just as important, the US annual loan became a grant, relieving the Israeli government from the burden of annual dollar-denominated debts. Israel began to receive $3 billion every year to enable it to counter exchange rate pressures (Shalev, 1992). The opposition to the EESP by the *Histadrut*, the powerful workers, the employers and some *Likud* ministers did not prevent the implementation of the plan but rather strengthened it by leading to negotiations over well-defined revisions, in other words, by opening up a political space for mediation, which ultimately was very useful to legitimize the implementation of the plan.

The strongest pressure the government had to face, however, was not employee demands for wage compensation—except, perhaps, for the prolonged nurses' strike in 1986—but the exporters' pressure to devalue the currency. Several months after the implementation of the EESP, it became clear that wages in the business sector rose more than in the public sector, since the employers expected the government to continue devaluating in order to erode the wages. It then turned out, however, that the new Bank of Israel Governor, Michael Bruno, intended to hold fast and keep the exchange rate constant. This policy, combined with a relatively high interest rate, caused many companies to go bankrupt, particularly in the agriculture and construction industries. And yet, despite the bankruptcies, the government successfully resisted pressures to devaluate the currency (Bruno and Piterman, 1987). Here, the role played by Bruno was critical, now not only as an expert consultant, but as the powerful Central Bank Governor (Maman and Rosenhek, 2011).

The most dramatic corporate collapses were experienced by the entities formerly dependent on the WS subsidized Financial Plan: *Solel Bone, Koor, Hasne* (insurance), the *Kibbutz* Movement, the collective agricultural communities (*Moshavim*) and the *Histadrut*'s HMO. These organizations suffered more than others from the high interest rate, because ever since 1980 they had been forced to return huge loans, originally taken without indexation, and to refinance them by the now expensive loans. (Interview with Horowitz, Grinberg, 1985, 1991) The extent of their financial woes was only revealed when the inflation was brought to a halt, because their balance sheets had been concealing this situation until then.

CHAPTER SIX

According to the political-economic analysis suggested here, the collapse of the *Histadrut* related economic organizations once inflation was stopped was the flip side of the state's regained autonomy. Inflation was a manifestation of the state lack of autonomy because it was the result of the state's growing inability to withstand subsidization demands by powerful stakeholder groups. The state's strengthening thanks to the unity government and the US financial support which enabled it to bring inflation to a halt debilitated WS, and later on the *Histadrut* as a fulcrum of the old political economy. EESP's resounding success has had far-reaching consequences for both Israel's economic structure and its politics. (Grinberg, 1995a; 2010; Shafir and Peled, 2000, 2002; Ram, 2008)

VII. Conclusion

The *Likud* government's first term in office surprised everyone. Politically, it made much more progress than the previous Alignment governments, and signed a peace treaty with Egypt involving the complete evacuation of the occupied Sinai Peninsula. In the economic sphere, on the other hand, its liberalization policy failed miserably, and the economy found itself struggling with hyperinflation. The political achievement of peace with Egypt was not enough to compensate for the economic crisis, and the *Likud* just barely achieved reelection in 1981 thanks to its unprecedented "electoral economy" campaign.

In its second term, the *Likud* government found itself in even more dire straits as its political credit ran out following a failed military campaign and three years of bloody occupation in Lebanon (1982-85). Economically, it found no partners to restrain hyperinflation and could not prevent the stock market from crashing. Worse, the stock market crash failed to bring inflation to a halt, and it reached a historic high in 1984.

Despite Israel's deteriorating economic and political situation, the Alignment failed to regain its strength and become a credible alternative for disgruntled voters, and the 1984 elections ended in a stalemate. Paradoxically, it was the NUG forced upon the two parties that carried out the profound structural reform required to implement the WC recommended structural adjustment reforms, turning Israel into a neoliberal economy, previously expected from the *Likud* government in

1977. The NUG put an end to the subsidization pressures by various stakeholder groups and secured its position as the exclusive manager of economic affairs. This meant empowering the Treasury Ministry and the Bank of Israel (Maman and Rosenhek, 2011) to take economic decisions regardless of other ministries' interests (particularly the Ministry of Security), or of partisan interests, not to mention other stakeholders.

This belated structural reform weakened the pressure groups, and these began to focus on narrower interests. However, the main accomplishment of the NUG was that it split the unified anti-government front formed by the *Histadrut*, the employers and the powerful worker groups. The *Histadrut* firms were no longer subsidized, and together with the cut in the security budget, this completed the long-term structural adjustment. The NUG managed to do so thanks to the support of the two main political partners, who could now back the Ministry of Treasury in unpopular policies without risking their political future. In fact, the two big parties were excluded from economic deliberations since 1985, turning the economic policy-making process into a matter for "objective" experts or technocrats (what Williamson, 1994, calls "technopols"), within the framework of a discourse that ignore the moral, social, and political aspects of the economic policy.

Although the key processes discussed in this chapter—the building of state autonomy by weakening the *Histadrut* and the de-politicization of the economy—were completed during the term of the NUG, they could not have taken place without the prior seven years of *Likud* rule. It was the *Likud* rule that dismantled the state relative embedded autonomy,[23] and consequently drove the economy into a crisis that required immediate and extreme action. Although the *Histadrut* initially grew stronger under the *Likud* as an organization confronting the state and representing the government-subsidized stakeholder groups, including the private capitalists, it eventually lost its lifeline when the non-indexed loans were eliminated in October 1980. Since then the *Histadrut* went on a downward spiral, with only the running inflation concealing the depth

---

23 For the concept of embedded autonomy, see Evans (1995). Successful state autonomy was secured thanks to its institutional connections with various class interests of capital and workers. This autonomy was limited by the internal split of state apparatuses between the Treasury and Security establishment, which facilitated private interests to penetrate the state. However, prior to the *Likud* ascent to power autonomy was relatively maintained thanks to the Labor Party close relations with the *Histadrut*, the security establishment, and employer organizations.

of its financial woes. Therefore, in 1981-84 it could no longer act as an aggressive opposition capable of mobilizing the masses, and this weakness was also manifested in the Alignment's failure to win the 1984 elections despite the *Likud*'s failure to deal with the country's economic and political crises.

The expected long-term consequence of the stabilization plan was a far-reaching structural change: the government's exclusion from the capital market, a more flexible labor market, privatization of government-owned corporations and public services, shrinking of the public sector and of the security budget, etc. These changes were in line with global economic trends and the goals of WC (Williamson, 1994; Filc, 2004; Ram, 2008; Maman and Rosenhek, 2011). However, the most far-reaching change was the collapse of the political-economic institutional complex constructed by ZLM as a result of the EESP implemented by the Labor Party. This collapse, combined with the dual regime that facilitated the divide-and-rule of the working class, prevented the emergence of new political actors able to represent the working class in the political arena. The autonomy of the state and the bureaucratic power concentrated in the hands of Treasury Ministry "technopols" led to the exclusion of political parties from the formulation of economic policy, now seen as a "professional" endeavor.

The implementation of the neoliberal reform that weakened Forum/13 was a reaction to the powerful position of strong workers in the public sector, among other important factors, as exposed during the resistance moment in 1980. The new neoliberal economic policy represented, in this sense, the most important counter-mo(ve)ment supported by both cartel parties that facilitated state institutional autonomy. Undoubtedly, when Forum/13 was organized in December 1979, its leaders could not foresee the long-term disastrous consequences for them. At that time, the *Histadrut*'s powerful position was in danger due to the government's threat to cut its subsidies. The lack of direct representation of workers in the *Histadrut*, its economic interests as a major employer and its political structure as a quasi-state ruled by the Labor Party were its downfall. In the discussions preceding the establishment of Forum/13, the worker leaders considered another option: an umbrella organization of trade unions and worker committees, representing all employees with no partisan affiliation and no linkage to WS (Interviews with Eli Ben-Menachem and Yoram Overkowitz, in Grinberg, 1985,

1991). However, this far-reaching option was subsequently dropped in favor of an option which resolved the *Histadrut*'s short-term difficulties but doomed it in the long run. Why did Forum/13 opt to save the *Histadrut*'s obsolete colonial structure instead of building a new worker organization, independent of partisan rule and WS capitalist interests?

According to my analysis, the *Histadrut*'s non-representative structure allowed the powerful worker committees considerable freedom of action and autonomy, and the ability to secure wage increases thanks to their strong position in the labor market. Reorganizing the entire working class would have also meant taking responsibility for the majority of salaried workers, who were weakened by the dual economy due to the competition with non-citizen Palestinians. Creating an umbrella organization for all Israeli workers was thus a bit too much for the powerful worker committees, because it meant challenging the dual economy that empowered them in the labor market. This was a political project that worker committees did not tend to lead because their main responsibility was towards their own members and their direct interests.

Such a political project could only have been designed by a political elite aiming to challenge the *Histadrut*'s traditional structure, the party controlling it, and the dual regime that weakened the majority of the workers. However, all worker parties benefitted from the *Histadrut*'s subsidization and jobs in its apparatus, and therefore actively maintained the quasi-state structures. The long-term implications of the workers' structural weakness and the absence of an alternative political leadership able to represent them were twofold: (1) the bolstering of state autonomy; and (2) the complete disappearance of organized opposition by workers balancing the joint power of private capital and the autonomous state. In other words, the counter-mo(ve)ment eventually closed down political space to collective worker identities and demands, and left them too divided and weak to face the powerful Treasury Ministry officials who served the empowered private capital. The unintended effect of the Forum/13 resistance mo(ve)ment was the most desirable political outcome for neoliberal economic reformers.

The cooperation of the powerful committees with the *Histadrut* leadership in order to prevent worker revolt against the EESP in 1985 is telling: in effect, they dug their own grave. The concept of political space helps us understand how the strength of workers in the labor market coupled with their lack of political representation proved disastrous for

CHAPTER SIX

them. The *Histadrut* was able to manipulate and prevent the workers' resistance to the neoliberal economic plan precisely because it was a political organization and could negotiate in the name of the workers, closing political space for their autonomous representation. The critical failure of Forum/13 was that their powerful position prevented them from realizing that the weakness of the working class as a whole could also weaken the organization. The absence of effective political elites committed to the working class independently of the *Histadrut*'s bureaucratic conservative interests was thus the key failure of the working class, but also of Israeli politics as a whole.

The 1984 elections[24] reflected the new structure of the political arena, which replaced the one-party monopoly of the 1950s and 60s with a "cartel" controlling a huge majority in the Knesset (Arian 1999). The two big parties were able to mobilize hostile identities of "left" and "right", the two major tribes that condensed class, ethnicity and religion and channeled their fears and anger to polarized tribes. Almost the entire repertoire of distortion was used by these parties, and the disconnection between patterns of mobilization and real state politics was demonstrated by the fact that immediately after one of the most hostile campaigns in the history of both parties, in 1984 they managed to collaborate for six years in a national unity government, until its unexpected breakdown in 1990 (see Chapter 7).

Without any viable political alternative to the cartel, and in view of its politically conservative tendencies, the Palestinians, who were the only element in Israel that did not benefit from any of the changes discussed above and was completely excluded politically and economically discriminated against, took to the streets. The new economic policies publicly exposed the fact that the Israeli/Palestinian dual regime could not function as a real neoliberal free market system so long as the Palestinian workers and producers were subjected to military rule. The next chapter analyzes their own resistance mo(ve)ment, the First Intifada.

---

24 Although the tribal polarization made its first appearance in 1977, and was key to the 1981 electoral campaign, it was only after the charismatic Begin retired that the intensive institutionalization of the cartel of tribal polarization became evident.

7.
1987-1993 — THE INTIFADA:
THE PALESTINIAN RESISTANCE MO(VE)MENT[1]

I. INTRODUCTION

The Israeli polity saw two major structural changes during the post-colonial era: the creation of the State of Israel in 1948 and the institutionalization of the dual democratic/ military regime after 1967. Despite these two tremendous transformations in terms of population, economy, territory and bureaucracies, the colonial Zionist Labor Movement (ZLM) proved strong enough to maintain its institutional structure and power. The only long-term political development occurred gradually, with the transition from a monopoly of a single ruling party to a bipartisan "left/right cartel" (see Chapter 5) made up of two Zionist party blocks. Although these two blocks competed for power, tribal channeling of polarized hostile feelings closed political space to new actors, while in fact both implemented similar economic policies and supported the dual regime (Ben Porath, 1982; Grinberg, 1991, 2010). The ruling Labor Alignment, in cooperation with the *Histadrut* and the security establishment, institutionalized the dual regime designed to maintain control of the economy and population on both sides of the Green Line separating sovereign Israel from the Occupied Territories. The Labor Movement ideology, however, was unequipped to legitimize the military occupation or reassert the state's institutional autonomy after 1967. The *Likud* government elected for the first time in 1977 was able to legitimize the occupation but unable to control the economy due to the lack of state autonomy and its incapacity to articulate economic interests, which became its most critical obstacle (see Chapter 6).

It is therefore no coincidence that precisely as a result of the state's newly established autonomy in 1985, in the context of profound eco-

---

[1] This chapter is based on my research published under the title *Politics and violence in Israel/Palestine* (Grinberg, 2010).

nomic and political crises (hyperinflation and the aftermath of the First Lebanon War), the two parties of the dominant cartel became weakened vis-à-vis the state technopols. The National Unity Government's (NUG, 1984-1990) neutralization of the traditional hostility between the two mythological parties enabled the state bureaucracy to act autonomously without any significant differences between the two parties. Shimon Peres (Labor party), as Prime Minister (1984-1986), dealt the worst blows to the *Histadrut* and its firms, ultimately weakening his own party in the process.[2]

Evidently, the policies of the two blocks, particularly when in power together, were not as different as experienced by their constituents on election days. The real decisions were not made by the voters or representative party organs, but were rather dictated by circumstances and bureaucracies. In that sense, the Israeli imagined democracy could never be materialized (Grinberg, 1999). Before 1967 a transition process to democracy started with the working class resistance mo(ve)ment and the empowerment of the middle and upper classes, but it was reversed by the institutionalization of the dual democratic/military regime (Grinberg, 1993, 2008). Since 1967, political space for mediation between civil society and state was closed by political actors who carefully manipulated national myths to mobilize social groups without actually representing their interests, identities, and political views (Shapiro, 1996).

The actors in the political field were exposed as unable to resolve the country's problems and as the "left/right" cartel waned, two new autonomous forces emerged. The first was a vibrant civil society in the form of protest movements against the Lebanon War and class struggles against the economic policies. The second was the state's autonomous bureaucracies—most notably the Bank of Israel and the technocrats in the Ministry of Treasury (see Grinberg, 1991; Maman and Rosenhek, 2011). The specific role of political parties in democratic processes—to act as a bridge between civil society and the state and represent new ideas, agendas and identities—was not fulfilled.[3] However, the shrink-

---

2   I thank Shaike Gavish (general manager of Koor) for this insight in an interview in 1988 (Grinberg, 1991). He explained that only a leader of the Labor party could dismantle the Workers Society, exactly as only the *Likud* leader could withdraw from Sinai and make peace with Egypt. His point was that they faced no serious opposition to their policies.
3   The combined power of *Likud* and Labor in the Knesset fell from 95 delegates in 1981 to 85 in

ing of political space was manifested clearly by the formation of the NUG which was detached from the Israeli civil society and crucially, prevented the opening of political space to the violently oppressed Palestinian civil society.

This chapter will analyze the opening of political space by Palestinian resistance in the Occupied Territories, demanding recognition of their legitimate claims, representation and negotiations. I will show that the Palestinian resistance mo(ve)ment succeeded in opening political space both for recognition and representation due to the demarcation of borders and a balance of power, and immediately opened political space also to class, ethnic, and civil society claims within sovereign Israel. It was the political failure to synchronize and coordinate the three political arenas (within either sovereign Israel or the Occupied Territories (OT) as well as between them) that ultimately led to the violent closure of political space in the three arenas.

II. The Intifada Resistance Mo(ve)ment

In the two and a half years ever since the inflation was halted, Israel's economy became stabilized and the NUG held fast. However, the growth promised by neo-liberal theory to follow stabilization never came. Instead, a popular Palestinian uprising, or Intifada, broke out, with massive demonstrations against the military government, accompanied by attempts to break free of the economic dependency on Israel by disrupting the exchange of workers and goods. Hence the resulting stagnation in the Israeli economy was not attributed to the economic plan, but to the inevitable "costs of the Intifada."

Undoubtedly, economic hardship was one of the main causes of the Intifada,[4] which broke out in December 1987, caused by the recession in Israel and the Gulf countries. It was pushed by the poorest elements in the refugee camps, who often forced the shopkeepers to strike and contribute to the national struggle.[5] Two additional contextual factors were

---

    1984, and has continued falling ever since.
4   After October 2000 this was renamed the First Intifada. Elsewhere, I have analyzed both events as diametrically opposed, despite their misleadingly similar names (Grinberg, 2010, 2013a).
5   For more on the First Intifada, see Gilbar and Sesser (1992); A. Shalev (1990); Nassar and Heacock (1990); Schiff and Ya'ari (1990).

related to the lack of political space for the Palestinians in the OT, not only vis-à-vis the State of Israel but also within the PLO. First, the IDF's success in removing the PLO offices from Beirut to Tunis—far away from Israel and the West Bank—was a key element in the uprising. The feeling that the PLO was incapable of coordinating a national struggle from across the Mediterranean galvanized the popular uprising. Second, the lack of any political initiative for peace from the Israeli side and the expansion of the Jewish settlements at the heart of the West Bank also contributed to a general sense of despair.[6]

Civil society mobilization against the background of hopelessness wasn't new in the OT. After the signing of the 1978 Camp David Accords with Egypt, which would eventually lead to the peace treaty between the two countries, the IDF attempted to impose a civil administration aiming to unilaterally implement the so-called "autonomy plan" rejected by the PLO. In order to confront IDF plans, an autonomous Palestinian civil society began to emerge, organizing trade unions, women's and students' organizations, youth movements and national committees during 1980-81.[7] Opposition to the unilateral Israeli imposition of civil administration fuelled a non-violent resistance movement (Younis, 2000). This civil society mobilization gained prominence especially after a cease-fire agreement signed indirectly between Israel and the PLO in Lebanon in July 1981, because the agreement did not include the Palestinian struggle against military occupation in the OT.[8] For almost one year, no violent struggle against the occupation took place, and almost all protests took the form of non-violent civil resistance (Younis, 2000).

This period of autonomous organization and mobilization of Palestinian civil society came to an abrupt end in June 1982 with the occupation of Southern Lebanon by the IDF and its siege of Beirut. The war and the ensuing three years of occupation of Southern Lebanon formed the immediate political context for understanding the Israeli reaction to the Intifada. Two main consequences of the war were particularly relevant to the outbreak of the Intifada. The first was the PLO's inability to attack

---

6   On the atmosphere of despair among the Palestinians on the eve of the Intifada, see Kimmerling and Midgal (1999: 222-32).

7   On the Intifada's organizational basis, see Luckman and Beinin (1990); Nassar and Heacock (1990); and Schiff and Ya'ari (1990).

8   The cease fire agreement included only the mutual firing in the North of Israel, namely Israeli air attacks in Lebanon and PLO Katyusha rocketing of the Galilee (Schiff and Ya'ari, 1984)

Israel directly due to the distant location of its headquarters in North Africa. This situation empowered the Palestinian civil society in the OT with its non-violent resistance strategy. The second consequence was the growing criticism within Israeli civil society regarding the use of the IDF not for purely defensive purposes but for the offensive purpose of foreign intervention indirectly designed to maintain the occupation and expand the settlements in the OT.

The Intifada was organized and directed by local civil society leadership and political parties. Its objective was limited: to push the Israelis out of the OT, not out of all Palestine. The occupied population sought self-rule, even at village and town level, with soldiers and Jewish settlers kept out. Economic independence through boycotting of Israeli products was part of this strategy, and soon enough all Israelis felt the economic impact of the Intifada. Civil right organizations that reacted by criticizing military repression and upholding liberal principles were supported by relatively broad sectors of civil society and media opinion leaders (Ezrahi, 1997; Peled and Shafir, 2002).

The Palestinian strategy demarcated the physical boundaries of the demand for independence: the boundaries of the dual regime, which separated the democratic sovereign state from the militarily occupied population. The distance from what came to be known as PLO Tunis, on the one hand, and the hatred against the occupation on the other enabled a process of nation building. This process was characterized by the formation of a differentiated Palestinian internal political space of representation and articulation, a space demarcated by the boundaries of the West Bank and Gaza Strip, whose delineation was facilitated by the confrontation and counterbalancing challenge against the IDF.

At first, the Intifada was purely about popular protest: men, women and children demonstrated, threw rocks and Molotov cocktails and went on strike in direct response to unfolding events, under the instructions of an underground central command (Younis, 2000; Nassar and Heacock, 1990). The low level of violence used in the demonstrations is exactly what was defined here as resistance; it was the necessary level to get recognition, but not too much violence that might be interpreted as terror by the Israeli political and military elites and legitimize the escalation of violent repression. The Intifada claimed a political space in a clearly defined area outside the borders of sovereign Israel, and represented an anti-colonial struggle aimed at kicking the IDF out of the

OT. The demarcation of the borders of resistance, combined with the relative law level of violence, facilitated the opening of political space for recognition and negotiations also by the State of Israel (Grinberg, 2013a).

The boycott on Israeli goods in the OT had some non-negligible effects on the Israeli economy, but the frequent absences of Palestinian workers created a more serious problem. One of the immediate steps taken by the IDF was to issue a magnetic ID card to control the border crossings. This policy proved effective, as many Palestinians were deterred from taking active part in demonstrations by the risk of losing the right to work in Israel. However, this did not put an end to absences during strikes called by the Intifada leadership, or punitive curfews by the IDF.

Israeli society was deeply shocked by the Intifada as it exposed the meaning of occupation in the eyes of the entire world. Despite the Palestinians' dependence on Israeli economy, it was now clear to all that the dependency was mutual, with the Israeli economy relying on Palestinian labor for blue-collar work. The moral price of occupation also became clearly evident, with soldiers often filmed oppressing civilians (Gal, 1990; Shalev, 1990). NGOs such as *B'Tselem* and the Association for Civil Rights in Israel often appealed to the High Court of Justice to challenge the legality of actions taken by the IDF.[9]

The IDF immediately realized that it was facing a new problem, with no ready-made solutions. About a month after the uprising started, the IDF began adopting a new attitude according to which the solution for Israel's relations with the Palestinians could not be purely military, but also required political leadership. In other words, the military realized the limits of its power when confronting women and children, and came to the conclusion that stepping up the oppression will not do. Senior officers began voicing those doubts in the media.

Widespread criticism against IDF's excessive use of force led Chief of Staff Dan Shomron to publicly declare that "there is no military solution for the Intifada—a political solution is required" (Shalom and Hendel, 2011). The phrase "no military solution" meant lack of public legitimacy for exerting the full might of the IDF. However, a political solution required Israeli leadership capable of opening up a political

---

9   Ezrachi (1996); Kretzmer (2002).

space for dialog with the Palestinian leadership. Thus, in order to better understand later developments, it is important to emphasize that it was the military that legitimized political negotiations right from the beginning. The Israeli public debate around the Intifada constrained the IDF's freedom of action and tarnished its apolitical image. Hence, the IDF required a political representative identified with its worldview; the most eloquent and best qualified representative was "Mr. Security"—the former Chief of Staff during the glorious Six Day War and present Security Minister, Yitzhak Rabin. Rabin became the IDF's political leader when he reiterated its pessimism regarding a military solution and went a step further by arguing that the uprising could prove useful should it foster partners to a political settlement (Grinberg, 1994). In other words, the positive aspect of the Intifada is that it has the potential to open political space for recognition, representation and compromise. The question was who would represent the Palestinians after 20 years of complete rejection of negotiations with the PLO.

The emergence of an explicit military attitude holding the politicians responsible for security was perhaps the most significant result of the Intifada. Ever since its establishment, the IDF never shied from dictating political moves in the name of "security" (Ben Eliezer, 1998). This blurring of the boundaries between security and political affairs characterized the IDF ever since the early 1950s, through 1967 and to the First Lebanon War. It always had contingency plans and ideas on how to manage the difficult relations with the neighboring Arab states and the Palestinians (Sharet, 1978; Ben Eliezer, 1998; Gluska, 2004; Levy, 2003; Peri, 2006). The Intifada forced the military, for the first time, to recognize the limits of its strength and to draw a clear line separating politics and security. This is an essential democratic assumption: the distinction between goals (determined by the elected government) and the means to achieve them (proposed by the bureaucracy). It is based on the realization that using force is a means rather than a goal.[10]

The Intifada's leadership emerged directly from the desperate occupied population. Although it was the local leadership that initiated the Intifada and directed it throughout in a culmination of the empowerment of Palestinian civil society—shaped around the dual regime's

---

[10] For a discussion of the political role of the military see in Chapter 2 and Introduction to Part 4 in Grinberg (2010).

boundaries of control—it was supported by PLO leadership in Tunis. The PLO quickly moved to regain its status as the Palestinians' exclusive representatives, and convened the Palestinian National Council, which declared the establishment of an independent Palestinian State in the occupied West Bank and Gaza Strip on November 15, 1988. The Independence Declaration and demarcation of borders implicitly recognized the State of Israel in the 1967 borders, and opened space for mutual recognition and negotiations. The US administration immediately reacted by welcoming the PLO resolution and started direct talks at low diplomatic levels, through its ambassador in Tunis.[11]

However, the questionof who Israel should recognize as legitimate representative of the Palestinian uprising remained. Since 1988, the PLO prevented direct negotiations with an autonomous OT leadership, demanding their submission to decisions made in Tunis. This attitude shrunk the internal political space opened by the autonomous civil society in the OT. The Israeli military and political elites argued that they preferred talking with local leaders under the occupation, but as a matter of fact closed their space by the policy of deportation of local leaders to Tunis. This policy supported the PLO claim to represent the occupied population by creating a dependency relation between the occupied population and the Tunis bureaucracy. This attitude led to the close dependency of the OT negotiators in the Madrid Conference (1991) and later on during the bilateral negotiations in Washington (Ashrawi, 1995). However, the strong organization of civil society in the OT continued to exert pressure on the State of Israel and the PLO until they were finally neutralized by the secret negotiations and accords in Oslo (Ashrawi, 1995).

III. The "Dirty Trick": Towards Opening Political Space to the Palestinians

The upheaval in Israel's civil and military society caused by the Intifada did not produce immediate political change, and the 1988 electorate campaign was once more characterized by the tribal "right-left" cartel mobilization, with the financial crumbling of *Histadrut*'s services and

---

11   "Arafat declares an independent state," *Yediot Ahronot*, November 15, 1988.

firms (caused by the EESP, see Chapter 6) at the center of the *Likud*'s propaganda. Following these elections, a new NUG was established, this time with no rotation, with *Likud* leader Yitzhak Shamir as a four-year prime minister, Yitzhak Rabin as Minister of Security, and Shimon Peres as Minister of Treasury.[12] The latter appointment was critical to the Labor Party, which wanted to save the Workers' Society companies from total collapse (Grinberg, 1991, 1995; Barzilay, 1996).

The constant strikes and curfews in the OT disrupted the labor market and the ability to ensure regular supplies of goods and services within sovereign Israel. The Intifada was causing heavy losses with no end in sight, precisely at a time when global economy was beginning to open up to capital and goods movements, following the 1989 global trade agreement (GATT). Under these circumstances, a rising business elite began to formulate a new political economic strategy: "the peace project."[13] This "project" meant that the new privatized economic elites were ready to give up control of the OT and the benefits it provided since 1967 (cheap labor, captive consumer market and demand by the security establishment) in return for its integration in the emerging global economy. The local conflict came to be viewed as a stumbling block (Peres, 1993; Shafir and Peled, 2000, 2002; Ram, 2008).

This new attitude by the economic elites was aligned with that of the military elite: both required a political solution for the Intifada, but both were dependent on the government. Military and economic elites can speak out and leverage personal contacts, but cannot directly make policy (unless the democratic rules of the game are broken and the military takes over).[14] They therefore required political mediators to represent their position, given the hawkish positions of PM Yitzhak Shamir and the concomitant closure of political space to new ideas and strategies vis-à-vis the Palestinians. Under the pressure of civil society and the economic and military elites, the political space for the debate was opened within the Labor Party, taking the form of internal rifts and

---

12 Although the *Likud* got 40 seats and Labor 39, the balance between them was broken by the empowerment of the *Likud* partners in the NUG: 18 seats of religious parties and 7 of secular extreme right.
13 The main corporation initiating the project was Koor, the privatized conglomerate previously owned by the *Histadrut* (Shafir, 1999). The new economic elites were the owners and managers of privatized big corporations.
14 This happens of course in many cases, when power elites form anti-democratic coalitions and take power by force, but they do so to *close* political spaces rather than *open* them.

personal conflicts between Peres and Rabin regarding the NUG, which ultimately caused the Labor to secede.

The changes caused by the Intifada were indeed far-reaching, but the NUG reflected the bi-partisan cartel inertia and paralysis. Ever since 1988, the PLO became legitimized as the Palestinians' representative almost all over the world, following its historic decision to establish a Palestinian state in the West Bank and Gaza Strip, and de facto recognition of the State of Israel in its pre-1967 borders. In response, as mentioned before, the US authorized its ambassador in Tunis to negotiate with the PLO, and began pressuring Israel to do so as well. The international upheavals of that time also had a significant effect on the local political scene. The Berlin Wall fell in 1989 and with it the Soviet Union's control of Eastern Europe. Eventually, the Soviet Communist Party was disbanded, and the Union broke apart. The collapse of the Soviet Empire coincided with the GATT, which reduced barriers to free trade. These developments created new economic opportunities as well as a new geopolitical configuration, supporting the response of Israel's economic and military elites to the Intifada. The collapse of the Soviet Union left the world with a single superpower—one supportive of Israel. Economically, the Israeli market was offered unprecedented opportunities in emerging markets in the former Soviet Union, China, and other previously hostile countries. It was also an opportunity to attract investors to a more open Israeli market (Shafir and Peled, 2000).

The NUG paralysis was reflected by its total rejection of negotiations with the PLO, it even outlawed any contact with its representatives ("enemy agents"). Consequently, Shimon Peres hatched a plan to form a government without the *Likud*, later immortalized by Rabin's label of "the dirty trick," because it was secretly planned in cooperation with *Shas* leaders but concealed from the public eye, including elected party organs and Rabin himself.

In the summer of 1990, two years after the establishment of Shamir's NUG, a group of young pragmatic leaders in the Labor Party (led by Haim Ramon, Yossi Beilin, Abraham Burg, and Amir Peretz) initiated a parliamentary move designed to form a new government coalition headed by Peres without the *Likud*, together with the (then) moderate religious party in the coalition, *Shas* (Barzilay, 1996). This move failed to make Peres prime minister due to pressure on individual KMs that suddenly became clandestine and hanged their partisan loyalties. However, the "dirty trick" pulled the Labor Party out of the NUG, and being the main opposition party, it was forced to make clear its distinct position regarding Israel's future control of the OT, in order to return to power. It was precisely the Labor Party sojourn in the opposition during 1990-92 which, for the first time, gave the Israeli voter a choice between two blocks with clearly defined and diametrically opposed strategies vis-à-vis the ruling of the OT.

In response to the "dirty trick" fiasco, masses demonstrated on the streets demanding reforms in the election system and legislation of a constitution[15] that would restrict the power of small parties and single parliament members to switch sides, unite and split as they wished. This public pressure helped the more dynamic and pragmatic Labor leaders complete an internal reform with far-reaching repercussions for the entire political system: the party convention decided to elect both its Knesset list of candidates and its prime ministerial candidate directly, according to the US model of open primaries among all party members, rather than indirectly through party bureaucratic committees.[16]

This change was a severe blow to the pre-state colonial party apparatuses of the LIC, as it could no longer dictate candidates or influence them after their election. In other words, the "dirty trick" fiasco had unintended positive long-term consequences for the internal democratization of the Labor Party: it forced it into the opposition at a difficult time for Shamir's coalition government, and further weakened the *Histadrut*'s financial situation because it no longer benefitted from government subsidies. The weakening of the *Histadrut* also reduced the influence of its bureaucratic apparatus within the Labor Party, helping the young reformist forces from within the party prevail. It was this reform that enabled the party's new leadership to face the crisis that was overwhelming Shamir's government, formulate a strategy for resolving Israel's new set of problems and present a fresh image to the Israeli voter. The opening of political space for new ideas and strategies made possible the effective activation of the Israeli imagined democracy, be-

---

15 The State of Israel's legal heritage originates in the British regime, and has no written constitution, leading to a relatively "fluid rules" within the Israeli political arena.
16 In the old system, the list of candidates was elected according to *Mapai*'s Bolshevik heritage: a party Commission prepared the list, and the Central Committee approved. The Prime Minister candidate was elected by the party Conference, with 2000 members not directly elected for this purpose by the Party members.

cause new groups and leaders were able to realize their ideas by means of public debate and mass mobilization towards the 1992 elections.

The internal democratization of the Labor Party could never have happened without the success of the Palestinian Intifada in demarcating the borders of the Israeli sovereign state and democratic politics, and counterbalancing the Israeli dominant military power by means of strikes and demonstrations. The reformist young leaders within the Labor Party, also influenced by the military and economic elites, sought to represent civil society vis-à-vis the state. The balance of power changed due to the mobilization of Israeli and international public opinion against the occupation, and most importantly, the change in the US administration's attitude that started to exert pressure on the Israeli government to recognize and negotiate with the Palestinians. There was a direct connection between the opening of political space for the Palestinians and for the Israelis, just as the closure of Palestinian space had also closed space for representation of Israeli citizens' demands (see Chapters 5 and 6).

IV. The Political Economy of 1992 Elections and Democratic Opening of Political Space

In 1992, various groups in Israeli society that saw themselves marginalized or felt insecure due to Shamir's economic policy gave their votes to the opposition parties: Rabin's Labor and the more left-wing *Meretz*. These groups included traditional *Likud* voters in the development towns as well as newly arrived voters from the former Soviet Union. The collapse of the Soviet Union opened its former territories to Jewish emigration, and as it turned out, the arrival of 100-150,000 immigrants per year would deal the *coup de grace* to the old political arena in Israel.

The new immigration wave affected Israel mainly in that it led to renewed growth. Government spending on absorbing the immigrants and the expansion of local demand reversed the slowdown trend even before the Jewish immigrants joined the labor market. However, this time absorbing this group in the labor market was different from the previous cases of mass integration of workers, namely the Oriental Jews of the 1950s or the non-citizen Palestinians in the 1970s: these had been skilled workers in the USSR, employed in technical, engineering, medical, and academic professions. The possibility of their employment in their original professions threatened powerful Israeli organized workers.

The competition between the native Israeli professional workers and the new immigrants was resolved in various ways, partly through the expansion of the economy, rapid growth and the creation of new jobs, and partly through the undervaluing of the immigrants' professional qualifications that caused some of them to seek an alternative career. The immigration wave facilitated the implementation of the structural adjustment reforms sought since 1985 by the senior technocrats in both the Israeli and US treasuries (Maman and Rosenhek, 2011). These reforms, which can be lumped together under the heading "labor market flexibilization," included various forms of precarious or indirect employment of workers unprotected by collective wage agreements, facilitated by the availability of unorganized workers, threatening to displace Israeli citizens. The displacement of (veteran) Israeli workers and "flexibilization" of the labor market were facilitated by the need to provide jobs to the unemployed new immigrants from the former Soviet Union, and legitimized by the Zionist ideology.

The flexibilization of labor markets is one of the main objectives of neo-liberal political economy, designed to weaken powerful, well-organized employee groups (protected by collective labor agreements) by tearing down boundaries obstructing the entrance of non-citizen employees and encouraging indirect forms of employment. The weakening of powerful worker organizations by the state autonomous Economic Emergency Stabilization Plan from 1985 (see Chapter 6) and the recession it caused, was augmented by the Intifada. After 1992 the Israeli workers were struck another blow with the immigration from the former Soviet Union and the import of non-Jewish immigrants as "migrant workers," living in Israel without any legal status or basic rights.

The sense of threat and lack of security were intensified during 1990-1992 due to internal as well as external political developments. Internally, due to the lack of political recognition and relative success of military repression, the *Intifada* started to deteriorate from its initial form of nonviolent popular uprising in the OT to attacks against Israeli citizens within sovereign Israel, particularly in the big cities. This new trend, called "knifesmanship" for the common use of knives in these attacks, created a prevailing sense that the government was helpless and lacking in any clear direction. In response to this wave of attacks, mostly perpetrated by individual workers with permits to work within sovereign Israel, the IDF began enforcing "closures," which meant hermetic sealing of the Green Line border for extended periods. This was a new form of collective punishment against the Palestinian population and a barbiturate for the Israelis, but nobody saw it as a viable long-term solution.

The closure policy had a strategic implication. If the Intifada forced Israel to draw a clear line and keep the Palestinians on its other side, there was no point in the *Likud*'s Greater Israel strategy. The far-reaching implications of the ideological crisis in the *Likud* caused by the Intifada were skillfully used by the new leader of the Labor party, Yitzhak Rabin. Rabin dared faced angry demonstrators following a knife attack on the eve of the elections and promised to "take Gaza out of Bat Yam."[17] In that, Rabin articulated a return to *Mapai*'s pre-1967 strategy that required a clear separation between the two populations. This strategy was also compatible with the IDF's conclusion that it could not suppress the popular uprising in the OT, but also could not protect the citizens of Israel proper without a clear boundary, hence its closure policy. This realistic discussion, so clearly opposed to the Greater Israel myth, helped to create, during the 1992 elections, an atmosphere that voters are deciding between a clear path that offers a solution and the existing situation characterized by individual insecurity.

In other words, the Intifada—including the violent stabbings within Israel—opened up political space for negotiations with the Palestinians by demarcating the borders between the sovereign State of Israel and the Occupied Territories in a way that enabled the Israeli public to imagine a two-state solution. Under these circumstances, the public opinion was overwhelmingly in favor of dealing with the real issues, mostly by way of clear separation. The parties that touted the Greater Israel myth either shrunk (*Likud*) or disappeared (*Tehiya*) and every party which offered practical solutions grew in strength,[18] including the Labor and *Meretz* to the left, and *Tzomet* and *Moledet* to the right (these were non-

---

17 Following the assassination of Helena Rapp in Bat-Yam on May 24, 1992. http://www.ynet.co.il/articles/0,7340,L-4136092,00.html.
18 The combined power of right-wing parties *Likud* (40) and *Tehiya* (3) in 1988 was 43 seats in the Knesset, with other right-wing parties *Tzomet* and *Moledet* gaining 2 seats each. In the 1992 elections, the *Likud* shrunk to 32, *Tehiya* disappeared, and *Tzomet* (8) and *Moledet* (3) went up.

mythical nationalist parties suggesting intensified oppression). In the 1992 elections, the public took part in a fateful decision to open political space to Palestinian representation and negotiations (Grinberg, 1994, 2007, 2010).

The momentous change in 1992 was mainly affected by the international atmosphere following the collapse of the Soviet Union, the rise of the US to single superpower status and the growing globalization of world economy (Shafir and Peled, 2000, 2002). Against this background, the 1991 Gulf War broke out between Iraq and a powerful international coalition led by the US, legitimized by the inclusion of several Arab partners. Following the war, the US influence in the region grew, and its relationships with its Arab coalition partners warmed up. Consequently, it pressured Israel to take part in a peace conference in Madrid, together with Arab delegates, as well as Palestinian representatives (in direct coordination with the PLO in Tunis, as noted above).

The US pressure on Shamir's government mounted when the US conditioned its agreement to provide Israel with $10 billion worth of guarantees for loans it urgently required to absorb the new immigrants on Israel's agreement to suspend all construction in the Jewish settlements in the West Bank. Shamir, who rejected the US terms, seemed completely out of touch with the so-called New World Order, as he seemed willing to sacrifice the Israelis' economic welfare for its mythological ideology. Rabin, on the other hand, seemed to offer a real solution that would not only improve relationships with the US and the Palestinians, but also enable Israel to become integrated in the global economy. Rabin and his supporters in the economic elite embraced the zeitgeist in the hope of material profit (Ram, 2008; Shafir and Peled, 2002). One of the prerequisites for joining the global economy was opening up new markets for Israeli exports, markets hitherto closed due to the prolonged conflict with neighboring countries. The new Labor government promised to put an end to Israel's isolation and allow broad sectors in Israeli society to share in the profits (Peres, 1993).

The 1992 elections were unique in Israeli electoral history, both in its propaganda messages and in its outcomes. The Labor Party's messages were not inflammatory or seditious, but focused on present-day issues and practical solutions. Its new-old leader, Rabin, proposed a clear plan for a settlement with the Palestinian leadership, as part of a general change of priorities that should channel government expenditure from the settlements in the OT to financing education, job creation, and welfare. The party associated socioeconomic difficulties within sovereign Israel caused by the Intifada with the *Likud*'s conservative policy in the OT, thus drawing a clear line between "here" (sovereign Israel) and "there" (the OT). This new discourse managed to undermine old loyalties and mobilize traditionally right-wing voters, as well as new immigrants resentful of their early absorption experience.[19]

Rabin and the Labor Party were faced with a prime minister who failed to deal with Israel's new economic and political problems. Most of the Israeli public voted against the *Likud*'s tattered image, and in favor of Rabin's campaign for dealing with the issues at hand. The results demonstrated the gap between the mobilization power of the Greater Israel myth and the new pragmatic discourse opening space for the Palestinians: the *Likud* won only 32 seats in the Knesset, while the Labor Party won 44.[20] With 56 votes to Zionist left-wing parties and only 45 to the right, the results broke the stalemate between the two cartel blocks. Just as importantly, the parties representing Israel's Palestinian citizens (5 seats) replaced the Jewish religious parties as the tie breakers in the Knesset. These outcomes facilitated a true policy change that was not possible in previous Knessets, a change that did not take long to occur.

V. The Formulation of an Alternative Strategy

The new government's first moves were not directed at the Palestinians in the OTs, but rather at "internal" issues. The new priorities promised in the electoral campaign were realized in the form of highway construction and large investments in education in rural areas. Talks with the Palestinian were held in Washington, but quickly ran into difficulties. The Palestinian delegation was composed of OT personalities—headed by Haidar Abdel-Shafi, Hanan Ashrawi, and Faisal Husseini—coordinated with the PLO leadership in Tunis (Ashrawi, 1995). The Palestinian delegation strongly rejected Israel's proposals for elections in the OT followed by a five-year transitional period during which the elected rep-

---

19   For a more detailed analysis of the 1992 elections, see A. Arian and M. Shamir (1995).
20   The detailed 1992 election results are: Labor 44, Likud 32, *Meretz* 12, *Tzomet* 8, *Shas* 6, NRP 6, United Tora Judaism 4, *Hadash* 3, *Moledet* 3, Arab Democratic Party 2. http://www.knesset.gov.il/history/eng/eng_hist13_s.htm.

resentatives would be delegated autonomous administrative authorities and negotiations for a permanent settlement would be held.

The Washington talks took advantage of the political space opened up by the Intifada and symbolized the formal recognition of the Palestinians' representatives, who were now able to negotiate as well as compromise. But their source of legitimacy was not based on the OT resistant population but mainly on their connection to the PLO, the national symbol of all Palestinians living outside their homeland since 1948. In that sense, the negotiations proved difficult, since Israel completely rejected the option of direct negotiations with the PLO. Every position stated by the Washington delegation required approval by the PLO HQ in Tunis, and the PLO was reluctant to authorize any compromise while it was not recognized by the US and Israel as the Palestinians' legitimate representative.

With the Washington talks stuck, various attempts were made to negotiate directly with PLO representatives in more confidential channels.[21] These backdoor talks focused on the original proposal to hold elections in the OT and grant them autonomy for a period of five years. A key element in this initiative was that all Jewish settlements would remain in place until a permanent agreement was reached; Arafat decided to accept this condition, despite the opposition of most of his close advisors and all of the Washington delegates.[22]

In the eyes of most Palestinians living in the OT, this early concession by Arafat, combined with the lack of any explicit commitment by Israel to freeze construction in the settlements, doomed the entire process from its inception. The Intifada broke out in 1987, among other things, due to the urgent need to stop Jewish construction in the West Bank that threatened to prevent any chance of establishing a territorially contiguous Palestinian state even in the West Bank. From the point of view of his Israeli negotiation partners, Arafat's concession was a huge success, perhaps too huge, as it perpetuated the original power relations and Israeli domination that the peace process was presumably designed to transform.

Obviously, Arafat was anxious to reach a preliminary agreement and secure Israeli withdrawal before the Hamas deportees returned to

---

21   See Beilin (1996); Hirschfeld (2000: 147-210).
22   See Lipkin-Shahak-Arafat talks after the Cave of the Patriarchs massacre, in Savir (1998: 156-7).

Gaza.²³ Consequently, the Declaration of Principles (DOP) agreement (which was not implemented at the time) stipulated that the IDF would start pulling out of Gaza on December 13, 1993, one week before the deportees were scheduled to return. This already shed a painfully clear light on the balance of power between the Israeli and Palestinian ruling elites and the powers opposing them: Rabin was afraid of the fanatic settlers and made sure no settlement would be evacuated, while Arafat was troubled by the internecine strife in Gaza and therefore sought to enter as soon as possible. However, after the Declaration of Principles (DOP) was signed in Washington, a dispute broke out regarding the control of the crossings between Egypt and Gaza and between Jordan and Jericho, delaying the implementation of the "Gaza-Jericho First" Agreement by five critical months, from December 1993 to May 1994.²⁴

As the secret talks in Oslo progressed, the different goals of the negotiators were revealed: while Rabin sought to bypass the "tougher" Palestinian delegation in Washington and reach a more convenient agreement, Arafat wanted above all to arrive in Gaza as soon as possible, to reinforce his position vis-à-vis the Hamas as the only one capable of bringing about real improvement in the lives of local Palestinians. He needed Rabin's consent for that, and was ready for painful concessions to obtain it.

While the agreement was being quietly formulated in Oslo, the formal charade in Washington continued. At one point, when the Palestinian delegates in Washington felt that the Tunis leadership was fooling them by ordering them to adopt positions that were too soft, they resigned collectively and flew to Tunis to explain their view (Ashrawi, 1995: 257). Suddenly, the Washington delegates appeared as extremists in comparison to Arafat, the leader willing to defer all key issues to future negotiations. Indeed, this is what Arafat agreed to do, despite the heavy criticism and substantial risk to his status as leader.

---

23 In response to the assassination of an Israeli Border Guard, and the Israeli Government reaction to deport 415 Hamas and Islamic Jihad leaders and activists to Southern Lebanon (then jointly controlled by the IDF and a local Christian militia called the South Lebanon Army), for a period of one year. (*Haaretz*, December 13-16, 1992; http://www.btselem.org/hebrew/deportation/1992_Mass_Deportation.asp [in Hebrew]).
24 See Savir (1998).

VI. The Declaration of Principles: Mutual Recognition in Exchange for Palestinian Concessions

The Oslo DOP was primarily an act of mutual recognition of the two peoples' legitimate rights, and the intention to end the conflict and live in peace and mutual respect. The agreement stipulated a five-year transitional period, during which a freely elected Palestinian government would take over the authorities of the Israeli military and civil government in the OT and negotiate a permanent settlement with Israel. These same principles were suggested by Menachem Begin to Anwar Sadat in 1978, and the latter rejected them. Rabin made almost the same offer in the Washington negotiations but was rejected by the OT Palestinian delegation. Only the PLO has the legitimacy to make such huge concessions.

The permanent settlement was supposed to implement UN Security Council Resolutions 242 and 338 and discuss the key issues deferred for the time being: Jerusalem's future status, the refugees, the settlements, security arrangements and borders. Negotiations on the permanent settlement were supposed to begin in two years and continue for three years.

The Declaration of Principles defined the West Bank and Gaza Strip as a single territorial unit to be governed by a Palestinian Authority (PA), with Israel retaining authority over the security of Israelis and foreign security during the transitional period. Israel would retreat from the Gaza Strip and Jericho where the PA would be initially installed. Within nine months after the declaration came into effect,[25] free elections for a legislative assembly would be held under international supervision, with Palestinian police officers responsible for public order. The elections were supposed to be held by July 1994, after the IDF's retreat from the urban areas. However, they were delayed by the Israeli government and IDF and eventually held only in January 1996, two months after Rabin's assassination.[26]

The PA was to be responsible for civil government of Palestinians in the West Bank and Gaza, including education, health, welfare, direct

---

25 The declaration became effective on October 13, a month after it had been signed.
26 For a detailed description and analysis of this period and the delays in implementing DOP, see Grinberg (2010: Part 2).

taxation and tourism. It also undertook to create a strong police force in charge of internal security,[27] while external security and the protection of Israeli citizens in the OT remained Israel's responsibility. The PA was authorized to create organizations designed to promote economic development, including an electricity company, a Gaza port authority, a development bank, an environmental protection agency, a land authority, a water administration, and so on.

Arafat's concessions seemed exaggerated not only to the Palestinian delegation and most PLO officials, but also to many Israelis, who began speculating about his ulterior motives. Some believed there were secret agreements in which Israel promised him a Palestinian state, while others thought he intended to enter the OT only to reignite the armed struggle against Israel "from within." Still others expected him to head a Palestinian Million Man March on Jerusalem. The reason for all the speculations was that Israel's concession was symbolic: recognizing the PLO. From Israel's point of view, this was nothing short of a bargain, with no mention of the Washington delegation's demands for real powers in the OT, including East Jerusalem, during the transitional period, and the prevention of any unilateral actions on the ground affecting the permanent settlement (i.e. Jewish settlements).[28] What allayed the Israeli governments' fears and encouraged it to recognize the PLO was the huge gap between Arafat's legitimacy to make far-reaching concessions and that of the OT delegates in Washington. While the latter showed no willingness to compromise on matters of principle, and even resigned collectively to protest against the moderate positions dictated to them by Arafat, the PLO went much further in the Oslo negotiations in return for mutual recognition. However, Israel gave no significant concession, since everything was still open for negotiation, including the evacuation of Gaza, Jericho and later other population centers in the West Bank.

In a very candid interview (following Netanyahu's election in 1996), Yoel Singer, the legal expert who formulated the agreements, argued that all the *Likud* had to do now was read the agreements and discover that Israel still had total control:

---

27 A formula originally included in the Autonomy Agreement between Begin and Sadat.
28 In the Washington talks there was no mention of the refugee issue. This was discussed in a multilateral committee, based on the assumption that resettling the refugees in Arab countries would require the latter's involvement in the settlement.

The agreement leaves the territory in our hands and grants them the populated areas that neither the *Likud* nor the Alignment ever wanted to control—and what's more, leaves them in charge of the dirty job of patrolling the towns and refugee camps. The permanent settlement will be what you want it to be. And in the transitional period, you still control most of the unpopulated area, you have all the utilities in your control, while they are in charge of security [...]. We are the strong party and they are the weak, this is absolutely clear. You need to go through us to get from Gaza to the West Bank. You need to go through us to enter, they depend on us for tax and customs revenues. We did not want to establish a conflict resolution mechanism through a third party. When the strong face the weak, the third party tends to support the weak.[29]

Arafat did not deny the fact that the agreement he had achieved was far from optimal, but insisted it was the best one available given the Palestinian weakness at the time. In the Jabalia Refugee Camp near Gaza, he put it into words any Palestinian could understand: "I realize many of you believe Oslo is a bad agreement. Indeed it is. But it is the best we could achieve in our bad situation" (Usher, 1995: 1). Subsequently, Arafat developed a strategy for appeasing his critics by making radical speeches, promising a future Palestinian state in all the OT, with Jerusalem as its capital. These speeches were designed to legitimize his concessions and reinforce his status within the OT, and indeed this is all that he managed to achieve.[30]

According to the theoretical framework of political spaces, Arafat's concessions may be interpreted as co-optation, because he was detached from the resisting Palestinian people and promised to restrain them. However, the concept of political spaces is dynamic, and includes the option of continued opening process. The failure of continued opening, as seen below, was not deterministic, and Arafat could assume he

---

29 *Haaretz*, August 18, 1996. Singer also said: "If the government ministers study the Oslo Agreement better, they will say it is excellent."
30 I thank Professor Salim Tamari of Bir-Zeit University for this insight.

would accomplish Palestinian statehood. The explanation for his failure is retrospective, based on historical contingencies, and not only on structures and institutions. Although the structural weakness of the Palestinians and their dependency on the Israeli economy were crucial factors, Rabin's assassination and the Labor party's subsequent loss of power were contingent events that contributed to the eventual closure of political space for further negotiations.

VII. Counter-Mo(ve)ment: Israeli Profits and Perpetuated Palestinian Dependency

Thanks to the Palestinians' far-reaching concessions, the Oslo DOP was commended in Israeli public discourse as an ideal deal that offers the chance of "painless peace."[31] The emphasis was on the agreement's endless potential economic benefits—Shimon Peres's "New Middle East"—achievable without conflict or struggle.[32] According to that version, which was also adopted by Israeli economic elites, the Palestinians were experiencing such severe economic conditions that all they needed was to improve their economic situation, and then they would be ready to restrain their political claims.

Although no one could really imagine how the promised "peace" would look in the future, the Israeli businessmen had a pretty good idea about their potential profits. Immediately after signing the Declaration of Principles, even before they were ratified or became effective, the gold rush was on. On his way back from Washington, Rabin's plane stopped in Morocco as an indication of the new atmosphere, and within five days the heads of the Chambers of Commerce and Manufacturers Association, Dan Gilerman and Dan Proper, called for a committee to promote regional cooperation in Morocco or Egypt.[33] On October 1, Finance Ministers from all over the world convened to secure financing for the PA for the next five years, based on a needs assessment by the World Bank which determined that it would require three billion dollars over that period.[34] On October 10, Rabin flew to Russia with a large entourage of

---

31 Hami Shalev, "Painless peace" (*Haaretz*, September 21, 1993).
32 Margalit, Gadot and Dechs (2004).
33 *Haaretz*, September 14 and 20, 1993.
34 *Haaretz*, September 12 and October 2, 1993. For the World Bank report, "Developing the Occupied

leading businessmen to open up the new emerging markets, and two weeks later he made an even more promising journey to China, Indonesia and Singapore.[35] As Koor's CEO, Benny Gaon, eloquently put it, the very handshake between Rabin and Arafat opened world markets to Israeli entrepreneurs.[36] One week later, the King of Spain came to Israel to discuss joint ventures with North African countries and Israel. By December, Israel approached the EU to renew the negotiations on upgraded trade terms, suspended since 1975.[37]

Many people around the world were busy constructing the peace process as an essentially economic project: economists from Harvard and the World Bank's research department, Israeli economists and Treasury Ministry officials, as well as conglomerates such as Koor.[38] The economic agreement (the Paris Protocol) was the first agreement signed after the DOP.[39] The guiding principle of the Paris Agreement was the political imperative not to draw a borderline between Israel and the Palestinians, so that Israel's economic borders remained the same as they had been since 1967, namely, the borders between Israel/Palestine and the neighboring Arab countries. The economic dependency relations were called now "customs union," resembling the economic relations among the members of the European Union, where the external border, its control, and customs collection defined a single economic unit. According to the Paris Agreement, Israel undertook the collection of customs for the PA's imports and transferred the revenues back to it. This was supposed to be one of the PA's main sources of income, albeit dependent on Israel's willingness to transfer the funds (Fischer, 2001). However, the main problem was not only this particular form of dependency, but Israel's accorded authority to dictate to the Palestinians a trade policy tailored to

---

Territories: An investment in peace," Vol. 1-6. See http://www-wds.worldbank.org/servlet/WDS_IBank_Servlet?pcont=details&eid=000009265_3970311123238.

35 *Haaretz*, October 11, 1993; *Maariv*, October 22, 1993.
36 See interview in Shafir and Peled (2000: 257-9).
37 *Haaretz*, November 1 and December 7, 1993.
38 See the report by the political negotiations' economic advisory team headed by Haim Ben Shahar (1993); Hausman and Karasik (1993).
39 They were signed in Paris six days *before* the Cairo Agreement on the Israeli evacuation of Gaza and Jericho (April 29, 1994), and a full eighteen months before the Interim Agreement on the evacuation of all the Palestinian towns in the West Bank and the elections was signed. The Israeli negotiators in Paris were equipped with a report submitted to the Treasury Minister by a committee headed by Professor Haim Ben Shahar. Professor Ben Shahar from Tel Aviv University's Department of Economics was known for his connections with the Labor Party, as well as with the business sector.

suit the needs of the Israeli manufacturers and importers, rather than those of the emerging Palestinian economy.

The 1993 World Bank Report stated explicitly that the relations between the Israeli and Palestinian economy ever since 1967, which were characterized as a "customs union," worsened the situation of the latter and thwarted its development.[40] Israel's interest is to deny the Palestinians' "small economy advantage" by preventing free flow of cheap goods to Israel, neither the products from the OT or those imported through the borders with Egypt or Jordan. When the Palestinians signed the Paris Agreement, their captive economy was under severe crisis for two main reasons: a) the Gulf War, which led to the deportation of 300,000 Palestinians (suspected to be pro-Iraqi) from Kuwait, and b) the Israeli policy of frequent closures and strict allocation of employment permits.

The Paris Agreement did not change this economic dependency regime, but created a hypothetic possibility of returning to the pre-Intifada economic conditions, apart from a few important amendments in favor of the Palestinians: allowing the export of agricultural goods to Israel (which threatened to compete with the Israeli farmers), allowing Israeli capital investments in ventures employing Palestinian workers in the OT (which threatened to compete with Israeli workers in the same industries), and transferring international aid to renovate infrastructures and establishing a quasi-state bureaucracy. However, the agreement was not implemented in full and the situation on the ground did not change: the Palestinians were not given tools to break free of their economic dependence on Israel, particularly due to their continuing inability to act independently in the global market.

The "peace" agreements weakened Palestinians' civil society in the OT because they became dependent on Israeli authorities for permits to travel, work, and do business. Their only power was in the form of armed opposition groups, which tried to channel the population's general frustration in support for their armed struggle. Each violent attack led the IDF to close the borders, preventing Palestinian workers from entering sovereign Israel and worsening their already fragile economic situation (Roy, 2001).

The closure of the OT borders to the entrance of Palestinian workers further pushed the neoliberal policy of labor market flexibilization. This

---

40   See World Bank Report (1993).

trend intensified after 1993 with the massive import of unskilled labor to replace the regularly absent Palestinian workers. Under pressure by the employers who wanted a stable source of cheap, non-unionized labor, workers were imported from dozens of countries in Asia, Africa, Latin America, and Eastern Europe. This phenomenon, which was threatening to spin out of control, changed Israeli economy irreversibly, and was one of the direct results of Israel's integration in the global economy through the "Peace Project" (Shafir and Peled, 2000, 2002; Ram, 2008; Kemp and Reijman, 2008; Rosenhek, 1999).

In the power structure created by the economic agreements there were winners and losers on both sides, but everyone suffered from the ensuing violence. The Israeli economic and military elites tightened their control, as did the Palestinian ruling elite. The latter was empowered by the population's dependence on it, but gradually lost legitimacy as widespread economic hardships meant increasing support for violence. Israel applied economic pressure in the form of IDF checkpoints within the OT and closure of the border crossings between the West Bank and Gaza, and between them and Jordan and Egypt, respectively, in order to force the PA to crack down on the opposition. This turned the "customs union" agreed upon in Paris into a meaningless paper, and as convincingly argued by Sara Roy (1995) the "development" of the Palestinian economy became a form of "de-development."

The economic agreements combined with the opening of world markets to the Israeli economy, the importing of migrant workers and the constant closure of borders constitute the counter-mo(ve)ment of the Intifada. The power of the Intifada resistance movement lay in the intermittent strikes that paralyzed Israeli economy, and in the illegitimacy of IDF repression. The Oslo Accords ended the strikes, revitalized Israeli economy, and re-legitimized IDF repression and constant closures as acts of "self-defense." Recognizing the PLO and establishing the Palestinian Authority became the most effective co-optation strategy.

VIII. The Unintended Counter-Mo(ve)ment: The New Post-Conflict Agendas

Rabin's election in 1992 was based on the Labor Party's successful campaign that linked the need to withdraw from the OT with the popular demand to invest resources within the sovereign borders of Israel ("changing the order of priorities"). According to this new approach, the new governmental coalition excluded parties opposed to territorial compromise. In addition, the two parties with majoritarian votes of Palestinian citizens[41] also supported the government in exchange for resources to their constituencies.

Once installed, the Rabin government carried out major changes in resource allocation. Even before any geopolitical moves, it greatly increased the education budget[42] and infrastructure investments—particularly road construction—as well as enacted a National Health Law. This policy had tangible effects: from an earlier peak of 11.2%, unemployment fell to 7.8%. Unemployment among the new immigrants fell even more drastically, from 39% to 11%. The map of national priority areas was redrawn to include 534 communities, and exclude most (albeit not all) Jewish settlements in the OT.[43]

Soon after the signature of the DOP with its Israeli recognition of the PLO, the new socioeconomic agendas erupted in full force in various political arenas. The first indication of the new political atmosphere was the outcome of the municipal elections in November 1993: coalitions emerged that spanned the tribal lines of "left" and "right," while the joint power of the *Likud* and Labor declined dramatically. The municipal elections revealed the rising power of *Shas*, the growing aspiration of the Russian-speaking immigrants to have a share of political power, and the tension between them and the *Mizrahi* lower classes, particularly in the peripheral areas (Brichta and Pedatzur, 2001). Tensions between *Shas* and the secular *Ashkenazi* parties also incited confrontations within the coalition.

The second and most significant and far reaching electoral upheaval took place in the *Histadrut*, which led to a significant structural reform,[44] In the May 1994 elections the Labor party lost control of the *Histadrut* after 74 years of rule (since its founding). The group that won 46% of the votes, was a list formed by an innovative coalition of Labor young

---

41 *Hadash* and *Mada* 5 Knesset members.
42 The budget rose from 6 to 14 billion NIS and 6,000 new classrooms were built (Ethan Haber, www.ynet.co.il, October 28, 2001).
43 "Proposal for new tax break areas approved," *Hadashot*, June 7, 1993.
44 As I already mentioned I took part in the effort to reform the *Histadrut* (see introduction). I would like to emphasize here that the goal of democratization, namely direct election of worker representatives in the *Histadrut* organs, was not achieved.

reformists (headed by Haim Ramon and Amir Peretz), that decided to split from their party towards the elections, and created a list together with *Shas* and *Meretz*. Ramon was nominated Health Minister by Rabin in 1992 with the explicit goal of formulating a National Health Law; however, he was blocked by the *Histadrut* apparatus within the Labor Party. This is the reason he decided to split and form an alternative list towards the May 1994 elections (Barzilay, 1996).

The whole campaign, which gained remarkable popularity, was around the demand of a structural reform of the *Histadrut*, claiming the separation between its trade union functions and its Health services. Only after the *Histadrut* elections, and the support of the new *Histadrut* leadership to the new National Health Law, it was enacted with unanimous support. After losing its Health function, and mainly after losing more than of two thirds of its members,[45] and losing the Health revenues, the *Histadrut* also was forced to privatize the Worker Society companies it owned until then (Grinberg and Shafir, 2000). The dismantlement of the *Histadrut* quasi-state structure deeply weakened the organizational capacities of the Labor Party, but also weakened the hostility against the labor party and right wing mobilization against its anti-democratic control of the Labor market, services and public companies. In other words, the *Histadrut* reforms weakened the tribal polarization of the "left/right" cartel.

The decline of the mythological "left/right" mobilization during the *Histadrut* and municipal elections revolved around the political role of *Mizrahi* Jews and their potential open participation in the coalition building processes. In the mythological discourse, *Mizrahim* were constructed as religious and right-wing supporters. This stereotyped vision was supported by spokespersons of both the "left" and "right" as part of the cartel cooperation designed to close the political space to new *Mizrahi* voices and representatives. The "left" defined itself as western, rational and secular, constructing an image of the modern Israeli, the "new Jew," as opposed to the diasporic, traditional and religious "old Jew" (Eisenstadt, 1967). Right-wing discourse, on the other hand, provides a space for *Mizrahim* by emphasizing collective Jewish identity, as reflected in the myth of the Land of Israel promised to the People of Israel. It is this

---

45 As I showed in Chapter 2, *Histadrut* membership was forced through the need to have Health insurance and the absence of a national insurance. See also Grinberg (1991, 1993).

dichotomous construction of identities that maintained the tribal mobilization and closed the option of identities out of the two poles.

Ethno-class tensions between *Mizrahi* lower classes and *Ashkenazi* middle and upper classes were channeled, ever since the *Wadi Salib* riots in 1959 (see Chapter 3) and Black Panther movement in 1971-73 (see Chapter 5), into the tribal polarization between "left" and "right." The 1992 Knesset elections, the new governmental coalition, the municipal and *Histadrut* elections opened the political space to *Mizrahi* voices, new coalitions and organizations.[46]

The initial election slogan of the Labor Party in the election campaign—"Changing the Order of Priorities"—focused on material questions of resource allocation. However, the new discourse also facilitated the opening of political space to symbolic struggles over collective identity and its relation to discrimination in resource allocation. The political space for both identity issues and its relation to the allocation of resources would abruptly close after Rabin's assassination in November 1995. The violence of the assassination would provoke fear, hostility, and uncertainty, and help the dominant *Ashkenazi* elites deny any political space to new identities and material claims. Such new agendas, identities, demands and coalitions emerged in full force after the DOP in September 1993, because the imagination of the Palestinian State facilitated the imagined demarcation of the borders of the sovereign State of Israel, and the framing of the "internal" political arena. During the years 1993–95, the "post-conflict" agendas included issues of religion and state, relations between *Mizrahi* and *Ashkenazi* Jews, the civil rights of Palestinian citizens, and class struggles. All these issues had more profound political and cultural implications than the simplistic and naïve slogan "changing the order of priorities," which alluded to shifting the allocation of public resources from the OT to within sovereign Israel in order to invest in infrastructure, education, health, and employment.

Within the Rabin government were two conflicting approaches to the dismantling of the "left/right" tribal cartel hostilities and the coalition with *Shas*. On one side were those who viewed the integration of *Mizrahim* into the halls of power as fundamental to breaking down the mythological discourse of the "left" and providing legitimacy to the gov-

---

46 In addition to *Shas* the most salient where David Levy split from the *Likud* and the establishment of *Gesher* and the formation of the Democratic *Mizrahi* Rainbow (Chetrit, 2004).

ernment. Rabin and his circles were prominent supporters of this view, forging an alliance with *Shas* and with Ramon and Peretz, who left Labor and brought *Shas* and *Meretz* into a list drawn from both camps for the Histadrut elections in 1994. On the other hand, some Labor leaders sought to preserve the mythological "left-right" tribal discourse by stressing symbolic and cultural differences with the "right," mainly *Shas*.

This last conservative approach within the government was voiced primarily by *Meretz* ministers,[47] but it was also shared by key Labor ministers (mainly Shimon Peres and Yossi Beilin). The main problem was, however, the attitude of many "leftist" tribal voters, and some of their opinion leaders—journalists, authors, and poets—because the tribal hostility expressed their collective sense of superiority. Thus, the ability of Rabin and his partners to break down the mythological "left/right" mobilization was limited by their voters' desire to preserve the "left" as a status symbol of *Ashkenazi*, upper-middle ethno-class superiority. After Rabin's assassination all the agendas and tensions remained open, but the political capacity to contain them through representation, mediation and compromise—namely through dynamic opening of political space—significantly shrunk.

To resume, the recognition of the Palestinians immediately opened space for new post-conflict agendas and contributed to the initial dismantling of the tribal "left/right" identities. These changes occurred rapidly and transformed the political arena by diminishing the power of the two cartel parties—Labor and *Likud*—from almost two-thirds of the Knesset (76 MKs) in 1992 to just over one-third (42) in 1999.[48] This dramatic political change had profound implications for the ability to turn an imagined peace into reality. The new agendas that the old cartel parties were unable to contain by representation, negotiation, and compromise were related to ethnicity, class, religion, and civil rights of the

---

47 Before moving to its post-conflict, *Ashkenazi*-secular identity, *Meretz* was identified with social democratic views and even socialism among some of its members, particularly those from *Mapam* and the former Communist Party. These were the *Histadrut* activists who made possible the seeming anomaly of a joint list with *Shas* for the *Histadrut* election, while tribal enmity prevailed between the parties in the national arena—the *Knesset* and the government.

48 The decline was rather moderate in the 1996 election, and together they won 66 seats, and continued the general trend since 1981 (95 in 1981, 85 in 1984, 81 in 1988, 76 in 1992). The big drop in 1999 was also the result of new electoral legislation that had been designed to halt the decline of the cartel by splitting the vote between the party and Prime Minister, but actually affected voters in the opposite way (see Grinberg, 2010).

Palestinian citizens. New parties representing new identities, ideas and demands arose to replace the tribal cartel. However, these new political formations marginalized Israeli-Palestinian relations and sometimes even completely ignored them (see Chapter 8). Therefore, the new post-conflict agendas became the unintended counter-mo(ve)ment of the Intifada, because they marginalized the need to negotiate and compromise with Palestinian representatives.

IX. Conclusion

Arafat was allowed to enter Gaza with a concrete purpose in mind: to suppress Hamas and put an end to terrorist attacks against Israelis. In Rabin's famous words, "I'd rather the Palestinians restore law and order to Gaza. Perhaps the Palestinians would do it better than us; don't worry—there will be no appeals to the High Court of Justice there. The Civil Rights Association will not go there to snoop around. They have their rules, but the point is that it won't be IDF soldiers who'll do it" (*Yediot Ahronot*, September 7, 1993).

The message was obvious: the IDF found itself unable to suppress the Palestinians because it was restrained by Israel's civil society critics, but also by critics within "military society" itself.[49] The PLO leader was just as interested in suppressing Hamas, and he was not constrained by democratic rules of the game. Thus, Rabin's main goal was not to open political space for Palestinian representation and compromise, but rather to find a Palestinian partner to suppress the Intifada from within; he found one in Tunis.[50] The young PLO leaders who emerged in the OT during the Intifada quickly realized their new situation and reacted against Arafat's nominations of PA bureaucrats designed to marginalize them (*Haaretz*, December 28, 1993; Usher, 1995: 16-18).

Rabin's intention was to open very limited space to Palestinian representation, enough to secure Arafat's cooptation based on economic de-

---

49   For a discussion of the civil society mobilization against the use of violence see Grinberg (2011, 2013a).
50   In a private conversation Rashid Khalidi told me a very telling story. In early March 1994, Khalidi and others were invited to a panel with Rabin's advisor Shlomo Gazit at Amherst College in Massachusetts. In response to a question about Arafat that seemed to have annoyed him, Gazit replied: "Arafat has a choice: he can be Lahd or super-Lahd." In other words Arafat choice was, according to him, to be a collaborator or a super collaborator.

pendency and military control of all borders. It was this dependency and this control which had enabled him to impose Israel's terms on the PLO. Arafat, however, had good reason to believe that the Israeli leader would have to compromise sooner or later. This reasoning is supported by the historical evidence of democratization processes. When authoritarian regimes recognize that they cannot continue ruling by violent repression they need to recognize the claims of subjugated social groups and open political space for negotiations with moderate leaders. The initial goal of this limited opening is to co-opt the leaders. However, it precipitates a process that finally leads to the transfer of power (Przeworsky, 1991; O'Donnell and Schmitter, 1986). This happens as soon as the process of negotiation reaches critical junctures requiring authoritarian leaders to finally choose to proceed with the transfer of power to the moderate leaders or risk losing their power to extremists who oppose the negotiations and demand intensified oppression.

I believe Arafat was a very astute leader, and did the "the best we could achieve in our bad situation," as quoted above. He expected that Rabin would make the right decisions in the future critical junctures and continue the process of transferring power to the PA, because the other option was to lose next elections to the extremist opposition. In other words, the coalition between moderate Israeli and Palestinian leaders would necessarily lead Rabin to go beyond his initial cooptation plan (Grinberg, 1994). Arafat's basic mistake was that he ignored the Palestinians' dependency on Israel, and the dependency of the entire Oslo process on Rabin's charismatic leadership.

The political success of the Oslo process mainly owed to Rabin's popularity, and much less to the power, strategy or discourse of the organizations supporting him. Hence, peace was imagined while all practical difficulties down the road were ignored by the peace supporters (Grinberg, 1994). The agreement's ambivalent and self-contradictory provisions—promising peace but allowing continued expansion of the settlements, the bypassing roads and the perpetuation of the PA's economic dependency—facilitated the creation of a "peace camp" that supported Rabin but was actually lacking in a clear plan to democratize (namely decolonize) Israeli-Palestinian relations. These contradictions could be contained within the leader's personality and the collective imagination that he was leading Israel the right direction. Thus, Rabin's charismatic leadership role (Weber, 1968) became critical under conditions of weakened institutionalized authority and changing power structures.

The concept of dynamic political space contributes to the understanding of charismatic leadership: the leader opens space to new ideas, interests, and identities and mediates between an emerging civil society and state institutions stagnating in the absence of new discourses and representative political actors. The charismatic leader contains the contradictions within society by using his body, voice and individual authority in order to legitimize his decisions and policies. The leader's followers identify with him in the absence of a new language of power or new structures able to contain the conflicts among them by political representation. The charismatic leader leads a process of change, and he is needed in order to open political space whenever there are no new recognized and legitimate goals, values, language and institutions. In the long range the charismatic leader builds new power and facilitates its institutionalization, and in the long run the new institutionalized power might conflict with the continued opening of political space to new ideas. This is often interpreted as the counter-mo(ve)ment, which was analyzed by Weber as the routinization of charisma (Weber, 1968).

However, Rabin had no time to build the new discourse, political power and institutions that would be able to continue his path and contain social conflicts in Israel/Palestine before his assassination, and had no guarantee of success if he remained alive. Nobody was really certain where Rabin had been taking the process, and after his assassination it proved impossible to continue the negotiations (Grinberg, 2000). Rabin's assassination immediately closed the legitimate political space for negotiation and compromise with the Palestinians, and later closed political space to all post-conflict agendas (Grinberg, 2010). According to the Interim Agreement signed in 1995, the PA had full control only in Area A, with the rest of the occupied population dispersed in enclaves surrounded by the IDF (Area B), which was authorized not only to close the border crossings between the OT and Israel, but also to prevent passage of Palestinian between their enclaves. The ultimately political meaning of this eventual outcome was that the Oslo process defused the Palestinian resistance mo(ve)ment with the help of the PLO and its historic leader, without an Israeli partner able to continue negotiations and legitimize the necessary compromise.

From the Palestinians' point of view, the process was pointless without complete decolonization—namely the evacuation of the Jewish settlements, retreat of the IDF, independent control of their own borders and economy. Without pushing for a permanent settlement, the Oslo Accords only ensured improved conditions for Israel's continued control of the OT, as argued by Singer (quoted above). This control, however, remained very unstable due to the presence of the PA in the cities (Area A). The presence of legitimately elected Palestinian authorities in the occupied cities thus represents both the success and failure of the Intifada resistance mo(ve)ment. This was the maximum autonomy that could be achieved given the uneven power relations with Israel.

Importantly, this outcome is not only the result of power imbalance, but also of the peculiarity of the borders in that they do not separate but also do not unite Israelis and Palestinians. The interpenetrated populations create three distinct political arenas—Israeli, Palestinian and interrelated. The main obstacle from the very beginning has been the need to articulate the three arenas and synchronize the opening of political space in those three spheres (Grinberg, 1994). This was the fundamental reason for the mutual dependency between the leaders.

The rise of post-conflict agendas, identities and interests in the Israeli political arena led to the "imagined peace," namely the peace illusion, which marginalized political debate on decolonization and ending the occupation in the Israeli public agenda (Grinberg, 2007). The political elites were weakened and became unable to carry out strategic moves vis-à-vis the Palestinians because of internal divisions over post-conflict agendas. Imagination transformed into illusion is a peculiar repertoire of misrepresentation, not necessarily the result of manipulation by political actors, but a kind of "coproduction" between leaders and followers who prefer to ignore their weakness and inability to change political structures. While imagination is a vital element in every political change, it becomes an illusion when it helps ignore the balance of power and weakness of social groups seeking change.

The counter-mo(ve)ment of the First Intifada was very peculiar, part and parcel of the legitimate process of negotiations. It started with the economic benefits for the Israeli elites, which resolved the initial pressure to recognize the PLO and negotiate a compromise to end the Intifada. It continued with the dismantling of the old tribal polarized "left-right" mobilization, which was a necessary pre-condition for designing new structures and new languages of power, but after Rabin's assassination it disarticulated the process and discontinued the negotiations.

CHAPTER SEVEN

Cooptation of the Palestinian leadership failed, but dependency on the Israeli economy and IDF continued, and was legitimized, creating the "unstable stability" situation, since October 2000.

The inability to coordinate the three political arenas after Rabin's assassination, combined with the interpenetration and erasure of borders created uncertainty and led to a collective fear of "national disintegration" among the Israelis.[51] In the absence of political mediation and compromise aiming to contain internal conflicts, new identities and agendas deteriorated into tribal hostility among the various sectors in the Israeli population. After dismantling the old cartel of tribal "left/right" polarized mobilization, Israeli politics remained unable to open political space for the containment of conflicts, neither internal nor external. Hence, renewed violence between Israelis and Palestinians became the only way to mobilize Israeli public opinion and legitimize the unstable situation created by the Oslo Accords (Grinberg, 2010).

The Palestinian resistance movement was contained by the cooperation between the Israeli and Palestinian moderate political elites. They shared the common interest of controlling the Palestinian population and weakening the radical Islamists. But Israeli and Palestinian political elites had contradictory ways of doing it. The compromise was an Interim Agreement that became a permanent temporariness (Azoulay and Ophir, 2013), which significantly improved the Israeli dual regime of domination, because after Oslo it became legitimized by the PLO leadership as part of a "peace process." The new permanent-temporary institutions that emerged from the counter-mo(ve)ment reflect the power relations between the Israeli state and the Palestinian subjugated population, but also the joint interests of the Israeli and Palestinian political elites to prevent the opening of political space to new Palestinian leadership representing the resisting people.

---

51 This phenomenon was analyzed from different sociological perspectives: Kimmerling (2001) called it the fall of "Israeliness," Shafir and Peled (2002) the weakening of "republican citizenship," and Ram (2008) the weakening of "Zionism" vis-à-vis post-Zionism and neo-Zionism. For my critical take of this debate see the introduction to part 3 in Grinberg (2010).

8.
THE J14 MO(VE)MENT:
THE EMERGENCE OF THE OCCUPY REPERTOIRE OF RESISTANCE[1]

Immediately after the fall of Hosni Mubarak in Egypt on February 2011, many Israelis raised a question: Why can't we do something like this in Israel? This was not an obvious question. After all, Israel is apparently a democracy: there are periodic free elections and changes of government. Nevertheless, the feeling was that, although popular discontent with the government was increasing, it was impossible to mobilize masses to affect politics. In a 30-minute interview for the Knesset public channel,[2] I analyzed the Egyptian success in reconstructing the people's sense of solidarity as they gathered in the public squares, and their ability to define common goals and demands in the name of the people.[3] In Israel, my analysis continued, no one can speak for the people because Israeli collective identity is divided into several sectors and tribes with opposed goals.

Half a year later, however, Israel was swept by a spontaneous pro-

---

1   The ideas for this chapter were presented in two lectures, the first in November 3, 2011, at Berkeley (http://cmes.berkeley.edu/there-chance-democratize-israelpalestine) and the second in Bilbao (http://www.ehu.es/argitalpenak/images/stories/libros_gratuitos_en_pdf/Ciencias_Sociales/From%20Social%20to%20Political_Conference%20Proceedings.pdf). They were also presented in several op-eds published mainly in Hebrew in *Haaretz*: "Protest against all," August 15, 2011 (http://www.haaretz.co.il/opinions/1.1372865); "Now the social protest must be political," April 9, 2012 (http://www.haaretz.co.il/opinions/1.1682328); "Netanyahu's trickle-down election anxiety" (English), December 18, 2012 (http://www.haaretz.com/news/features/netanyahu-s-trickle-down-election-anxiety.premium-1.485529). In Haokets: "What is the new Israeliness?" September 6, 2011 (http://www.haokets.org/2011/09/06/%D7%9E%D7%94%D7%99-%D7%94%D7%99%D7%A9%D7%A8%D7%90%D7%9C%D7%99%D7%95%D7%AA-%D7%94%D7%97%D7%93%D7%A9%D7%94/); and "B is the generation that fights for a home," July 28, 2011 (http://www.haokets.org/2011/07/28/%D7%91-%D7%96%D7%94-%D7%93%D7%95%D7%A8-%D7%A9%D7%A0%D7%9C%D7%97%D7%9D-%D7%A2%D7%9C-%D7%94%D7%91%D7%99%D7%AA/). A preliminary version, not including the analysis of the counter-movement, was published in *Current Sociology* (Grinberg, 2013b).
2   "Breaking the tools," Knesset Channel, February 17, 2011 (http://www.youtube.com/watch?v=POlM_jsLqmk, http://www.youtube.com/watch?v=OBa8zETgDJU).
3   "Democracy is no Panacea," Al-Jazeera, February 28, 2011 (http://www.aljazeera.com/indepth/opinion/2011/02/2011225181951493541.html).

test movement called J14, and masses of young people occupied public spaces all over the country, two months before Occupy Wall Street movement emerged in the US (Gitlin, 2012; Chomsky, 2012) This was a sudden eruption of "popular" inclusive social protest against the government that took place in the "quiet" (warless) summer of 2011, inspired by the Egyptian democratic mobilization in Cairo's Tahrir Square and the Spanish M-15 movement of *indignados*.

This unexpected movement saw 10% of Israel's total population go out on the streets, probably more people in relative terms than all other global mass mobilizations in 2011, except Egypt. Over a period of 52 days (July 14-September 3), demonstrators protested against the unaffordable housing and increasing socio-economic inequality, and their call for social justice was supported by 85% of the population (according to a YNET poll, August 2, 2011). Mainstream media covered the movement sympathetically and facilitated the mobilization of more than half a million demonstrators (Shechter, 2012).

The movement's popularity forced the government to acknowledge its responsibility for the crisis. Following recommendations by the especially appointed Trachtenberg Commission (2011) the Government made some important decisions, including new taxation of the rich, military budget cuts, and new policies aiming to reduce poverty and social gaps. After the September 3 "One Million March," the leaders of J14 announced the dismantling of the tent camps, and most protesters were demobilized. Thus, when the government reverted to its neo-liberal policies, movement leaders and activists found themselves unable to remobilize the masses. The moment of the movement had passed.

During 2011, the repertoire of Occupy resistance movements spread all over the world by contagion. However, despite their common resistance to neo-liberal economic policies, their political context was always local. The more striking differences were between Egypt and Spain: while in Egypt the most overwhelming and clear demand was free elections, in Spain the protest was against the absence of any political alternatives to neo-liberal policies *despite* free elections.[4] The Israeli version combined features of both, due to the peculiar local mix of democratic regime for Israelis and military regime for Palestinians

---

4   The movement occupied public spaces one week before the elections and protested against the entire political establishment.

(Grinberg, 2008). Here lay the main obstacle for popular mass mobilization: while political space for representing Palestinians under occupation was and still is clearly closed, the closure of political space for representation of Israeli citizens' interests and demands was and still is much more subtle.

This chapter discusses both unusual phenomena: Why was J14 so successful in the summer of 2011, and why did it fail to mobilize supporters later on? I will suggest an explanation for the movement's sudden emergence and no less sudden disappearance. To do so I will briefly analyze the historical context of the Israeli political crisis of representation and economic neo-liberalization, the generational class that led the J14 movement, and the unique window of opportunity opened in the summer of 2011. Next, I will analyze the counter-mo(ve)ment of institutionalized political actors, and the emergence of new actors who distorted the resistance movement's message during the 2013 electoral campaign.

I. A Local Path-Dependent Political Context: The Disintegration of Israeli Solidarity

The lack of recognized state borders that define the citizen body, combined with the legitimation crisis of the Israeli regime, gave birth to two political blocks that legitimized the 1967 occupation with different national myths and mobilized opposing social groups without any open representation of their interests, claims, and opinions. In the previous chapters, I analyzed the peculiar political process that created two blocks misnamed the "left" and the "right": the "left" mobilized the middle and upper classes, while the "right" mobilized the lower classes. Although the "left" was seen as supporting territorial compromise and the "right" as an expansionist movement claiming the entire Occupied Territories (OT), both excluded the Palestinians from the legitimate political space, and cooperated in expanding Israeli settlements and institutionalizing the dual democratic-military regime.

The hostility between the "left" and "right" was tribal and polarized, with no space for representation, debate, compromise or middle ground; in other words, without political space to contain the economic, cultural and social conflicts between Israeli citizens. The most important container was the "enemy," consisting of either neighboring countries or the Palestinians under occupation. The risk represented by this enemy silenced other discourses. However, during quieter periods, the reduced saliency of this enemy gave rise to resistance mo(ve)ments that facilitated the emergence of socio-economic conflicts to the public surface (see Chapter 5).

A significant change in this pattern took place after the first Intifada. The demarcation of Palestinian claims in the OT facilitated majority support for opening political space to negotiations with Palestinian representatives, but also opened up "internal" conflicts between Israelis over issues of representation and negotiation (Grinberg, 2013). After the 1992 elections and mutual recognition of Israel and the PLO in September 1993, many Israelis were able to imagine, for the first time since 1967, a democratic state framed by the 1967 borders. The imagination of the democratic Israel gave birth to new "post-conflict" agendas, and new coalitions emerged (Shafir and Peled, 2000, 2002; Ram, 2008). The entire political party system became reshuffled under the assumption that negotiations with the Palestinians would lead to an agreement and the end of occupation.

However, in 1995 Prime Minister Yitzhak Rabin was assassinated. This proved to be a crucial turning point in the political process (Peri, 2000; Grinberg, 2010), foreshadowing the disintegration of Israeli society into hostile tribes, mobilized by political parties that capitalized on the increasing feelings of hostility and fear. Between Rabin's assassination and the 1999 elections, the combined strength of the two main parties (*Likud* and Labor) shrank from almost two thirds of the Knesset seats to just under one third. The main concern of most Israelis was the disintegration of Israeli society,[5] and the most salient critical sociologists suggested theories to explain it (Kimmerling, 2001; Shafir and Peled, 2002; Ram, 2008).

The Second Intifada broke out in 2000, at a moment when no political power in Israel was able to negotiate a compromise and the majority of the population was willing to unite and rediscover a shared identity when the "enemy" reappeared (Grinberg, 2013). In this political context, the military elites were able to mobilize significant popular support for repression and neutralize political negotiations aimed at

---

5   See *Yediot Ahronot* polls, September 28, 2000.

containing the violence (Peri, 2006; Ben Eliezer, 2012). The Second Intifada gave birth to a new national myth: Israel had "no partner for peace", and under these circumstances had no choice but to continue fighting (Grinberg, 2010). The continued military domination of the Palestinians was legitimized by this new myth, which combined the myths of the "left" (security) and "right" (divine promise), facilitating consensual use of violence in the Intifada (2000-2004), the Second Lebanon War (2006), and operations Cast Lead (December 2008-January 2009) and Pillar of Cloud (November 2012) against Gaza. This new myth also provided wide support for the unilateral withdrawal from Gaza in 2005 and its blockade since 2007.

However, in the "quiet" interwar periods, the marginalized "internal" conflicts reemerged. This included a popular movement of single mothers in the summer of 2003; but more important was the case of the 2006 elections held after the withdrawal from Gaza and before the Second Lebanon War. These were elections with a clear socio-economic emphasis: new parties were formed, old parties changed their platforms and discourses, and the neo-liberal *Likud* led by Treasury Minister Benjamin Netanyahu crashed from 38 to 12 (out of 120) Knesset members, forcing him to the opposition. As detailed in the next section, the socio-economic agenda, which had been submerged by the violent conflict with the Palestinians, reemerged in July-August 2011 due to the disenchantment with the government's neo-liberal policies.

II. Political Economic Context: Implementing the Neo-Liberal Program

The J14 window of opportunity began to open in the 2003 parliamentary elections. Netanyahu had been Prime Minister in 1996-1999, and towards 2003 he tried again to oust Prime Minister Sharon in the *Likud* primary. Given the US invasion of Iraq and its pressure on Israel to resume negotiations with the Palestinians, Netanyahu's economic agenda remained marginal. However, after the elections Sharon nominated Netanyahu as Minister of Treasury and gave him full support for his radical neo-liberal reforms (Peled, 2004).

Netanyahu proved to be the classical political leader dreamed of by neo-liberal economists: he thought in neo-liberal terms and identified his political success with the implementation of reforms.[6] Netanyahu's rapid privatization and de-regulation moves provoked immediate social protests. These were made possible by the Palestinian declaration of unilateral cease fire, which reduced the sense of "existential threat" in Israeli discourse and opened the political space. In retrospect, the summer of 2003 was the precursor of 2011, with a single mother's long march and her subsequent encampment in front of the Ministry of Finance.[7]

The most important confrontation at that time was with the trade unions forced to invest most of their pension fund savings in the stock market instead of government bonds guaranteeing a stable interest. The tax and capital market reforms were the first significant moves, followed by budget cuts. The most significant opposition to Netanyahu's policies was led by the *Histadrut* and its chair, Amir Peretz.[8] After the withdrawal from Gaza in 2005, and thanks to expectations for another "quiet" period, economic agendas dominated the Israeli public debate, and Peretz was elected by the Labor Party as its prime-ministerial candidate. Immediately afterwards, PM Sharon split from his own party, dissociating himself from both Netanyahu's neo-liberal policies and the *Likud*'s opposition to the withdrawal. Together with the former Labor veteran Shimon Peres, who had lost to Peretz, they formed a center party named *Kadima* ("forward"), criticizing Netanyahu's economic policies as "piggish capitalism,"[9] and suggesting further unilateral withdrawal from the West Bank based on the "no partner" discourse.

The 2006 elections were mainly a vote of repudiation of neo-liberal policies to the almost total neglect of the Palestinian issue (Grinberg, 2008a).[10] A center-left coalition led by *Kadima* was formed, preventing Peretz from being nominated as Minister of Finance. Peretz thereupon deeply disappointed his supporters by accepting the nomination of Minister of Security, and was subsequently responsible, together with

---

6 On the characteristics of the ideal political reformer, see Williamson (1994).
7 See Daniel Ben Simon, "A mother against Netanyahu" (*Haaretz*, July 18, 2003).
8 For transparency purposes I must state that I had been Peretz's personal advisor in 1994-1997 and remained his friend.
9 This was Shimon Peres' contribution to *Kadima*—creating the image of moderate neo-liberals (YNET, June 20, 2004, [http://www.ynet.co.il/articles/0,7340,L-2934863,00.html]).
10 The election results in 2006 were as follows: *Kadima* 29, Labor 19, *Likud* 12, *Shas* 12, *Yisrael Beiteinu* 11, The National Union 9, The Pensioners List 7, Torah Judaism 6, *Meretz* 5, The United Arab List 4, *Hadash* and *Balad* 3 each.

Sharon's successor, Ehud Olmert, for the controversial Second Lebanon War. The disenchantment from the center-left coalition that actually pursued Netanyahu's neo-liberal policy was rapidly suppressed by the renewed agenda of war and conflict. This suppression was increased towards the 2009 elections, when the *Kadima*-Labor government initiated a ruthless attack on Gaza (Operation Cast Lead). Nevertheless, public disenchantment with neo-liberal policies remained strong enough to fuel the 2011 resistance mo(ve)ment.

Almost no agenda was discussed in the 2009 elections: neither socio-economic issues nor war and peace. A strong anti-Arab message was expressed by *Yisrael Beiteinu*, a party representing new Jewish immigrants from the former Soviet Union, headed by Avidgor Lieberman. This party demanded that "disloyal" demonstrators—such as those who had protested against the attack on Gaza—be denied citizenship (Grinberg, 2010a). *Yisrael Beiteinu* (meaning "Israel is our home") became the third strongest force in the Knesset, with 15 members, after *Kadima* (28) and the *Likud* (27), with the Labor Party winning only 13. The resulting right-wing coalition excluded *Kadima*, but included the Labor Party, now led by once more by Ehud Barak.[11]

Netanyahu's new government initiated a series of anti-democratic laws, particularly against Israel's Palestinian citizens.[12] A racist discourse became legitimate in the open public sphere (De Malach, 2009), and Netanyahu rolled out an ambitious economic plan. For the first time the Treasury's bureaucratic elites found themselves opposing more neo-liberal reforms, and the media began criticizing Netanyahu's plan.[13] In the long run, it was this split in the elites which fueled the 2011 resistance movement.[14]

In the meantime, the main agenda remained focused on the external "enemy": US pressure to resume negotiations with the Palestinians,

---

[11] Barak, who had led the repression of the Second Intifada as Prime Minister, blurring the distinction between left and right, also led Operation Cast Lead in 2008 as Minister of Security. Barak was interested in retaining that position after the 2009 elections, and was supported by 8 Labor party KMs, while a minority of 4 KMs opposed the government. In 2011, Barak split from the party, taking 5 KM with him and leaving 8 in the opposition.

[12] For a detailed description of this legislation see a report by the Association for Civil Rights in Israel (http://www.acri.org.il/he/?p=1231).

[13] Nechemia Stressler, a popular economic reporter called a senior Finance Ministry official a "socialist" following his opposition to the renewed tax exemptions for capital and cuts in social services (*The Marker*, May 9, 2012)

[14] I owe this insight to an exchange of ideas with Avia Spivak.

the continued Jewish settlement in the West Bank, and the economic blockade of Gaza. Given their total mistrust of the new Israeli government, the PA in the West Bank[15] decided to opt for a diplomatic initiative in the UN aiming to mobilize international support for statehood.

The Palestinian initiative helped Netanyahu to once more suppress socio-economic unrest with the pretext of a new external threat. Catastrophic forecasts of the dangers involved in Palestinian statehood started leaking, and the government began an international campaign against the Palestinian efforts in the UN. Throughout almost the entire first half of 2011, Israeli media were concerned with this "threat," culminating in Netanyahu's May 24 speech before the two Houses of the Congress, which won 29 standing ovations.[16] The image was that Netanyahu defeated Obama on his home turf.

Despite the media preoccupation with the so-called Palestinian threat, Israeli public opinion was apparently much more concerned with a more tangible, realistic threat: the high prices of basic goods. A massive Facebook campaign against the price of cottage cheese mobilized almost half a million supporters for a consumer strike and succeeded in forcing government intervention (*Haaretz*, June 30, 2011). Later on, the threat of strike against the increase in fuel prices led to the reversal of a government decision. This was the atmosphere when Netanyahu returned from his triumphant speech in Congress, the climax of his anti-Palestinian campaign. Thus, the climax turned out to be an anti-climax, with nothing to report on the impending "threat" in anticipation for the real "confrontation" in the UN, scheduled for September. It is my argument that some awareness of the narrow window of opportunity affected significant decisions by the J14 leaders: the initiative in July, the quick mobilization, the scheduling of the Million March to September 3, and the immediate dismantling of the tent camps afterwards. The movement's short lifecycle serves to explain its "carnival" features,[17] and the misguided expectation that it would re-

---

15 The Palestinian Authority was split in 2007 between Hamas which won the 2006 elections and subsequently gained control of the Gaza Strip, and Fatah which remained in in control of the West Bank.
16 ABC News, May 24, 2011 (http://abcnews.go.com/blogs/politics/2011/05/israeli-prime-minister-gets-20-standing-ovations-in-congress-sends-message-to-white-house/).
17 See Yehuda Shenhav, "Carnival: Protest without a sting," *Haoketz*, February 20, 2012 (http://www.haokets.org/2012/02/20/%D7%94%D7%A7%D7%A8%D7%A0%D7%91%D7%9C-%D7%9E%D7%97%D7%90%D7%94-%D7%9C%D7%9C%D7%90-%D7%A2%D7%95%D7%A7%D7%A5/).

turn the next summer, based on the assumption that its success had been due to the summer holiday. In fact, the Israeli mo(ve)ment in the 2011 Summer was framed by the Palestinian refusal to play the role of enemy before September and Netanyahu's tour de force in Congress, not only by the student holiday.

III. The Disenchanted B Generation

The symbol of the J14 movement was the Hebrew letter Beth (B), which also means "home." When the first tents were erected on July 14 the protesters wrote on them: "B is a tent."[18] I called them the B Generation[19] and associated them with a combination of deep political and economic disappointment. The B Generationers were 25-35 years old in 2011 (Shalev, 2012; Shalev and Rosenhek, 2013). They had been politically traumatized by Rabin's assassination at age 10-20, having lost their fervent hope to live in peace. As we have seen, the assassination marked the beginning of the process of social disintegration, and five years later the no-partner myth became dominant. B Generation is also the informal name of the collective wage agreements signed during the 1990s and 2000s, which discriminated against new workers in terms of salary, social rights and pension rights. In line with the neoliberal adjustment of Israeli society, this created a background in which B Generationers could clearly see the rising economic inequality in general, and particularly the deterioration of their position compared to their parents: skilled and well-educated employees now had less chance of reaching highly paid positions and their incomes fell (Shalev and Rosenhek, 2012).

In reaction to their collective experience, members of the B Generation started to differentiate themselves from established political parties and develop their own distinct views and attitudes. They organized mainly in civil society organizations, activist groups and NGOs, which were also one of the main forms of organization in the world under globalization in the 1990s and 2000s (Gidron et al., 2003), a world charac-

---

18 This is a Hebrew pun. A nursery rhyme for teaching the ABC goes: "A is a tent and B is home."
19 Lev Grinberg, "B is the name of a generation fighting for a home"; http://www.youtube.com/watch?v=KqFzb48qiQ8.

terized by increasing alienation between civil society and politics.

One of the first appearances of the B Generation in the Israeli public sphere was the 1998 students' strike, which lasted 50 days and paralyzed academic studies in all public universities and colleges. This movement had several similarities with the future J14 movement: the media was very supportive, public support was almost 80%, and the PM was Netanyahu. Some of the leaders of 2011 had taken part in this strike and remained highly suspicious of Netanyahu's manipulative skills.[20] Another important similarity was one of the slogans of the 1998 strike that reappeared in 2011, claiming that the students include everyone: Jews and Arabs, left and right, religious and secular, Oriental and European Jews, new migrants and long-time Israelis (Grinberg, 2007).

This slogan was crucial for the B Generation's ability to gain public support: while all the parties were active contributors to the disintegration of society by inciting hostility among the "tribes," the students in 1998 and J14 in 2011 claimed to represent all social groups and their shared interests, building a new formula for Israeli peoplehood. The slogan was also used in another prolonged and popular student strike in 2007. This time the country was ruled by the disappointing "center-left" coalition that had promised social-democratic reforms but continued the neo-liberal economic policy dictated by the economic elites, the Treasury, and the Central Bank technocrats (Maman and Rosenhek, 2011). After prolonged negotiations a compromise was reached in 2007, but the significance of this second major strike lay in the politicization of the students who had a direct impact on the activists of 2011. The 2007 activists underwent a process of radicalization: they started talking about an "educational revolution," and even "social revolution," criticizing the shrinking of the welfare state, not only the education budget. Some activists started working with non-unionized workers who suffered from the neo-liberal labor market flexibilization and privatization, and established a new trade union called "Power to the Workers."[21]

---

20 In 1998 Netanyahu effectively manipulated the media, bringing pizzas to the negotiators when some of them were supposed to be on a hunger strike, making it appear as though the hunger strike were a fiction. In 2011 he tried to split J14 by a very attractive package of benefits for the students, hoping that the National Student Federation would accept it and abandon the movement. The rejection of the offer was crucial to the further success of J14 (Smoli, 2012).

21 This is a very peculiar organization that organizes both the lower strata workers, like public building cleaners, and middle class workers in temporary jobs, like teaching assistants and adjunct

The "revolutionary" spirit of the 2007 strike affected the young generation of skilled workers in several strikes, most importantly those of the secondary teachers (2007), social workers (2011), and physicians (2011). In all these strikes, B Generation members rose against their former union leaders, mainly because the agreements discriminated against them. The tendency of trade unions to compromise the interests of young workers and sign the B Generation agreements was a result of neo-liberal policies aiming to reform the labor markets, lower wages, and reduce tenured positions and pension funds. The new phenomenon was that the B Generation rejected the option to continue compromising in the name of younger workers and revolted against their own unions.[22]

My interpretation of the B Generation is that they are the product of a double political economic crisis, global and local. The local political crisis is related to the disintegration of society into "tribes" and the complete suppression of socio-economic agendas by means of "external enemies" and tribal hostility. The global crisis is the crisis of representation caused by the neo-liberal economy that weakens middle and lower classes as well as the state's capacity to redistribute (Amin, 1997). In the absence of a balance of power between dominant and dominated classes, and with a weak state, political parties cannot fulfill their promises and are unable to represent the majority. As shown in previous chapters, tribal hostility is one of the counter-mo(ve)ment repertoires used by political actors to mobilize the anger and fears of voters without representing their social and economic needs and demands (See also Grinberg, 2010).

The B Generation suffered the effects of precariousness caused by the neo-liberal political economy and became the generational-class category Standing (2011) called the precariat. The generational class suffered all the negative effects of the neo-liberal economy, with no promise for stable jobs or any jobs at all, no stable and increasing salaries, and decreasing social rights, including pensions. In Israel, the B Generation also suffered from the implications of a dual democratic-

---

professors in the universities.

22 See Grinberg, Lev "Tahrir Square in Arlosoroff Street," *Haoketz*, March 31, 2011 (http://www.haokets.org/2011/03/31/%D7%90%D7%9C-%D7%AA%D7%97%D7%A8%D7%99%D7%A8-%D7%91%D7%A8%D7%97%D7%95%D7%91-%D7%90%D7%A8%D7%9C%D7%95%D7%96%D7%95%D7%A8%D7%95%D7%91/).

military regime and the tribal hostility. In this context, the prospects for mobilizing a popular resistance movement did not seem promising. The J14 movement managed to emerge with very opportune timing, however, thanks to the coming of political age of an entire generation.

IV. J14's Imagined People

The story of J14's inception is well known. Daphne Leef, a 25 year-old student, was evacuated from her rented apartment because she had refused to pay a higher rent. She decided to move to a tent on the street, in protest against the rising cost of housing (30% in four years).[23] She asked a small group of friends to join her and posted an event on Facebook. Dozens of tents were erected on the very first day in Tel Aviv's trendy Rothschild Boulevard, and within days the entire boulevard was filled with tents. New encampments appeared every day in Tel Aviv and all over Israel (*Haaretz*, July 19, 2012). While the Rothschild encampment and the movement leaders were characterized as middle-class students of European descent, other encampments in Tel Aviv and in peripheral areas of Israel were more representative of the Israeli class structure, including homeless families. Several encampments were also organized by Arab citizens,[24] and one in downtown Tel Aviv was populated by migrant workers. No encampment was erected in the OPT by either Jewish settlers or Palestinians: the protest movement clearly demarcated the borders of the Israeli sovereign state, although its leaders avoided any reference to the military occupation, the erasure of state borders, housing subsidies for Jewish settlers or house demolitions targeting Palestinians.

At first there was an attempt to delegitimize the protestors as radical leftists due to their middle class, secular background, and the encampment's fashionable location and carnival atmosphere. This overused strategy (e.g. Lev and Shenhav, 2010) orchestrated mainly by the

---

23 These are real prices, the nominal rise over the same period (2007-2011) was 50% (Trachtenberg Report, 2011: 195).
24 On the participation of Arabs see Avi Klein, "Then summer came and we shouted together," *Haoketz*, May 16, 2012 (http://www.haokets.org/2012/05/16/%D7%95%D7%90%D7%96-%D7%91%D7%90-%D7%94%D7%A7%D7%99%D7%A5-%D7%95%D7%A6%D7%A2%D7%A7%D7%A0%D7%95-%D7%91%D7%99%D7%97%D7%93/).

government and supportive media failed. The rapid joining of other social groups and the non-partisan student associations neutralized this attempt to delegitimize the movement's leadership. Nevertheless, the tension and differences between the European (*Ashkenazi*) middle classes in the center and the peripheral ethno-classes were real, and never completely disappeared (Bernstein, 2012).

Many civil society organizations joined the movement, including the youth movement affiliated with the Histadrut trade union federation (Dror Israel), Power to the Workers, the New Israel Fund and the medical interns who were in the middle of their own strike. The rapid growth and expansion of the movement took the country by surprise: within ten days 20-40,000 people were mobilized, and by August there were already 300,000. (*Haaretz, Yediot Ahronot, Maariv*, July 24, 31, August 7, 2011). Finally, in the One Million March more than half a million protestors went to the streets in 12 cities (*Haaretz, Yediot Ahronot Maariv*, September 4, 2011). There is no Israeli precedent for such massive and rapid mobilization on socio-economic issues; the only comparable movement was the opposition to the First Lebanon War in 1982.[25]

The movement expanded not only numerically and geographically, but also in terms of its agendas. Every group felt free to raise their own issue and join the movement, be it education, prices, women and minority rights, or health (Schechter, 2012). The common denominator was inequality and discrimination within the 1967 borders; however, Jewish settlers were also welcomed when they joined the protestors in Tel Aviv (Haaretz, August 12, 2011). Everyone could camp in Rothschild Boulevard, including also racist activists. This apparently a-political attitude contributed to the mo(ve)ment's carnival atmosphere,[26] also affected by the timeframe of the summer, which would end when the students returned to school.

As already mentioned, however, the truly significant timeframe was not the academic but the Palestinian calendar: the students went back to school on October 30, but the Rothschild encampment was dismantled on September 7, a few days before the UN discussion of the Palestinian statehood proposal. The a-political and carnival image was obviously a

---

[25] In mid-September 1982, following the massacre in the Sabra and Shatila Refugee Camps near Beirut, an unprecedented 400,000 demonstrators protested in Tel Aviv.
[26] Shenhav, "Carnival."

crucial element of J14's success, but not everyone can mobilize such a carnival. The question therefore remains: why did so many join the movement?

I argue that the political space for representation of socio-economic issues in Israel is closed not only by the salience of the Israeli-Palestinian conflict and the manipulations of the external "threat," but also by internal tensions and hostility between ethno-classes, instigated by the institutionalized political actors and constructed as "tribal" conflicts. No universal claim can be made within the framework of neo-liberal economic policy, and only sectorial parties representing specific, privileged social groups are able to provide some benefits to their voters. These differential benefits only exacerbate tribal hostility in turn.

Against the background of a political discourse focused on tribal hostility (facilitated by a weakening of the external threat), the non-religious middle and lower classes had no representation or political space. They responded by going to the streets and avoiding the tribal hostility discourse, which would have rapidly prevented any mass mobilization. The inclusive discourse and open-ended agenda of the B Generation reconstructed peoplehood in inclusive terms, inspiring the movement's most chanted slogan—"The people demand social justice"—and contributing to a sense of "togetherness" in the streets (Talshir, 2012).

The movement's a-political aspect is obviously the pretention to represent all the people, with the inclusive construction of the borders and boundaries of the people acting as a precondition for democratization (Rustow, 1970; Linz and Stepan, 1996; Mann, 2005). While J14 succeeded for a short time in imagining and reconstructing the people inclusively and a-politically, it also added two very radical innovations crucial for democratizing the Israeli dual regime: (1) the borders were tacitly demarcated by the places where housing was demanded to the exclusion of the OT; and (2) the boundaries of the people included the entire citizen body, Jews and Arabs alike.[27]

The discourse of "togetherness" and the willingness to discuss every idea upset many political activists. However, these were, in my opinion, essential for mobilizing the people, opening political space to socio-economic claims, and starting a democratization movement (Talshir, 2012). The catch of this strategy was that it was very difficult to move

---

27 See Klein, "Then summer came and we shouted together."

on without taking any clear democratic stands in order to prevent the future closure of political space. Consequently, the dismantling of the camp ended the mo(ve)ment. At the moment the "people" did not meet each other in the occupied public space, each community returned to its original isolation and was subjected to the pre-J14 tribal manipulations. This isolation of the ethno-classes facilitated the work of the political actors who started the counter mo(ve)ment.

V. Counter-Mo(ve)ment 1: In Search of Threats

The J14 huge mobilization provoked strong responses and an incredibly inventive repertoire of misrepresentations and distortions by political actors, due to the unprecedented impact in the public discourse and its collective memory. The old actors cannot ignore the resistance movement, and in this broad sense mo(ve)ments of resistance have always had a significant effect on politics, albeit sometimes in the opposite direction.[28] In the present case, the immediate reaction by the old political guard was followed by the emergence of new political actors claiming to represent the social protest movement and seeking to gain power despite their distortion of the movement's socio-economic demands and inclusive collective identity. I will analyze here the main repertoire of old political (re)actors and new (pro)actors during the counter-mo(ve)ment.

The counter-mo(ve)ment started immediately and was anticipated in advance by the protesters and their leaders, given the peculiar window of opportunity opened by the temporary suspension of the "security" agenda and the "Palestinian threat." The most striking evidence that the leaders and activists of J14 were aware of the danger posed by violent escalation manipulated by the counter-mo(ve)ment was during their last attempt to keep the masses on the streets, after the UN General Assembly. Symbolically, this demonstration took place in Tel Aviv's Rabin Square, the scene of the 1995 assassination, and was attended by more than 50,000 demonstrators, an impressive number given the fact that it took place at a time of renewed hostilities in the Gaza area (*Haaretz*, October 30, 2011). The central drama was a sketch by five famous come-

---

28 The most radical reactions I found involved working class movements. See Chapters 4, 6 and 9.

dians[29] who directly referred to the danger that a belligerent countermovement could kill the movement ("We smell war").

Indeed, immediately after the Palestinian "threat" had vanished Netanyahu started manipulating the old and trustworthy Iranian nuclear "threat."[30] When the seemingly more "reliable" Iranian threat failed to suppress the socio-economic agendas, new issues, dangers and divisions were constantly introduced by the veteran political actors supporting the government. The first wave took the form of intensive anti-democratic and anti-Palestinian legislation. Within a few months almost all social actors who supported J14 during the summer were attacked by some kind of special legislation, including civil rights organizations, the media, and courts, but especially the Palestinian citizens.[31]

When external threats and anti-democratic legislation proved insufficient, a new "external-internal" threat was "discovered" among the refugees and asylum seekers from South Sudan and other conflict areas in Africa. A racist demonstration against them in the inner city Tel Aviv neighborhood where they were concentrated flamed ethno-class tensions among J14 activists (*Haaretz*, May 23, 2012). While the J14 mobilization had previously succeeded in containing tensions between the *Ashkenazi* middle classes and the *Mizrahi* lower classes by means of joint collective action and popular assemblies with open debates in the occupied squares, after the encampments were dismantled, ethnic and class tensions reappeared. In May 2012, the differential reactions to the anti-African demonstration emphasized socio-cultural gaps and divergent everyday experiences. Many members of the *Ashkenazi* middle classes condemned the racist riots, whereas some *Mizrahi* activists criticized the former's arrogant position, given the fact that they did not experience the less pleasant aspects of coexistence in poor neighbourhoods in South Tel Aviv.[32]

After the "hot May days" of anti-African riots came the "despairing June days," which culminated with the self-immolation of Moshe Silman and the complete split of the movement into two core groups of *Ashkenazi* middle-class activists. Silman's mourning parades in fact la-

---

29 These were the members of the "Chamber Quintet," a very popular satiric TV program in the late 1990s.
30 Yossi Melman, "The nuclear spin," *Haaretz*, November 4, 2011.
31 Report of the Association for Civil Rights in Israel (See note 12).
32 See for example the Miri Regev Saga: http://news.walla.co.il/?w=/90/2535681.

mented the end of the mo(ve)ment itself. As shown below, the January 2013 Knesset elections reflected the sorry state of the May-June 2012 counter-mo(ve)ment: the complete marginalization of the peripheral *Mizrahi* lower classes and the split among the *Ashkenazi* middle classes, the decay of the old political re-actors and emergence of new political pro-actors. However, no representation of the new agendas, claims, and identities succeeded in penetrating the political arena. This remained so even given the significant new power accumulated by new actors manipulating the J14 symbols and language against the old-new "internal enemies" discourse, which distorted the mobilizing symbols of new inclusive Israeli collective identity—solidarity and social justice. This distortion started in June 2012.

At the background of the May-June days were the rising expectations created leading up to the summer of 2012, when a new protest carnival was expected to remobilize the masses. These expectations were based on the symbolic violence of a government that ignored the protesters' demands and did not change its policies, did not stop the spiraling housing prices and failed to implement even the recommendations of its own Commission. While the repression and counter-mo(ve)ment of extreme right-wing political parties was only to be expected, the more surprising sabotage of J14 came from central and left-wing parties. These prevented the movement's resurgence in their attempt to "help" the movement set more "realistic" goals by channeling its demonstrations to support their own sectorial agendas and co-opting their leaders and activists.

The first attempts to reorganize the protest towards the next summer were rapidly and violently repressed by the police (*Haaretz*, June 3, 2012); however, it was the channeling of the movement's demands by political actors and the neutralization of the social activists that really prevented the expected mass remobilization. Indeed, activists and supporters of center-left parties—the majority of the J14 protestors (Shalev, 2012)—had realized in 2011 the value of the movement's inclusive collective identity, designed to mobilize "left and right" constituencies, mainly *Ashkenazi* middle classes and *Mizrahi* lower classes. Accordingly, the "center" and "left" parties did not impose their parties' signs, colors or flags on demonstrators. By the summer of 2012 this tolerant attitude disappeared, provoking tensions with the activists who sought to continue the inclusive discourse of 2011, which sometimes deteriorated into violence between activists.³³ By 2012, each group regained its separate identity and the sense of "togetherness" was gone. The carnival never even started, and different activist groups demonstrated separately, unable to join forces and to mobilize the second ring of supporters.

The most successful attempt to channel the protest movement was initiated by the "center" political actors—the decaying *Kadima* and a new party called *Yesh Atid*, which organized following J14, claiming to represent the middle class. These two parties shifted the claim for equality of rights towards equality of obligations, fanning the old hostility against the ultra-Orthodox Jews and Arab citizens who are legally exempt from military service. They adopted the egalitarian discourse of the 2011 protest, co-opted some of the leaders, and organized demonstrations taking up the place and time planned by the J14 movement for renewing the carnival.

The first tensions appeared during the global demonstration called by M-15 on May 12, when leftist parties attempted to occupy the square with their flags and signs, and violent clashes with party orderlies were uploaded to YouTube.³⁴ The anti-African demonstrations amplified these tensions. However the main split took place when two different and extremely opposed demonstrations took place on June 2. The expectations of the activists and media for a new hot summer in 2012 were very high, and the failure to unite the movement drove many to despair. As mentioned above, the veteran disability rights activist, Moshe Silman, died of self-immolation in the middle of one such demonstration, sacrificing his life in the hope that it would help unify the movement. Unfortunately, it did not.

The splintered demonstrations continued and led to violence among the activists. The "equal [military] service camp" was supported by the National Student Federation and Dror Israel, two key organizations that had played a crucial role in the 2011 mobilizations. This camp's tribal attack against the poorest segments of Israeli society (ultra-Orthodox Jews and Palestinian citizens) by the more wealthy middle class failed to mobilize the masses and rapidly vanished. Thus, the center's political identity became tribalized as well, at the moment it defined itself by merging the hostilities of the "right" and "left" against Arabs and

---

33 See *Haaretz*, August 4, 2012; http://www.themarker.com/news/protest/1.1793445.
34 http://www.youtube.com/watch?v=72z5rKxJJX0; http://www.youtube.com/watch?v=WrdutR1I8IE.

ultra-Orthodox Jews, respectively. Whereas the tribal polarized discourse closed political spaces to discussing any political issue, the new tribal center joined the club and built a new political identity closing all political spaces for recognition, representation, negotiation, and compromise, including issues it pretended to raise, involving military service and the participation of Arabs and ultra-Orthodox Jews in the mainstream education system and labor markets.[35]

VI. COUNTER-MO(VE)MENT 2: CLOSURE OF POLITICAL SPACES IN THE 2013 ELECTORAL CAMPAIGN

The most salient phenomenon in the summer of 2012 was the constant attempt and failure to mobilize the masses again despite the fact that several thousands of activists took to the streets almost every week. Even the reversal of some economic policies, such as new taxes on the middle and lower classes, did not provoke any significant mobilization. The active intervention of political actors to prevent mass mobilization was obviously related to the approaching elections. In principle, the official timing of the elections was November 2013, but the 18 months left until the elections threatened to facilitate the opening of political spaces by social actors able to organize independent political parties representing the new identities, agendas, and demands of the J14 movement. The point is that the transition from civil society to the political arena is complex and time-consuming. The old political actors were aware of that and sought to close the space by shortening the time until the elections. The control of the agenda and schedule is one of the advantages of power holders.

The summer of 2012 was the time for the obstruction of new political identities. This was carried out with full cooperation between the old reactive political parties and the new proactive parties of those middle classes serving in the armed forces. The latter were indeed part and parcel of the motivations of the middle classes going to the streets in the summer of 2011. The feeling of middle classes was that they worked hard and did their military duties, but lacked recognition and repre-

---

35   Aluf Benn, "The coalition of minority haters," *Haaretz*, February 25, 2013 (http://www.haaretz.co.il/opinions/1.1936880).

sentation. However, instead of the creative inclusive identity of Israeli solidarity around the values of social justice, the new political pro-actors channeled the anger against the encapsulated and isolated poor Arab and ultra-Orthodox Jewish communities, which are indeed represented by sectorial political parties.

Netanyahu feared that his new budget would upset the entire population and sought to hold the elections before the approval of a new budget, a strategy designed to abort any autonomous political organization of social activists. His first partners in closing political space were old, declining reactors, and his challengers were the new distorting pro-actors. As I will show here, this was the main issue during the elections and the negotiations to form the new government.

The Prime Minister's first move to advance the elections was supported by the leader of the Labor Party, which was also threatened by the entrance of new political actors. The leaders of *Likud* and Labor agreed on May 2, 2012 to advance the elections to September 4, 2012, aiming to occupy summertime with the electoral agenda.[36] This was a real threat to *Kadima*, the major opposition party, which was about to disappear according to the polls.[37] Netanyahu, however, got cold feet and suspended the move, because he was also afraid of the dynamics of the elections due to his experience in 2006, when the *Likud* under his leadership shrank from 38 seats in 2003 to 12 seats in 2006.[38] In order to continue his term and secure a majority on the budget, he decided to build a new coalition with *Kadima* solely on one basis: the promise to pass a new conscription law that would apply to all citizens. However, it soon became clear that such law was not going to pass, due to the strong opposition of other members of Netanyahu's coalition. Hence, it was impossible to maintain the coalition government, which includes both *Kadima* and the ultra-Orthodox parties vehemently opposed to such legislation. The new coalition with *Kadima* was dismantled within 71 days, and early elections were declared.

The January 2013 elections were the opposite political phenomenon to the mass mobilization of civil society against the political actors. Now

---

36 http://www.ynet.co.il/articles/0,7340,L-4223897,00.html.
37 http://www.haaretz.co.il/news/politi/1.1701222.
38 Grinberg, "Netanyahu's trickle-down Election Anxiety," (English) *Haaretz*, December 18, 2012 (http://www.haaretz.com/news/features/netanyahu-s-trickle-down-election-anxiety.premium-1.485529).

the political actors occupied the public sphere and managed to neutralize civil society, which remained perplexed and alienated, and felt manipulated. During the electoral campaign, political commentators attempted to explain the strange atmosphere that accompanied the elections, characterized by the extreme ambivalence of voters, their distrust of politicians, the absence of clear agendas and expected coalitions based on them. The campaign was full of tricks and manipulations of public opinion and the media. Instead of actively involved citizens influencing the agenda and making clear demands, like they were during the mo(ve)ment of resistance, we got the opposite: passive and alienated citizens, watching the elections as if they were a reality show, on which they were expected to vote for the next newborn star ("Israeli Idol"), or the one who would form the best team of survivors. Indeed, the new pro-actors behaved like TV stars, and the old parties seemed like survivor teams.

The first failed manipulation to usher in the electoral campaign was Operation Pillar of Cloud in November 2012, which was rapidly dubbed by many citizens as the "Elections War." After eight days of mutual bombing resulting in 162 Palestinians and Israelis killed, it became clear that the operation would not produce the victory photo needed to support Netanyahu's slogan: Israel is strong with Netanyahu. The IDF's inability to stop the Palestinian rockets was evident, and the operation was halted, suffering harsh criticism. The most striking element is that immediately after the cease-fire all major parties collaborated in ignoring the event; indeed, throughout the ensuing campaign hardly anyone raised any fundamental issues like the blockade of Gaza, the absence of political negotiations or the continued Israeli settlement in the West Bank.

Given the threat of a coalition of anti-*Likud* forces, Netanyahu announced a block between the *Likud* and Lieberman's Party, *Yisrael Beiteinu*, making sure that no other block of parties could gain more votes. This block was indeed the biggest survivor team, and they won the competition, despite having lost more than 25% of their power in former elections.[39] The block was strongly criticized by *Likud* activists and supporters precisely in the context of the J14 critique of Netanyahu's policies, because the *Likud* voters identified with the critics of Netanyahu's economic policies, while Lieberman was also identified with

---

39   In 2009, the *Likud* got 27 seats and *Yisrael Beiteinu* 15; in 2013 they got 31 together.

the pro-capital neo-liberal economic policies and the Russian-speaking ethnic group. The danger of alienation of lower-class *Likud* supporters was imminent, but no other party attempted to represent them, except *Shas*, which was deeply delegitimized by the parties of the *Ashkenazi* middle classes due to their rejection of mandatory military service for all. Four parties appealed to the secular *Ashkenazi* middle classes: two old survivors parties—Labor and *Meretz*—a new group of survivors from different parties (the Movement),[40] and the new centrist party—*Yesh Atid*—headed by Israeli Idol Yair Lapid. These parties failed to unite and form a block of their own. *Yesh Atid* offered the voter an attractive list of newborn stars, composed of social activists, journalists, businessmen and popular mayors, with nothing in common except the demand for equality in conscription and the desire to gain political power.

The right had its own new born stars, oddly enough in the extremist settler party Jewish Home, which decided to win votes using the images and discourses of the new generation, and the claim for equal obligations, agitating against the Arabs and ultra-Orthodox. In order to do so, they chose for their leader a young hi-tech professional with a modern, almost secular look, who avoided extremist ideological language and instead spoke the new language of social discourse, talking about housing prices and economic inequality. The election results reflected the maintenance of power by the marginalized community parties (*Hadash*, *Balad*, and *Raam* 11, and 17 for *Shas* and *Agudat Yisrael*). The survivor parties shrank: *Likud-Yisrael Beiteinu* from 42 to 31, and *Kadima*, Labor and *Meretz* from 42 to 29). The newborn parties gained 31 seats, 19 for *Yesh Atid*, and 12 for the Jewish Home.

The election results and the following negotiations to form a coalition seem to indicate four phenomena: (1) the rise of the newborn proactive parties; (2) the fall of the old reactive parties; (3) the marginalization of the Arab and ultra-Orthodox parties despite their success in retaining their seats in the Parliament; and (4) the complete disregard of the *Mizrahi* lower classes interests, identities, and expectations by all parties, except *Shas*, which maintained its power but was powerfully delegitimized. The newborn parties formed a block after the elections towards

---

40 The Movement attracted survivors from *Kadima* and *Likud*, Livny and Shitrit (former candidates to lead these respective parties), as well as two former Labor leaders: Amir Peretz and Amram Mitzna.

the formation of the new coalition, making clear that their joint demand was a new law of conscription for all, seeking to block the option of a coalition with ultra-Orthodox parties. No other agendas concerned them, completely distorting the social justice demands of the 2011 resistance mo(ve)ment.

VII. Conclusion

The J14 movement of resistance was an unprecedented, albeit short-lived movement: the window of opportunity opened after Netanyahu's speech in Congress, and closed when the UN General Assembly started discussing Palestinian statehood. Like all other movements analyzed in this book, J14 emerged as a response of social groups to the lack of political space for their interests, agendas and identity. In order to be recognized, they must penetrate the public sphere and demonstrate their presence. The resistance movement adopted a new repertoire of collective action imported from Tahrir in Cairo and Puerta del Sol in Madrid—encampment in city squares. They did it only within the legitimate and recognized borders of the State of Israel. This framing tacitly emphasized that the government did build and subsidize housing, but only beyond its legitimate borders, forcing its Jewish citizens to move to the OT.

In this chapter I have analyzed the peculiar moment of resistance, when relative calm in the Israeli-Palestinian violent routine opened a window of opportunities to social protest. The analysis of the time framing of the moment helps comprehend the success of both the mo(ve)ment and the counter-mo(ve)ment. It explains why the mass mobilization was so short lived, and failed to remobilize the masses, to organize a social movement or be represented by the political system towards the elections held only 18 months later. I have shown how they indirectly influenced the elections, but failed to gain representation of their new definition of the inclusive Israeli identity, and why the old phantom of tribal politics re-occupied the political arena, against the Israeli Occupy resistance movement. The effective separation between the occupied Palestinian people and the Israeli people subordinated to the global capital is at the core of Israeli local politics. However, despite these peculiar features, the phenomenon of weakening state institutions and social solidarity leading to narrowing political space for representation is a global one.

Just like most other 2011 movements, the Israeli movement emerged by way of contagion. Events in Tunisia and Egypt fuelled strong emotions in the Israeli media and public opinion, and Tahrir Square became a byword in local public discourse. In July 14, when the first tents were erected in Rothschild Boulevard, one of the most visible posters read "Rothschild at the corner of Tahrir" (MAKO, August 7, 2011). The key strategy in the J14 repertoire, occupying the main square, was adopted from the Egyptian uprising, and its main slogan—"The people demand social justice"—was the Hebrew version of the most chanted slogans in Egypt.

However, the Israeli demonstrators' repertoire borrowed also from Spain. The Spanish M-15 movement inspired not only the sister movement's name (J14) but also key forms of organization, communication and discourse. As in Spain, the Israelis organized general assemblies and constantly attempted to listen to everyone and make consensual decisions; even the hand signs language was copied from Madrid's Puerta del Sol. Most crucial was the strategic refusal to negotiate with the government and compromise with the political establishment. The Spanish experience was critical for mobilizing Israeli protesters because it gave the protest movement its global image: more than local discontent against Arab dictators, it now became a protest in democratic regimes against the crisis of political representation.

This is perhaps the most salient feature of the global wave of protests in 2011, from Egypt to Spain, from New Delhi to New York, from Chile to Israel: all were resistance movements against political systems unable to represent the masses, against ruling governments and established opposition parties. Everywhere, the uprising was led by a skilled young generation[41] crushed by neo-liberal economic policies, increasing inequality and the precariousness of their economic position who protested against the linkage between big capital and national elites.

---

41   The concept of political generation is obviously not new, having been first suggested by Mannheim (1952). It has been also used to analyze the social movements of the 1960s (Wilson, 1973).

9.
CONCLUSION: ON THE DYNAMICS OF POLITICAL SPACES: TIME, MOVEMENT, ACTORS AND MASSES

I. INTRODUCTION

This book is designed to provide tools for analyzing political dynamics provoked by movements of resistance, and the reactions of the powerful—whether with or without democratic rules of the game. The types of resistance selected here are concerned with the collective identity and demands of subordinated social forces, and how they influence the decision making process.[1] In my previous work I've shown that some balance of power between the dominant and dominated is a necessary precondition for the opening of political space (Grinberg, 2010, 2013a). However, this is a highly complex concept that originates a set of new questions, which are explored here by the comparative analysis of seven historical cases of mass resistance to dominant power and political elites. The research presented here analyzes a variety of mass mobilizations seeking the opening of political space for recognition and representation of demands, identities, and agendas of subordinated populations, and discusses different responses of political actors aiming to maintain and expand their power.

This chapter seeks to expand the analytical framework of dynamic political spaces by suggesting abstractions and generalizations anchored in the comparative analysis of the historical cases presented in the book. The comparison of the cases is helpful in characterizing the different social forces involved in movements of resistance, their distinct successes and failures; and repertoires of political distortion and misrepresentation used by conservative political actors, in addition to the institutional and structural adjustments orchestrated by the powerful political actors

---

[1] I have excluded cases of violent repression and resistance that escalate into a vicious circle of violence, which I discussed elsewhere (Grinberg, 2010, 2013a), as well as collective mobilizations claiming peace, or violent revolutions.

and state actors in counter-mo(ve)ments.

No straightforward dichotomy is involved in the concept of political space elaborated here, be it politics/violence, open/closed political space, or democracy/autocracy. In the cases analyzed here, categories tend to be more nuanced and subtle, and in the transition from open presence of resistance movements in the public sphere to their symbolic representation in the political arena, everything can be transformed, distorted, manipulated, misrepresented or coopted. The transition from recognition to representation is never direct, smooth or obvious, and it reflects the gap between civil society and social actors on the one hand, and the political arena on the other. While resistance movements demonstrate their presence in the public sphere and may gain recognition, the transference of their power to the political field of representations is obstructed by competing political actors threatened by the potential emergence of new competitors.

Sophisticated containment of subordinated groups and their demands takes place in both so-called democratic and authoritarian regimes. Accordingly, the concept of political space is designed to analyze and criticize political power and its dynamics in cases where governments do not rely on heavy-handed control and violent repression of civil society. As seen in Chapters 2 and 7, externally imposed regimes (the British Mandate in historic Palestine or the Israeli military occupation in the West Bank and Gaza Strip) often attempt to contain resistance by way of recognition and negotiations. This has been the case also in many other colonial, dictatorial and military regimes. The exceptions to this rule (not discussed in this book) are extremely repressive regimes, which regularly use violence and secret services to penetrate civil society and prevent its organization, arresting and often killing their opponents.

*

Before embarking on a comparative analysis, I would like to clarify the methodological use of concrete cases and their relation to theory. I have no theoretical assumptions about the structure of "society" or the "state." I see both, and their interrelations, as historical contingent constructs in constant dynamic flux. This is why my focus is on the political mediation between state and civil society as a tool of analysis of

Conclusion: On the Dynamics of Political Spaces: Time, Movement, Actors and Masses

these changing relations, and of the concrete forms they take in specific times. This approach is based on a path-dependent vision of history and eventful sociology (Sewell, 1996, 2005).

I have asked questions aiming to understand the relation between the moment and movement. For example, why have ethnic riots sparked in previously Palestinian neighborhoods settled in 1948 by Jewish migrants from Arab countries? Why have the powerful workers organized the struggle in 1980? And why did the Arab transportation companies organize the joint anti-colonial struggle in 1931? I have not looked for agents of social change expected by macro-theories of society and change; rather, I have looked for the social actors that organized to present their demands vis-à-vis the state, and also succeeded in mobilizing mass support.

My comparative research focuses on the social actors and masses that present their resistant power without making any assumptions on the nature of the conflict (social, ethnic, or national) is about; sometimes these were workers, sometime middle classes leading the entire civil society, sometimes ethnic or nationalist mobilization. All these categories are seen here as contingent mobilizations that in certain moments may generate collective mass movements.

The sequence of events helps us comprehend why these were the actors and social forces mobilized, and to discover the ruptures and tensions in state-society relations. This analysis is not a deductive one based on a-priori macro theory of society, but it is also not inductive, arising only from the specific historical cases. It is abduction, namely the readiness to be surprised by the dynamic power relations uncovered by mo(ve)ments of resistance.[2] Here lies the importance of analyzing resistance to power: its capacity to uncover what is usually unseen in ordinary social and political daily life. The abstractions and generalizations, like all interpretations, are based on my own imagination, assisted by the imaginations of the actors—either social actors seeking change, or political and state actors seeking to contain the conflicts and maintain their power, who proved to be no less creative.

The reader may get some idea of the very peculiar sequence of events that shaped historical turning points in Israel/Palestine and produced such a different outcome from the original visions of Zionist leaders and

---

2   See Handelman (2005).

competing political currents. No one achieved all their goals. The present political situation is the unintended consequence of multiple struggles between dominant forces and the resistance of the dominated.

II. Forms of Resistance: Social Actors and Mass Mobilization

The cases analyzed in this book can be divided into four forms of resistance, each with different goals, demands and agendas. They differ in their repertoires of presentation, in the capacity of social actors to organize and mobilize, and in the collective imagery of mobilized masses. They also differ in the obstacles faced by social actors seeking to transfer the collective identity, agendas, and demands presented in the public sphere to the political arena, transforming it into legitimate representation recognized by state institutions and other competing political actors. The analysis of each form of collective action and its specific obstacles on the way to gaining political representation is used to comprehend Israel's political peculiarities and to make some generalizations of characteristics of each form of resistance and obstacles preventing its representation in the political arena.

I refer to representation of the subordinated social groups as the establishment of one or more autonomous political organizations (usually political parties) capable to articulate the identity, interests, agendas, and demands of the social groups that have publicly presented their resistance to power. Misrepresentation, which will be analyzed later, is based on manipulations and distortions of the identities, agendas and demands by conservative political actors, and the cooptation of individual actors.

a. The working class struggle: Institutional obstacles and weakening structures. Working class resistance is the first form of collective action provoked by the establishment of the capitalist nation-state in Europe. It is characterized by the mobilization of rank and file workers who pressurize their direct leaders in the workplace and from there bottom up to regional, industrial, or national trade union leaders (Crouch, 1983; Pizzorno, 1978). This form of resistance is led by trade union leaders at different levels, and its trajectory or path is significantly influenced by local institutional settings: the relations between the different levels of organization, and between them and political institutions, both parties and the state (Maier, 1984; Collier and Collier, 1991; Grinberg, 1991; Shalev, 1992). The institutional links between worker trade unions and parties constitute what activists called the labor movement, and some sociologists labeled as the "old" social movements based on material claims and class bases.[3] This form of resistance was seen as cyclical movements of protest because instead of being revolutionary, as Marx predicted, it became reformists within the capitalist nation-state.

The Israeli cases discussed here are exemplar of the path-dependent institutional features of the workers' struggle: it started from strong pressure from below on worker organizations, but then it diverged. The first wave in 1960-1965 was characterized by decentralized strikes that were supported also by opposition parties seeking to weaken the ruling party (*Mapai*) in both institutions—the central union (*Histadrut*) and the state. However, the attempt to articulate working class power with representative political actors failed due to *Mapai*'s successful cooptation of working class leaders through the new alignment with *Ahdut Haavoda*. In 1980, the strong worker committees organized a centralized struggle "in the name of the weak workers" unable to organize autonomously. In so doing, they took the power of the entire Jewish working class for themselves, in order to maintain the structure of the split Israeli-Palestinian labor markets and the *Histadrut*'s non-democratic institutions.

The specific timing and repertoire of working class mobilization was shaped by labor market business cycles of full employment and economic recession, the structure of the markets and state, political institutions and opportunities. All of these factors are relevant for the analysis of the two cases discussed in this research, and we can define the different repertoires of resistance according to the historical contingencies. In favorable times of full employment, workers sought to improve their working conditions, income and rights, and in dangerous times of economic recession, hyperinflation, and liberalizing economic policies, they acted to protect their employment and wages and accumulated rights.

This distinction shaped two different repertoires of resistance. In the period of full employment (1960-1965) working conditions became homogeneous, weakening previous ethnic divisions between Jews and Arabs and between *Ashkenazi* and *Mizrahi* workers, facilitating class soli-

---

3   For an effective refute of this distinction, see Calhoun (1993).

darity and a "proactive offensive" wave of rank-and-file wildcat strikes leading to significant improvement of real wages. The general phenomenon of working class power benefiting from full employment is that the social actors organizing working class struggles are less concerned with political organization and state policies, precisely due to their power at labor market level (Sturmthal, 1973). The concern with working class political organization comes from political actors, both conservative actors threatened by the resistance mo(ve)ment, and those seeking working class support.

Chapter 4 provides a detailed discussion of the dynamics between social forces, political institutions, and social and political actors. I have argued that this is the relevant context to understand the struggle between *Histadrut* General Secretary Pinhas Lavon and Prime Minister Ben Gurion, which ended with the replacement of both leaders by Treasury Minister Levi Eshkol, who became Prime Minister in 1963. The importance of this crucial political struggle, alongside the historical turning point in 1967, has been obscured and misunderstood by Israel's dominant security discourse.

The wave of "reactive defensive" resistance rose under hyperinflation, recession, and a new Treasury Minister who threatened to dismiss public sector workers and lower their wages. Under these conditions, the main repertoire of working class resistance cannot be offensive strikes, so they use "warning strikes," solidarity strikes and mass demonstrations. The defensive workers' repertoire uses their main source of power: their big numbers, which when organized have potential political power. Given the workers' weakness in the labor market, the promise of political protection by state intervention becomes the most useful venue for political actors to mobilize the workers.

While political articulation of workers and their organizations is crucial in periods of defensive resistance, the previous institutional interrelations between trade unions and political parties are a crucial factor in the political dynamic. Chapter 6 discusses in detail the dismantling of worker committees and the Histadrut, the workers' split both in the labor markets and in terms of political affiliations, and the different attitudes towards *Likud* governments (1977-1984) and the later National Unity governments. It shows that the economic liberal reforms implemented by the *Likud* government and the resulting hyperinflation, which had terrible effects on labor and the mobilization of the working class in 1980, encouraged Labor party opposition. However, when Labor returned to power in 1984, it implemented even more radically neo-liberal economic reforms designed by state elites, and legitimized by the National Unity government that conferred relative economic autonomy to the Treasury Ministry reformers.

Both cases analyzed in this book ended with the defeat of the working class and the structural weakening of their collective power. The principal political powers reacting to worker resistance in both cases were the Labor institutions seeking to maintain their dominant position in the labor market—*Mapai*, which ruled the state, and the *Histadrut*, which controlled the workers in the 1960s. These ended up empowering the military institutions in 1967 and restructuring state borders and labor markets that divided the working class along national and ethnic lines (Chapter 4); and with the Labor party policies during the 1980s, when it formed a National Unity government with the *Likud*, empowering private capital and the state bureaucrats to design the neo-liberal restructuration of the state (Chapter 6).

These two repertoires of breaking up working class power were evident globally and almost at the same time: ethnic splitting of workers in the 1960s and 1970s; and neo-liberal policies and institutions designed to break the strong skilled workers in the public sector, services and big industries during the 1980s and 1990s. Working class power is based on their indispensable role in the economy. The fluctuations between periods of empowerment and enfeeblement depend on business cycles in labor markets, which are not determined only by internal politics, but also by the world economy, namely the international competition between workers and firms (Grinberg, 1991a), and between hegemonic powers (Balibar and Wallerstein, 1991).

The main obstacle to political representation of the working class is the disarticulation of global markets and local politics, and the always complex organizational links between trade unions and parties. In addition to organizational links, workers are mobilized through discourse, symbols and collective imaginations (often called ideology) that promise state protection from their economic weaknesses. These symbols and discourses are not always the expected working class solidarity according to Marxian traditions. In their weakness, workers might be mobilized by populist or nationalist ideologies claiming the displacement or unequal subordination of other workers (Bonacich, 1979; Collier and Collier,

1991). This was the case of Labor Zionism discussed in Chapter 2 (Shafir, 1989; Shalev, 1992; Sternhell, 1998).

The fundamental obstacle preventing workers from opening up political space to their interests and agendas has to do with their "human condition": namely, their dependence on their body. In order to promote their interests, workers must somehow compromise on their individual views and interests and subordinate them to the collective worker organization. However, such an organization—committee, union or party— has its own institutional interests, which might conflict with individual workers' interests (Offe and Weisental, 1980). These features of the working class transform its political articulation into a phenomenon that is unstable, historically contingent and subject to strong cycles of empowerment and weakening. This is why we can find workers supporting a very wide variety of political formations and ideologies (Collier and Collier, 1991; Maier, 1984), most of them looking for peaceful incorporation of the working class in the capitalist economy, instead of changing the structures that construct labor as the dependent variable of the economy.

b. The anti-colonial repertoire: (Local) civil society vs. (external) state institutions. I suggest here that the organization of civil society is the result of the imposition of centralized authority in a delimited territory on a civil population.[4] While social actors are able to organize civil society activities, interests and communities autonomously, the state attempts to penetrate civil society, regulate its activities and extract its resources (Mann, 1986; Tilly, 1992). In certain moments of friction, civil society organizations react against state authorities demanding voice to their interests and participation in the decision-making process. These typical struggles of democratization within nation-states occur when there is an imagined correlation between the local population's collective identity and the goals of state authorities. Transitions to democracy, which institutionalize the rules of the game for the dynamic opening of political spaces, are outside the scope of this research; the main difficulty in opening up political space occurs when the State's explicit goals are related to

---

[4] This is an operative definition. The concept of civil society deserves a much deeper discussion due to the variety of its interpretations. For a comprehensive discussion of the concept, see Cohen and Arato (1994).

the interests of an external power. The anti-colonial repertoires analyzed here refer to two different cases of civil society resistance to an externally imposed state that extracts resources without opening space to the representation of civil society interests.

Contrary to Weber's definition of the modern state,[5] I suggest here that colonial (and post-colonial) states are characterized by external enforcement of an *il*legitimate monopoly of violence on a population within a given territory. In these cases the original conditions that facilitated capitalist development, the organization of strong centralized states and the imagination of national communities did not exist (Chatterjee, 1993). Despite the absence of the fundamental requisites of capitalist nation-states, the isomorphic imposition of central state administrations in delimited territories framed a civil society bound by the state and opposed to it. The modular adaptation of nationalism in colonial states (Anderson, 1991) provided the legitimacy to the claim of local political actors for legitimate monopoly over the use of violence, namely the struggle for replacing the foreign elites ruling state institutions with indigenous or creole political actors. When local political actors succeeded in articulating the local civil society and claim the representation of their identity and interests it was usually called "self-determination" or "independence."

As shown in Chapters 2 and 7 the ability of political actors to articulate the interests of the different social groups that constitute the local civil society framed by the borders of the colonial state is crucial to the successful claiming of self-rule and independence. The focus here is on the local dynamics that lead local civil society to oppose the unilateral decisions of colonial administrations, and the reactions to them by local political actors and external state apparatuses. The comparison of the short-lived transportation strike in 1931 and the prolonged Palestinian uprising in 1988-1992 demonstrates clear differences of colonial situations (moments) and resistance repertoires (movements).

Both anti-colonial mobilizations, against the British Mandate in 1931, and against Israeli military occupation in 1988-1992, sparked due to worsening economic conditions that damaged the entire civil society,

---

5   "A human community that (successfully) claims the monopoly of the legitimate use of physical force within a given territory" (Max Weber, *Wirtschaft und gesellschaft*, 1921: 29) obviously refers to European states and excludes colonial states and empires.

and the symbolic violence of the colonial state that ignores their interests and needs, and does not recognize their representatives. However the cases markedly differ in the actors, goals and demands, the repertoire of public acts of presence, and the articulation of interests between social actors, the mobilized masses, and political actors.

The 1931 anti-tax revolt was initially organized by private providers of a vital public service—transportation. They managed to paralyze the entire economy and to mobilize the support of the entire civil society affected by the state's unilateral decision to raise transportation taxes. As a result, the organization of the Arab and Jewish drivers was recognized by the government and it accomplished the material goals of the strike. However, after the successful strike the social actors were unable to agree on a common political goal for Jews and Arabs claiming self-rule, or even participation in decision making processes (Grinberg, 2003). On the contrary, the British Mandate effectively succeeded to divide and rule civil society along ethno-national divisions, strongly supported by nationalist political actors, who managed to build their power over civil society on the confrontation between Jews and Arabs.

The Intifada was framed by the dual regime that defined the boundaries of the Palestinian population that was subordinated to Israeli military rule. The resistance movement succeeded in achieving collaboration among various classes, including peasants, workers, and merchants, and to mobilize mass demonstrations and general strikes of the entire population with a shared collective goal of claiming recognition, representation, negotiation and self-determination. The reaction to the Intifada was mixed, combining immediate violent repression and later on recognition and negotiations. This was followed by the establishment of self-ruled institutions that effectively co-opted the dominant Palestinian political actors. The Palestinian anti-colonial resistance had dual power: (1) it caused economic damage by denying workers from the Israeli economy and by boycotting Israeli products; and (2) it raised public awareness through popular mass demonstrations of presence.

In 1931 and 1987, the strikes succeeded in disrupting the economy and the government had to recognize their representatives and negotiate. In 1931 there was no violent repression, and the British Government simply revoked the taxes. In 1987, after the initial repressive reaction, Minister of Security Yitzhak Rabin attempted to find interlocutors, and finally decided to recognize the PLO and sign an agreement aiming to put an end to Palestinian resistance. The Oslo Accords, signed after the mutual recognition, eventually ended in co-opting the PLO leadership by establishing the PA under Israeli military and economic domination (Grinberg, 2008). This move divided the Palestinian civil society under occupation and established a much more effective and stable regime. This was because during 1993-2000, Israel radically transformed its economy by finding new global markets for its products and importing migrant non-Palestinian and non-Jewish workers (Shafir and Peled, 2002; Kemp and Raijman, 2008). Therefore the potential disruptive effects of any Palestinian strike were significantly contained, as evident during the Second Intifada of 2000-2005. As shown by Younis (2000), one of the crucial differences between the successful resistance movement in South Africa and the limited achievements of the Palestinian Intifada lies precisely in the differential dependence of the dominant state on the supply of labor.[6]

c. The ethnic riots repertoire: (Discriminated) citizens against the (nation) state. Chapters 3 and 5 analyze a distinct form of collective action and resistance understood by the actors as ethnic protest against discrimination. Having no stable or homogeneous position in the economy, ethnic protests cannot disrupt the public order by strikes like the previous cases, and they usually erupt as riots. Ethnic discrimination is exerted against certain citizens marked as different by the power holders without having anything in common except their marker. Discrimination may be at different and not mutually exclusive levels: formal or informal discrimination by the state, economic discrimination in the markets, or symbolic degradation by the dominant social group. The dominant social groups define the boundaries of their higher culture by the attribution of an inferior culture to the marked citizens, and by doing so they legitimize their own privileged positions. Ethnic discrimination may occur in European nation-states and post-colonial states, the marked populations may be formally equal citizens; however, in all cases the state is considered responsible for continued discrimination, which is attributed to the dominant elites.

---

6   There were obviously other significant differences. The opposite reactions provoked by the two Intifadas are discussed in "Resistance, politics and violence: The catch of the Palestinian struggle" (Grinberg, 2013).

CHAPTER NINE

The violent riots are a moment of explosive outrage, which seeks recognition of discrimination in response to the symbolic violence exerted by the dominant elites (Auyero, 2003); in some cases they could deteriorate into ethnic wars. The state is the ultimate arena for ethnic clashes precisely because it can privilege or discriminate different social categories. The social construction of an ethnic group is not deterministic, it is an eventual historical development, and the process of nation-state formation has a crucial role, both in the construction of a homogenizing national identity, and in the discrimination of certain subjects, "ethnicized" by the treatment of the state (Brubaker, 2004). The process of acknowledgement of the discrimination of certain citizens due to some shared marker is always a political process, independently of whether the discrimination is by the state, the market or the symbolic power of the dominant group. In any case the arena of change is the state and the organization is political (Hechter, 1975; Rothschild, 1980).

The initiative for the riots may come from social actors, but they rapidly see the need for political articulation and become political actors: they claim representation of the discriminated group and attempt to enter the political arena. The violent presentation in form of ethnic riots appears when political recognition is denied, and the basic goal is opening political space for recognition and representation. According to my analysis of the 1959 and 1971 cases, the riots provoked some level of recognition, but no representation. In both cases the physical proximity to Arab and *Ashkenazi* neighbors was crucial in flaming up the sense of injustice.

The *Mizrahi* migrants have been discriminated against by the state at all levels, mainly in unequal allocation of lands, their settlement in the periphery, and differential levels of education, jobs and housing. They have also seen discrimination in the labor markets, which placed them in between the privileged Europeans and the further subjugated Arabs (Swirski and Bernstein, 1980; Swirski, 1981; Semyonov and Levin-Epstein, 1987; Yiftachel, 2005; Chetrit, 2010). The dominant cultural elites constructed them as inferior, due to their non-modern, religious, and Arab culture (Shohat, 1988; Shenhav, 2006).

The Black Panthers mo(ve)ment of resistance sparked precisely when they could directly see the discrimination against Palestinians on the one hand, and the resources invested in housing new Russian migrants on the other. Within less than one kilometer from their poor overcrowded neighborhood of Musrara (previously a well-to-do Palestinian neighborhood, emptied in 1948) they could see the occupied Palestinians in the so called "slave market" in front of Nablus Gate in the Old City of Jerusalem, and the nice new houses built for the *Ashkenazi* migrants (mainly from Russia) in Ramat Eshkol on empty lands in northern Jerusalem. These new houses were much more comfortable than the housing conditions of the old *Mizrahi* migrants. Both Wadi Salib and the Black Panthers riots took place at a moment of economic expansion and integration of Palestinians in the Israeli economy. This economic dynamic created competition between *Mizrahi* and Palestinian workers, in Haifa in 1959 and in Jerusalem in 1971, and highlighted the privileged position of *Ashkenazi* skilled workers and employers.

Obviously the most oppressed group of citizens that mobilized ethnic riots were the Palestinian citizens living within the sovereign borders of the State of Israel, which were not included in the cases analyzed here. The features of their collective action are typical of mo(ve)ments of resistance, although shorter (one day on March 30, 1976 and one week in October 2000) and more violently repressed (6 citizens death in 1976 and 13 in 2000). They had direct political effects: a shift in the voting patterns of the Palestinian citizens towards anti-Zionist parties since 1977, and massive abstention in the 2001 elections. Discrimination of non-Jews is the very definition of the State of Israel, and its Palestinian citizens are therefore in a very tricky situation: they are apparent equal members of the state but are officially excluded from the nation, and legally discriminated (Lustick, 1980; Zureik, 1979). They have rights to vote and parties claiming their representation, but are always ignored and never included in the government coalition.

The state is the main organ of discrimination in Israel, evident in the legal distinctions it draws between Jews and non-Jews, through land confiscations, the support of Jewish immigration and Palestinian emigration, and finally in the military service. All these forms of discrimination are justified and rationalized as part of the "national conflict" between Jewish settlers and Arab local population, but it also affects the different privileges and discriminations among Jews. Not only Arabs are excluded in the military recruiting, but also ultra-orthodox Jews; not only Arabs suffer in terms of land rights, as the redistribution of Lands between European and *Mizrahi* settlements has been extremely unequal. The treatment of Jewish migrants when they arrived to Israel was also discriminatory, privileging European vis-à-vis *Mizrahi* Jews in the 1950s-1960s or vis-à-vis Ethiopian Jews in the 1990s-2000s.

The main difference between the *Mizrahi*-marked citizens and all the "others" marked by their distinctions from the dominant *Ashkenazi* secular Jews is that the legitimacy of the *Mizrahi* collective identity is denied, and their political representation is constantly coopted or channeled. In both resistance mo(ve)ments, the leaders of the riots attempted to organize parties and to enter the political arena but failed, due to the conservative reactions of the existing political actors in the run-up to the elections: *Mapai* in 1959, and *Likud* in 1973 and 1977.

Both major parties indirectly defined themselves as representing one of the main ethno-classes that constitute the large majority of the Jews in Israel. Both parties have different symbols representing myths of the imagined nation, each of them hinting at the particular ethno-class they seek to gain their identification. *Mapai* constructed the Israeli imagined nation inspired by the myth of a modern, rational, and implicitly European "new Jew" working the land and fighting, contrasted to the image of the traditional, "weak" Diasporic "old" Jew (Eisenstadt, 1967; Ram, 2008).

Likud presented the collective imagined nation with a completely different rhetoric based on the religious myth of the Promised Land. The collective identity is Jewish, old and new, religious and secular, *Ashkenazi* and *Mizrahi*—all part of the nation that had been promised the land. This was the Revisionist discourse from the beginning. However, Menachem Begin's speeches became very effective in mobilizing *Mizrahi* support after the occupation of the ancestral sites in the West Bank in 1967, and the *Mizrahi* protests against their exclusion from *Mapai*'s imagined nation in 1971 (Shapiro, 1991).

These two reactions to *Mizrahi* protest shaped Israel's political arena and closed the political space to the ethnic question because it remained covered by a carpet of national imaginations. The symbols, myths and discourses of the "left" and "right" after the 1977 elections hid any explicit reference to ethno-classes but mobilized their mutual hostilities. This tribal polarized political channeling also hid the fact that both parties represented something very different: the labor party representing the interests of the *Histadrut*'s conservative bureaucracy and economic interests, and the *Likud* representing the drive to expand Jewish settlements in the West Bank, aiming to prevent any future territorial compromise.

However, despite the different symbols of the nation, both left- and right-wing national discourses legitimize the privileges of the Jewish settlers by the Orientalist discourse vis-à-vis the local Arabs (Eyal, 2005). This construction of national identity in conflict with the Orient is arrogant and denigrates also ultra-orthodox and *Mizrahi* (Oriental) Jews, because they are constructed as "inferior," and subject to the state's institutions designed to modernize them (Bernstein, 1978). The de-legitimization of *Mizrahi* symbols and culture is deeply related to the conflict between the European settlers and the local Arab population, but it effectively neutralizes *Mizrahi* political representation.

Here lies the most crucial obstacle to ethnic representation of *Mizrahi* Jews in the Israeli context. The option of a *Mizrahi* political articulation of their collective identity is dangerous to the ruling elites because it is the flip-side of the Zionist construction of a collective national identity in conflict with the Orient. All non-dominant communities have their legitimate representative political parties: Palestinian citizens, ultra-Orthodox, nationalist-religious and Russians.[7] The only "forbidden" identity is *Mizrahi*, and when coopted *Mizrahi* leaders talk about their collective discrimination, they are immediately silenced as manipulatively using their identity to gain power (to silence them, they are routinely blamed for "taking the ethnic demon out of the bottle"). For sure they cannot unite and form their own party, except if they camouflage it under the guise of an ultra-Orthodox party, like *Shas*; but in that case their continued marginalization as non-modern, non-Zionists or non-fighters and non-workers is an easy feat.

The Jewish migrants from Arab countries had nothing in common except their discrimination by the dominant *Ashkenazi* former migrants, who saw them as an inferior type of Jew, to be modernized. They were unequally incorporated in Israeli society, but could benefit from the privileges of being Jewish, serving in the military and being integrated in the expanding economy. During the years, some of these migrants joined the middle classes through jobs, education, and marriage. However, the feeling of cultural illegitimacy, the persistent poverty of those who remained in the peripheries, and the continued closure of political space by the ethno-class polarization between left and right prevented the total

---

[7] Migrants from Ethiopia do not have their own party not because it is not considered illegitimate, but because they are a small group.

disappearance of the ethnic tensions even in the 2013 elections.

d. The (new) Occupy repertoire: The people vs. institutionalized political actors. As mentioned in Chapter 8, the Israeli J14 movement emerged by way of contagion. Events in Tunisia and Egypt fuelled strong emotions in the Israeli media and public opinion, and Tahrir Square became a byword in local public discourse.[8] On July 14, when the first tents were erected in Rothschild Boulevard, one of the most visible posters read "Rothschild, corner of Tahrir" (MAKO August 7, 2011). The key strategy in the J14 repertoire—occupying the main square—and the main slogan—"The people demand social justice"—were both adopted from the Egyptian uprising. The Spanish M-15 movement inspired not only the sister movement's name (J14) but also key forms of organization, communication and discourse. As in Spain, the Israelis organized general assemblies and constantly attempted to listen to everyone and make consensual decisions; even the hand signs language was copied from Madrid's Puerta del Sol (Shushan, 2012). Most crucial was the strategic refusal to negotiate with the government and compromise with the political establishment.

The most salient feature of the worldwide wave of protests in 2011 is that all were movements against political systems unable to represent the masses, including both ruling governments and established opposition parties. Everywhere, the uprising was led by skillful youngsters crushed by neo-liberal economic policies,[9] growing inequality, and the precariousness of their economic status (Standing, 2011), who protested against the linkage between big capital and national elites.

In 2011 a new repertoire of mass protest has crystalized, having emerged in Egypt and traveled to Spain, Israel, and the US. Although the name "Occupy movement" was coined by the latecomers from Wall Street, this was the proper conceptualization of the new repertoire of local protests against the unruly power of financial capital (Castells, 2012; Gittlin, 2012; Chomsky, 2012; Harvey, 2012). Despite the fact that the neo-liberal economic policies had similar effects in all the economies that implement them, the closure of political space to the opposition to neo-liberalism was always contingent on the local political situation.

---

8 See "Tahrir, corner of Rothschild" photo exhibition (*Haaretz*, September 29, 2012).
9 On the concept of political generation see Mannheim (1952), and in the context of social movements, Wilson (1973).

Although neo-liberalism's socio-economic effects and the fluidity of the uncontrolled financial capital were similar, the political manifestations of the protest against them were strikingly different. In Egypt, protesters cried in the name of the people to replace the dictator and called for democratic elections and free competition between parties. Three months later, the demonstrators in Spain protested against the elections and against all parties, opposition and coalition alike, in the name of the masses of young middle and lower classes unemployed and under-employed called "indignados."

The Occupy movements that crystalized in 2011 were part of a new form of civil society mobilization against the very peculiar linkage between globalized financial capital and the local deflated political bodies of the nation-state. The two fundamental elements of the Occupy repertoire, the protest against both government and opposition, and the physical occupation of the public space were not new to the movement. Encampment in public spaces, for example, was used in 1999 by anti-globalization protesters in front of the G-7 Conference in Seattle (Levi and Murphy, 2006). Mass protests uniting the middle and lower classes against all parties because of their failure to represent protect them against financial capital were the most salient feature of Argentinian popular revolt: in December 2001, millions of protestors took to the streets calling for the ousting of the elected president and crying against all parties ("que se vayan todos")[10] and succeeded in forcing the resignation of five presidents within a month.

The Occupy repertoire merges protest against global capital and against local politics. The Occupy movements oppose the powerful coordination between uncontrolled globalized financial capital and the local political elites due to shrinking state capacities to redistribute national resources, which weakens the big majority of local population ("99%" or "the people"). Within the neo-liberalized state, no one can represent the views, demands and interests of the majority of the people affected by neo-liberal policies. There is no political space to represent the demands of the sovereign people vis-à-vis the state, because the state has lost its sovereignty and is no longer the locus of policy making. Political parties are no longer the institutional link between civil society and the state because, notwithstanding their rhetoric, discourse, or economic ideology,

---

10   Everyone must go.

when in power they submit to the interests of capital.

Physical occupation of public space is the most salient form of peaceful physical presentation of the underrepresented, much more than sporadic demonstrations, strikes, or riots. The Occupy repertoire is less violent and disruptive of social order, but much more persistent and difficult to ignore when big masses join the encampments and the demonstrations grow from one to the other (Gitlin, 2012). The Egyptian model is the most striking due to its perseverance, peaceful message, and mushrooming support. The Israeli case is also impressive in the increasing support the protestors managed to mobilize, but it was totally vague in terms of political demands, especially when compared to the simple Egyptian demand to topple Mubarak.

The occupation of public spaces is obviously not new. However, it became the salient feature of these new movements in 2011, when the masses immediately joined by occupying public spaces all over the country. It is the contagious feature of the Occupy movement that emphasizes its global meaning, contagion both within and beyond state borders. The Israelis started looking for options of similar popular revolt against local political institutions almost immediately after the Mubarak's fall. It started with a revolt of social workers against their union in March,[11] and continued in May-June with a Facebook boycott against the price of cottage cheese, culminating with the contagious encampment in Rothschild Boulevard against the price of housing. "We build tents in the streets because we don't have money to rent an apartment," explained the social actors. Very soon, however, the resistance movement began focusing its criticism on the linkage between the state and political elites and big private capital. These were defined in a very concrete way, called the "tycoons," ten families that own almost all financial institutions, industries, marketing, etc. The owners of almost all big business in Israel are local families, but their capacity to transfer capital elsewhere is global.

The agendas expanded as soon as the encampments spread, and many marginalized groups joined the protest, each with their own agenda, demands and identity. Here we can find the reason for the strategy of occupying public space to mobilize the entire civil society against externally

---

11 See my op ed "Tahrir Square in Arlossoroff streets," *Haoketz*, March 31, 2011 (http://www.haokets.org/2011/03/31/%d7%90%d7%9c-%d7%aa%d7%97%d7%a8%d7%99%d7%a8-%d7%91%d7%a8%d7%97%d7%95%d7%91-%d7%90%d7%a8%d7%9c%d7%95%d7%96%d7%95%d7%a8%d7%95%d7%91/).

Conclusion: On the Dynamics of Political Spaces: Time, Movement, Actors and Masses

imposed economic policies: the logic of collective action is to reconstitute local civil society. At the moment that capital is global and uncontrolled and economic policies are externally imposed, civil society has no terms of reference, it is divided in various social identities and agendas, and suffers from atomization. Workers in particular are split, their unions weakened, the labor conditions and employment terms unstable. The result of this situation has been the flourishing of small NGOs filling the empty space of politics: bridging specific civil society demands regarding state policies. Neo-liberal economy and uncontrolled capital succeeded in destroying social solidarity and cooperation, including the nation and the state, the two original forms created by capitalism, which framed civil society and facilitated the bridging of particular social interests by opening political spaces of representation.

The concrete physical encounter in the city square is the moment when the feeling of peoplehood is recreated and re-invented, claiming recognition first, and hopefully representation later. Given the legacy of the globalization years, the expectations for representation are weak, except in places that still lack democratic rules of the game, where the demand is for free elections, as in the Arab Spring of 2011. However, when the formal rules of the game in democratic regimes are already in place, the Occupy resistance movements are against the existing parties in government and opposition, claiming recognition of their demands and agendas.

The Occupy resistance movements re-invent the people claiming representation, and those who join them are the citizens who feel under-represented, a broad coalition of marginalized classes and ethnic identities. The crucial questions are how these groups are articulated, presented and represented, who the social actors are and how they work together, and what the attitudes of the actual political actors and the potential new political actors are. All these factors are crucial in the political dynamics of Occupy movements.

The Israeli case is telling. The occupation of Rothschild Boulevard provoked immediate mobilization of masses that joined the encampment and also started new encampments all over the country, but not in the Occupied Territories. The feeling was that the movement represented the majority of the population, despite internal divisions between ethno-classes. Not all sectors were equally active. Those who had their own legitimate representation felt less identified with the movement. The most salient absentees were the new Russian-speaking Jewish migrants, the ultra-Orthodox, and the Palestinians. The most salient activists were members of the two big ethnic groups, the dominant *Ashkenazi* middle classes and the *Mizrahi* lower and middle classes, who were under-represented by the "left" and "right" parties.

However, the special excitement provoked by J14 was related to the new inclusive Israeliness created by the physical occupation of public space, and it was in my opinion the most powerful mobilizing force. Young activists believed that they could overcome the divide-and-rule regime of hate between different ethno-classes created and constantly maintained by the political elites of the left and right. There were obviously tensions and mistrust between activists who have never met before. However, the striking point is that during the moment of the encampment they managed to overcome these tensions, while immediately after the dismantling of the encampment all the tensions re-emerged and no further social movement could be organized. The movement did not survive the moment.

As shown in Chapter 8, towards the elections a new party used the discourse of the J14 movement to appeal to the middle class voters, but recreated the divide-and-rule regime of hate, constructing the center as the merger of "left" and "right" hatred against the poorest populations, Palestinians and ultra-Orthodox Jews. This unhappy end of the J14 movement requires us to discuss the various strategies used by political actors to manipulate the claims and discourses of resistance movements after the end of the moment, seeking to maintain and expand their own power.

II. Political Actors: Counter-Mo(ve)ments, Repertoires of Distortion and Misrepresentation

a. Challenges to institutionalized political actors. Political actors cannot ignore movements of resistance because they might lose power if social actors leading the movement manage to enter the political arena. The actual political actors are challenged by the resistance movement because the social forces mobilized want to demonstrate presence precisely due to lack of representation. The legitimate speakers of the resistance are the social actors leading the movement, but they are not yet considered legitimate political actors: they have no stable and articulated organization, have no strategy and discourse able to mediate between social demands and state institutions, and have not entered the political arena according to the legitimate rules of the game. In other words, they are still not recognized political actors, although they may be transformed into political actors as an outcome of successful resistance and effective use of the rules of the game if they exist, or demand the establishment of such rules if they do not.

Actual political actors seek to prevent the maturing of resistance movements into new political actors, discourses, strategies, and agendas; struggles in the political arena are strongly influenced by the challenge posed by resistance movements. The political field has its own actors, rules of the game, and struggles, and they are not direct reflections of society (Bourdieu, 1992; Eyal, 2003). Nevertheless, as I suggest here, the fact that the political field does not reflect society does not mean it is not influenced by it. The political field is not autonomous and political actors cannot ignore resistance movements; they must actively work to contain them lest they lose power, and even disappear. Political actors are aware of their own fragile and unstable position mainly when social forces are mobilized and demonstrate their power in the public sphere. This is why political actors are so creative, assertive and sometimes overactive in their attempts to maintain and expand their power. The leading social actors of the resistance movement usually fail to enter the political field because actual political actors have several means to obstruct their entrance. They apply a rich repertoire of distortions, in addition to the well-known cooptation. This repertoire is influenced by the struggle with other actors in the political field, by the legitimate discourses and languages of power, and by the rules of the game that determine legitimate access to the political arena by the regime.

The social movement literature (e.g. McAdam, 1982) argues that a split among the ruling elites is necessary in order to open political opportunities for protest. The comparison of the cases discussed here, however, suggests that such a split is not a necessary precondition for the emergence of a resistance movement. The crucial drive to resist is a reaction to the closure of political space to representing the claims of a subordinated social group in distress, combined with some political-economic contingency that frames the moment and facilitates the movement. This is true of the Black Panthers and the Intifada movements, which sparked in moments of national unity that ignored their respective ethnic and national claims. In these cases, the split and hostility between the leading parties were a *reaction* to rather than a *precondition* for the resistance movement. In the cases of class mobilization—the action committees and Forum/13—there were strong divisions among the ruling elites; however, the key drive for the resistance movement was the lack of political representation of the working class, either by the *Histadrut* or the Labor party. In these cases the hostility and split between the parties was the main obstacle to worker representation because some of them identified with labor parties and others with Herut (and later *Likud*). To succeed, class resistance had to overcome partisan divisions among the workers in order to prevent de-legitimization of their demands. It is therefore no coincidence that the counter-mo(ve)ments of actual political actors crystalized with the establishment of National Unity Governments (in 1967 and 1984), which were able to neutralize the workers' market power. It is not at all an accident that the J14 movement emerged in the absence of a split among the ruling political elites, and used the same strategy of Forum/13 to overcome the left-right tribal polarization, aiming to legitimize their collective identity and demands.

In short, the common feature of resistance mo(ve)ments is not any preexisting split among the elites, but rather the fact that each movement affected the political arena precisely because its collective action articulated in the public sphere the lack of political space and the underrepresentation of social claims, identities, and agendas. Nevertheless, the reaction in all cases was never direct representation of the movement in the political arena except in the case of the Intifada, which succeeded precisely due to the existence of a border that located the PLO's demands outside the sovereign State of Israel, and the previous existence of an internal Palestinian political space and political parties. Nevertheless, despite the space opened for Palestinian recognition, representation, and negotiation, the most powerful political force succeeded to convert the compromise into a new regime of cooptation.

b. Recognition and cooptation. As we have seen, resistance movements provoked struggles between key political actors. When transferred to the political arena, the social conflicts have become transformed. This process of transformation is shaped by political actors who interpret the resistance movement and seek to maintain or expand their political power vis-à-vis other competitors, as well as to deny entrance to new actors. It is possible to comprehend crucial political dynamics and historical processes as the reaction of powerful political actors to resistance movements, such as those analyzed in this book. Although such a historiography is obviously lacking in many factors, my argument is that there is constant tension between dominant and subordinated groups, and that resistance to power provokes struggles between the actual political actors, leading to changes in the political field. Resistance movements have the power to influence politics, but not necessarily in the direction they want. This is due to the gap between civil society and the state on the one hand, and between the concrete forms of present social actors and their symbolic representation in politics, on the other hand. In order to expand the concept of dynamic political spaces it is necessary to conceptualize this gap, and how the political power holders seek to exploit it.

Cooptation is the first and most common manipulation used by dominant groups to neutralize opposition. All the resistance movements analyzed here were countered by some form of cooptation. After Wadi Salib, *Mapai* employed many *Mizrahi* officials in party and *Histadrut* apparatuses, while at the same time delegitimizing the leaders of the resistance movement (Chetrit, 2010). During the 1960s workers' revolt, *Mapai* decided to co-opt the workers through its Alignment with *Ahdut Haavoda*. In the 1970s the leaders of the Black Panthers rejected cooptation, but the *Likud* successfully co-opted other *Mizrahi* leaders in the peripheral development towns, which occupied their position as legitimate representatives (Grinberg, 1989). The *Histadrut* co-opted the strong worker leaders within its institutions, both before and after Forum/13. The establishment of a Palestinian Authority instead of an independent sovereign state represented a creative attempt at cooptation, which created a "permanent interim" regime of partially autonomous decision-making institutions. During the 2013 elections, several parties courted the leaders of J14 movement, but only the Labor party succeeded to coopt two of them, the same two leaders that joined the tribalized condensation (Eyal, 2003) repertoire of distortion (see below).

The effectiveness of cooptation as a means of neutralizing resistance depends on the ability of dominant political actors to detach the coopted leaders from the social group they are supposed to represent, thereby weakening it. The coopted leaders may believe that they will use their new power position in order to empower their social bases, and they are not necessarily driven solely by self-interest. However, if they are detached from the subordinated social group they seek to represent, or if the group has been weakened, they will probably fail to represent it and lose credibility. By analyzing cooptation we can better understand the meaning of representation as the effective articulation between social forces, actors and organizations, and the leaders speaking in their name. In the original model of mass-membership political parties, the articulation is assumed to take place within the party, where social and political actors meet and negotiate in a constant dynamic, shaped and reshaped by the organization, mobilization and collective action of social groups.

The neo-liberal global economy significantly weakened this pattern of articulation capacities of political parties. The most obvious reason is the weakening of the state institutions as the locus of social struggles over reallocation of resources. However, I would like to emphasize two additional phenomena: the weakening of the working class and "old" social movements, and the emergence of the new social movements and politics of recognition (Melucci, 1985).

For the purposes of political representation or coopted misrepresentation, the main difference between ethnicity, identity, and class is that identity representation or cooptation of the former must be performed by people possessing the marker, while working-class representation may be performed either by people who have never been workers or workers who have to leave the assembly line for the sake of a political career.[12] Members of the middle classes do not necessarily need to abandon their position in order to develop a political career as workers do. As shown below, this distinction has far-reaching implications for the dynamics of resistance and counter-resistance.

The first goal of ethnic resistance that suffers from symbolic violence is recognition, aiming to change their inferior image. Recognition of ethnic discrimination has its own value, and it even may be sufficient to reduce material discrimination. On the other hand, workers (and other classes) have some market power based on their economic contribution.

---

12   In his insightful analysis, "The 18th Brumaire of Louis Bonaparte," Karl Marx comments in Chapter 3 on the relations between class and their representation by parties, saying, "What makes them [social democrats, LG] representatives of the petty bourgeoisie is the fact that in their minds they do not get beyond the limits which the latter do not get beyond in life, that they are consequently driven, theoretically, to the same problems and solutions to which material interest and social position drive the latter practically. This is, in general, the relationship between the political and literary representatives of a class and the class they represent."

Their goal is not symbolic recognition but concrete material gains; therefore, they seek representation at the market-level in order to negotiate collective agreements. Class organizations can more easily disrupt the social order either thanks to their strategic economic position—like Forum/13's 24-hour strike in 1980 or the 10-day transportation strike in 1931—or thanks to contingent power in periods of full employment and economic expansion, as in 1960-1965.

The distinction between ethnic and class resistance helps understand the different dynamics and types of reactions, the success and failures of the various resistance movements. The typical class movements, the Action Committees and Forum/13, won immediate success in terms of wages and employment. They did not seek political representation, however, and in the long term proved unable to resist the counter-mo(ve)ments that structurally weakened their position in the markets: the splitting of the working class in 1967 and the economic neo-liberalization of 1985. The typical ethnic resistance movements, Wadi Salib and Black Panthers, on the other hand, were initially repressed violently, but on the longer run won significant success in opening space for recognition of *Mizrahi* identity and material claims, and the economic situation of the *Mizrahi* ethno-class relatively improved despite the failure of the resistance movement organizers to achieve representation by establishing autonomous political parties.[13] To conclude, the counter mo(ve)ments were divergent: ethnic resistance movements had partial success in the long term after suffering short-term violent repression, while class resistance movements won short-term success but suffered long-term structural dismantling of their power.

c. Repertoires of distortion and misrepresentation. In the cases compared here, political actors have used four repertoires of symbolic distortion of social resistance in addition to the cooptation of individuals, as discussed above, and structural and institutional reforms, as discussed below. These strategies are complementary rather than mutually exclusive, and when combined they may be extremely effective in shrinking the political space for the entrance of new actors. The fact that I have found four types does not mean that there are no additional repertoires wait-

---

13 The lack of legitimacy to directly represent *Mizrahi* identity—an important and interesting subject—is discussed below.

ing to be discovered in different political settings, which may enrich the theoretical framework of dynamic political spaces. Eyal (2003), using Bourdieu's theory of the political field, suggests four forms of transposition from the social field to the political field, one of them also appeared in the Israeli case (condensation).[14]

Channeling feelings of fear and hate was the repertoire used in reaction to both ethnic resistance movements. This repertoire's power lies in its use of the memory of some real element of danger and threat to the group in the past, and reactivates its memory in a decontextualized manipulative way, consigning any real conflicts in the present to collective oblivion. In 1959, the Mapai ruling party channeled the feelings of *Ashkenazi* voters by identifying *Mizrahi* violence with their fears of "Arab violence."[15] The *Mizrahi* threat could easily be merged with the external enemy due to their shared cultural background as Arabs. This is why military calm along the borders was a prerequisite for ethnic *Mizrahi* protests: Wadi Salib could emerge two years after the IDF's withdrawal from Sinai, and the Black Panthers more of half a year after the cease-fire agreement with Egypt. Despite the opportune timing of the *Mizrahi* protests, the ruling elites were so effective in constructing the *Mizrahi*m as dangerous, that when demonstrations started repression was considered legitimate. Thus, channeling *Ashkenazi* fears mobilized their support of the ruling party in the 1959 elections. This effective channeling constructed the Labor movement as the protector of *Ashkenazi* Jews from the *Mizrahi* collective threat.

Following the Black Panthers movement, the *Likud* channeled *Mizrahi* feelings against the ruling Labor Party and *Ashkenazi* elites after the 1973 War by demanding equal rights between "brothers in arms"—Jews who fought together against the common Arab enemy. This discourse channeled the discontent of Jewish immigrants from Arab countries following their unequal integration in the 1950s and 1960s, while obscuring their economic discrimination in the present, and denying them any distinct collective identity. The *Likud*'s discourse successfully integrated

---

14   The four forms that transpose from the social and economic to the political field are: reflection, condensation, polarization, and inversion. The first is the most similar to representation, and the third is apparently similar to my suggested concept of polarization but differs in its meaning.

15   Morrocans were symbolically marked by their violence called "Morroco knife," and in one case the legendary Mayor of Haifa compared the riots with the Nazis, calling them "Kristallnacht" (*Leil Abdulach*). I have analyzed in my previous work the channeling of fears from Palestinians using the images of Nazis (Grinberg, 2010).

Mizrahi collective identity within Jewish identity, not as a social group with legitimate symbolic and material claims of its own.

*Condensation is defined by Eyal (2003: 140) as "a transposition that obscures a certain social antagonism by locating it within the party." Both blocks' parties used condensation by mobilizing both employers and workers within the party and obscuring the economic conflicts between them. The Labor Alignment between *Mapai* and *Ahdut Haavoda* in 1964 condensed the mainly *Ashkenazi* public employers and powerful workers, while the *Likud* (starting in 1965 with the Liberal-Herut block) condensed private employers and mainly *Mizrahi* weak workers. The powerful workers were mainly employed in the powerful public sector and state- and *Histadrut*-owned corporations. The weak workers were mainly employed in agriculture, construction, services and low tech industries (Semyonov and Levin Epstein, 1987; Grinberg, 1991). The majority of the Jewish weak workers were *Likud* supporters, as were private employers in small-size businesses.[16]

The condensation repertoire was related to the mobilization of different classes. It appeared in reaction to the empowerment of the unified working class during the full employment period of the early 1960s, and the autonomous organization of private capital in reaction to them. In the run-up to the 1965 elections, both parties created condensed blocks—the "left" through the Alignment of *Mapai* and *Ahdut Haavoda*, and the "right" by joining together Herut and the Liberal Party (Shapiro, 1991). The distinction between the "left" and the "right" was central to their discourse and symbols, but in both cases the condensation repertoire served the same purpose: preventing representation of class conflict in the political arena and its containment within the parties. The different capacities of the two condensed blocks to contain class contradictions between Labor and capital became clear after the ascent of *Likud* to power in 1977, when its liberal reforms immediately provoked hyperinflation, and later on when the need to bring the Labor Party into the government in order to halt inflation became clear in 1985.

*"Tribal" mobilization is an upgraded, extreme variation of the channeling repertoire. It takes at least two to tribally mobilize: this repertoire of political mobilization against the Other has to be reciprocal, fed

---

16 Big, concentrated private capital developed in Israel only towards the end of the millennium, outside the scope of this research.

by a mutual sense of tangible collective threat. While channeling fears and anger was already at work in 1959 (through the *Ashkenazi* vote for Mapai) and in 1973 (through *Mizrahi* voting for *Likud*), tribal mobilization appeared in the run-up to the 1977 elections, and culminated in the 1981 and 1984 electoral campaigns based on extreme mutual hostility. Tribal mobilization is based on fear and hostility towards another social group (tribe), mainly its leader (chief), who is seen as the embodiment and symbol of all threats. Tribal mobilization is highly effective in that it closes the political space to discuss the issues of conflict and the real dangers to collective identity, focusing on mobilizing the tribe and convincing it that there is another tribe that represents an existential threat. The political field may be composed of several tribes: the Israeli dual tribal field that contained all ethnic, religious and class conflicts in the late 1970s and 1980s (see below the repertoire of polarization) eventually disintegrated into seven tribes, mutually hostile (Kimmerling, 2001) based on the dichotomies of Jews vs. Arabs, religious vs. secular Jews, *Mizrahi* vs. *Ashkenazi*, and new migrants vs. locals, in addition to the "old" left-right tribal hostility.[17]

* *Polarization* occurs when only two tribes are occupying the whole political space, creating a dichotomy. Sometimes it is based on historic civil wars—Republicans and monarchists in Spain, for example—in other cases it is encouraged by the electoral system—like republicans and democrats in the US. However, the levels of mutual hostility vary in different historical contexts, and depend on the feelings of threat posed by non-polarized new political actors. Polarization is the most effective barrier against the entrance of new political actors. It is based on the presentation of two options, and complete de-legitimization of any other, either in the middle or in the extremes. The implication is that you must vote for "our" tribe, or else be deemed a "traitor," and there is no room for people seated at the borders. As we have seen in the Israeli case, polarization resulted from the tribal mobilization of two party blocks, which co-operated on the discursive and political levels to form what Arian (1998) called a cartel.

The crucial distinction between tribalism and polarization is that

---

17 This process of social disintegration is out of the scope of this book, and took place following the Oslo process of mutual recognition, which opened space to internal social conflicts. I have discussed the national disintegration as one of the main factors that prevented the Israeli-Palestinian compromise in *Politics and violence in Israel/Palestine* (Grinberg, 2010).

the former allows the entrance of new "tribes" (Russian migrants, for example) while the latter closes political space much more hermetically against any form of intermediary positions, ideas and identities outside the "us or them" formulation. This is the basic form of national hostility—friend or foe—however, it is very effective also in internal politics, manipulated by historical memory and the crucial importance of collective identity building in the symbolic political field. The polarization left-right that picked to its highest hostility during the first years of *Likud* rule, continued also during the six years of National Unity Government (1984-1990). It was weakened by Rabin's ascent to power, but reached a new peak with Rabin's assassination in 1995, and was calmed down only thanks to the reappearance of the "real" enemy in 2000, the Palestinians. The objects of hate were extreme representations of "otherness": for the modern secular Jews of the left the ultimate object of fear and hate were the nationalist and ultra-orthodox Jews, while for the Jewish collective identity of the "right" tribe the extreme opposite object of hate were "the Arabs" and "Goyim."

*

By comparing and defining the different repertoires of political actors, we can formulate a more accurate definition of distortion: the symbolic construction of collective identities by political actors seeking to mobilize constituencies by appealing to their weaknesses, frustrations, fears and hatreds, and in doing so neglecting and suppressing their direct claims, interests, ideas, agendas, and power. Distortions and misrepresentations disempower mobilized subordinated citizens by establishing their dependency on political actors. The objective is to deny representation, that is, articulation by and dialogue between social forces, social and political actors, thereby shrinking political space for negotiated containment of social conflicts.

III. State Actors: Institutional Reforms, Languages of Power and Technopols

Every challenge of subordinated groups to the ruling power holders in Israel, as analyzed in this book, has provoked the reshaping of the political arena. The resistance of the working class and anti-colonial national movement (Chapters 4, 6 and 7) was followed by significant institutional or structural reforms, designed to weaken the uprising of dominated forces and prevent or at least delay its resurgence. These reforms entailed active participation of state actors and were influenced by their interests and agendas. Following the neo-liberal terminology, I suggest the term "structural adjustments."

I will focus in this section mainly on the participation of state elites in the shaping of institutions designed to control economic and social forces of civil society. The overt political actions of state elites (state actors) are considered illegitimate interventions in politics, namely in the mediation between state and civil society, precisely because the legitimacy of their actions is based on the appearance of the state as a neutral, impartial and universal service for all citizens. This is the reason that state actors must camouflage the promotion of their institutional power interests and struggles as professional, apolitical and disinterested interventions. Hence, the understanding of long term institutional and structural adjustments in response to mo(ve)ments of popular resistance to power must include the study and analysis of the intervention of state actors (Skocpol et al., 1985).

Following the World Bank economist John Williamson (1994), who suggested the term "technopols" to refer to state experts who design economic policies and structural adjustments as apolitical solutions, I suggest calling the state actors "technopols" and viewing the apolitical professional speech as languages of state power. It is important to analyze the actions of technopols in order to comprehend the complex relations between different state institutions, political actors, and civil society. The analysis of institutional redesign processes during counter-mo(ve)ments must take into consideration the distinctions between different state actors, because they have their own goals, strategies, language, and power. Much like political and social actors, technopols can recognize opportunities and challenges.

I would like to focus here on a peculiar form of closing political space that was blatant during the National Unity Governments (NUG) in 1984-1990 (Chapter 6). The NUG had considerable successes, most notably in formalizing the state's autonomous economic policy making and partially rebuilding the apolitical image of the IDF, damaged during the Lebanon War. In the process, both cartel parties facilitated autonomous state decisions regarding the most critical problems the government was expected to solve: hyperinflation and military withdrawal from Lebanon. The autonomy of state actors was facilitated by the suspension of internal struggles between Labor and *Likud* on both agendas, and the authorization of economic and military technopols to work out solutions to both problems. The legitimacy of the decisions taken by the NUG on these issues was not political—the citizens demands from the state—but professional, legitimized by technical economic and security expertise. Thus, political space was effectively shrunk.

As a general observation, I suggest that the de-politicization of economy and security is facilitated when dominant political actors have no clear idea how to face major state crises and have no language to legitimize new policies. These types of conjunctures gave birth in other times and places to revolutionary and charismatic movements. However the Israeli case shows that institutionalized political actors can protect their powerful positions by relying on professional experts of the state (technopols) in order to obtain bailout plans and nonpolitical, expert legitimacy for the decisions they make. The cooperation between political (re)actors and state technopol actors is at the core of the institutional redesign during counter-mo(ve)ments.

I suggest here to expand the use of the term technopols to the political intervention of state elites in the decision making process in the name of their professional expertise. Military professionals do exactly the same in the security domains: they occupy the political space of decision-making, closing the space for civil society demands, and relying on the support of political actors, touting their expertise as apolitical (Grinberg, 2010). In the Israeli case the total success of the economic technopols since the 1990s and of the security technopols since 2000 has been crucial in the emptying of democratic political spaces which provoked the 2011 resistance movement.

Now we return to the NUG in 1985. The emergency economic plan to halt hyperinflation, and the military plan to withdraw from Lebanon, both were designed and implemented by technopols, within their fields of expertise, economics, and security. These plans were supported by the National Unity Government formed in 1984, and were implemented in 1985, bailing Israel out from the *Likud*'s disastrous failures during 1977-1984. These technopols anchored their legitimacy in their respective languages of legitimacy of power: security and economic stability.

However, the condition for their effectiveness is the historical contingency of political backing of the NUG for their autonomous functioning.

Theda Skocpol (1985) argued that there are three fundamental conditions for the state institution's willingness and capacity to act autonomously from social and political actors: a crisis, a well-trained professional team, and autonomous financial resources of the state. The Israeli case shows that a fourth condition is crucial: the interests and support of dominant political actors on the autonomous intervention of state actors. However, as long as political actors defined the field (economic or security), as a matter of political disputes the actions of technopols were interpreted as illegitimate political interventions. The interventions of military technopol elites were interpreted either as a matter of disinterested security, or as interested political actions, depending on the political contexts, civil society resistance, and political articulations: in 1982 and 1987 the violence used by the IDF against the Palestinians was criticized as a matter of biased political interests and goals, while the political negotiations led by the military technopols during the 1990s and the further violent repression since 2000 were considered a matter of apolitical disinterested security. In all the cases, however, the military technopols were actors seeking to promote their institutional power interests (Grinberg, 2010, 2013a). I have discussed a similar phenomenon with relation to halting inflation in the early 1980s, when various plans to halt inflation were delegitimized as politically biased, and only after the 1984 elections, the formation of NUG, and the political support of the *Histadrut* was the professional economic team of technopols designing the economic plan legitimized as an apolitical actor (Grinberg, 1991).

Understanding the legitimacy of state actors to make political decisions—namely articulating civil society claims and state policies—highlights the second crucial condition for successful political intervention by state actors: the existence of languages of power legitimized by civil society. While political actors constantly produce symbolic languages aiming to legitimize their demands from the state, also state actors have their own capacity to produce languages of legitimate power, like security and economic stability.

The articulation of languages of power by political actors, state technopols and social actors is at the core of the dynamic opening or closure of political spaces for the representation of social conflicts. Without legitimate symbols there is no social force, identity or claim that may succeed to penetrate the political arena, even after wide mobilizations of resistance movements. The cases discussed in chapters 2, 4, 6, and 8 are all cases of massive mobilizations and total inability to gain representation in the political arena; they refer to cases of class and civil society mobilization. Here is one of the most striking conclusions of this research project: there is a clear distinction between recognition and representation. While all movements of resistance gained some level of recognition at their active moment, direct representatives of the movement could be prevented from entering the political arena by various strategies: co-optation, discursive distortions and structural adjustments. In order to comprehend this dynamic, I will proceed to discuss the main symbolic articulation between civil society and the state (the nation) and its most salient institution of articulation between social conflicts and authoritative state decisions (democracy).

IV. Democracy, the Nation and Political Imagination

The gap between the different social interests, identities, and cultures subordinated to the authoritative state institutions is bridged by images of the national community, namely a symbolic homogeneous collective identity of the civil society framed by the state borders and attribution of rights. National collective identities may be imagined by political, state, or social actors seeking mass identification with their leading position given concrete historical situations. Politics, namely the articulation of civil society and the state, is at the core of national imaginations and movements, and competing actors may imagine the nation in very different and opposed ways according to their positions, goals, and interests. Competing political imaginations of the nation differ on the definition of the content of national identity, who is included and excluded, who is the most important social carrier of the national goals. These questions also shape a hierarchy within civil society among those social forces formally included as equal members of the nation. As I discussed in various chapters here, the political struggle over the definition of the nation—who are we and what is our collective goal?—is at the core of the dynamic opening and closure of political spaces to subordinated social forces.

CHAPTER NINE

Collective national identity is probably one of the most salient and intriguing phenomena related to political hegemony, domination and resistance. The emergence of national communities has been studied extensively and produced very creative theories that show that it is a social construct, imagined through homogenizing mass media, and consciously invented by dominant elites; it differs according to contingent conditions, and despite being path-dependent it spread in a modular and isomorphic manner all over the globe. (Hobsbawm, 1983; Anderson, 1991; Brubaker, 1996). National political movements emerged in Europe in very peculiar conditions of huge concentration of economic and military power, competition and wars between the emerging capitalist states (Tilly, 1992; Mann, 1987; Balibar and Wallerstein, 1991). At the same time that capitalist states expanded their borders to contiguous territories, subjugated new populations and fought against rival states they also expanded overseas, imposing their administration on local populations and extracting their material resources, mainly for their capitalist and war industries in Europe. However, the unintended consequence of the colonial expansion was the adoption of national mobilization as a legitimate political strategy of local elites to displace the foreign occupiers and take the power of the state in the name of popular sovereignty.

In all cases, national identities were articulated by political and state actors that define its content and meaning according to the interests and views of their institutions and social supporters, attributing them a central historical role in building the nation. As I have shown in this book, in the Israeli case Labor Zionism before 1948 defined the nation according to the interests of the Jewish workers in rural areas, and after 1967 the national identity split between the "left," which identified the nation with security and the military, and the "right," which identified Zionism with the divine Promise of the Land, transforming a myth of a nationalist religion into the historic subject of nation building. The Palestinian Arabs failed to consolidate a national movement before 1948 due to the opposed interests of rural peasants and urban bourgeoisies vis-à-vis Zionist colonization. Since 1948 they were divided into different areas of Israeli rule and control. The military occupation in 1967 facilitated the consolidation of a Palestinian national movement with a common goal within the borders of the occupied areas against the Israeli rule imposed on them.

Conclusion: On the Dynamics of Political Spaces: Time, Movement, Actors and Masses

I have learned from the Israeli-Palestinian case that if the nation is the product of political imagination, democracy is imagined twice: the sovereign people are imagined—but so are political actors—as representing different interests and collective imaginations among the civil society. However, democracy is a successful container of social conflicts when it is not only imagined but can also be materialized by citizens' actions: when citizens can organize, express themselves, vote and influence policies, or have recourse to courts. When the imagination of the nation excludes, both at the symbolic and institutional level, parts of the population, democracy cannot work. The major advantage of democracy over other types of regimes lies in the rejection of violence as legitimate means of resolving social conflicts, and in the imagination that oppressed groups have at least potential formal equal rights to organize, influence policies and improve their situation.

The obstacles to political representation, given democratic rules of the game, lie in the gap between the capacity of social actors to organize and mobilize their constituencies on the one hand, and the ability of political actors to manipulate citizens on the other. The repertoire of manipulations includes cooptation, discursive distortions, and institutional design aiming to weaken the subordinated groups and prevent their representation. In these cases democracy is not only imagined—it becomes an illusion, legitimizing policies that run counter to the wishes of citizens. In the absence of political space, social groups that have some contingent power at a given historical moment may try to express their claims through resistance movements.

The modern democratic rules of the game and institutional framework are social constructions designed in historical conditions of recognized borders of the nation and the state and some balance of power both between state institutions and civil society, and among social forces in civil society. These conditions first appeared in Western Europe, when wars developed technology, the financial system and capitalism, and imposed arbitrary borders on civilian populations, subjugating them to sovereign state apparatuses (Tilly, 1992). The balance of power between dominant and dominated was generated by the development of capitalism, which empowered the working and middle classes vis-à-vis the dominant economic groups, and civil society vis-à-vis the state (Rueschemeyer et al., 1992; Andrews and Chapman, 1995).

Given the adverse structural conditions of capitalist development and the political capacity to prevent representation of subordinated citizens, it is puzzling that the working class ever succeeded in the past to open political space for representation of its interests and agendas in so many places in the world. How did it gain any recognition of its interests and rights? This question is relevant to understanding the general phenomenon of representation of subordinated groups under democratic rules of the game. In addition, the analysis of the working class success may help us comprehend its weakening during the last twenty years, and the possible ways to revert this anti-democratic process that imposed the will of the economic elites not only the working class, but on the large majority of the civil society, either if we call it "the 99%" (US style) or "the people" (Middle eastern style). Understanding how the working class managed to enter the political arena in the past is necessary in order to conceptualize the empowerment of civil society and effective confrontation with economic elites and technopols, aiming to re-democratize the political field by resistance mo(ve)ments.

Using the analytical tools provided by the present research, I would suggest that in the past the working class succeeded in gaining recognition and representation in the political arena by applying two successful strategies: institutional articulation between social and political action and symbolic construction of a collective identity of the working-class in terms of general interest of the whole society. Both strategies have suffered significant setbacks during the last twenty years.

The important lesson that can be learned from the Israeli case is the path-dependent influence of institutional linkages between trade unions and parties: once the linkages are established it is very difficult to change them. Institutional rigidity might prevent proper responses of the labor movement to changes both in the global economy and labor markets and in local economic conditions. The institutional rigidity is especially salient when compared to the flexibility and dynamism of global financial capital, its free movement guaranteed by neo-liberal institutions and legitimized by powerful and creative technopols. The institutional rigidity of union-party relations and the conservative interests of organizations were at the core of the retrocession of the working class despite their significant achievements.

According to working-class history, the condition for representation in the political field is apparently the construction of an inter-subjective collective identity of the movement supporters and the institutionalization of the dialogue and mutual influence between civil society organizations and political actors. Historically, the collective identity of the working class was shaped by the use of common symbols, discourses, myths and language, called all together "ideology."[18] Through "ideologies" and trade unions, political parties forged stable linkages with the working class, claiming representation of their interests even if the individual political actors were not workers. The "ideological" and institutional linkages with trade unions not only reinforced workers' identification with the party, but also established trust in their political actors, and commitment of the social classes supporting them. "Ideology," however, can be just as rigid as institutional linkages, and may find it difficult to adapt to changing conditions.

Here we can define the specific symbolic role of political actors seeking to articulate a conflicted civil society with authoritative state decisions: political actors produce the languages of power able to legitimize the interests of their constituencies and present them in terms of general public interest that will be implemented by state authoritative decisions. When they refer to class struggles, the languages of power are usually called ideology, like liberalism, social-democracy, socialism or communism. Opposed to them, the neo-liberal language of technopol power presents itself as being out of the class struggle, as a technical matter of economic stability. When the languages of power articulate the claims of discriminated groups, they are usually called identity politics or politics of recognition, and are seen as particularistic, contesting the legitimate national languages of power. In order to represent discriminated communities, the new political actors must imagine the collective identity of their constituencies using a legitimate language of power in order to transform them into a legitimate political collective identity.

The symbolic construction of political collective identities may merge elements of class ideology, national identity, and democratic equal rights depending on the constantly changing political conditions. However, when marginalized and discriminated communities with distinct markers, culture, or values have the capacity to imagine their own collective identity and language of power, they need to challenge the nation's

---

18   I find the term "ideology" controversial and problematic. I use it as a convention, and not at all as a concept with any specific theoretical meaning.

homogeneous imagination. In Israel, the different political actors were labeled as "ideological," when they speak in the name of a legitimate image of the nation, or "sectorial" when representing a particular identity based on a legitimate language of power. These are communities based on religious collective identity (represented by ultra-Orthodox parties), *Ashkenazi* (European) migrant collective identities, or a merger of religion and Zionist colonization (represented by the national religious parties). The marginalized sectorial parties are those representing the Palestinian citizens, that reject the state Jewish identity and symbols, and are almost completely isolated from the legitimate political arena.

The most salient illegitimate collective identity is, however, the *Mizrahi* collective identity, which were analyzed in chapters 3 and 5. I suggest that the *Mizrahi* collective identity failed to articulate a legitimate collective political identity for the citizens marked as *Mizrahim* because their collective imagination immediately becomes the opposite of the national identity forged by the secular *Ashkenazis*. The common cultural denominator of Jews that migrated from Arab countries (in addition to their shared discrimination) is not European and modern, it is not either secular or religious, and it is not in necessary conflict with the Orient. *Mizrahi* collective identity is delegitimized by the *Ashkenazi* elites precisely because it is not just a sectorial collective identity of a particular discriminated community claiming representation; it is rather a collective identity able to contain the tensions within the Israeli civil society between secular and religious, Orient and Occident, Arabs and Jews. In other words, it is an alternative national identity for the Israeli civil society, challenging the dominant power of secular *Ashkenazi* elites. The *Mizrahi* political actors are the only ones that might challenge the dominant *Ashkenazi* elites capable to contain civil society tensions, hence they are not only non-recognized as such but also constantly actively delegitimized or coopted.

*

To resume, competing political actors may open political spaces of representation for the interests, identities and agendas of non-represented parts of the civil society only if and when they are capable of producing a symbolic language of power that articulates social forces with state authoritative policies. Following successful experiences of the working class in various places, we learn that this process may occur when distinct actors are independently organized both within civil society (social actors) and the political field (political actors) and some institutionalized dialogue between them produces the language that legitimizes their claims from the state. This is a process that takes time and does not necessarily take place following mo(ve)ments of resistance; on the contrary, the counter-mo(ve)ments initiated by already organized political actors are designed to prevent such a process of politicization of civil society mobilizations.

The means to prevent the articulation between social actors and new political actors leading to representation are: a) cooptation, which disconnects potential political actors from the social forces that might support them; b) discursive distortions, which prevent the political imagination of new collective identities; and c) institutional and structural adjustments, carried out in cooperation between political and state actors aiming to disempower the resistant social forces. Democratic rules of the game are not a guarantee to the opening of political spaces to new identities, ideas, demands, and agendas. Rather, they might be an effective tool that facilitates and legitimizes the closure of political spaces of representation, as shown in chapters 3, 4, 5, 6, and 8. Chapters 2 and 7 show that non-democratic impositions of unilateral rule are more vulnerable to movements of resistance. However, the effective opening of political spaces is in both situations a real challenge to social actors, both due to the conservative reactions of actual political actors and due to the need to transform mass mobilization into political power. Comparing mo(ve)ments of resistance has been the tool I have used in this research, both to uncover the means of domination used by political rulers, and to comprehend the obstacles faced by dominated social forces seeking representation. This method, as well as the concept of dynamic political space, can help guide future research programs and may encourage critical reflections among social and political actors.

LIST OF SOURCES

NEWSPAPERS
Davar
Hadashot
Maariv
Yediot Ahronot

WEBSITES
Association for Civil Rights in Israel, http://www.acri.org.il/
Btselem, http://www.btselem.org/
Golda Meir's archive, http://www.golda.gov.il/archive
Haokets, http://www.haokets.org/
Knesset Website, http://www.knesset.gov.il/
Walla, http://news.walla.co.il/
World Bank, http://www-wds.worldbank.org/
Y-net, http://www.ynet.co.il/

ARCHIVES
LA—Lavon Institute Archives, Tel Aviv.
National Archives, London.
ZA—Zionist Archives, Jerusalem.

Bibliography

Abu-Sitta, S. H. (2004). *Atlas of Palestine, 1948*. London: Palestine Land Society.
Aharoni, Y. (1991). *The political economy in Israel*. Tel-Aviv: Am-Oved. (Hebrew)
Aharonson S. (1999). *David Ben-Gurion: The renaissance leader who declined*. Kiryat Sde-Boker: the Institute for Ben-Gurion's legacy. (Hebrew)
Amin, S. (1997). *Capitalism in the age of globalization*. London and New York: Zed Books.
Anderson, B. (1991). *Imagined communities: Reflections on the origin and spread of nationalism*. Revised Edition, London and New York: Verso.
Andrews, G. R, and Chapman, H. (eds.) (1995). *The social construction of democracy, 1870-1990*. New York: New York University Press.
Arendt, H. (1970). *On violence*. New York: Harcourt, Brace& World.
Arian, A. (1973). *The choosing people: Voting behavior in Israel*. Cleveland: Press of Case Western Reserve University.
------. (1998). *The second republic: Politics in Israel*. Chatham, NJ: Chatham House Publisher.
Arian, A., and Shamir, M. (eds.) (1995). *The elections in Israel*. Albany, NY: SUNY Press.
Arnon, A., and Weinblatt, J. (2001). Sovereignty and economic development: The case of Israel and Palestine. *The Economic Journal*, 111, F291-F308.
Arnon, Y. (1979). The Israeli economy 1953-1978 and forecast for 1979. *Economic Quarterly*, 100, 27-45. (Hebrew)
------. (1981). *Economy in turmoil*. Tel-Aviv: Hakibutz Hameuhad. (Hebrew)
------. (1984). The national economy in 1983 and the forecast for 1984. *Economics Quarterly*, 120, 3-21 (Hebrew)
Ashrawi, H. (1995). *This side of peace: A personal account*. New York: Simon and Schuster.
Auyero, J. (2003). *Contentious lives*. Durham: Duke University Press.
Azoulay, A., and Ophir, A. (2013). *The one-state condition, occupation and democracy in Israel/Palestine*. Stanford: Stanford University Press.

Baharal, U. (1965). *The effect of mass immigration on wages in Israel*. Jerusalem: Falk Project. (Hebrew)
Bahat, S. (1979). *Structural relations between trade unions and labor parties: A comparative study*. (Unpublished MA thesis). Tel Aviv University, Tel Aviv. (Hebrew)
Balibar, E. (2004). *We, the people of Europe?: Reflections on transnational citizenship*. Princeton: Princeton University Press.
Balibar, E., and Wallerstein, E. (1991). *Race, nation, class: Ambiguous identities*. London: Verso.

Bar-El, R., and Michael, A. (1977). *Strikes in Israel*. Tel-Aviv: The Institute of Labor Relations. (Hebrew)

Barkai, H. (1987). The military industry in the cross-road. *Monthly Review*, 43 (9). (Hebrew)

Bar-Zohar, M. (1977). *Ben-Gurion*. Tel-Aviv: Am-Oved. (Hebrew)

------. (1980). *Ben-Gurion: Biography*. Jerusalem: Keter. (Hebrew)

Barzilay, A. (1996). *Ramon*. Tel Aviv: Schocken Publishing House. (Hebrew)

Becker, A. (1982). *Of time and men*. Tel Aviv: Am Oved. (Hebrew)

Beilin, Y. (1985). *The price of unification*. Tel Aviv: Revivivm. (Hebrew)

------. (1996). *Peace at hand*. Tel Aviv: Yediot Ahronot. (Hebrew)

------. (2001). *Manual for a wounded dove*. Tel Aviv: Miskal — Yediot Ahronot Books and Chemed Books (Hebrew).

Ben Eliezer, U. (1998). *The making of Israeli militarism*. Bloomington, IN: Indiana University Press.

------. (2012). *Old conflict, new war: Israel's politics toward the Palestinians*. New York: Palgrave Macmillan.

Ben-Gurion, D. (1974). *From class to nation*. Tel-Aviv: Ainot. (Hebrew).

Ben-Porath, Y. (1966). *The Arab labor force in Israel*. Jerusalem: Palk Institution. (Hebrew)

------. (1975). The years of plenty and the years of famine: A political business cycle? *Kyklos*, 28(2), 400-403.

------. (1982). The conservative turnabout that never was: Ideology and economic policy in Israel since 1977. *Jerusalem Quarterly*, 115, 3-10. (Hebrew)

Ben-Porath, Y. (ed) (1986). *The Israeli economy: Maturing through crises*. Cambridge, MA: Harvard University Press.

Ben-Shahar, H. (1993). *The report of the economic consulting team to the political negotiations*. Jerusalem. (Hebrew)

Benziman, U., and Mansour, A. (1992). *Subtenants*. Jerusalem: Keter. (Hebrew)

Berglas, E. (1989). The burden of security and the Israeli economy. In Y. Ben-Porath (ed.), *The Israeli economy: Maturing through crises* (199-229). Tel Aviv: Am Oved. (Hebrew)

Bernstein, D. (1976). *The Black Panthers of Israel, 1971-1972: Contradictions and protest in the process of nation building*. (Unpublished PhD dissertation). University of Sussex, England.

------. (1978). Sociology absorbs immigration. *Notebooks for Research and Critique*, 1, 5-21. (Hebrew)

------. (2000). *Constructing boundaries: Jewish and Arab Workers in mandatory Palestine*. Albany: SUNY Press.

------. (2012). Paper presented in the Conference of the Israeli Sociological Society, Hebrew University, February 2012. (Hebrew)

------. (Forthcoming). The Black Panthers: The personal and collective narrative as a political act and arena of politicization. In K. Schlesinger, Y. Ezrahi and G. Algazi (eds.), *Baruch Kimmerling Memorial Volume*. Jerusalem: Kibutz Hameuchad and Van Leer. (Hebrew)

Bichler, S. (1991). *The political economy of national security in Israel.* (Unpublished PhD dissertation). Hebrew University, Jerusalem. (Hebrew)
Biger, G. (1984). The development of built urban area in Tel Aviv, 1909-1934. In M. Naor (ed.), *Tel Aviv's beginning 1909-1934* (42-61). Jerusalem: The Rachel Yanait Ben-Tzvi Center for Jerusalem Studies. (Hebrew)
Blumenthal, N. (1984). The influence of defense industry investment of Israel's economy. In E. Lanir (ed.), *Israel society planning in the 1980s* (166-180). Tel-Aviv University: Praeger Publishers.
Bonacich, E. (1972). A theory of ethnic antagonism: The split labor market. *American Sociological Review*, 37, 547-559.
------. (1979). The past, present, and future of split labor market theory. In *Research in Race and Ethnic Relations*, 1, 17-64.
Bourdieu, P. (1992). *Language and symbolic power.* Cambridge, MA: Harvard University Press.
Brauer, D. A. (1989). *Histadrut in Israeli economy: Centralized collective bargaining and wage restraint.* (Unpublished PhD dissertation). University of California, Berkley.
Brichta, A., and Pedhazur, A. (eds.) (2001). *Elections to the local authorities in Israel, 1998: Continuity or change.* Tel Aviv: Ramot and University of Tel Aviv. (Hebrew)
Brubaker, R. (1996). *Nationalism reframed: Nationhood and the national question in the new Europe.* London: Cambridge University Press.
------. (2004). *Ethnicity without groups.* Cambridge: Harvard University Press.
Bruno, M. (1986). Sharp disinflation strategy: Israel, 1985. *Economic Policy*, 2, 380-402.
Bruno, M., and Piterman, S. (1987). *Israel's stabilization: A two year review.* Discussion Paper 87.05, Bank of Israel Research Department. (Hebrew)
Brynen, R. (2000). *A very political economy: Peacebuilding and foreign aid in the West Bank and Gaza.* Washington, D.C.: United States Institute of Peace Press.
Burawoy, M. (1989). Two methods in search of science: Skocpol versus Trotsky. *Theory and Society*, 18, 759-805.

Calhoun, C. (1993). "New social movements" of the early nineteenth century. *Social Science History*, 17(3), 385-427.
Cardoso, F. H., and Faletto, E. (1979). *Dependency and development in Latin America.* Berkeley: University of California Press.
Carmi, S., and Rosenfeld, H. (1976). The privatization of public means, the state-made middle class, and the realization of family value in Israel. In J. G. Peristiany (ed.), *Kinship and modernization in Mediterranean society* (131-159). Rome: Center for Mediterranean Studies.
------. (1989). The emergence of militaristic nationalism in Israel. *International Journal of Politics, Culture and Society*, 3(1), 5-49.
Castells, M. (2012). *Networks of outrage and hope: Social movements in the internet age.* Cambridge: Polity Press.
Chalamish, A. (2004). *From national home to a state in the making: The Jewish Yishuv*

in *Eretz Israel between the wars*. Tel Aviv: The Open University (Hebrew)

Chatterjee, P. (1993). *The nation and its fragments: Colonial and post-colonial histories*. Princeton: Princeton University Press.

Chetrit, S. S. (2004). *The Mizrahi struggle in Israel: Between oppression and liberation, identification and alternative, 1948–2003*. Ra'anana: Am-Oved/Ofakim Series. (Hebrew)

------. (2010). *Intra-Jewish conflict in Israel: White Jews, black Jews*. London: Routledge.

Chomsky, N. (2012). *Occupy*. Brooklyn: Zuccotti Park Press.

Cohen, A. (1969). *Population dispersal and "integrating the exiles": Two conflicting tasks*. Jerusalem: Magnes. (Hebrew)

Cohen, E. (2009). *My own private Wadi Salib*. Tel Aviv: Miskal — Yediot Ahronot and Chemed. (Hebrew)

Cohen, H. (2003). Land, memory and identity: The Palestinian internal refugees in Israel. *Refuge: Canada's Periodical on Refugees*, 21(2), 6-13.

------. (2008). *Army of shadows: Palestinian collaboration with Zionism, 1917-1948*. Berkeley: University of California Press.

------. (2010). *Good Arabs: The Israeli security agencies and the Israeli Arabs, 1948-1967*. Berkeley/Los Angeles: University of California Press.

Cohen, J. L., and Arato, A. (1994). *Civil society and political theory*. Cambridge, MA and London: MIT Press.

Collier, R. B., and Collier, D. (1991). *Shaping the political arena: Critical junctures, the labor movement and regime dynamic in Latin America*. Princeton: Princeton University Press.

Crouch, C. (1983). Pluralism and the new corporatism: A rejoinder. *Political Studies*, 31, 452-60.

Dahan Kalev, H. (1991). *Self organizing systems: Wadi Salib and the Black Panthers; implications on the Israeli society*. (Unpublished PhD dissertation). Hebrew University, Jerusalem. (Hebrew)

Dan, H. (1963). *On an unpaved road*. Tel-Aviv: Shoken. (Hebrew)

Dayan, A. (1999). *The story of Shas*. Jerusalem: Keter. (Hebrew)

De Malach, D. (2009). Where are the occupation, discrimination and imperialism: Comments to the discussion of globalization in Israel. *Theory and Critique*, 35, 111-140. (Hebrew)

Diskin, A. (1988). *Elections and voters in Israel*. Tel-Aviv: Am-Oved. (Hebrew)

Dor, D. (2004). *Intifada hits the headlines: How the Israeli press misreported the outbreak of the second Palestinian uprising*. Bloomington, IN: Indiana University Press.

Eisenstadt, S. N. (1967). *Israeli society*. London: Weidenfeld and Nicolson.

Eisinger, P. (1973). The conditions of protest behavior in American cities. *American Political Science Review*, 81, 11-28.

Eliav, A. (1972). *Land of the Hart*. Tel Aviv: Am Oved. (Hebrew)

Elroi, G. (2004). *Immigrants: Jewish immigration to Eretz Israel in the early 20th cen-

tury. Jerusalem: Yad Yitzhak Ben Tzvi Press. (Hebrew)

Eshel, N. (1994). *The seamen's strike*. Tel-Aviv: Am-Oved. (Hebrew)

Eshel, T. (2002). *Abba Hushi: Man of Haifa*. Tel Aviv:Ministry of Defense Press. (Hebrew)

Evans, P. (1995). *Embedded autonomy: States and industrial transformation*. Princeton: Princeton University Press.

Eyal, G. (2003). *The origins of post-communist elites*. Minneapolis: University of Minnesota Press.

--------. (2005). *The disenchantment of the Orient: A history of Orientalist expertise in Israel*. Tel Aviv: Hakibbutz Hameuchad and Van Leer Jerusalem Institute. (Hebrew)

Ezrachi, Y. (1996). *Rubber bullets: Power and conscience in modern Israel*. New York: Farrar, Straus and Giroux.

Fanon, F. (1967). *Black skin white masks*. New York: Grove Press.

------. (1968). *The wretched of the earth*. New-York: Grove Press.

Filc, D. (2004). Israel model 2000: Neoliberal post-Fordism. In D. Filc and U. Ram (eds.), *The power of property: Israeli society in the global age*, 34-56. Tel Aviv: The Van Leer Institute in Jerusalem and Hakibbutz Hameuchad Publishing House.

Fischer, S., Alonso-Gamo, P., and Von Allmen, U. (2001). Economic developments in the West Bank and Gaza since Oslo. *The Economic Journal*, 111, 254-275.

Fourcade, M. (2009). *Economists and societies: Discipline and profession in the United States, Britain, and France, 1890s to 1990s*. Princeton: Princeton University Press.

Forman, G., and Kedar, A. (2004). From Arab lands to "Israel lands": The legal dispossession of the Palestinians displaced by Israel in the wake of 1948. *Environment and Planning D: Society and Space*, 22, 809-830.

Fredrickson, G. (1997). Nonviolent resistance to white supremacy. In *The comparative imagination*, Chapter 10, 173-212. Berkeley, L.A. and London: University of California Press.

Friedman, A. (1963). *Worker committees' research*. Tel Aviv: The Histadrut Institute for Social and Economic Research. (Hebrew)

Gal, R. (1990). *The Intifada's influence on Israeli society*. Zikhron Yaakov: The Israeli Institute for Military Research. (Hebrew)

Galin, A., and Taub, Y. (1971). The "package deal" as a turning point in labor relations. *Economic Quarterly* 69/70, 106-113. (Hebrew)

Gat, M. (2008). Retaliatory raids as an accelerating factor leading to the Six-Day War. *Historian*, 70(3), 462-485.

Gazit, S. (1985). *The carrot and the stick: The Israeli administration in Judea and Samaria*. Tel Aviv: Zamora-Bitan. (Hebrew)

Gidron, B., Katz, H., Bar-Mor, H., Katan, J., Silver, I., and Telias, M. (2003). Through a new lens: The third sector and Israeli society. *Israel studies*, 8(1), 20-59.

Giladi, D. (1973). *Jewish Palestine during the fourth Alia period (1924-1929): Eco-*

nomic and social aspects. Tel Aviv: Am Oved. (Hebrew)

Gilbar, D., and Sesser, A. (eds.) (1992). *In the eye of the conflict: The Intifada*. Tel Aviv: Tel Aviv University and Hakibbutz Hameuchad. (Hebrew)

Ginor, I., and Remez, G. (2006). Unfinished business: Archival evidence exposes the diplomatic aspect of the USSR's pre-planning for the Six Day War. *Cold War History*, 6(3), 377-395.

Gitlin, T. (2012). *Occupy nation: The roots, the spirit, and the promise of Occupy Wall Street*. New York: HarperCollins Publishers.

Gluska, A. (2004). *Eshkol give the command!: IDF and the Israeli government towards the Six Days War, 1963-1967*. Tel Aviv: Maarachot. (Hebrew)

Goldthorpe, J. (1978). The current inflation: Towards a sociological account. In *The political economy of the inflation*, 186-212. London: Robertson.

------. (1984). *Order and conflict in contemporary capitalism*. Oxford: Clarendon Press.

Gordon, D., Reich, M., and Edwards, R. (1982). *Segmented work, divided workers*. Cambridge: Cambridge University Press.

Greenberg, Y. (1984). *From Hevrat Ovdim to the workers economy: The development of the Hevrat Ovdin idea during 1909-29*. (Unpublished PhD dissertation). Tel Aviv University, Tel Aviv. (Hebrew)

------. (2011). *Pinchas Sapir: An economic and political biography*. Tel Aviv: Resling. (Hebrew)

Greenwald, C. S. (1972). *Recession as a policy instrument: Israel 1965-1969*. London: Hurst.

Grinberg, L. L. (1985). *The revolt that never was: The forum of thirteen big workers' committees; A test-case for Israeli corporatism*. (Unpublished MA thesis). Hebrew University, Jerusalem. (Hebrew)

------. (1989). Public activists of Histadrut and local authorities: The ethnic dimension. *Jerusalem Institute for Israel Research*, 33. (Hebrew)

------. (1991). *Split corporatism in Israel*. Albany: SUNY Press.

------. (1991a). Are dualism and corporatism compatible patterns of political economy? Some implications of the Israeli case. *International Sociology*, 6, 211-225.

------. (1993). *The Histadrut above all*. Jerusalem: Nevo. (Hebrew)

------. (1993a). The crisis of statehood: A weak state and strong political institutions. *Journal of Theoretical Politics*, 5, 89-107.

------. (1994). A theoretical framework for the analysis of the Israeli Palestinian conflict. *Revue internationale de sociologie*, 1(1994), 68-89.

------. (1995). The Jewish-Arab drivers organization strike: A contribution to the critique of the sociology of the national conflict in Palestine. In I. Pappe (ed.), *Jews and Arabs in the mandate period: New perspectives on historical research* (157-178). Tel Aviv: Givat Haviva Publications. (Hebrew)

------. (1995a). The political economy of the old Histadrut crumbling. *Economic Quarterly*, 42, 1. (Hebrew)

------. (1996). The political economy of Zionist Labor during the British colonial period. *ISSR*, 11(2), 1-20.

------. (1999). Imagined democracy in Israel: Theoretical background and historic perspective. *Israeli Sociology*, 2(1), 209-240. (Hebrew)

------. (1999a). Labor, democratization and dconomic stabilization in Argentina. *Political Economy in Latin America*, 11, 13-38. Truman Peace Institute Publications.

------. (2000). Why we didn't continue his path? On peace, democracy, political assassination and the post-conflict agenda. In L. L. Grinberg (ed.), *Contested memory: Myth, nationalism and democracy* (123-152). Beer Sheva: Humphrey Institute. (Hebrew)

------. (2001). Zionism and political economy in Israel. In E. Yaar and Z. Shavit (eds.), *The Israeli society: Structure and processes* (585-706). Tel Aviv: The Open University Publishers. (Hebrew)

------. (2001a). Mapai between democratization and liberalization: On the questionable dichotomy of state/civil society. In A. Ophir and Y. Peled (eds.), *Israel drom mobilized society to civil society*, 244-261. Tel Aviv: Hakibbutz Hameuchad/ Van Leer Institute. (Hebrew)

------. (2003). An historical slip of the tongue, or what can the Arab-Jewish transportation strike teach us about the Israeli-Palestinian conflict? *International Journal of Middle East Studies*, 35(3), 371-391.

------. (2007). *Imagined peace, discourse of war: The failure of leadership, politics and democracy in Israel:1992-2006*. Tel Aviv: Resling. (Hebrew)

------. (2007a). *Imagined peace: On borders and discourse, politics and violence*. Ramalla, MADAR. (Arabic)

------. (2008). Israel's dual regime since 1967. *MIT-EJMES (Electronic Journal of Middle East Studies)*, 3, 59-80.

------. (2009). Speechlessness: In search of language to resist the Israeli "thing without a name." *International Journal of Politics, Culture and Society*, 22, 105-116.

------. (2010). *Politics and violence in Israel/Palestine*. London and NY: Routledge.

------. (2011). The reversal of citizenship: The Lebanon War and Intifada in the 1980s and the 2000s. In Y. Peled, N. Levin-Epstein, G. Mundlak, and J. Cohen (eds.), *Democratic citizenship and war*, 218-230. London: Routledge.

------. (2013). Resistance, politics and violence: The catch of the palestinian struggle. *Current Sociology*, 61(2), 206-225.

Gross, E. (1983). On wages in the public and business sectors. *Iyunim Bakalkala*: 157-173. (Hebrew).

Hacohen, D. (2003). *Immigrants in turmoil: Mass immigrants to Israel and its repercussions in the 1950s and after*. Syracuse, NY: Syracuse University Press.

Halevi, N., and Klinov-Malul, R. (1968). *The economic development of Israel*. New York: F. A. Praeger in cooperation with the Bank of Israel.

Handelman, D. (2005). The extended case: International foundations and prospective dimensions. *Social Analysis*, 49(3), 63–86.

Harel, A., and Galin, A. (1978). *Developments and changes in the Israeli labor relations system*. Ramat-Gan: Massada. (Hebrew)

Harel, A., and Issacharoff, A. (2004). *The seventh war*. Tel Aviv: Yediot Ahronot (Hebrew).

Harvey, D. (2012) *Rebels cities: From the right to the city to the urban revolution*. London: Verso.
Hassin, E., and Horowitz, D. (1961). *The affaire*. Tel-Aviv: Am Hasefer. (Hebrew)
Hattis, S. L. (1970). *The bi-national idea in Palestine during mandatory times*. Haifa: Shikmona.
Hausman, L. J., and Karasik, A. D. (1993). *Securing peace in the Middle East: Project on economic transition*. Cambridge, MA: Harvard University Press.
Hechter, M. (1975). *Internal colonialism: The Celtic fringe in British national development, 1536-1966*. Berkeley: University of California Press.
Helman, S. (1999). Negotiating obligations, creating rights: Conscientious objection and the redefinition of citizenship in Israel. *Citizenship Studies*, 3, 45-69.
Helman, S., and Levy, A. (2001). Shas in the Israeli press. In Y. Peled (ed.), *Shas: The challenge of israeliness*, 390-424. Tel Aviv: Miskal (Hebrew).
Herzog, H. (1986). *Political ethnicity: The image vs. the reality*. Tel-Aviv: Hakibbutz Hamehukhad. (Hebrew)
Hever, H., Shenhav, Y., and Moutzafi-Heller, P. (eds.). (2002). *Mizrahim in Israel: New critical perspectives*. Jerusalem: Van Leer Institute. (Hebrew)
Hirschfeld, Y. (2000). *Oslo: Formula for peace*. Tel Aviv: Rabin Center and Am Oved. (Hebrew)
Hirschman, A. (1970). *Exit, voice and loyalty: Responses to decline in firms, organizations and states*. Cambridge, MA: Harvard University Press.
Hofnung, M. (2006). *Protest and butter: The Black Panthers demonstrations and allocations for social needs*. Sarigim-Leon: Nevo. (Hebrew)
Horowitz, D. (1948). *The Palestinian economy in development*. Tel-Aviv: Dvir for Mossad Bialik. (Hebrew)
Horowitz, D., and Lissak, S. (1978). *Origins of the Israeli polity: Palestine under the mandate*. Chicago: University of Chicago Press.
Hughes, M. (2009). The banality of brutality: British armed forces and the repression of the Arab revolt in Palestine, 1936-39. *English Historical Review*, 507, 313-354.
------. (2010). From law and order to pacification: Britain's suppression of the Arab revolt in Palestine. *Journal of Palestine Studies*, 39(2), 6-22.

Kassem, F. (2011). *Palestinian women: Narrative histories and memory*. London: Zed.
Keisar, I. (1973). The composition of the Israeli manpower: Trends and transformations. *Economics Quarterly*, 20(78-9), 283-297. (Hebrew)
Kemp, A., and Raijman, R. (2008). *Migrants and workers: The political economy of labor migration in Israel*. Jerusalem: Van Leer Institute. (Hebrew)
Khalidi, R. (2006). *The iron cage: The story of the Palestinian struggle for statehood*. Boston: Beacon Press.
Khalidi, W. (1992). *All that remains: The Palestinian villages occupied and depopulated by Israel in 1948*. Washington, D.C.: Institute for Palestine Studies.
Khamaisi, R. (2006). Mechanism of land control and territorial Judaization in Israel. In M. Al-Haj and U. Ben-Eliezer (eds.), *The name of security: The sociology

of peace and war in Israel in changing times, 421-448. Haifa: University of Haifa Press and Pardes Press. (Hebrew)

Kimmerling, B. (1982). A model for analysis of reciprocal relations between the Jewish and Arab communities in Mandatory Palestine. *Plural Studies*, 13(1): 45-68.

------. (1983). *Zionism and territory: The socioterritorial dimension of Zionist politics*. Berkeley: Institute of International Studies, University of California.

------. (1983b). *Zionism and economy*. Cambridge, MA: Schenkman Publishers.

------. (1992). Ideology, sociology and nation building: The Palestinians and their meaning in Israeli sociology. *American Sociological Review*, 57, 446-460.

------. (2001). *The invention and decline of Israeliness*. Berkeley: University of California Press.

Kimmerling, B., and Midgal, Y. S. (1999). *Palestinians: A nation in the making*. Jerusalem: Keter. (Hebrew)

------. (2003). *The Palestinian people: A history*. Cambridge, MA: Harvard University Press.

Kleinman, E. (1967). The place of manufacturing in the growth of the Israeli economy. *Journal of Development Studies*, 3, 226-248.

Kochavi, A. J. (1998). The struggle against Jewish immigration to Palestine. *Middle Eastern Studies*, 34(3), 146-167.

Kretzmer, D. (2002). *The occupation of justice*. Albany: SUNY Press.

Kriesi, H., Koopmans, R., Duyvendak, J. W., and Giugni, M. G. (1995). *The politics of new social movements in western Europe: A comparative analysis*. Minneapolis/London: University of Minnesota Press/University College of London Press.

Lakatos, I. (1978). *The methodology of scientific research programmes*. J. Worrall and G. Currie (eds.). Cambridge: Cambridge University Press.

Lamdani, R. (1989). Emigration from Israel. In Y. Ben-Porath (ed.), *The Israeli economy: maturing through crises*, 179-197. Tel Aviv: Am Oved. (Hebrew)

Lehman-Wilzig, S. (1990). *Stiff-necked people, bottle-necked system*. Bloomington, IN: Indiana University Press.

Lev, T., and Shenhav, Y. (2009). "Don't call me worker, call me Panther": The Black Panthers and identity politics in the early 1970s. *Theory and Critique*, 35, 141-164. (Hebrew)

------. (2010). The construction of the internal enemy: The Black Panthers as objects of moral panic. *Israeli Sociology*, 12(1), 135-158.

Levi, M., and Murphy, G. H. (2006). Coalitions of contention: The case of the WTO protests in Seattle. *Political Studies*, 54, 651–670.

Leviatan, O. (1982). *Development in COLA agreement and wage-prices correlation*. Jerusalem: Bank of Israel Research Department, Discussion Paper 82-89. (Hebrew)

Levine, M. (1998). Conquest through town planning: The case of Tel Aviv, 1921-48. *Journal of Palestine Studies*, 27(4), 36-52.

Levy, Y. (2003). *The other army of Israel*. Tel Aviv: Yediot Ahronot. (Hebrew)

------. (2010). The tradeoff between force and casualties, Israel's wars in Gaza: 1987-2009. *Conflict Management and Peace Science September*, 27(4), 386-405.

Lewin-Epstein, N., Elmelech, Y., and Semyonov, M. (1997). Ethnic inequality in home-ownership and the value of housing: The case of immigrants to Israel. *Social Forces*, 75(4), 1439-62.

Linz, J., and Stepan, A. (1996). *Problems of democratic transitions and consolidation*. Baltimore: John Hopkins University Press.

Lockman, Z. (1996). *Comrades and enemies: Arab and Jewish workers in Palestine, 1906-1948*. Berkeley: University of California Press.

Luckman, Z., and Beinin, J. (1989). *Intifada: The Palestinian uprising against Israeli occupation*. Boston: South End Press.

Lustick, I. (1980). *Arabs in the Jewish state: Israel's control of a national minority*. Austin: University of Texas Press.

Maier, C. (1984). Preconditions for corporatism. In J. Goldthorpe (ed), *Order and conflict in contemporary capitalism*, 39-59. Oxford: Clarendon Press.

Maman, D. (1997). The elite structure in Israel: A socio-historical analysis. *Journal of Political and Military Sociology*, 25(1), 25-46.

Maman, D., and Rosenhek, Z. (2011). *The Israeli Central Bank: Political economy, global logics and local actors*. Abingdon, Oxon: Routledge.

Mann, M. (1986). *The sources of social power*. Cambridge: Cambridge University Press.

------. (2005). *The dark side of democracy: Explaining ethnic cleansing*. New York: Cambridge University Press.

McAdam, D. (1982). *Political process and the development of black insurgency, 1930-1970*. Chicago: University of Chicago Press.

------. (1996). Political opportunities: Conceptual origins, current problems, future directions. In D. McAdam et al. (eds.), *Comparative perspectives on social movements* (23-40). Cambridge: Cambridge University Press.

Margalit, E. (1991). Mapam's social and economic ideology, 1948-1954. In E. Margalit, *The united left: The social road of Mapam during the State's outset*. Givat Haviva: The Center for documentation and research of Hashomer Hatzair, Yad Yaari Press. (Hebrew)

Margalit, M., Gadot, I., and Dechs, S. (2004). *Constructing the Oslo discourse*. Seminary Paper, Ben-Gurion University's Behavioral Sciences Department.

Marx, K., and Engel, F. (1969 [1848]). Manifesto of the communist party. In *Marx/Engels selected works*, Vol. one, 98-137. Moscow: Progress Publisher.

Medding, P. Y. (1972). *Mapai in Israel: Political organisation and government in a new society*. Cambridge: Cambridge University Press.

Meital, Y. (2005). *Peace in tatters: Israel, Palestine and the Middle East*. Boulder, CO: Lynne Reiner Publishers.

Melucci, A. (1985). The symbolic challenge of contemporary movements. *Social Research*, 52(4): 789-816.

Mendeltzweig, R., and Magor, N. (1984). *Immigration and absorption: Development and trends*. Jerusalem: Center of Propaganda, Ministry of Immigration and Absorption. (Hebrew)

Metzer, J. (1991). *Jewish economy and Arab economy in Palestine (1919-1946)*. Tel-Aviv: Peretz. (Hebrew)

------. (1998). *The divided economy of mandatory Palestine*. Cambridge: Cambridge University Press.

Michels, R. (1915). *Political parties: A sociological study of the oligarchical tendencies of modern democracy*. New York: The Free Press.

Mintz, A., and Ward, M. D. (1988). The evolution of Israel's military expenditures: 1960-1983. *The Western Political Quarterly*, 41(3), 489-507.

Morris, B. (1987). *The birth of the Palestinian refugee problem, 1947-1949*. Cambridge: Cambridge University Press.

------. (1993). *Israel's border wars 1949-1956: Arab infiltration, Israel retaliation and the countdown to the Suez War*. Oxford: Claredon Press.

------. (2008) *1948: A history of the first Arab-Israeli war*, New Haven: Yale University Press.

Nahon, Y. (1993). Occupational status. In S. N. Eisenstadt, M. Lissak, and Y. Nahon (eds.), *Ethnic communities in Israel: Socio-economic status* (50-75). Jerusalem: The Jerusalem Institute for Israel Studies. (Hebrew)

------. (1993a). The expansion of education and occupational opportunity structure. In S. N. Eisenstadt, M. Lissak, and Y. Nahon (eds.), *Ethnic communities in Israel: Socio-economic status*. Jerusalem: The Jerusalem Institute for Israel Studies. (Hebrew)

Naor, M., and Giladi, D. (1990). *Eretz Israel in the 20th century: From the yishuv to a state, 1900-1950*. Tel Aviv: Ministry of Defense. (Hebrew)

Nassar, J. R., and Heacock, R. (1990). *Intifada: Palestine at the crossroads*. New York: Praeger.

Neubach, A. (1986). *Conclusion after one year of economic stabilization program implementation*. Prime Minister's Office, Jerusalem, June 29, 1986. (Hebrew)

O'Donnell, G., and Schmitter, P. C. (1986). *Transitions from authoritarian rule: Tentative conclusions about uncertain democracies*. Baltimore: Johns Hopkins University Press.

Offe, C., and Weisenthal, H. (1980). Two logics of collective action: Theoretical notes on social class and organizational form. *Political Power and Social Theory*, 1, 67-115.

Osnat, D. (2004). "Of tailors and shoemakers we built here a port": Class, nationalism and ethnicity among Ashdod port workers, 1961-1967. (Unpublished PhD dissertation). Ben Gurion University, Beer Sheva. (Hebrew)

Pappe, I. (2006). *The ethnic cleansing of Palestine*. Oxford: Oneworld.

Patinkin, D. (1993). Israel's stabilization program of 1985, or some simple truths of monetary theory. *Journal of Economic Perspectives*, 7(2), 103-128.

Peled, Y. (1992). Ethnic democracy and the legal construction of citizenship: Arab citizens of the Jewish state. *The American Political Science Review*, 86, 432-443.

------. (2004). Profits or glory? The 28th Elul of Arik Sharon. *New Left Review*, 29, 47-70.

Peres, S. (1993). *The new Middle East*. New York: H. Holt.

Peres, Y., and Shemer, S. (1984). The ethnic factor in the election to the tenth Knesset in Israel. *Megamot* 2-3, 316-331. (Hebrew)

Peri, Y. (1983). *Between ballots and bullets*. Cambridge: Cambridge University Press.

------. (2000). *The assassination of Yitzhak Rabin*. Stanford: Stanford University Press.

------. (2006). *Generals in the cabinet room: How the military shapes policy*. Washington: U.S. Institute of Peace Press.

Peri, Y., and Neubach, A. (1984). The military industrial complex, interim report. Tel Aviv: The International Center for Peace in the Middle East.

Pinard, M. (2011). *Motivational dimensions in social movements and contentious collective action*. McGill-Queen's University Press.

Piore, M. and Doeringer, P. B. (1971). *Internal labor markets and manpower analysis*. Lexington, MA: Heath Lexington Books.

Pizzorno, A. (1978). Political exchange and collective identity in industrial conflict. In C. Crouch and A. Pizzorno (eds.), *The resurgence of class conflict in western Europe since 1968* (277-298). London: MacMillan.

Porath, Y. (1976). *From riots to revolt: The Palestinian national movement, 1929-1939*. Tel-Aviv: Am-Oved. (Hebrew).

Przeworski, A. (1991). *Democracy and the market*. Cambridge: Cambridge University Press.

Rabin, Y. (1995). *Pursuing peace: The peace speeches of Prime Minister Yitzhak Rabin*. Tel Aviv: Zmora Beytan. (Hebrew)

Ram, U. (2008). *The globalization of Israel: McWorld in Tel Aviv, Jihad in Jerusalem*. New York: Routledge.

Ratner, Y. (1956). The martial law. *Mibefnim*, 19(1). (Hebrew)

Razin, E. (1984). *The location of industrial firms in Israel*. Report No. 7. Jerusalem: The Jerusalem Institute for Israel Studies (Hebrew).

Reshef, T. (1996). *Peace Now*. Jerusalem: Keter (Hebrew).

Reshef, Y. (1981). *The impact of political change on patterns of political exchange*. (Unpublished MA thesis). Tel Aviv University, Tel Aviv. (Hebrew)

Rex, J. (1970). *Race relations in sociological theory*. London: Weidenfeld and Nicolson.

Roniger, L., and Feige, M. (1992). From pioneer to freier: The changing models of generalized exchange in Israel. *European Journal of Sociology*, 33, 280-307.

Rosen, G. (ed.) (1983). *The Lebanon war: Between protest and compliance*. Tel Aviv: Hakibutz Hameuchad. (Hebrew)

Rosenhek, Z. (1999). Migrant workers in the Israeli welfare state: Trends of exclusion and inclusion. *Bitahon Sotziali* [Social Security], 56, 97-112. (Hebrew)

Rothschild, J. (1981). *Ethnopolitics: A conceptual framework*. New York: Columbia University Press.

Roy, S. (1995). *The Gaza Strip: The political economy of de-development*. Beirut: Institute for Palestine Studies.

------. (2001). Decline and disfigurement: The Palestinian economy after Oslo. In R. Carey (ed.), *The New Intifada*. London: Verso.

Rubinstein, A. (1982). *Some political experience*. Jerusalem: Idanim. (Hebrew)

Rueschemeyer, D., Stephens, E. H., and Stephens, J. D. (1992). *Capitalist development and democracy*. Chicago: University of Chicago Press.

Rustow, D. A. (1970). Transitions to democracy: Toward a dynamic model. *Comparative Politics*, 2, 337-363.

Sagi, E., Sheinin, J., and Perlman, M. (1992). *The Palestinian economy and its affinity to the Israeli economy*. Tel Aviv: University of Tel Aviv, Pinhas Sapir Development Center (Hebrew).

Said, E. (1978). *Orientalism*. New York: Pantheon Books.

Savir, U. (1998). *The process: Behind the scenes of a historic decision*. New-York: Random House.

Sayigh, R. (1979). *Palestinians: From peasants to revolutionaries*. London: Zed Books.

Schechter, A. (2012). *Rothschild: Chronicle of the protest*. Tel Aviv: Hakibbutz Hameuhad (Hebrew)

Schiff, Z., and Yaari, E. (1984). *Israel's Lebanon war*. New York: Simon and Schuster.

------. (1990). *Intifada: The Palestinian uprising—Israel's third front*. New York: Simon and Schuster.

Schmitter, P. C. (1974). Still the century of corporatism? *The Review of Politics*, 36, 85-131.

Schwartz, M. (1995). *Unlimited guarantee*. Beer-Sheva: University of Ben-Gurion in the Negev. (Hebrew)

Segev, T. (1986). *1949: The first Israelis*. New York: Free Press.

Semyonov, M., and Lewin-Epstein, N. (1987). *Hewers of woods and drawers of water: Noncitizen Arab in the Israeli labor market*. Ithaca, NY: ILR Press.

Sewell, W. H. (1996). Three temporalities: Toward an eventful sociology. In T. J. McDonald (ed.), *The historic turn in the human sciences* (245-280). Michigan: University of Michigan Press.

Shafir, G. (1989). *Land and labor in the making of Israeli nationalism*. Cambridge: Cambridge University Press.

------. (1999). Business in politics: Globalization and the search for peace in South Africa and Israel/Palestine. In D. Levy-Faur, G. Shefer and D. Vogel (eds.), *Israel, the dynamics of change and continuity*, 103-120. London: Frank Cass.

------. (1999a). The Jaring program. *Theory and Critique*, 12-13, 205-214 (Hebrew).

------. (2011). Capitalist bi-nationalism in mandatory Palestine. *IJMES*, 43(4), 611-633.

Shafir, G., and Peled, Y. (2000). *The new Israel: Peacemaking and liberalization*. Boulder, CO: Westview Press.

------. (2002). *Being Israeli: The dynamics of multiple citizenship.* New York: Cambridge University Press.

Shalev, A. (1990). *The Intifada: Causes, characteristics and consequences.* Tel Aviv: Papirus. (Hebrew)

Shalev, M. (1984). Labor, state and crisis: An Israeli case study. *Industrial Relations,* 23, 362-386.

------. (1992). *Labor and the political economy in Israel.* Oxford: Oxford University Press.

Shalev, M., and Rosenhek, Z. (2013). The political economy of the 2011 protest: A class-generational analysis. *Theory and Critique,* 41. (Hebrew)

Shalom, Z., and Hendel, Y. (2011). The specific features of the Intifada II in Israel's wars. *Military and Strategy,* 3(1), 15-24. (Hebrew)

Shapira, A. (1977). *The futile struggle: Hebrew labor 1929-1937.* Tel Aviv: Kibbutz Meuchad. (Hebrew).

------. (1980). *Berl: Biography.* Tel Aviv: Am Oved Press. (Hebrew)

Shapiro, Y. (1975). *The historic Achdut Havoda.* Tel-Aviv: Am-Oved. (Hebrew)

------. (1976). *The formative years of the Israeli labour party: The organization of power, 1919-1930.* London: Sage Publications.

------. (1977). *The Israeli democracy.* Ramat Gan: Masada (Hebrew).

------. (1991). *The road to power: Herut party in Israel.* Albany, NY: State University of New York Press.

------. (1996). *Politicians as a hegemonic class: The case of Israel.* Tel Aviv: Sifriat Poalim. (Hebrew).

Sharett, M. (1978). *Private diary.* Tel Aviv: Sifriat Poalim (Hebrew).

Shaw commission of inquiry report. (1930). Jerusalem, British Mandate.

Shenhav, Y. (2006). *The Arab Jews: A postcolonial reading of nationalism, religion, and ethnicity.* Stanford: Stanford University Press.

Shiffer, S. (1984). *Snow ball: The story behind the Lebanon war.* Tel Aviv: Yediot Ahronot/Edanim. (Hebrew)

Shils, E. (1957). *Center and periphery: Essays in macrosociology.* Chicago: The University of Chicago Press.

Shohat, E. (1988). Sephardim in Israel: Zionism from the standpoint of its Jewish victims. *Social Text,* 19-20, 1-35.

Shumsky, D. (2010). *Between Prague and Jerusalem.* Jerusalem: Leo Beck Institute.

Skocpol, T. (1980). Political response to capitalist crisis: Neo-Marxist theories of the state and the case of the New Deal. *Politics and Society,* 10, 2.

------. (1985). Bringing the state back in: Strategies of analysis in current research. In P. B. Evans, D. Rueschemeyer, and T. Skocpol (eds.), *Bringing the state back in,* 3-43. Cambridge: Cambridge University Press.

Smith, H. (1969). *Israeli elections.* Tel-Aviv: Adi. (Hebrew)

Smoli, Y. (2012). Sapir college conference, January 2012. (Hebrew)

Smooha, S. (2002). The model of ethnic democracy: Israel as a Jewish and democratic state. *Nation and Nationalism,* 8(4), 475-503.

Snow, D. (2004). Social movements as challenges to authority: Resistance to an

emerging conceptual hegemony. *Research in Social Movements, Conflicts and Change*, 25, 3-25.
Standing, G. (2011). *The precariat: The new dangerous class*. London and New York: Bloomsbury Academic.
Sternhell, Z. (1998). *The founding myths of Israel: Nationalism, socialism, and the making of the Jewish state*. Princeton: Princeton University Press.
Stiglitz, J. (2003). *Globalization and its discontents*. New York: Norton.
Sturmthal, A. (1973). Industrial relations strategies. In A. Sturmthal and F. G. Scoville (eds.), *The international labor movement in transition: Essays on Africa, Asia, Europe, and South America*, 1-20. Urbana: University of Illinois Press.
Susman, Z. (1974). *Wage differentials and egalitarian ideology of the Histadrut*. Ramat Gan: Masada. (Hebrew)
Sussman, Z., and Zakai, D. (1983). *Changes in the wage structure of the civil service and rising inflation: Israel; 1974-1981*. Jerusalem: Bank of Israel Research Department. (Hebrew)
Swirski, S. (1979). Comments on the Historical Sociology of the *Yishuv Notebooks for Research and Critique*, 2, 5-42. (Hebrew)
------. (1981). *Orientals and Ashkenazim in Israel: The ethnic division of labor*. Haifa: Notebooks for Research and Critique.
Swirski, S., and Bernstein, D. (1980). Who worked, where and for how much? *Notebooks for Research and Critique*, 4, 5-66. (Hebrew)
------. (1982). The rapid economic development of Israel and the emergence of the ethnic division of labor. *British Journal of Sociology*, 33, 64-85.

Talshir, G. (2012). Social democracy beyond identity politics: An ideological analysis of the protest summer, Israel 2011. Paper presented in Open University Seminar, Beyt Daniel, September 10-11. (Hebrew)
Tarrow, S. (1989). *Democracy and disorder: Protest and politics in Italy, 1965-1975*. Oxford: Clarendon.
------. (1998). *Power in movement*. Cambridge: Cambridge University Press.
Temkin, B., and Ben Hanan, U. (1986). The overload juggler: The electoral economic cycle in Israel, 1951-1984. In A. Arian and M. Shamir (eds.), *The elections in Israel, 1984*, 15-36. Ramot: Ramot Publishing Company.
Tevet, S. (1992). *Shearing time/Calaban*. Israel: Ish-Dor. (Hebrew)
Tilly, C. (1978). *From mobilization to revolution*. Reading, MA: Addison-Wesley.
------. (1992). *Coercion, capital and European states, AD 990-1992*. Cambridge: Basil Blackwell.
------. (1993). *European revolutions, 1492-1992*. Oxford: Blackwell.
------. (2006). *Regimes and repertoires*. Chicago and London: The University of Chicago Press.
Tokatli, R. (1979). *Political patterns in labor relations in Israel*. (Unpublished PhD dissertation). University of Tel Aviv, Tel Aviv. (Hebrew)
Trachtenberg, M. (2011). *Report of the committee for socio-economic change*. Jerusalem. (Hebrew)

Trotsky, L. (1964 [1879-1940]). *The age of permanent revolution: A Trotsky anthology*. Isaac Deutscher (ed.). New York: Dell.

Usher, G. (1995). *Palestine in crisis: The struggle for peace and political independence after Oslo*. London: Pluto Press.

Weber, M. (1968). *On charisma and institution building*. Chicago: University of Chicago Press.
Williamson, J. (1994). *The political economy of policy reform*. Washington D.C.: Institute for International Economics.
Wilson, J. (1972). *Introduction to social movements*. New York: Basic Books.
Winograd, E. (2008). Final report of the commission of inquiry into the events of military engagement in Lebanon 2006. Jerusalem: Government of Israel. (Hebrew)

Yadlin, A. (1980). *Testimony*. Jerusalem: Yediot Ahronot. (Hebrew)
Yanay, N. (1969). *Split in the elite: The crisis that shocked Mapai and led to the formation of Rafi*. Tel Aviv: A. Lewin-Epstein. (Hebrew)
Yiftachel, O. (2006). *Ethnocracy*. Philadelphia: University of Pennsylvania Press.
Yishai, Y. (1978). *Factions in the labor movement: "Siah B" in Mapai*. Tel Aviv: Am-Oved. (Hebrew)
Yizhar, U. (2005). *Between vision and power: The history of Ahdut-Ha'Avoda-Poalei-Zion Party*. Kfar Habad: Yad Tabenkin. (Hebrew)
Yona,Y., and Saporta, I. (2004). Pre-vocational education: The making of Israel's ethno-working class. *Race Ethnicity and Education*, 7(3), 251-273.
Yoran, Y. (1989). Dynamics of anti-growth: The Israeli market after the oil crisis and the Yom-Kippur war. In S. Stempler (ed.), *People and state: Israeli society*, 348-377. Israel: Ministry of Defense Press. (Hebrew)
Younis, M. N. (2000). *Liberalization and democratization: The South African and Palestinian national movement*. Minneapolis: University of Minnesota Press.

Zakaria, F. (1997). The rise of illiberal democracies. *Foreign Affairs*, 76, 22-43.
Zalmanovitch, Y. (1981). *Histadrut, Kupat Holim, government: The conflictual and concensual exchange approach as a political explanation; A macroeconomic, social and political analysis; Processes of change*. (Unpublished MA thesis). University of Haifa, Haifa. (Hebrew)
Zureik, E. T. (1979). *The Palestinians in Israel: A study in internal colonialism*. London: Routledge.

INDEX

Abargil, Reuven, 171(n21)
Abdel-Shafi, Haidar, 232
Absentee Property Law, 91, 92(n3), 96(n7)
Acco, 104, 112
Acre (see Acco)
Action committees (Ch.4)
Anti-government demonstrations, 139
    General strike, 132
    Resistance, 123, 125, 132-133, 146, 148-150
Agudat Yisrael, 272
Ahdut Haavoda, 94-95, 116, 124-125, 127, 129, 132-136, 142, 148-149, 161-163, 165-166, 279, 297, 301
Aliyah,
    Second, 61-62
    Fourth, 70
Almogi, Joseph, 112, 128
Alon, Yigal, 162
Anti-African demonstration, 266, 268
Anti-colonial repertoire, 282-283
Anti-globalization protest, 291
Anti-Semitism, 63, 78
Arab,
    Absentee, 96
    Bourgeoisie, 73, 82-84, 86, 308
    Citizens, 93, 97-98, 100, 106, 119-120, 262, 268
    Economy, 63, 157
    Strike of 1936, 71, 78-79, 81, 87
    Labor, 61, 63, 69, 83, 122
    Lands, 61, 64, 83, 92, 105, 107
    Middle class, 71, 78(n23)
    Peasants, 67, 72, 84-86, 308
    Products, 80
    Revolt, 60, 79-80, 82, 86, 88
    Second class citizens, 106
    Spring, 59, 293
    States, 223
    Workers, 61-64, 69, 80-81, 83, 122
Arafat, Yasser, 30, 33-34, 233-234, 236-237, 239, 246-247
Aridor, Yoram, 201-202
Arlosoroff, Haim, 75, 77
Ashdod, 159, 165, 168,
Ashkenazi,
Apparatchik, 114
Ashkenazim, 90, 153, 170, 174-175, 181, 312
    Cooperative settlements, 106
    Elites, 90, 106, 175, 178, 244, 300, 312
    Employers, 106, 287, 301
    Holocaust victims, 93
    Leadership, 92
    Left, 176
    Middle-class, 14, 93, 105, 111, 114, 117, 178-179, 181, 244, 263, 266-267, 272, 294
    New immigrants, 93, 105, 171, 287
    Parties, 242
    Secular, 179, 242, 272, 288, 312
    Upper-class, 110, 174, 176, 244
    Veteran, 90, 93, 105-106, 114, 118
    Workers, 93, 122, 174, 279, 287, 301
Ashrawi, Hanan, 232
Authoritarian regimes, 24, 38, 49, 54, 247, 276
Autonomy plan, 220
Avoda ivrit, 63-64, 66, 69, 71, 140, 158
Ayarot Pituach, 105-107, 114-115, 148, 174-176, 181, 228, 297

Bak'a neighborhood, 169
Balad, 256(n10), 272
Bank Hapoalim, 66, 163, 189
Bank of Israel, 205, 207-208, 211, 213, 218

Barak, Ehud, 32-33, 257
Bat Yam, 230
Becker, Aaron, 130
Beer Sheba, 112
Begin, Menachem, 116, 133-134, 175, 178, 182, 200, 202, 235, 288
Beilin, Yossi, 29, 226, 245
Beirut, 220
Ben Aharon, Yitzhak, 165
Ben Gurion, David, 71, 76-78, 108, 111, 113-114, 118, 124-129, 132, 134-136, 151, 158, 161, 280
Ben Gurion's juniors (see Tzeirei Ben Gurion)
Ben Harush, David, 114, 168
Ben Menachem, Eli, 185, 214
Berglas, Ethan, 205
Berlin Wall fall, 226
Bitton, Charlie, 171(n21)
Black Panther, (Ch. 5)
    Ethnic riots, 19, 40, 90
    Mass demonstration, 169, 173
    Protest, 154, 169, 171, 174, 176, 178
    Resistance moment, 153, 171, 173
    Resistance movement, 153-154, 170, 173, 175-176, 178
Borders,
    1967, 157, 224, 254, 263
    British mandate, 122, 147
    Cease fire, 89
    Economic, 239
    National, 48
    Of resistance, 222
    Of society, 15
    Pre-1948, 89
    Pre-1967, 177, 226
    Recognition, 30, 32, 35, 42, 51, 147, 273, 309
    State, 13-14, 18, 26, 42, 47-48, 88, 92-93, 95-97, 99, 119, 122, 147, 149, 162, 228, 253, 262, 281, 292, 307
    Symbolic, 29, 35, 68, 88, 92
Boycott, 221-222, 284, 292
British Mandate, 13, 39, 62, 65, 70, 72, 78, 82-83, 85-86, 92, 94-95, 119, 122, 143, 147, 276, 283-284
British colonial,
    Government, 22, 143
    Rule, 17, 60, 98
Bruno, Michael, 192(n12), 205, 207, 211
B'Tselem, 222
Burg, Abraham, 226

Cairo, 252, 273
Camp David, 33, 220
Capital,
    Accumulation, 107-108, 110, 189
    Flux, 82, 107
    Global, 273, 291, 310
    Imports, 91, 151, 184
    Influx from US, 155
    Injection system, 163
    Investment, 105, 155, 164, 240
    Market, 94, 208, 214, 256
    Private, 63, 71, 121, 133, 136, 163-164, 183, 189, 191, 213, 215, 281, 292, 301
    State, 58
    Transfer, 61, 158, 201
Cartel parties, 214, 245, 304
Cease fire agreement, 153, 171, 200, 271, 300
Central Bank, 211, 260
Chalutzim, 62, 90
Chambers of commerce, 75, 83, 87, 238
Charismatic leadership, 165, 203, 247-248
Chile, 274
Citizenship, 25, 36, 48, 66, 89, 96-97, 102-103, 147, 154, 175, 177-178, 257
Civil right organizations, 221-222
Civil society organizations, 26, 30, 259, 263, 282, 311
Cohen, Shalom, 172, 175
COLA, 151, 185, 189-190, 208-209
Collective action, 19, 25, 53-54, 107, 199, 204, 266, 273, 278, 285, 287, 293, 296, 298

Index

Collective identity, 23, 54, 82, 119, 136, 153, 179, 244, 251, 265, 267, 275, 278, 282, 288-289, 296, 300-303, 307, 310-312
Colonial
Colonialism, 15, 85, 105
    expansion, 14, 308
    regime, 72, 99, 147
Conscription law, 270, 272-273
Constitution, 29(n12), 51, 227
Constructivism, 63, 69, 71
Cooptation, 116-120, 133, 135, 176, 246-247, 250, 278-279, 295-299, 309, 313
Corruption affairs, 164, 186
CPI, 164, 185, 189-190
Crystal night, 112
Cultural capital, 116, 153-154
Customs union, 239-241

Dash, 180, 181, 187
Dayan, Moshe, 113-114, 120, 141, 151, 160-162
Dead Sea Works (DSW), 197
Decision-making process, 19, 37-39, 72, 275, 282, 284, 305
Declaration of Principles (see DOP)
Democratic regime, 21, 28, 31, 36, 38-39, 46, 48-52, 59, 293
Democratization, 14, 27, 30, 32, 40, 45, 47-48, 120, 122, 166, 227-228, 247, 264, 282
Development towns (see Ayarot Pituach)
DOP, 234, 235, 238-239, 242, 244
Dror Israel, 263, 268
Dual,
    Colonialist regime, 64
Democratic/military regime, 39, 158, 173, 175-177, 180, 182, 217-218, 252-253, 261
    Israeli/Palestinian Political economy, 146, 149-150, 153-154, 157-158, 164
    Society, 13-14
    Structure of domination, 141, 150, 155, 159-160, 250
Economic,
    Assimilation, 77
    Blockade, 258
    Conflict, 15, 20, 254, 301
    Crisis, 26, 70-71, 75, 79, 86-87, 137-138, 146, 183, 191, 202, 212, 218, 261
    Dependency, 122, 219, 239-240, 247
    Development, 84, 102, 108, 125, 137, 156, 236
    Elite, 16, 22, 82, 87, 143, 183, 225, 228, 231, 238, 260, 310
    Inequality, 252, 259, 272, 300
    Integration, 27, 142-143, 156-157, 162, 170, 175, 178, 287
    Organizations' Coordination Bureau (see EOCB)
    Restraint, 138, 192
    Segregation, 64, 67, 72, 74, 85
    Stability, 187, 305-306, 311

Economy,
    Apolitical image, 213, 304, 306
    Balance of Payments, 130, 137-138, 151, 184, 206-207
    Bankruptcy, 70, 211
    Bonds, 140, 167, 208, 256,
    Budgetary deficit, 73, 191, 205-206
    Commerce, 75-76, 78, 83, 87, 100, 106-107, 238
    Commodification, 184
    Credit, 108, 140, 189, 191, 193, 200, 205, 212
    Customs, 73-74, 131, 144, 201, 237, 239-240
    Debt, 140, 151, 164, 211
    Devaluation, 123, 184, 206-208, 211
    Exchange rate, 123, 184, 187, 204, 206-208, 211
    Export, 75, 138-139, 144, 159, 184, 191, 197-199, 206-208, 211, 231, 240
    Fiscal deficit, 123, 138-139, 155,

164, 206, 210
Free market, 62-64, 67, 76, 81, 88-89, 119-121, 124, 134, 143, 148, 157, 177, 216
Global market, 83, 86, 240, 281, 285
Growth, 78, 107, 124, 131, 151, 155-156, 158, 184, 207-208, 219, 228-229
GNP, 151, 156
Hyperinflation, 25, 58, 108, 146, 155, 164, 183, 193, 204, 212, 218, 279-280, 301, 305
Import, 63, 75, 138, 155, 159, 167, 186, 191, 239, 240-241, 285
Inflation, 23, 26, 94, 137-138, 155, 163-164, 167-169, 182, 184-185, 188-193, 196, 198-202, 203-208, 211-213, 219, 301, 306
Interest rate, 206-208, 211
Local currency, 123, 191, 205
Local demand, 107, 123, 137, 139, 228
Low-cost production, 107
Mark-denominated transfers, 138
Monetary crisis, 210
Nominal wage, 208
Non-indexed loans, 141, 163, 184, 189, 192, 200, 213
Production, 65, 107, 137, 139, 141, 144, 190, 206-207, 249
Real wage, 123, 188, 190, 199, 205, 208, 280
Recession, 27, 70, 79, 107, 137-140, 142, 144-145, 149-150, 152, 154, 160-161, 163, 170, 177, 190-191, 193, 196, 200, 207, 219, 229, 279-280
Separated, 142, 144, 146
Stagnation, 219
Standards of living, 130, 156
Stock market, 202, 212, 256
Trade deficit, 155, 193, 205
EESP, 204-212, 214-215, 225, 229
Egged, 77
Egypt, 74, 111, 126, 144, 151, 153, 155-156, 171-172, 182, 200, 202, 212, 220, 234, 238, 240-241, 251-252, 274, 290-292, 300
Egyptian uprising, 274, 290
El-Al, 185, 193, 196-198
El-Dajani, Hasan Sidqi, 74, 77, 79, 84, 87
Ehrlich, Simcha, 187-190
Elad, Avri, 127(n5)
Elections (Knesset),
    of 1959, 90, 111, 114, 117-118, 127, 174, 288, 300, 302
    of 1961, 129
    of 1965, 27, 130, 133-134, 136, 140, 148-149, 161, 165, 301
    of 1969, 141-142, 149, 154, 166, 177
    of 1973, 155, 168, 172, 175, 183, 288, 302
    of 1977, 23, 103, 173, 177, 180-181, 186, 288, 302
    of 1981, 179, 200-201, 212, 302
    of 1984, 179, 203, 212, 214, 216, 302, 306
    of 1988, 224, 245(n48)
    of 1992, 30, 228, 230-231, 232(n19), 241, 244, 254
    of 1996, 235-236
    of 1999, 32, 133, 245, 254
    of 2001, 287
    of 2003, 255, 270
    of 2006, 255-256, 270
    of 2009, 257
    of 2013, 58, 253, 267, 269-270, 290, 297
Elections War, 271
Electoral system, 125, 302
Emergency Economic Stabilization plan (see EESP)
Emigration, 139, 228, 287
EOCB, 189-190, 204
Eshkol, Levy, 108, 126-130, 134-136, 143, 161-163, 280
Ethnic
    Demon, 117, 289
    Mobilization, 117

Index

Riots repertoire, 285-287
Segregation, 89, 95
Ethno-classes, 14, 58, 67, 80, 82, 85-86, 93, 105-106, 110, 115, 122, 143, 148, 150, 152-154, 169, 173-174, 178-179, 183, 200, 203, 244-245, 263-266, 288-289, 293-294, 299
Ethno-national confrontation, 22, 58, 73, 88, 97
European Union, 239

Fatah, 34, 258(n15)
Forum/13, (Ch.6)
    24-hour strike, 194, 198, 299
    General strike, 194, 209-210
    Resistance moment, 214
    Resistance movement, 182, 199, 201, 209, 215
French colonialism, 105
Frenkel, Mordechai, 205

G-7 Conference, 291
Gahal, 136-137, 151, 166, 168
Gaza, 32, 58, 96, 122, 133, 141, 144, 221, 224, 226, 230, 234-237, 241, 246, 255-258, 265, 271, 276
Gaza-Jericho First Agreement, 234
General Security Service (Shabak), 156
Geographic segregation, 23, 64, 70, 95
German reparation payments, 93, 137-138
Germany, 20, 77-78, 107, 137-138
Gilerman, Dan, 238
Global trade agreement (GATT), 225-226
Global wave of protests, 268, 274
Globalization, 16, 231, 259, 291, 293
Golan Heights, 141
Gorochowsky, Shraga, 74
Government investment resources, 107, 137
Government spending, 139, 190-192, 228
Greater Israel myth, 34, 175-177, 230, 232

Green line, 160, 178, 217, 230
Gulf countries, 219

Hadash, 187(n6), 205(n18), 242(n41), 272
Haganah, 66, 70, 95
Haifa, 78-79, 83, 90, 104, 111-112, 148, 287
Hakibbutz Hameuhad, 94
Hamas, 233-234, 246, 258(n15)
Hamashbir Hamerkazi, 66
Haolam Haze, 172
Hapoel, 68
Hapoel Hatzair, 62, 66
Hashomer Hatzair, 68(n6), 94(n6), 95
Hasne, 211
Hebrew labor (see Avoda ivrit)
Hebron, 70
Herut, 116-117, 132-134, 136, 148, 151, 296, 301
Hevrat Haovdim, 65-67, 101, 108, 110, 139-141, 144-145, 159, 162-165, 184, 189-191, 194-195, 198-200, 209-212, 214-215, 225, 243
High Court of Justice, 222, 246
Histadrut,
    1935 elections, 78
    1965 elections- 27, 94, 134-135, 137
    1973 elections, 165, 172-173
    1977 elections, 181-182
    1985 elections, 204-205
    1994 elections, 103, 242-243, 245
    Bureaucracy, 95, 194, 288
    Central committee (see Vaada Merakezet)
    Centralist federation, 130
    Comprehensive pension agreement, 189-190
    Collective wage agreements, 165, 186, 196, 229, 259
    Corporations, 65-66, 136, 187, 301
    Cost-of-living allowance agreement (see COLA)
    Employment exchange, 67, 97, 101

Index

Executive committee (see Vaad Hapoel)
Firms, 164, 186, 213
General strike, 188, 190
Governance structure, 66
Health maintenance organization (HMO), 104, 200, 211
Institutional enterprise (see Meshek Mosadi)
Leadership, 123, 129-131, 134, 185, 187, 193, 204, 209-210, 215, 243
Meshek Mosadi, 65-66
Owned economy, 140
Package Deal, 164, 166-167, 186, 190, 199, 201, 204-206
Pre-state, 100, 102-103, 111, 136
Public services, 24, 66, 101-102
Restraining workers, 204
Secretary General, 76, 78, 108, 124, 126, 130, 165, 186, 188, 194
Structural reform, 213, 242-243
Trade Union department, 130, 141
Umbrella trade union, 29
Vaad Hapoel, 21, 66, 173(n23), 194, 209
Vaada Merakezet, 66, 76, 209-210
Welfare state, 65, 69, 100, 125, 129, 137, 169, 260
Worker council, 112-113, 130-131, 134, 148, 185, 192, 195-196, 209
Worker troops (see Plugot Hapoel)
Histadrut-IDF cooperation, 147, 161-162, 217
Historical
    Cases, 19, 275, 277
    Contingencies, 56, 238, 279
    Turning point, 13-14, 18, 20, 277, 280
Homology, 44-45, 91
Horowitz, Yigal, 190-191, 193, 196, 199-201, 203-204, 211,
Housing minister, 186
Hushi, Aba, 112, 120
Husseini, Faisal, 232

IAI, see Israeli Aviation Industry
IBA, see Israeli Broadcasting Authority
IDF, 66, 95-98, 113, 146-147, 156-157, 159, 161, 205, 220-223, 230, 234-234, 240-241, 246, 248-250, 271, 300, 304, 306
IEC, see Israeli electric Company
Illusionary democracy, 31, 41, 52, 58, 309
Imagined,
    Democracy, 31-32, 49-50, 218, 227, 309
    Nation, 31, 51, 119, 288, 307
    Peace, 31-32, 245, 247, 249
    People, 31, 49-50, 262, 309
IMF, 140
Indexing insurance, 163, 170, 189-190
Indignados, 252, 291
Industrial peace, 151
Industrialization, 90, 107, 111, 131, 148, 156
Institutional
    Flexibility, 102
    Rigidity, 28, 310
Intifada (ch.7),
    Civil society mobilization, 220, 246(n49)
    Counter movement, 241, 246, 249
    General strike, 284
    Leadership, 222-223
    Mass demonstration, 284
    Non-violent resistance, 220-221
    Political solution, 222, 225
    Resistance movement, 58, 216, 219, 241, 249, 295
    Second Intifada, 17, 57, 157(n6), 254-255, 285
Iran, 266
Iraq, 93, 115-116, 118, 231, 240, 255
Islam, 234(n23), 250
Israel,
    Aviation Industries (IAI), 193, 196-198
    Broadcasting Authority (IBA) IBA, 197, 210
    Electric Corporation (IEC) 109,

131, 196-198, 209-210
Israeli,
    Communist party, 97, 132, 148, 183
    Democracy, 14, 31, 59, 97
    Economy, 13, 58, 118, 122, 142, 144, 146, 163, 167, 174, 190, 219, 222, 238, 241, 250, 284, 287
    Goods, 144, 151, 155, 222
    Intelligence, 126
    Products, 141, 144, 221, 284
    Quasi-citizenship, 102
Israeli-Arab conflict, 169, 182
Israeli/Palestinian,
    History, 12, 17, 88
    Joint economy, 26, 157
    Polity, 18, 153
    Society, 15-16
Israeli-Palestinian,
    Arena, 30, 249
    Matrix, 30
    Negotiation, 29, 33

J14 movement (Ch.8)
    Apolitical image, 263-264
    Assemblies, 266, 274, 290
    B Generation, 259-261, 264
    Carnival image, 262-264
    Civil society mobilization, 291, 307
    Consumer strike, 258
    Crisis of representation, 253, 261
    Equal [military] service camp, 268
    Facebook campaign, 258, 262, 292
    Inclusive identity, 252, 264-265, 267, 270, 273, 294
    Middle class, 262-263, 266-269, 272
    One Million March, 252, 263
    Peoplehood, 260, 264, 293
    Resistance moment, 252, 273
    Resistance movement, 253, 257, 265, 273
    Social justice, 252, 264, 267, 270, 273-274, 290,
    Socio-economic agenda, 255, 261, 266

Tent camps, 252, 258
Jabalia, 237
Jabotinsky, Ze'ev, 67
Jaffa, 78, 83, 104
Jericho, 234-236
Jerusalem, 70, 78, 83, 104, 111-112, 145, 151, 169-172, 178, 193, 235-237, 287
Jewish,
    Agency, 75, 78, 80, 92, 94, 98, 100
    Anti-Jewish violence, 70
    Capital, 61, 71, 80, 160
    Colonist, 62, 84
    Economic interests, 157
    Economy, 63-65, 157
    Employers, 62, 64, 143
    Employment, 67, 69, 79, 84, 119
    Ethiopian, 288
    European, 15, 50, 58, 64, 69, 90, 92, 104-105, 109, 153, 260, 262-263, 288
    Farmers, 63, 83
    From Arab countries, 14(n2), 15, 92-93, 104, 115, 120, 153, 277, 289, 300, 312
    Home (party), 272
    Identity, 154, 174, 243, 301, 312
    Immigrants, 15, 63-64, 77, 92, 96, 104-105, 120, 148, 171, 228, 257, 300
    Middle class, 14, 69, 71, 73
    Nation-state, 18, 124
    National fund (JNF - Keren Kayemet)
    Nationalist, 21, 284, 289, 303, 308
    New Jew, 105, 243, 288
    North African, 90, 105, 111-112, 114-117, 221
    Old Jew, 243, 288
    Polish, 70
    Post-1948 Immigration, 105, 140
    Religious, 32, 64, 70, 179, 232, 243, 260, 286, 288, 302, 312
    Russian, 228-229, 242, 257, 272, 286, 294, 303
    Secular, 12, 302-303, 243, 260,

262, 288, 312
Separated economy, 157
Settlements, 16, 34, 61, 67, 75, 80, 83, 89, 193, 220-221, 231, 233, 236, 242, 253, 288
State, 13, 15, 22, 24, 26, 28, 60, 66, 80-81, 83, 88-89, 90-92, 94-95, 97, 100-101, 119, 144, 154, 158, 177-178
Ultra-orthodox, 268-270, 272-273, 287, 289, 294, 303, 312
Workers, 24, 62-64, 66, 68, 79, 81, 84, 148, 152, 154, 308
Yemenite, 63, 118
Jewish-Arab,
   24-hour strike, 74
   Anti-colonial strike, 23, 57-58, 72, 87
   Bi-national cooperation, 76-77, 87-88
   Civil Society (ch.2), 13, 39, 60, 73
   Commerce strike, 76
   Common economic interest, 71, 82-83
   Economy, 88
   General strike, 75
   Identity, 178
   Inter-ethnic, 75-77, 81
   Joint motor transportation organization, 74
   Matrix, 76, 82, 85
   Resistance moment, 77, 88, 283
   Resistance movement, 22, 77
   Transportation strike, 22, 72, 76, 283, 299
Jibli, Binyamin, 126
Jordan, 144, 155-156, 171, 234, 240-241
Judea and Samaria, 175

Kadima, 256-257, 268, 270, 272
Karmi, Raed, 34
Katamon neighborhood, 169
Katz, Israel, 172
Katzenelson, Berl, 71
Keisar, Israel, 209-210
Keren Hayesod, 64
Keren Kayemet, 64
Kibbutz, 64, 69, 83, 94-95, 104-106, 135, 139, 145, 148, 211
Kiriat Shmona, 112
Knesset, 27, 95, 111-116, 125, 134, 166, 172-173, 175, 181-182, 187, 201, 216, 227, 232, 244-245, 251, 254-255, 257, 267
Koor, 200, 211, 225(n13), 239
Kuwait, 240

Labor Institutional Complex (LIC), 103, 128, 133-134, 146-149, 227
Labor Market,
   Business sector, 145, 165, 186, 188, 191-193, 196, 198-201, 211
   Construction sector, 70, 139
Cultural division, 90
   Dual labor market theories, 16, 25-26, 109, 152 (n3)
   Flexibilization, 214, 219, 240, 260
   Full employment, 24, 28, 58,78, 90,111, 118, 122-124, 127, 129-135, 138-140, 145, 147-149, 152, 154-155, 174, 279-280, 299, 301
   Homogenization, 148, 154
   Industrial workers, 123, 131, 174
   Low-cost labor, 119, 138
   Low-tech industry, 146, 301
   Manufacturing sector, 156, 190, 193
   Migrant workers, 16, 229, 241, 262
   Neo corporatist theories, 16, 24-26
   Non-unionized workers, 136, 145, 165, 241, 260
   Powerful worker, 25, 58, 109, 165, 167, 183, 185, 194-196, 201-202, 209-211, 213, 215, 229, 277, 301
   Primary sector, 25, 152, 155
   Private sector, 138-140, 164-165, 174, 185, 189-190, 192, 210
   Professional trade unions, 131-132, 146, 166
   Professional workers, 109, 168, 191, 229

Public sector, 131, 136, 138, 165-167, 184, 186, 188, 190-191, 193, 196-197, 199-201, 207-208, 211, 214, 280-281, 301
  Rank and File workers, 23-24, 125, 130-132, 148, 174, 185, 198, 278, 280
  Secondary sector, 152
  Segmentation, 152, 154, 164, 166, 168, 175
  Service sector, 106, 146, 168, 170, 193, 281, 301
  Skilled workers, 81, 228, 261, 281, 287
  Split corporatism, 23, 26, 166(n15), 181(n1)
  Structural change, 151-152, 214
  Tenured positions, 261
  Transportation sector, 74, 77
  Unemployment, 67, 70, 90, 109, 122, 139, 145, 151- 152, 174, 190, 193, 196, 199, 242
  Unskilled workers, 109, 123, 145-146, 166, 241
  Wage increase, 123, 134, 137, 166-167, 192-193, 195-196, 198, 201, 207, 215
  Wage restraint, 24, 130-131, 135, 183-186
  Weak worker, 25, 149, 166, 185-186, 279, 301
Labor party, 14, 16, 26, 58, 103, 117, 142, 161, 163-164, 168-169, 186, 203-204, 214, 218, 225-228, 230-232, 238, 241-244, 256-257, 270, 281, 288
Labor unions, 67, 110
Language of power, 116, 175, 179, 248-249, 295, 303, 306, 311-312
Lapid, Yair, 272
Latin America, 52, 59, 241
Lavon affair, 124-126, 128-129, 134-135
Lavon, Pinhas, 108, 124-135, 148, 158, 280
Lebanon, 96, 156, 202-203, 205, 212, 220, 305
Leef, Daphne, 162
Left/Right cartel, 217-218, 243-244
Levi, David, 184, 200, 202, 208
Liberal party, 133, 136, 151(n1), 183-184, 301
Lieberman, Avigdor, 257, 271
LIC, (see Labor Institutional Complex)
Likud, 14, 16, 18, 34, 117, 155, 168, 173-180, 181-184, 187, 192-195, 197, 200-205, 207-208, 211-214, 217, 225-226, 228, 230, 232, 236-237, 242, 245, 254-257, 270-272, 280-281, 288, 296-297, 300-303, 305
Likud Iotzei Tzfon Africa, 112, 114, 116, 168.
Local organization of North Africans (see Likud Iotzei Tzfon Africa)
Lod, 104, 112
London, 74-75

M-15 movement, 252, 274, 290
Maabarot, 104-105, 169
Ma'arach, 161
Madrid Conference, 224, 231
Mafdal, 182, 187(n6)
Mandatory mediation bill, 186
Manufacturers Association, 189-190, 193, 210, 238
Mapai, 70-71, 77-79, 81, 92-95, 98, 100-103, 108-109, 111-114, 116-118, 123-136, 138, 140-142, 148-149, 154, 158-159, 161-163, 166, 178, 191, 230, 279, 281, 288, 297, 300-302
Mapam, 68(n6), 95, 98, 124-125, 127, 129, 132-133, 135, 148, 161, 166, 183, 245
Marciano, Saadia, 171(n21), 173(n24)
Matzpen, 171
Meir, Golda, 143, 163, 172
Melting pot, 105, 117
Meretz, 228, 230, 243, 245, 272
Meshel, Yeruham, 130, 186, 188, 190, 195, 198

Index

Middle East, 58, 85, 238, 310
Migdal Haemek, 112
Migration wave, 61-62, 86, 103-105, 119, 139-141, 159, 228-229
Military,
    Apolitical image, 42, 144, 147, 157, 223, 304-306
    Administration, 89, 96, 98, 142
    Control of Palestinian movements, 155
    Elites, 33-34, 41, 96, 221, 225-226, 241, 254
    Expansion, 13, 47, 80
    Government, 144, 156-157, 162, 219
    Institutions, 97, 281
Martial law, 15, 93, 97-99, 106, 119-120
    Public Jewish support, 33-34, 156, 160, 254
    Political role, 41, 99(n9), 144, 147, 155
    Regime, 17, 146, 252, 276
    Rule, 17-18, 31, 58, 102, 147, 152, 158, 174-175, 216, 284
    Service, 97, 170, 268-269, 272, 287
    Supervision of the labor market, 97
Military occupation,
    Employment permits, 101, 240
    Industry, 141, 159
    Temporary image, 156-157
Minister of Commerce, 107
Minister of Foreign Affairs, 29, 99, 126, 205
Ministry of Security, 127(n4), 159-163, 165, 205, 213
Ministry of Treasury, 108, 126, 146, 155, 159-161, 163, 182, 188-189, 205, 213, 218, 225, 255
Mizrahi,
    Activists, 174, 266
    Citizens, 170, 173, 178,
    Collective identity, 153, 174, 179, 288-289, 301, 312
    Discrimination, 153-154, 169-170, 174, 286-287
    Immigrants, 104-106, 110, 114, 122, 136, 146, 148, 153, 168, 174-176, 242, 267, 297
    Leaders, 117, 175-176, 202, 289, 297,
    Lower classes, 93, 174-175, 179, 181, 242, 244, 266-267, 272
Marginalization, 15, 267
Mizrahim, 90-93, 105-106, 110, 117-118, 146, 153, 168-170, 172, 174-177, 243-244, 132
Mobilization, 178
    Peripheral, 14, 93, 105-106
    Plugot Hapoel, 113
    Protest, 181, 288, 300
    Representation, 117, 173, 176, 289
    Resistance movement, 14, 117, 168, 175
    Settlements, 93, 105, 175, 287
    Veteran, 170
    Workers, 106, 122, 136, 148, 170, 174, 279
Moledet, 230, 232(n20)
Morocco, 93, 105, 171, 238
Moshav, 64, 80, 83, 104, 106, 211
Movement of single mothers, 255-256
Movementism, 111, 118, 123, 129, 162
Mubarak, Hosni, 251, 292
Multi Class blocks, 136-137
Musrara neighborhood, 111, 169, 171, 178, 287

Nablus Gate, 287
Nakba, 82, 88
Nasser, 126
Nation Building strategy, 60, 68-69, 81, 84, 101, 122, 142, 157, 221, 308
National,
    Health Law, 242-243
    Identity, 16, 25, 44, 47, 85, 178, 286, 289, 307-308, 311-312
    Movement, 23, 42, 72, 83-84, 304, 308
    Religious party, 116, 182, 202
    Sport association (see Hapoel)

Student Federation, 268
Unity government (NUG) 203-205, 210, 212-213, 216, 218-219, 225-227, 280-281, 296, 303-306
Water Carrier, 159
Neo-Liberal policy, 18-19, 40, 183, 214, 252, 255-257, 260-261, 272, 274, 281, 290-291
Netanyahu, Benjamin, 31, 236, 255-260, 266, 270-271, 273
Neubach, Amnon, 205
New Delhi, 274
New Israel Fund, 263
New Middle East, 238
New social movements, 298
New state
    Democracy, 27, 61, 119
    Histadrut, 100, 111
    Institutional boundaries, 99
    Mapai control, 95, 98
    Palestinians, 93-97
    Settlement policy, 104
    Tools of domination, 90, 100
    Triangle of dependence, 27, 101
New York, 274
NGOs, 222, 259, 293
No partner myth, 255-256, 259
NUG, see National Unity Government

Obama, 258
Occupied Territories (OT) 32, 141-144, 149, 152, 154-155, 159, 162, 164, 170-171, 177-178, 217, 219-222, 224-225, 227, 229-230, 232-233, 235-237, 240-242, 244, 246, 248-249, 253-254, 264, 273, 293, 308
Occupy,
    Movement, 18-19, 40, 59, 252, 273, 290-293
    Wall Street, 252, 290
Offer, Abraham, 186
Old social movements, 279, 298
Olmert, Ehud, 257
Olshan-Dori Committee, 126
Open Bridges Policy, 144
Orientalism, 15, 90, 93, 115, 289

Oslo accords, 224, 234-238, 241, 247-250, 285, 302(n17)
    Area A, 248-249
    Area B, 248
OT, see Occupied Territories
Ottoman Empire, 61-62
Overkowitz, Yoram, 214

PA, see Palestinian Authority
Palestine,
    Occupied areas or territories (see OT)
Partition plan, 81
Palestinian,
    Anti-Palestinian campaign, 258
    Authority (PA) 58, 235-236, 238-239, 241, 246-249, 258, 285, 297
    Captive market, 58, 141, 144, 149, 151, 155, 162
    Citizens, 31, 146, 154, 157, 183, 232, 242, 244, 246, 257, 266, 268, 287, 289, 312
    Delegates, 234, 236
    Dependency, 146, 155-156, 238, 240
    Economy, 26, 94, 142, 155-156, 240-241
    Elites, 88, 234, 241
    Independence declaration, 224
    Liberation Organization (see PLO)
    Merchants, 156
    Military control of movement, 155
    National Council, 224
    Nationalism, 23, 54, 72, 85, 87, 96, 308
    Non-citizens, 142, 152, 155, 165, 215, 228-229
    Peasants, 22-23, 82
    Population, 17, 99, 122, 143-144, 174, 230, 250, 284
    Produce, 143-144
    Refugees, 91, 93, 96, 99, 103-104, 106, 156, 235
    Resistance, 147, 156, 219, 248, 250, 285
    State, 32, 224, 226, 233, 236-238,

244, 258, 263, 273
Statehood proposal, 263
Terrorism, 156-157, 221
Under military occupation, 31, 58, 154
Uprising, 89, 219, 224, 283
Workers, 27, 143, 145, 152, 155, 159, 162, 165, 171, 216, 222, 240-241, 287
Palmach, 66, 95
Paris Agreement, 239-240
Parsons, Talcott, 12
Path dependent, 12, 14, 18, 25, 47, 100, 277, 279, 308, 310
Peace,
  Agreement, 30, 171, 182, 200, 212, 220, 240
  Now movement, 33(n16), 182
  Process, 16, 29-33, 233, 239, 250
Peel commission, 79-81, 87
Pension fund, 108, 110, 145, 163, 189, 200, 256, 261
Peres, Shimon, 127(n4), 204-205, 207, 210, 218, 225-226, 238, 245, 256
Peretz, Amir, 226, 243, 245, 256, 272(n40)
Physical,
  Resistance, 39, 294
  Violence, 39, 41, 50, 53, 116
Pioneers (see Chalutzim)
PLO, 18, 178, 220-221, 223-224, 226, 231-233, 235-236, 241-242, 246-250, 254, 284-285
Poaley Zion, 62, 66
Political,
  Arena, 27-28, 30, 32, 35, 42-45, 47, 49, 51-52, 55, 88-90, 120, 137, 168, 183, 219, 244, 249-250, 269, 276, 278, 286, 288, 294-296, 301, 304, 307, 310, 312
  Business cycle, 138, 201
  Compromise, 20, 24
  Crisis, 123, 186, 202, 253, 261
  Dynamics, 12, 17, 20, 22, 28, 34, 38-39, 56, 275, 280, 293, 297
  Field, 44-46, 91, 98, 107, 133, 149, 218, 276, 295, 297, 300, 302-303, 310, 313
  Identity, 268-269, 311-312
  Junctions, 39
  Mediation, 20, 28, 34, 41, 46, 225, 250, 276
  Negotiation, 20, 77, 81, 223, 254, 271, 306
  Opportunities structure, 46, 56, 120, 295
  Power holders, 12, 38-39, 297
  Recognition, 229, 286, 298
  Representation, 41, 72, 149, 153, 180, 215, 248, 274, 278, 281, 288-289, 296, 298-299, 309
  Society, 45, 52
Political space (Ch.1),
  Close, 21, 28, 33, 35, 38, 41, 43-47, 49-50, 51-53, 55, 58-59, 65, 68, 87-88, 92, 97, 101, 117-120, 134, 136, 146-149, 157-158, 171-172, 176, 179, 199, 203, 215-219, 225, 228, 238, 243, 248, 264-265, 269-270, 288-290, 295, 302-307, 313
  Dynamic, 19-20, 39-40, 46-47, 54, 59, 248, 275, 297, 300, 313
  Open, 20-21, 27-28, 35, 38, 40-43, 45-52, 53-54, 58, 60-61, 87, 91, 100-101, 103, 107, 116-117, 119-120, 132, 146-148, 152, 173, 176, 178, 195, 211, 219, 223-224, 230, 233, 244, 248-250, 264, 275, 282-283, 286, 293, 306-307, 312-313
Post-1948 state (see new state)
Post-conflict agendas, 32, 241, 244-245, 248-249, 254
Postcolonial regime, 99
Postwar, 142, 145, 155-156, 161, 171
Power to the Workers, 260, 263
Pre-1948 (see also pre-statehood institutions)
  Borders, 89
  British mandate, 13
  Colonial state, 15
  Features of the Period, 86, 93, 142-143

Pre-statehood institutions, 13, 63, 88, 98-104, 108-109, 111, 117, 125, 129, 133-135, 146-148, 157
Precariat, 261
Prime minister, 32, 99, 108, 123, 126, 129, 161, 172, 175, 182, 186, 202, 205, 207, 210, 218, 225-227, 232, 254-256, 270, 280
Proactive,
Parties, 269, 272
    Resistance, 39, 280
Proper, Dan, 238
Public health bill, 125
Puerta Del Sol in Madrid, 273-274, 290

Raam, 272
Rabin, Itzhak, 16, 30, 33, 186, 205, 223, 225-226, 228, 230-232, 234-235, 238-239, 241-250, 254, 259, 265, 284, 303
Rabin Square, 265
Rafi, 135, 142, 151, 161-163, 166
Ramat Eshkol neighborhood, 171, 287
Ramla, 104, 112
Ramon, Haim, 226, 243, 245
Reactive
Parties, 272
Resistance, 280
Recession policy, 137-140, 154, 160-161, 170
Refugee camps, 219, 237
Religious myth of the Promised Land, 175, 288
Repertoire,
    Channeling 118-119, 155, 244, 267-270, 288, 300-301
    Condensation, 136, 149, 179, 297, 300-301
    Of distortion, 118, 178, 216, 295, 297, 299
    Of misrepresentation, 36, 91, 118, 176, 249, 265, 275, 294, 299, 303
    Of subjugation, 54
    Polarization, 179, 216(n24), 243-244, 289, 296, 302-303
Resistance Mo(ve)ment, 55-56, 58, 119, 288, 296, 310
Counter mo(ve)ment, 55-56, 276, 294, 296, 299, 305, 313
Resistance moment, 54-57, 214, 277, 282, 295, 307, 309
Resistance movement, 12, 19-20, 36, 39, 47, 49-50, 54, 56-57, 120, 276, 284-285, 294-297, 299-300, 305, 307, 309
Resolution committee, 186
Revisionists, 67
Rothschild Boulevard, 262-263, 274, 290, 292-293
Rural areas, 23, 65, 67, 83, 87, 106, 232, 308
Russia, 19-20, 61, 238

Saadat, Anwar, 171, 235
Sabra and Shatila Refugee Camps, 202, 263(n25)
Safed, 70
Sapir, Pinhas, 107, 136, 140-141, 159-161, 163
Seattle, 291
Sectorial parties, 264, 312
Security,
    Budget, 160, 162, 213-214
    Industry, 152, 159, 162
    Minister, 108, 126, 141, 151, 160, 163, 202-203, 223, 225, 256, 284
    Myth, 144, 157-158
Sequence of events, 12, 18-19, 25-26, 56, 142, 277
Settler societies, 47, 49-50, 86
Shamir, Yitzhak, 202, 204-205, 225-228, 231
Sharet, Moshe, 77(n17), 99, 126,
Sharon, Ariel, 32, 202, 255-257
Sharon, Immanuel, 205-206, 210
Shas, 32, 179-180, 226, 242-245, 272, 289
Shavit, Abraham, 190, 193, 196
Sheli, 173(n24), 187(n6)
Shemesh, Cochabi, 171(n21)
Shomron, Dan, 222
Silman, Moshe, 266, 268

Sinai, 141, 155, 161, 202, 212, 300
Singapore, 239
Singer, Yoel, 236, 237(n29), 249
Social-democratic party, 127
Social movement, 12, 46, 55-57, 116, 173-174, 273, 279, 294-295, 298
Solel Bone, 66, 70, 200, 211
Sovereign Israel, 143, 154-155, 160, 164, 169, 217, 219, 221, 225, 229, 230, 232, 240, 244
Soviet Union, 95, 169, 226, 228, 231, 257
Spain, 239, 252, 274, 290-291, 302
State
    Autonomy, 25-26, 99, 140-141, 146, 161, 164, 191, 210(n22), 212-215, 217-218, 229, 304-305
    Budget, 108, 119, 159, 191, 206
    Building strategy, 60, 68-70, 82, 99, 142
    Bureaucracy, 159, 218, 240, 281
    Crisis of statehood, 119, 122, 177
    Elites, 281, 304-305
    Financial resources, 26, 138, 306
    Owned companies, 146, 164, 196
    Quasi-state institutions, 24, 28, 92, 98, 100-101, 143, 147, 162
    Resources, 137, 160, 173
Sovereign state, 14, 47, 140, 149, 221, 228, 230, 244, 262, 296-297, 309
Statism, 95, 98, 100, 111, 118, 123, 129, 162
Strikes,
    24-hour, 74, 194, 198, 299
    Consumer, 258
    General, 72, 75, 87, 132, 185, 188, 190, 194, 209-210, 284
    Lockout, 206
    Offensive, 280
Solidarity strike, 280
Student, 260
    Warning, 74-75, 139, 280
    Wildcat, 123, 130, 280
Structural adjustments, 275, 304, 307, 313
Student associations, 263

Subordinate social groups, 21, 28, 39, 47, 49, 54, 57, 101, 275, 278, 295, 298, 307
Subsidies, 24, 69, 80, 107-108, 123, 137-141, 159-164, 169-170, 183-184, 189-193, 195, 205, 207, 209, 211-215, 227, 262, 273
Sudan, 266
Suffragettes, 48
Symbolic,
Space, 21, 35
    Violence, 21, 36, 39, 47, 50, 53, 116, 267, 284, 286
Syria, 74, 156

Tahrir square, 252, 261(n22), 274, 290, 292(n11)
Talbiya neighborhood, 169
Taxes, 22, 60, 71-75, 87, 127, 131, 145, 155, 166-167, 184, 186, 198, 205-206, 208, 236-237, 252, 256, 269, 284
Technopols, 192(n12), 206(n20), 213-214, 218, 303-306, 310
Tehiya, 205(n18), 230
Tel-Aviv, 65, 78, 148, 199, 262-263, 265-266
Tel Hanan, 112
Territorial compromise, 95, 242, 253, 288
The Alignment, 133, 135-136, 138, 140, 149, 161-162, 165-166, 177, 181-183, 185, 187, 192, 194, 200-201, 203-204, 212, 214, 237, 301
The Movement (party), 272
Tiberias, 70
Tnuva, 66
Tower and Stockade, 80
Trachtenberg Commission, 252
Transition camps (see Maabarot)
Tribal,
    Channeling, 90, 118, 149, 174, 176, 179, 203, 217, 288
    Left-right, 30, 179, 201, 224, 242-243, 245, 250, 253, 296, 302
    Mobilization, 176, 179, 203, 244,

Index

301-302
Tunis, 220-221, 224, 226, 231-234, 246
Tunisia, 93, 274, 290
Two-state solution, 32, 144, 178, 230
Tzomet, 205(n18), 230, 232(n20)
Tzeirei Ben Gurion, 126, 134

UN, 81, 96, 235, 258, 263, 265, 273
Unilateral decision, 34, 37-38, 72, 76, 201, 220, 236, 255-256, 283-284, 313
Unionization, 77, 81, 107, 110, 131, 148, 154
United,
    Israel appeal (see Keren Hayesod)
    Kibbutz Movement (see Hakibbutz Hameuhad)
US,
    Government, 126, 169, 189, 210
    Treasury, 140

Vicious Triangle (Mapai-Histadrut-State), 28, 102-103, 108, 126, 129, 131, 148, 159, 191
Violent repression, 28, 33, 35, 39, 47, 53, 153, 221, 247, 276, 284, 299, 306

Wadi Nisnass, 111
Wadi Salib (Ch.3)
    Ethnic riots, 19, 39, 54, 58, 90, 114, 117, 277
    Inquiry committee, 113
    Resistance moment, 111
    Resistance movement, 115, 120, 123
Wailing Wall, 70
War
    1948, 92(n3), 95, 99, 119
    First Lebanon war, 29(n13), 202, 218, 263, 304
    First World War, 65
    Gulf War, 231, 240
    June 1967 (Six day war), 99, 122, 133, 141, 146, 149, 151, 154, 157, 166, 223

    October 1973 (Yom-Kippur War), 153, 171, 173-177, 184, 300
    Operation Cast Lead, 255, 257
    Operation Pillar of Cloud, 255, 271
    Of Attrition, 151, 153, 171
    Second Lebanon war, 255, 257
    Second World War, 94-95, 104
    Sinai campaign of 1956, 111, 113
Washington,
    Consensus (WC) 140, 183, 212, 214
    Delegates, 224, 232-236
WB, 140, 238-240, 304
WC, see Washington Consensus
Weitzman, Ezer, 203
Weizmann, Haim, 63
West Bank, 16, 32, 58, 96, 122, 133, 141, 144, 170, 175, 220-221, 224, 226, 231, 233, 235-237, 241, 256, 258, 271, 276, 288
White house, 30
Worker,
    committee, 24, 37, 109, 165, 167, 182, 193-196, 198, 209-210, 214-215, 279-280
    Industrial, 123, 131, 174
    Migrant, 16, 229, 241, 262
    Non-unionized, 136, 145, 165, 241, 260
    Powerful, 25, 58, 109, 165, 167, 183, 185, 194-196, 201-202, 209-211, 213, 215, 229, 277, 301
    Professional, 109, 168, 191, 229
    Rank and File, 23-24, 125, 130-132, 148, 174, 185, 198, 278, 280
    Skilled, 81, 228, 261, 281, 287
    Unskilled, 109, 123, 145-146, 166, 241
    Weak, 25, 149, 166, 185-186, 279, 301
Workers' school system (see Zerem Haovdim)
Workers Society (WS –see Hevrat Haovdim)
Working class,
    24-hour strike, 198, 199

Collective identity, 310-311
General strike, 132, 185, 194, 209-210
Homogenization, 122
Ideology, 311
Mass demonstration, 280
Mobilization, 23, 40, 279-280
Political front, 149
Resistance, 13, 27, 125, 148, 150, 154, 218, 278, 280, 296, 304
Revolt, 18, 27, 57-58, 130
Solidarity, 22, 280-281
Strike wave, 19, 23, 39, 54, 148
Struggle, 21, 23, 48, 51, 148, 181, 278, 280
Wage demands, 127, 132, 184, 188, 198
Wildcat strike, 123, 130, 280
Warning strike, 139, 280
World,
    Bank (see WB)
    Energy crisis, 184
    Zionist Organization (see WZO)
WS Financial plan, 108, 163-164, 189-190, 200, 210-211
WZO, 62-63, 65-66, 69-71, 77-78, 86

Yemen, 93, 115-116
Yesh Atid, 268, 272
Yiddish, 93
Yishuv (see also pre-statehood institutions)
    Full employment, 78
    Institutions, 101, 119
    "Left" organizations, 95
    Military organization, 65, 80, 95

ZLM power, 69
    Yisrael Beiteinu, 257, 271-272
Zerem Haovdim, 68
Zionist Labor Movement (ZLM)
    Dominant position, 69, 82, 84, 86
    Historical moments, 182
    Ideology, 12, 14, 18, 26, 62, 68, 105, 142, 157, 217, 229
    Institutions, 89, 124, 146, 203
    Leadership, 71, 77-78, 82, 84, 88, 146
    Legitimacy, 146, 158
    Non-democratic and non-representative institutions, 146, 149
    Policies, 23, 81
    Political-economic institutional complex, 214
    Political parties, 60, 64, 68-69, 79, 148
    Settlements, 67, 75, 83
    Strategy of separation, 23, 26, 65, 71, 77, 79, 81-82, 84-86, 88, 122, 144, 157-158, 177